OKANAGAN UNIV/COLLEGE LIBRARY

P9-EJI-635

Multiple Identities
& False Memories

Multiple Identities & False Memories

A SOCIOCOGNITIVE PERSPECTIVE

Nicholas P. Spanos

American Psychological Association
Washington, DC

Copyright © 1996 by the American Psychological Association. All rights reserved. Except as permitted under the United States Copyright Act of 1976, no part of this publication may be reproduced or distributed in any form or by any means, or stored in a database or retrieval system, without the prior written permission of the publisher.

Published by
American Psychological Association
750 First Street, NE
Washington, DC 20002

Copies may be ordered from
American Psychological Association
Order Department
P.O. Box 92984
Washington, DC 20090-2984

In the UK and Europe, copies may be ordered from
American Psychological Association
3 Henrietta Street
Covent Garden, London
WC2E 8LU England

Typeset in Goudy by PRO-Image Corporation, Techna-Type Div., York, PA

Technical/Production Editor: Olin J. Nettles
Printer: United Book Press, Inc., Baltimore, MD
Cover Designer: Amy Stirnkorb, San Diego, CA

Library of Congress Cataloging-in-Publication Data
Spanos, Nicholas P.
    Multiple identities and false memories : a sociocognitive perspective /
Nicholas P. Spanos.
        p.   cm.
    Includes bibliographical references and index.
    ISBN 1-55798-340-2 (alk. paper)
    1. False memory syndrome.   2. Multiple Personality.   I. Title.
RC455.2.F35S67 1996
616.85'236—dc20
                                                                                    96-9772
                                                                                    CIP

British Library Cataloguing-in-Publication Data
A CIP record is available from the British Library.

Printed in the United States of America
First edition

CONTENTS

III. MULTIPLE IDENTITIES IN OTHER CULTURES AND TIMES

IV. THE THEORY OF MULTIPLE PERSONALITY DISORDER

V. CONCLUSION

PREFACE

Nicholas P. Spanos died on June 7, 1994, when the plane he was piloting crashed shortly after takeoff from Martha's Vineyard. His death brought a premature end to an astonishingly productive and influential career. His research and writing focused primarily on hypnosis, where his contributions have fundamentally altered our understanding. His cognitive–behavioral model of hypnosis is now the most influential perspective in the field, largely replacing the earlier "altered state" conception. Nick Spanos also made significant contributions to our understanding of a wide variety of related topics, including false memories, demonic possession, the Salem witchcraft trials, reports of alien abductions by UFOs, and multiple personality disorder.

We are fortunate that in the year before his death he took advantage of a sabbatical leave from Carleton University to write this book, which effectively ties together these apparently disparate interests. While drawing on the work of many scholars, the book confronts in a critical and highly original manner some of the most controversial issues in contemporary psychopathology, including multiple personality disorder, the recovery of repressed memories of childhood, physical and sexual abuse, and the phenomenon of dissociation. Many of the critical experiments that provide the foundation for the theoretical conclusions reached here were the results of studies that were conducted in Spanos's own laboratory and that were reported in approximately 250 scientific articles and chapters, as well as in two previous books that he authored or coauthored during his extraordinary career.

The present book had been submitted for publication prior to Nick's death, and, of course, he had no opportunity to make any of the revisions that he might have wanted after the book had undergone editorial review. He would certainly have responded to editorial suggestions on matters of style and organization. Although his opinions were strongly held, and usually controversial, he was always responsive to valid criticism. However, we feel confident that he would have made at the most minor changes to the text. Nick's writings have always displayed the virtues of clarity and explicitness. It is unlikely that he would have succumbed to pressures to use euphemisms or to substitute tactful turns of phrase to please the reader, if to do so would in any way have distorted his meaning. Those who know and value Nick's frankness in his other writings will not be disappointed in this book. We also believe that none of the empirical findings that have appeared since his death have controverted his fundamental conclusions.

Within the past two decades, a growing number of mental health professionals and laymen have come to accept the validity of the dramatic and counterexpectational notion that a single body may in some sense be said to serve as simultaneous host to more than one personality. Historically, this phenomenon has been referred to as *multiple personality disorder* (MPD), an expression used throughout the book and one that we shall continue to use here, notwithstanding the most recent relabeling of the phenomenon in the fourth edition of the *Diagnostic and Statistical Manual of Mental Disorders* of the American Psychiatric Association (1994) as *dissociative identity disorder*. Because what is challenged in this book is the validity of MPD, however called, as a distinct psychiatric entity, we need make no effort to bow to transient nosological fashion.

At the level of clinical practice and theory, the links among MPD, false memories, and hypnosis are reasonably obvious. Repressed memories of early childhood physical and sexual abuse are thought by therapists to set the stage for the emergence of MPD. The tool of choice to recover the memories and uncover the multiple personalities has been clinical hypnosis. The core belief that MPD provides a barrier to otherwise intolerable memories of abuse is now taken for granted by a number of therapists who have, in turn, influenced the more widely disseminated, and perhaps the more sensational, popular accounts. The debate in the scientific literature and, increasingly, in courtrooms in North America has had a somewhat more sceptical tone. This book, we believe, will be seen as a central contribution to the scientific debate and will undoubtedly begin to change how our legal culture responds to the problem of MPD.

Spanos critically examines the prevailing assumptions about MPD, repressed memories of abuse, and hypnosis and demonstrates that the received view is in each case incorrect. He argues that the idea that MPD is a naturally occurring mental disorder is fundamentally flawed. Rather, he proposes that multiple identities can be understood as rule-governed social constructions established, legitimated, and maintained through social interaction. Moreover, he shows that neither a history of abuse nor severe psychopathology is necessary for the development or maintenance of multiple identities. For us, this book provides the most powerful challenge yet published to the prevailing views of MPD and related phenomena. The implications for treatment and for theory are challenging and undoubtedly disturbing to some. We hope that this work will lead to the sort of fundamental change in the scientific understanding of MPD that Nick Spanos earlier achieved in relation to hypnosis. We are confident that this is how he would wish to be remembered.

We both had the privilege of knowing Nick and working closely with him for many years. He was among the most productive and influential workers in the area of scientific hypnosis during the last half of this century. During his career, he produced approximately 250 publications, including three books and 214 journal articles. A complete bibliography and a collection of appreciative reminiscences by his colleagues were published in a special issue of the journal *Contemporary Hypnosis* (volume 12, number 1) that is dedicated to his memory. As we have argued, his publications have played a major role in shaping scientific thought about hypnosis and related areas of interest for more than a quarter of a century.

Nick was born in Boston and graduated from Boston University with an A.B. in 1964. He attended graduate school in the department of psychology at Northeastern University, where his interest in hypnosis first developed. In 1967, he joined a group of Northeastern graduate students working with Theodore X. Barber at the nearby Medfield Foundation. We were all impressed by the research that Barber was doing. It appeared to us that he was revolutionizing the field of hypnosis research. Ted's interest and encouragement played a key role in stimulating Nick's work and shaping his approach to the topic. In graduate school, Nick had been unclear about his focus of interest. Once he committed himself to work in hypnosis, this remained the essential focus of the rest of his career.

Nick remained at Medfield until 1975. By that time, he had earned a PhD at Boston University and had gained significant clinical experience at Medfield State Hospital and in private practice. Research was his primary interest, however, and its pursuit led him to accept a position in the psychology department at Carleton University, where he remained for the rest of his career.

At Carleton, Nick built an empire. He established a laboratory for hypnosis research that was probably the most productive in the world. At times, he might have had up to 45 students working with him. In less than 19 years, he graduated 17 doctoral students and more than 60 master's students. His research productivity was astonishing. By one count, Nick was the author or coauthor of 7% of the entire world literature on hypnosis during the 10 years from 1979 to 1988. His research was consistently published in the most prestigious journals in the field and was characteristically ingenious and bold. He seemed to have the ability to design complex and imaginative research studies at will. His research was always historically rooted and revealed an extraordinary breadth and depth of scholarship. To be his intellectual adversary was a daunting task. He would know your research at least as well as you did, and probably better. He had an uncanny way of exploiting weakness in the arguments of his adversaries. In argument, he was often strongly confrontational, although he would usually go to some lengths to avoid personal conflict. People who first got to know him in debate in the journals or on the platform were likely to be surprised that in person he was usually shy and unassuming, without any of the affectations of the eminent scholar. It seems to us that his confrontational professional style can be best understood as a deeply committed search for truth, coupled with a more than usually low tolerance for the inane. Nick did not suffer fools gladly, and one always knew when he thought you the fool.

His intellect, curiosity, and passion combined to make him an inspirational teacher and mentor for his graduate students. As with his adversaries, he would force his students to confront their assumptions explicitly. A vast array of dissertation research resulted that has stimulated another generation of students who have themselves gone on to make important contributions.

Nick's contributions to hypnosis research have fundamentally changed the field. His constant reminders of the critical role of context effects are fundamental, as is his insistence that we keep in mind that human behavior in research or in psychotherapy is always strategic, always directed toward goals. Graham Wagstaff (1995) said it best when he noted that with Nick's passing we had "not just lost one of the greatest names in hypnosis research, we have lost one of the great psychologists of modern times" (p. 41).

Although the manuscript for this book was completed before Nick's death, some revisions were necessary, mostly to improve readability. The organizational structure was changed somewhat. Additional introductory material was added to chapter 1 to help clarify the relationships among the subsequent chapters. Some of the chapters were reordered, and summaries were added where they had not been provided.

We owe a debt of gratitude to Cheryl A. Burgess, PhD, of Carleton University and Suzy Conway of the St. Louis University Medical Center Library for their assistance in locating some very obscure references and helping to assemble the bibliography. Finally, we thank Judy Nemes, development editor for APA Books, who made many helpful suggestions regarding the book's organization.

John F. Chaves
Indiana University School of Dentistry
Indianapolis, IN

Bill Jones
Carleton University
Ottawa, Canada

ABOUT THE AUTHOR

Nicholas P. Spanos, PhD, was Professor of Psychology and Director of the Laboratory for Experimental Hypnosis at Carleton University from 1975 until his death in 1994. A graduate of Boston University, he received his MA from Northeastern University and his PhD from Boston University. He had been a senior research associate at the Medfield Foundation and Medfield State Hospital and clinical director at Boston Psychological Associates before assuming his position at Carleton. In the course of his career, he attained the position of fellow of the American Psychological Association and served on the editorial boards of a number of professional journals. His scholarship is evident in the more than 250 articles, chapters, and books published during his career. His articles have appeared in such publications as *Science, Psychological Bulletin, Journal of Abnormal Psychology, American Psychologist,* and *Contemporary Hypnosis,* and his previous books include *Hypnosis, Imagination, and Human Potentialities,* with T. X. Barber and J. F. Chaves; *Hypnosis: The Cognitive–Behavioral Perspective,* with J. F. Chaves; and *Hypnosis and Imagination,* with R. G. Kunzendorf and B. Wallace.

1

INTRODUCTION

People who receive the diagnosis of multiple personality disorder (MPD) behave as if they possess two or more distinct identities. They convey the impression of multiplicity by exhibiting a relatively integrated interpersonal style (i.e., a distinct personality) when calling themselves by one name and different interpersonal styles when calling themselves by other names. Frequently, MPD patients behave as if their different identities have their own unique memories and experiences, and many of the identities claim amnesia for the other personalities with whom they co-reside.

Modern MPD patients are usually women with a wide range of chronic psychiatric problems that predate their MPD diagnosis (Coons, Bowman, & Milstein, 1988; Ross, Norton, & Wozney, 1989). These patients usually claim to have been physically or sexually abused—often horrendously—in childhood (Coons & Milstein, 1986; Ross, Miller, Bjornson, Reagor, & Fraser, 1991; W. C. Young, Sachs, Braun, & Watkins, 1991). Moreover, it is now common for investigators (e.g., Bliss, 1986; Braun, 1990; Putnam, 1989; Ross, 1989) to argue that MPD is a distinct mental disorder caused by severe childhood abuse. According to this hypothesis, severe trauma during childhood produces a mental splitting or dissociation as a defensive reaction to the trauma. These dissociated "parts" of the person develop into alter identities or personalities that, in adulthood, periodically manifest themselves to help the individual cope with stressful situations, express resentments or other feelings that the primary personality disavows, and so on. Supposedly, one function of alter personalities is to "hold" memories of severe childhood abuse of which the host personality is unaware. During psychotherapy, these forgotten memories are recovered when the alters reveal them to the therapist.

The proponents of this perspective have been highly vocal, and despite much and varied criticism, this view has become highly influential. Thus, from this perspective, displays of multiple identities reflect a mental disorder—something that happens to the person as a result of early traumas and other experiences over which he or she has no control and often no memory, rather than something that the person does in response to current contingencies, goals, and understandings.

Despite its current popularity, the notion that MPD is a naturally occurring disorder that results from severe child abuse is fraught with difficulties. A detailed examination of these difficulties will take up much of this book. Nevertheless, the following brief preview concerning the characteristics of MPD, and the historical changes that have occurred in these characteristics, should provide some idea of the difficulties faced by those who conceptualize this phenomenon from a disease perspective.

Modern cases of MPD have tended to take on truly bizarre characteristics. For example, early cases rarely involved more than two or three alter personalities per patient. On the other hand, many modern cases involve 20 or more alter personalities per patient, and in some cases the alters number in the hundreds. Child sexual abuse was not a prominent feature of MPD cases reported before 1970. However, cases reported after 1975 have almost always involved descriptions of childhood sexual abuse, and the kinds of abuse purportedly experienced by these patients have grown progressively more lurid and more extensive. Some patients not only report such "conventional" forms of abuse as father–daughter incest but also tell tales of having been subjected to bizarre sexual torture at the hands of secret satanic cultists and of having been forced to endure multiple pregnancies and births only to see their newborn infants torn away and sacrificed at obscene rituals. Typically, patients have no memories of such sexual abuse when they enter therapy, but they recover increasingly outlandish and implausible abuse "memories" as their treatment proceeds. Until around 1980, MPD was considered to be a very rare disorder, and only a relatively few cases had been reported in the world psychiatric literature. Since 1980, the number of cases has mushroomed, some investigators speak of an MPD epidemic, and thousands of cases have been reported. However, some clinicians appear to run across these cases much more frequently than others. Many highly experienced clinicians claim never to have seen a case after many years of practice, whereas other clinicians report having seen literally hundreds of cases each.

Even this brief preview makes it obvious that the form taken by modern cases of MPD, and the historical changes that have occurred in the manifestations of MPD, requires an analysis of the social and historical contexts in which this phenomenon has evolved. No matter how thorough, the psychodynamic evaluation of individual patients can never provide an adequate account of the MPD phenomenon. Moreover, conceptualizing this phenomenon as a disease deflects attention away from the obvious cultural and historical frameworks that give meaning to MPD enactments and that explain the multifaceted changes that have occurred in the characteristics of these enactments.

In this book, I argue that viewing MPD as a naturally occurring mental disorder is fundamentally flawed. Instead, I describe a sociocognitive alternative to the disease model that suggests that MPD is a sociohistorical product (Hacking, 1986, 1992; Kenny, 1986; Shorter, 1992; Spanos, 1989). In the past two centuries, a number of psychiatric syndromes have developed, spread, and then all but disappeared as a function of changing conceptions held by both doctors and patients concerning the ways in which distress may be legitimately expressed (Shorter, 1992). In the past 20 years, the notion of multiple personality has become commonplace in North American culture, and it is now a legitimate way for people to understand and express their failures and frustrations. In short, the sociocognitive perspective suggests that patients learn to construe themselves as possessing multiple selves, learn to present themselves in terms of this construal, and learn to reorganize and elaborate on their personal biography so as to make it congruent with their understanding of what it means to be a multiple. These patients are conceptualized as actively involved in using available information to create a social impression that is congruent with their perception of situational demands, with the self-understandings they have learned to adopt, and with the interpersonal goals they are attempting to achieve (Spanos, Weekes, & Bertrand, 1985).

According to this perspective, psychotherapists play a particularly important part in the generation and maintenance of MPD. Some therapists routinely encourage patients to construe themselves as having multiple selves, provide them with information about how to convincingly enact the role of "multiple personality patient," and provide official legitimation for the different identities that their patients enact.

Central to the notion of MPD is, of course, the idea of multiple identities. Throughout this book, I use experimental, cross-cultural, and historical findings to argue that multiple identities can develop in a wide variety of cultural contexts and serve numerous different social functions. In our culture, the development of multiple identities is usually conceptualized in terms of mental disorder, and multiple identity enactments are frequently accompanied by symptoms of distress and psychopathology. In other cultures, such enactments can occur in the absence of psychopathology or symptoms of distress. More specifically, I argue that (a) multiple identities are usefully conceptualized as rule-governed social constructions; (b) neither childhood trauma nor a history of severe psychopathology is necessary for the development or maintenance of multiple identities; and (c) multiple identities are established, legitimated, maintained, and altered through social interaction.

IDENTITIES: SINGULAR AND PLURAL

In all cultures, people exhibit wide variability in their behavior across time and situations. Nevertheless, in our culture almost all people hold a subjective sense of unitary identity and view their diverse behavior as the product of a single self (Epstein, 1973). The concepts that people hold of themselves are social products. These concepts are generated through interaction with others and involve a series of interrelated construals made about the first-person singular by the first-person singular (Deaux, 1993). These self-construals reflect the feedback people have received from others and from their own behavior, filtered through the categories that each culture uses to describe its members. Thus, self-construals involve socially derived attributions that people apply to themselves. The way that people view themselves reflects the way that they are viewed by others, and it is others who provide or withhold legitimation for the varied self-presentations that people enact (Goffman, 1959). Individuals typically present themselves as a unitary self, enacting different roles because they are reinforced for doing so. In fact, the social, economic, and legal institutions of our culture are premised on the notion that each person is a unitary self who is accountable for his or her own diverse behaviors, and this view of unitary self is routinely legitimated in social interaction (Halleck, 1990; Mancuso & Sarbin, 1983; M. S. Moore, 1984).

Social products are, of course, subject to social change. There is nothing inevitable about the notion of a unitary self, and the same social processes that validate the conception people hold of themselves as unitary selves can be used to validate the alternative conceptualization that people consist of multiple selves. In other words, people can learn to think of themselves as possessing more than one identity or self, and can learn to behave as if they are first one identity and then a different identity. People can learn to behave in these ways regardless of whether they were abused as children and regardless of whether they are suffering high levels of distress and exhibiting symptoms of psychopathology. On the other hand, people are unlikely to think of themselves in this way or to behave in this way unless their culture has provided them with the idea of doing so and provided models from whom the rules and characteristics of multiple identity enactments can be learned. Along with providing rules and models, the culture, through its socializing agents, must also provide legitimation for multiple self enactments.

Identity enactments require the tacit, ongoing validation of others. Such validation is provided when people treat a person in terms of the identity that that person presents through his or her role enactments. My identity enactment as a "professor giving a lecture" is routinely validated by students who attend class, convey the impression of listening, take notes, ask course-related questions of me rather than the person sitting next to them, and so forth. Relatedly, a person's identity enactment as an MPD alter personality, an indwelling demon, the spirit of a departed relative, or a reincarnated past-life personality requires the validation of others who share at least a tacit understanding of what the identity enactment entails and who, through their interactions with the actor, treat the identity that is presented as real or genuine.

From a sociocognitive perspective, the importance of social learning and social validation in the generation and maintenance of multiple identity enactments would be difficult to overemphasize. Consequently, I will underscore the importance of these factors in numerous chapters by examining cross-cultural as well as experimental and historical examples of such enactments. These examples are designed to illustrate the very wide range of forms that multiple identity enactments can take and to demonstrate the crucial role of social factors in the generation and maintenance of such enactments, as well as in the historical changes that occur in the manifestation of such enactments.

ROLE ENACTMENT, MULTIPLE IDENTITIES, AND SELECTIVE RECALL

Recall from memory is selective and geared to the role demands associated with particular tasks (Neisser, 1976). For example, when enacting the role of "private pilot," the task demands of landing my aircraft absorb my full attention, and the information I recall is specifically geared to the goal of getting the aircraft safely on the ground. Consequently, I am continuously involved in integrating and comparing current incoming information from the flight instruments with information retrieved from memory, in order to make the ongoing corrective movements of the controls that will keep the airplane oriented in the appropriate landing configuration.

While landing the aircraft, I do not recall my role enactments as a professor giving a lecture. Keeping memories associated with my role of professor from intruding on the task of landing the airplane requires no special effort. Instead, my absorption in the role of pilot, by and large, prevents the recall of role-unrelated events. If, as I try to compensate for a stiff crosswind on the final approach, my passenger asks me how my morning lecture went, I am likely to respond with "I can't think of that now, I've got to land the plane." Taken literally, my response to the passenger is simply incorrect. Of course I could, if I chose to do so, think back to and recall my morning lecture in some detail. However, I could not simultaneously recall the lecture and safely land the plane. Thus my statement "I can't think of that now" is simply a shorthand way of indicating that I choose not to recall details of my lecture in order to maintain attention to the current role demands involved in landing the airplane safely.

The primary personalities of MPD patients frequently claim amnesia for the enactments of alter personalities. To a substantial degree, such "amnesia" may simply involve the kind of selective recall that prevents me from remembering my role as professor while landing my airplane. In other words, absorption in the enactment of identity A may, to a substantial degree, function to prevent the recall of memories associated with the enactment of identity B. But what if identity B, when asked to recall identity A, claims an inability to do so? An "inability" to recall identity A may be a requirement of the MPD role in the same sense that my "inability" to recall my professor role is a requirement of landing my airplane. The goal of landing safely takes precedence over recalling my role as professor. Consequently, I ignore requests to recall my morning lecture and, instead, maintain attention to the task requirements demanded by my role as pilot. In the pilot scenario, the goal of landing safely is intuitively obvious to everyone. It is equally obvious that this goal is incompatible with reminiscing about my earlier class and that the goal of a safe landing is more important than, and should take precedence over, the goal of vividly remembering my morning lecture. Because all of this is obvious, special explanations for my failing to recall the lecture by positing amnesia are not required.

As I will emphasize in several chapters, amnesia for the behaviors enacted by alter identities is an important component of the MPD role. I will suggest that understanding this "amnesia" does not require the positing of special or pathological memory mechanisms. According to this argument, the amnesia associated with MPD appears to be more unusual than my failing to recall my professor role when landing my aircraft because, in the MPD case, the goals involved in not recalling, and in claiming an inability to recall, are not nearly as obvious as the goal of preventing an aircraft accident. However, rather than requiring information about unusual memory processes, understanding the amnesia enacted by MPD patients requires information about the goals MPD patients are attempting to achieve by enacting between-alter amnesia. It also requires information about the contextual factors that define those goals and that legitimate the enactments of memory failure that are designed to meet them. To a substantial degree, the relevant contextual factors required to understand MPD amnesia are embedded in the procedures used to diagnose and treat MPD. Consequently, understanding the identity enactments and between-alter amnesic displays that constitute the MPD role involves examining the diagnostic and therapeutic interactions that serve to define and legitimate that role.

AUTOBIOGRAPHY, MEMORY, AND IDENTITY

Psychoanalytic thought has had a profound effect on Western European and American thinking, far in excess of the small number of professionals who actually practice psychoanalytic psychotherapy (Torrey, 1992). For example, the idea that adult problems stem from early experiences with parents and others is, in many circles, so common and so ingrained as to be taken for granted. Psychodynamic psychotherapies of almost all stripes assume the validity of this proposition and are frequently aimed at helping the client to reorganize and reorder his or her biography so as to make current concerns and problems intelligible in terms of a new understanding of the past. Under these circumstances, making a biography intelligible means organizing it so that it corresponds more closely than before to the tacit or explicit conception held by the therapist (and eventually by the client as well) concerning what the client's biography should be like. Obviously, such a process of reorganization involves some give and take between the conceptions of the client and therapist, but oftentimes, the success of therapy is defined in terms of the extent to which the client gains "insight," that is, overcomes "resistances" to viewing his or her biography in the light considered appropriate by the therapist (Frank, 1973).

At the very least, the reorganization of a biography means reinterpreting and reframing the significance of memories of the past. In many cases, however, such reorganization also involves the partial invention of the past. Thus, in searching their past, clients frequently recover "memories" that were previously forgotten and that serve to buttress the new view of themselves that they and their therapist are in the process of constructing. In some cases, the recovered memories may well be real; the events remembered correspond, with varying degrees of closeness, to events that actually occurred. In other cases, the recovered "memories" are unadulterated fantasies; the events "remembered" never happened. In still other cases, the recovered memories are an indecipherable mix of fantasy and reality (Spence, 1982).

The past 20 years have witnessed the discovery of child sexual abuse as a social problem in North America. The notion that such abuse is relatively common, and that it is often perpetrated within the family, has captured the popular imagination, led to pervasive changes in the functioning of legal and social welfare agencies, and served as a rallying point for political activism by a number of groups, including feminist groups on the one hand and conservative religious groups on the other (Brooks, Perry, Starr, & Teply, 1994; Bulkley & Horwitz, 1994).

One consequence of the attention focused on child abuse has been the development of a psychotherapeutic specialty for treating the adult "survivors" of such abuse. Incest-resolution therapists frequently contend that many people who exhibit unhappiness or other signs of psychological distress were sexually abused as children but have forgotten the abuse. One goal of such therapy involves the recovery of these hidden memories (Blume, 1990; Fredrickson, 1992). In other words, incest-resolution therapy, like other therapies, involves clients coming to see their problems in the same light as do their therapists. This involves the clients reconstructing their biographies to correspond to the therapist's conception of what caused their current problems. If patients in incest-resolution therapy have no memories of sexual abuse when they enter therapy, the appropriate reconstruction of their biographies requires that such memories be recovered during the course of therapy. In a number of places throughout the book I will argue that the "memories" recovered under these circumstances are, sometimes, not memories at all. They are fantasies that are legitimated as memories by the therapist.

The notion that sane people can generate complex, vivid, detailed, emotionally charged fantasy experiences, and confuse those fantasies with memories of real occurrences, seems counterintuitive. Consequently, I devote several chapters to a discussion of this issue, provide evidence from various sources that just such confusion between fantasy and memory occurs, and delineate some of the important social processes that lead people to experience and describe fantasies as memories.

MPD began to come to prominence both for the general public and for the psychiatric community during the 1970s, the period of awakening social interest in the problems and consequences of sexual abuse. In the later chapters of this book, I shall argue that the development of interest in MPD, during this period of societal interest in sexual abuse, indelibly shaped both the theories concerning the causes of MPD and the characteristics associated with modern MPD enactments.

The therapists who diagnose and treat MPD are usually trained in psychodynamic forms of psychotherapy that emphasize both the importance of early experience in shaping adult behavior and personality, and the importance of hidden (i.e., repressed or dissociated) memories in creating and maintaining adult psychopathology. Given the growth of the sexual abuse survivor movement and the development and popularity of incest-resolution therapies in the 1970s, it was probably inevitable that the MPD cases that most strongly captured the attention of both the public and the mental health community at this time involved recovered memories of horrendous child sexual abuse. During this period, MPD therapists also became incest-resolution therapists, and by the 1980s, the alter personalities of MPD patients began increasingly to be conceptualized as the repositories of memories of sexual abuse that were hidden from the main or host personality (Mulhern, 1991b). In short, the enactment of MPD came increasingly to involve the recovery of more and increasingly horrendous abuse memories that were "held" by more and more alter personalities. I will argue that, in many cases, the recovered "memories" of MPD patients are fantasies that are shaped to fit the shared construals that they and their therapists develop about the causes of their MPD enactments. This sociocognitive view is based on the notion that memory involves reconstructive processes and cannot be adequately understood as a simple "playing back" of previously stored information. To explicate these ideas, a number of chapters are devoted to the ways in which memory reports can be distorted by suggestion and expectation, and to the role of therapeutic legitimation in leading fantasies to be defined and treated as memories.

HYPNOSIS, HISTORY, AND MPD

MPD did not develop suddenly and in a historical vacuum after 1970. Long before the advent of the notion of multiple personality, it was believed in Western societies that demons could enter people and take over their functioning. Demonically possessed people sometimes enacted demon identities and later claimed amnesia for the period of time during which the demon was "in control." Exorcism and other procedures were sometimes used to expel the indwelling demons. During the 18th century, demonic explanations for unusual behavior increasingly gave way to medical ones, and medical treatments replaced exorcism and other religious therapies.

Cases in which people appeared to manifest different states of being and different personalities separated by amnesia were reported periodically in the medical literature of the late 18th and 19th centuries, and many of these cases were associated with mesmerism and, later, hypnosis. Frequently, mesmeric practices resembled semisecularized exorcisms, and the notion of mesmerism and hypnosis became associated with the occult and with the idea that mesmeric and hypnotic practices both cured diseases and produced unusual changes in memory, consciousness, and personality. The modern idea of multiple personality developed in the last quarter of the 19th century among medical investigators who were studying hypnosis and its relation to psychopathology. These investigators generated a small spurt in the number of MPD cases in the years shortly before and after the turn of the 20th century, but for a variety of reasons that will be discussed in some detail in several chapters, psychiatric interest in MPD was not sustained, and consequently, cases of MPD went into decline.

It is important to emphasize that the histories of MPD and hypnosis have been intimately intertwined since the late 18th century. For this reason, several chapters will be devoted to examining the historical interrelations between these phenomena and their joint emergence from the demonological ideas that, by the late 18th century, were sputtering toward scientific obsolescence. The relationship between MPD and hypnosis is important for still another reason. Throughout the book I argue that influential modern conceptions of MPD are frequently based on outmoded and inaccurate views of hypnotic phenomena. Thus, to understand both modern conceptions of MPD and the serious limitations of those conceptions, it is important to examine modern sociocognitive views of hypnosis and the research that supports those views.

ORGANIZATION OF THIS BOOK

This section provides a preview of the book's structure. It is intended as a guide for those readers who may not be familiar with each of the diverse topics covered or with their relationship to the central topics of multiple personality and false memories.

Part I of the book, The Use of Hypnosis as a Therapeutic Tool (chapters 2–4), presents commonly held views about hypnosis, together with evidence to support some substantial revisions in our thinking about hypnosis. Much of this evidence is derived from research conducted at the Laboratory for Experimental Hypnosis at Carleton University. What emerges is a comprehensive sociocognitive perspective on hypnotic phenomena that is radically different from traditional "special state" views. Hypnotic behavior, including so-called hypnotic amnesia, is shown, at its core, to be strategic behavior enacted to fulfill the subject's beliefs and expectations about hypnosis. Hypnotic subjects should not be seen as the passive automatons of the popular literature, but as voluntary actors striving to fulfill their role as they define it or as it is defined for them by the experimental or clinical situation. The notion that hypnosis can be understood as an altered state of consciousness is thus rejected.

To the extent that theories of MPD are based on the premise that hypnotic behaviors occur during some altered state or that hypnotic and nonhypnotic experiences are processed and stored in different ways, they must be equally invalid. Take, for example, the purported amnesia of some patients for their other personalities, frequently said by MPD theorists to resemble hypnotic amnesia. For such theorists, amnesia becomes the marker for an altered, involuntary state of consciousness following precisely the formulation in the hypnosis literature. The amnesia both of the MPD patient and of the hypnotic subject may be understood as goal-directed, purposive activity. Moreover, as chapter 4 notes, the enactment of multiple roles or "identities" (such as the "femme" role enacted with varying degrees of public success by male transvestites) is, in reality, only rarely associated with amnesia for the alternative roles.

One of the more alarming claims about MPD is that some patients have been subject to ritualistic abuse at the hands of satanists or some other cultic group. It is often asserted that these patients have been exposed to powerful brainwashing techniques that have transformed them into robotic automata. Chapter 4 argues, however, that so-called brainwashing is much less effective than usually supposed. Accordingly, "brainwashing" by ritualistic or cult abusers cannot provide an explanation for MPD. Moreover, the very existence of satanic groups cannot be established beyond the harmless fantasies of the followers of Wicca. The clinical interest here lies, in truth, in the paranoid delusions and conspiracy theories that sustain belief in a vast underground of satanists. Chapter 9 (see below) continues this theme.

Part II, Creating False Memories, begins with an examination of the nature of memory and the complex issues surrounding the reported recovery of memories of childhood sexual abuse during the course of psychotherapy (chapter 5). Chapter 6 examines the origins in psychoanalytic thought of the notion that childhood sexual trauma, real or imagined, plays an important role in the development of certain forms of psychopathology. The chapter marshals the evidence for the view that memory is essentially reconstructive and schema-based. In this regard, the manner in which therapists may inadvertently lead their patients to generate abuse fantasies consistent with the therapists' own presuppositions about early childhood traumas is given particular attention.

The prevalence of child sexual abuse and the fate of abuse memories are considered in chapter 7. Widely held assumptions regarding the prevalence of incest are critically examined. Many of the studies that purport to establish the validity of repressed memories of early sexual abuse are shown to suffer from crippling methodological problems. Just as hypnotic procedures have been used to demonstrate other personalities, the same procedures play the same role in the recovery of repressed memories of abuse. This application of hypnosis is critically examined in chapter 8. Beginning with an examination of the use of hypnosis to "refresh" eyewitness testimony, this chapter suggests that the use of hypnosis, while not improving accuracy of recall, can lead to greater, and unjustified, confidence in what is recalled. Age regression, one of the hypnotic strategies commonly used to facilitate memory retrieval, leads to outcomes that are strongly influenced by context effects as well as by the expectations and beliefs of the subject.

Chapter 9, "Complex False Memories, Body Memories, and Hypnosis," tries to explain why so many psychotherapists come to believe the false memories of MPD patients that often entail bizarre, complex, and elaborate scenarios including ritual abuse and torture, as well as human and animal sacrifice perpetrated by many people over a long period of time. Therapists frequently assume that the detail and the elaboration of these usually intensely emotional stories, often accompanied by "body memories," demonstrate their essential veracity. This chapter shows, through an analysis of some fascinating research, that other explanations, much less exciting than ritual abuse, are inherently more plausible. This and the following chapter suggest that equally puzzling reports of UFO abduction may be seen as examples of complex false memories sustained by a social network of therapists and other "abductees." The elaboration in these cases of intricate, internally coherent, and emotionally charged scripts, which perhaps few of us would take at face value, may help us to better understand the formation of memories of abuse in MPD patients.

This theme is further advanced in chapter 11, which documents the ease with which multiple identities may be both created and modified in the laboratory in focused response to the experimental context. The chapter describes research in which past-life identity enactments were concocted following hypnotic age regression. The essential features of these created "identities" varied in ways predictable from the particular experimental procedures. In other words, such past-life enactments may be readily understood as social creations that may be obtained without much difficulty from many normally imaginative individuals. The implication is that multiple identities may be created with equal ease. In practice, such identities ordinarily display attributes and features strongly dependent on both the social context and the existing beliefs of the subject.

Part III, Multiple Identities in Other Cultures and Times, examines the phenomenon of multiple identities from a broad cross-cultural perspective. The reader will find here important and provocative discussions of the phenomena of spirit possession (chapter 12), demonic possession (chapter 13), witchcraft (chapter 14), and hysteria (chapter 15). These chapters provide detailed analyses of the usual social background of each of these phenomena and place MPD in a relevant historical context. The usefulness of a historical understanding is demonstrated in chapters 16 and 17. Chapter 16 presents some of the earliest case studies of contemporary MPD and relates its emergence to spiritism, whereas chapter 17 examines the history of the concept of dissociation, a concept initially invoked to explain manifestations of multiplicity.

Part IV, The Theory of Multiple Personality Disorder, begins with a critical examination of contemporary accounts of MPD (chapter 18). It spells out the ways in which the role of the multiple is now taught in our culture and relates such teaching to the recent and dramatic increase in the frequency with which the diagnosis of MPD is made, as well as to the sensational spiralling in the reported number of "alters" per patient. Perhaps increases in detection rates result from improved diagnostic methods in the manner of tests for physical disease. More likely, we are dealing with the epidemiology of a more mundane social contagion. The chapter suggests that most cases of MPD are provided by a small number of clinicians, adding to the plausibility of the social-learning hypothesis. Any comprehensive theory of MPD must explain these demographic phenomena.

Chapter 19, "Correlates of Multiple Personality Disorder," critically examines studies that purport to show that the alters hosted by one body are physiologically distinct. It also examines the extent to which MPD patients can be distinguished from non-MPD patients by such factors as preexisting psychopathology, hypnotizability, dissociative capacity, and fantasy proneness, as well as by experiential factors, including the occurrence of early trauma. The chapter illustrates the complexities of research in these areas and alerts us to the need for caution in interpreting the research results. This chapter interprets these studies in terms of those factors that facilitate or inhibit the enactment of multiplicity and cautions us that these factors are likely to be culturally specific.

Chapter 20 critically examines widely held notions regarding the connection between child abuse and MPD. The connection of MPD to child abuse is a relatively recent development and one that requires critical evaluation. Similarly, reports of satanic ritual abuse sometimes reported by MPD patients are also further evaluated. Again, the role that therapists play in eliciting the reports of sexual abuse from their MPD patients is examined. Factors contributing to the dissemination and acceptance of the satanic abuse myth among professionals are also scrutinized.

Chapter 21 offers an account of the sociopolitical context of the MPD phenomenon. It discusses our growing tendency to medicalize ordinary problems of living and the resulting economic rewards for psychotherapists as they expand the domain of psychopathology. In this climate, bad habits are redefined as "addictions" requiring expensive psychotherapeutic intervention. Allegations based on recovered memories are related to significant cultural–sexual issues, including the resurgence of evangelical Christianity and the recent conservative backlash against the movement by women toward social, political, and economic equality. The chapter explores how medical explanations of MPD may serve a political purpose that parallels those served by spirit possession explanations provided in other cultures and at other times. The final chapter, chapter 22, concludes that MPD can be understood only in specifically cultural and historical terms. Theories of MPD that neglect culture and history are likely to be misleading at best and radically deforming at worst.

I

THE USE OF HYPNOSIS AS
A THERAPEUTIC TOOL

2

HYPNOSIS: MYTHOLOGY VERSUS REALITY

Historically, MPD has been closely tied to hypnotic phenomena. Some modern investigators (e.g., Bliss, 1986; Braun, 1990) have argued that, in predisposed children, trauma produces a "hypnotic state" that facilitates the development of alter personalities. Purportedly these alters remain outside of awareness, separated from normal consciousness by a process akin to hypnotic amnesia. In addition, these alters are often first contacted by using hypnotic age regression as a means of helping patients to recall early traumas that purportedly led to the formation of alters. Some investigators contend that some MPD patients were abused in satanic cults and that cult members "programmed" the patients with posthypnotic suggestions to respond automatically in specified ways to cues that the cult members later presented.

All of these ideas are based on the taken-for-granted notions that the term *hypnosis* refers to a readily identifiable altered state of consciousness and that the causes of hypnotic phenomena differ fundamentally from the causes of the mundane social behaviors that people carry out in everyday life. As I will demonstrate in this chapter, this view of hypnosis is inaccurate. Nevertheless, it is the view commonly held in our culture, and it exerts a powerful influence on what people are willing to believe about the behavior of hypnotic subjects and, by extension, about the behavior of MPD patients.

THE MYTH OF HYPNOSIS

Suppose B., whom you know to have excellent vision, looks at a piece of paper held two feet from her nose. The paper has printed on it a large number 8 that you and others in the room can all see very clearly. B., however, insists that the piece of paper is blank and has nothing on it, and continues to insist that it is blank despite your proddings to describe everything that she sees. B. is able to accurately describe other objects that she looks at; it is only the "8" printed on the piece of paper that she claims not to see. Most people would probably react skeptically to B.'s reports that the paper was blank. They would be likely to think that B. was playing a joke or that she had some other motive for lying about what she could see. Most people would not believe that B. had somehow succeeded in making herself selectively blind to something she was focusing her eyes on. After all, it strains common sense to believe that people can make themselves selectively blind in this way. Moreover, we are all aware that people sometimes lie and exaggerate in order to play jokes, call attention to themselves, and so on. It is much more parsimonious (and sensible) to believe that B. is, for whatever reasons, inaccurately describing her experiences than it is to believe that she can selectively influence her nervous system to stop processing the supraliminal visual stimuli that she focuses her eyes on.

Now suppose you learn that before you entered the room B. had been hypnotized. She had been given a hypnotic induction procedure and then told that when she opened her eyes she would see nothing on the piece of paper held before her eyes. She would see the paper as completely blank. Many people who initially refused to believe that B. was selectively blind would probably be willing to believe it after learning that she had been hypnotized. Why? Because the idea that hypnosis is an altered state of consciousness that enables people to have unusual experiences and to do things that they could not normally do is a powerful cultural myth that exerts a strong hold on the modern imagination. This mythology includes the ideas that hypnotic suggestions can cause people to become temporarily blind or deaf, that hypnotic amnesia involves the automatic and complete forgetting of complex experiences, that hypnotic age regression leads to the accurate recall of forgotten memories (even long-forgotten memories from early childhood), and that posthypnotic suggestions cause people to automatically carry out orders given during hypnosis whenever they are presented with a cue that "activates" the suggestion. In addition, it is commonly believed that hypnotic subjects do not lie or misrepresent their experiences, and for this reason, outlandish reports like not being able to see the number "8" on a page are often given much greater credence that they deserve.

These taken-for-granted cultural beliefs about hypnosis are now known to be wrong (Baker, 1992; Spanos & Chaves, 1989). Moreover, most of them have been known to be wrong for over 30 years (Barber, 1969; Barber, Spanos, & Chaves, 1974; Sarbin, 1950; Sutcliffe, 1960). Nevertheless, these beliefs persist and are often perpetuated by some of the researchers investigating hypnotic phenomena and many clinicians who regard hypnosis as an unusual altered state with special therapeutic properties (Yapko, 1994a). These common but erroneous beliefs about hypnosis are often accepted uncritically in the MPD literature, and their acceptance provides strong support for disease theories concerning the origins and treatment of MPD. Therefore, before examining whether it is sensible to believe that hypnosis enables therapists to contact previously hidden selves, that a process akin to hypnotic amnesia enables such selves to remain hidden from conscious awareness for decades, that hypnosis enables the accurate recovery of previously repressed memories, or that posthypnotic suggestions can transform people into automata who are "programmed" to react without remembering why, it behooves us to look briefly at an alternative to the traditional view of hypnosis and at the empirical findings that support this alternative perspective.

THE SOCIOCOGNITIVE PERSPECTIVE

Criticism of the traditional notion that hypnosis involves special psychological processes has a long history (Sarbin, 1962; Spanos & Chaves, 1991). During the latter half of the 20th century, this critical tradition culminated in modern formulations that view hypnotic phenomena as similar to other forms of social behavior and that account for these phenomena without recourse to special psychological processes (Baker, 1992; Barber, 1969; Lynn & Rhue, 1991; Sarbin & Coe, 1972; Spanos & Chaves, 1989; Spanos & Coe, 1992; Wagstaff, 1981). Common to these formulations is the idea that the term *hypnosis* refers not to a state or condition of the person but to the historically rooted conceptions of hypnosis and hypnotic responding that are held by the participants in the mini-drama that is labeled the hypnotic situation. According to this perspective, hypnotic responding is context dependent; it is determined by the willingness of subjects to adopt the hypnotic role, by their understandings of what is expected of them in that role, by their understanding of how role requirements change as the situation unfolds, by how they interpret the complex and sometimes ambiguous communications that constitute hypnotic suggestions, by their willingness and ability to use their imaginal and other cognitive skills to create the subjective experiences called for by suggestions, and by how feedback from the hypnotist and from their own responding influences the definitions they hold of themselves as hypnotic subjects and the interpretations they apply to their hypnotic experiences (Spanos & Chaves, 1989). Taken together, these ideas constitute a sociocognitive perspective toward hypnotic phenomena that challenges the traditional ideas that hypnosis is a special state and that hypnotic responding involves special processes. The fundamental tenets of the sociocognitive position were outlined by R. W. White (1941) more than a generation ago:

> Hypnotic behavior is meaningful, goal-directed striving, its most general goal being to behave like a hypnotized person as this is continuously defined by the operator and understood by the subject. (p. 483)

Before examining the evidence that has led proponents of the sociocognitive position to reject traditional views of hypnosis, it is important to describe basic components of the hypnotic situation.

COMPONENTS OF HYPNOTIC SITUATIONS

Hypnotic situations frequently involve two components. The first is a hypnotic induction procedure that explicitly defines the situation as hypnotic and that bolsters this definition of the situation by unfolding in a manner that is consistent with the preconceptions that most people hold about hypnosis (Sarbin & Coe, 1972; Spanos, 1982). For example, standard hypnotic induction procedures include interrelated suggestions that the subject is becoming relaxed, going to sleep, and entering an hypnotic state. Furthermore, these suggestions are usually phrased in such a way that it is implied that the suggested events are happening to the subject rather than initiated by the subject (e.g., "you are drifting deeper and deeper asleep").

The second component of the hypnotic situation involves the administration of suggestions that call for relatively specific behavioral and/or subjective responses. In clinical settings, suggestions are usually aimed at overcoming the problems of the patient. In some cases, the suggestions are relatively direct and aimed at modifying specific problematic behaviors. Suggestions to stop smoking, to eat less, to feel better about one's self, or to feel less pain are common examples. However, depending on the purposes and theoretical orientation of the clinician, the suggestions can vary widely and include requests to regress to an earlier age, to uncover hidden memories, to experience supposedly unconscious selves, or even to remember back beyond one's birth and experience past-life personalities. Regardless of their contents, however, suggestions typically imply that the suggested experiences and behaviors are emerging or occurring automatically and effortlessly (e.g., "your hand will be numb, dull, and insensitive, like a piece of rubber" and "you are becoming younger and younger, going back in time further and further, now you are 10 years old").

In experimental settings, subjects are frequently administered a standardized series of suggestions preceded by a hypnotic induction procedure. Each suggestion requires a simple behavioral response. Subjects are scored as passing the suggestion if they make the requisite response and failing the suggestion if they do not make the response. For instance, the arm levitation suggestion on one frequently used scale informs the subject that his or her outstretched arm is getting lighter and lighter and rising in the air. The subject is also instructed to imagine that his or her arm is being pumped up with helium that makes it feel lighter and lighter. If the subject raises his or her arm six or more inches within the requisite time, he or she is scored as passing this suggestion (Spanos, Radtke, Hodgins, Stam, & Bertrand, 1983). The number of suggestions out of the total that the subject passes is summed to yield a hypnotizability (also called hypnotic susceptibility) score for the subject. On some scales subjects rate their level of subjective experience to the suggestions, and these scales provide subjective as well as behavioral indexes of hypnotizability (Bertrand, 1989). A number of different hypnotizability scales are currently used in experimental settings and sometimes in clinical settings as well. All of them tend to be structured similarly, assess similar responses, and correlate to substantial degrees with one another (see Bertrand, 1989, for a review). People who respond to most or all of the suggestions on these scales are labeled highly hypnotizable, whereas those who respond to none or only a few of the suggestions are labeled as low hypnotizables.

If people are not exposed to training aimed at changing their level of hypnotizability, then, at least in adults, hypnotizability remains fairly stable. When the interval between hypnotizability tests is only a day or two, the test–retest correlations are fairly high (e.g., $r = .70$; Hilgard, 1965). More impressive, the test–retest correlations remain moderately high even when the retest interval is measured in decades rather than in days (Gwynn, Spanos, Gabora, & Jarrett, 1988; Morgan, Johnson, & Hilgard, 1974; Piccione, Hilgard, & Zimbardo, 1989; Spanos, Liddy, Baxter, & Burgess, 1994). As we shall later see, several different theories have been proposed to account for the stability of hypnotizability, and these bear on theories of multiple identity.

In short, in both experimental and clinical situations, hypnotic suggestions are communications that invite subjects to construct imaginary or "as-if" situations (e.g., imagine an arm pumped up with helium), to define those as-if situations as real, and to enact behaviors that are congruent with the definition of the imaginary situation as real (e.g., lifting the "helium-filled" arm). Subjects are implicitly instructed to convince themselves as well as the hypnotist that they are unable to bend their arm, that a cat is in their lap, that they are unable to recall well-known facts, that they have reverted to childhood, that they possess previously hidden selves or personalities, and so on. In effect, hypnotic subjects are asked to temporarily set aside the rules and assumptions usually used to differentiate imagined (as-if) situations from real events and, in so doing, to define the ongoing situation in terms of the as-if events described in the suggestions (Bertrand, 1989; Sarbin & Coe, 1972; Shor, 1959, 1970; Spanos, 1971, 1982).

TRADITIONAL VIEWS OF HYPNOSIS

Traditional views of hypnosis hold that subjects respond to suggestions when hypnotic procedures induce a "trance state" or a split between various mental processes called *dissociation* (Bliss, 1986; Fromm, 1992; Hilgard, 1965, 1986, 1991). According to such views, hypnotic subjects experience their responses to suggestions as feeling involuntary because the responses really are involuntary; they are under the control of an unconscious agency or process. On the other hand, sociocognitive views hold that responses to hypnotic suggestions do not stem from a trance state or from dissociated mental processes (Spanos & Chaves, 1989). Instead, responding to suggestions, like most other behavior in everyday life, is a social product. Such responding reflects the expectations and attitudes that people bring to the hypnotic situation, the interpretations they make of that situation, and the goals they are attempting to achieve by the manner in which they present themselves in that situation. The sociocognitive perspective recognizes that hypnotic subjects sometimes experience their responses as feeling involuntary (Spanos, 1971; Spanos, Rivers, & Ross, 1977). Nevertheless, according to this perspective, hypnotic subjects retain control over their behavior and guide it in terms of their understandings of what is expected. Subjects sometimes report that their behavior feels involuntary, not because they have lost control over their behavior, but because they interpret their goal-directed behavior as involuntary in line with the expectations conveyed in suggestions (Lynn, Rhue, & Weekes, 1989; Spanos, 1971; Spanos & Gorassini, 1984).

CHALLENGES TO TRADITIONAL VIEWS OF HYPNOSIS

In the past 40 years, a great deal of empirical evidence has challenged traditional views of hypnosis (for reviews, see Baker, 1992; Spanos, 1986b; Spanos & Chaves, 1989; Wagstaff, 1981). Contrary to the assumption frequently found in the MPD literature, over a century of research has failed to uncover unambiguous behavioral, physiological, or subjective report criteria for denoting a uniquely "hypnotic state" (Barber, 1979; Fellows, 1986; Kirsch, 1992; Radtke & Spanos, 1981; Sarbin & Coe, 1972). For example, subjects to whom hypnotic induction procedures have been administered do not differ from people who have simply been instructed to relax or to sit quietly on such physiological indexes as electroencephalographic (EEG) responding, electromyographic (EMG) responding, eye movements, electrodermal responding, heart rate, respiration rate, and so on (for reviews, see Edmonston, 1981, 1991; Perlini & Spanos, 1991). Hypnotic and non-hypnotically relaxed subjects also fail to differ in their reports of unusual subjective experiences such as changes in body image, experienced sensory changes (e.g., voices sounding distant, feelings of floating), experienced cognitive changes (e.g., thoughts slowing down), and degree of experienced relaxation (for reviews, see Barber, 1969; Edmonston, 1967, 1991). In short, the available evidence fails to support the hypothesis that hypnotic procedures produce a unique or unusual state of consciousness, or physiological and subjective changes that reflect anything other than simple relaxation and situationally induced expectations.

COMMON FALLACIES ABOUT HYPNOTIC RESPONSES

The idea that hypnotic responding involves special or unusual psychological processes has been fostered by several persistent but erroneous propositions. These include the notions that (a) hypnotic subjects typically exhibit higher levels of responsiveness to suggestions than do nonhypnotic subjects, (b) hypnotic subjects undergo unique cognitive changes that constitute the essential feature of hypnosis, and (c) highly hypnotizable subjects achieve highly unusual distortions in perception.

Heightened Suggestibility

The notion that hypnotic procedures are intrinsically more effective than nonhypnotic (control) procedures in inducing heightened responsiveness to suggestions persisted until the 1960s. During that decade and those that followed, an extensive series of studies carried out primarily by Barber and his associates demonstrated that short instructions aimed at motivating subjects' performance (i.e., task-motivating instructions) usually produced increments in suggestibility that matched (and sometimes exceeded) the increments produced by hypnotic induction procedures (for reviews, see Barber, 1979; Barber & Ham, 1974; Barber, Spanos, & Chaves, 1974; M. J. Diamond, 1974). For instance, Barber (1965) found that subjects who were administered either a hypnotic induction procedure or task-motivational instructions exhibited equally high levels of responsiveness on a scale that measured such suggested behaviors as body immobility, arm levitation, and postsuggestion response. Equivalent levels of response in hypnotic and motivated nonhypnotic subjects have also been obtained in studies that assessed responsiveness to suggestions for pain reduction (Barber & Hahn, 1962; M. B. Evans & Paul, 1970; Spanos, Barber, & Lang, 1974; Spanos, Perlini, Patrick, Bell, & Gwynn, 1990; Spanos, Perlini, & Robertson, 1989; Spanos, Radtke-Bodorik, Ferguson, & Jones, 1979), amnesia (Barber & Calverley, 1966; Norris, 1973; Spanos & Ham, 1973; Stam, 1989), source amnesia (Spanos, Gwynn, Della Malva, & Bertrand, 1988), auditory and visual hallucination (Barber & Calverley, 1964a; Graham, 1970; Ham & Spanos, 1974; Spanos & Barber, 1968; Spanos, de-Groot, & Gwynn, 1987; Spanos, Ham, & Barber, 1973; Spanos, Mullens, & Rivers, 1979), time distortion (Barber & Calverley, 1964b; Casey, 1966; Edmonston & Erbeck, 1967), deafness (B. Jones & Spanos, 1982; Spanos, Burgess, & Perlini, 1991), enhanced salivation (Spanos, Brice, & Gabora, 1992), age regression (Spanos & Bures, 1994), and memory and abstract reasoning (Salzberg & DePiano, 1980).

Some investigators dismiss experimental studies like those outlined above as irrelevant to the clinical situation (Graham, Wright, Toman, & Mark, 1975). According to these investigators, the artificial nature of the experimental laboratory produces findings that cannot be generalized to the clinic.

Until relatively recently, clinical research on hypnotic treatments was so methodologically unsound that few, if any, reliable conclusions were possible. However, the past 15 years have witnessed a gradual improvement in the quality of clinical research concerning hypnosis. Importantly, examination of the methodologically sound studies in this area indicates that in clinical settings, as in laboratory settings, nonhypnotic suggestions are typically as effective as hypnotic suggestions (for reviews, see Spanos, 1991, 1994). For instance, nonhypnotic suggestions have been shown to be at least as effective as hypnotic suggestions in the treatment of warts (Spanos, Stenstrom, & Johnston, 1988), smoking (Hyman, Stanley, Burrows, & Horne, 1986; S. W. Rabkin, Boyko, Shane, & Kaufert, 1984; Spanos, Mondoux, & Burgess, 1995; Spanos, Sims, de Faye, Mondoux, & Gabora, 1992), weight control (Devine & Bornstein, 1980; Deyoub & Wilkie, 1980; Wadden & Flaxman, 1981), headache (Nolan, Spanos, Hayward, & Scott, 1994; Spinhoven, Linssen, Van Dyck, & Zitman, 1988), chronic pain (Edelson & Fitzpatrick, 1989), temporomandibular joint pain (Stam, 1989; Stam, McGrath, & Brooke, 1984), pain and distress associated with bone marrow aspiration and lumbar puncture in pediatric cancer patients (Wall & Womack, 1989), fear reduction (Lang, 1969), public speaking anxiety (Spanos, Burnley, Burgess, & Lacene, 1994), insomnia (Graham et al., 1975) and posttraumatic stress disorder (Brom, Kleber, & Defares, 1989).

With respect to these studies, it is also worth noting that both hypnotic and nonhypnotic procedures are largely ineffective in producing long-term reductions in smoking, that the reductions in headache activity seen with both hypnotic and nonhypnotic procedures are often small and sometimes transient, that most subjects whose warts are treated with hypnotic or non-hypnotic suggestions do not lose their warts, and that the reductions in speech anxiety produced by nonhypnotic and hypnotic procedures often fail to produce any noticeable changes in objective speech-giving perform-ance.

In the studies cited above, explicit hypnotic suggestions were com-pared with explicit nonhypnotic suggestions. Other studies have compared hypnotic suggestions with placebos in the treatment of various disorders. The results have been mixed. For instance, hypnotic (and nonhypnotic) suggestions were more effective than placebos in reducing warts (Spanos, Gwynn, et al., 1988; Spanos, Williams, & Gwynn, 1990) and irritable bowl syndrome (Whorwell, Prior & Faragher, 1984). However, hypnotic and placebo treatments failed to differ significantly in the treatment of head-ache (Spanos, Liddy, et al., 1993) and failed to differ in the extent to which they reduced discomfort during and after surgery (Bonke, Schmitz, Verhage, & Zwaveling, 1986; L. Snow, 1979).

In summary, the common belief that hypnotic procedures are partic-ularly effective at facilitating responsiveness to suggestion, and much more effective in this regard than nonhypnotic procedures, is simply untrue. Moreover, this belief is untrue with respect to the clinical use of hypnotic suggestions as well as with respect to the use of hypnotic suggestions in experimental contexts.

Unique Cognitive Processes

Despite emphasizing the social psychological nature of hypnotic re-sponding, White (1941) continued to believe that hypnosis involved an altered state of consciousness that was characterized by subtle changes in cognitive functioning. This aspect of White's ideas was pursued most sys-tematically by Orne (1959, 1979a) and his associates (e.g., Orne, Sheehan, & Evans, 1968). Orne (1959) contended that much of hypnotic behavior could be explained in terms of social compliance, and like sociocognitive theorists, he described highly hypnotizable subjects as motivated to please the hypnotist and to respond in terms of the suggestions and other social demands that constitute the hypnotic situation. Unlike sociocognitive the-orists, however, Orne argued that hypnotic responding involves a trance state that possesses unique or essential cognitive characteristics. Suppos-edly, these cognitive characteristics, which Orne labeled "trance logic," involved a tolerance for logical incongruity that was hypnosis specific.

To assess these ideas, Orne (1959) used an experimental paradigm that compared the behavior of highly hypnotizable subjects with the behavior of low hypnotizables who were explicitly instructed to fake hypnosis to fool the hypnotist (i.e., simulators). The highly hypnotizable nonsimulators and the simulators were then exposed to the same hypnotic procedures and suggestions, and the hypnotist was not told which subjects were which. Because simulators and nonsimulators were exposed to the same hypnotic procedures, Orne argued that these subjects were exposed to identical social demands. According to this argument, differences in the behavior of the simulators and nonsimulators had to result from variables or processes other than social demands. Orne attributed such differences to the operation of a trance state in the nonsimulators and to its absence in the simulators.

In many experiments, however, the objective performance of simulators and nonsimulators was indistinguishable. These findings are important because they indicate that behaviors that were once assumed to be unique to hypnotic subjects and probably unfakable actually reflected contextual demands and could be easily faked. For instance, these experiments indicated that simulators were as effective as highly hypnotizable hypnotic subjects at giving convincing demonstrations of age regression (O'Connell, Shor, & Orne, 1970; Spanos & Bures, 1994), pain reduction (Hilgard, Hilgard, MacDonald, Morgan, & Johnson, 1978), optokinetic nystagmus (F. J. Evans, Reich, & Orne, 1972), source amnesia (Spanos, Gwynn, et al., 1988), and visual field narrowing (Leibowitz, Lundy, & Guez, 1980; R. J. Miller & Leibowitz, 1976). Simulators were also as likely as high hypnotizables to perform dangerous or "immoral" suggested behaviors (Coe, Kobayashi, & Howard, 1973; Levitt, Aronoff, Morgan, Overley, & Parrish, 1975; Orne & Evans, 1965). Although these findings do not necessarily mean that hypnotic subjects are simply faking their responses, they certainly indicate that many overt responses that were once considered to be beyond the abilities of the unhypnotized (e.g., age regression, optokinetic nystagmus, and high levels of pain tolerance) or unlikely to be performed by people in their "normal state" (e.g., dangerous or self-destructive behaviors) are within normal limits and a function of the social demands generated in experimental settings.

Orne's (1959) primary theoretical interest, however, was in those experiments that did find differences in the behavior of highly hypnotizable hypnotic subjects and simulators. For instance, when it was suggested that they visually hallucinate a person sitting across the room, nonsimulating hypnotic subjects often described their hallucinated person as transparent, whereas simulators usually reported that their hallucination was solid rather than transparent. Orne contended that this and other relatively subtle differences between the behaviors of simulators and nonsimulators indicated that "real" (as opposed to faked) hypnotic responding is characterized by a tolerance for logical incongruity (i.e., reporting that one can both see and see through a hallucinated object is, according to Orne, illogical).

A good deal of experimentation was conducted on trance logic responding during the 1970s and 1980s (for a review, see de Groot & Gwynn, 1989). Many of the behavioral differences between simulators and hypnotic nonsimulators that Orne touted as indexes of trance logic could not be replicated by other researchers (e.g., Obstoj & Sheehan, 1977; Sheehan, 1977; Spanos, de Groot, & Gwynn, 1987). In addition, as research on trance logic responding progressed, it became increasingly clear that the assumption that simulators and nonsimulators were exposed to the same social demands was untenable (e.g., de Groot & Gwynn, 1989; Sheehan, 1971). Instead, the administration of simulation instructions had a very substantial influence on how subjects interpreted and responded to the demands associated with test suggestions. Spanos (1986b) hypothesized that nonsimulating subjects given suggestions (with or without hypnotic induction) are exposed not only to demands for compliance but also to demands for responding honestly and for reporting accurately about their experiences. According to this hypothesis, nonsimulators tend to report transparent hallucinations not because they are exhibiting "trance logic," but because they are reporting more or less accurately that the suggested images they conjure up with their eyes open tend to be nonvivid, incomplete, of short duration, and transparent. Simulators, on the other hand, are explicitly instructed to ignore demands for honesty and to lie about their experiences so as to fool the experimenter into thinking that they are hypnotized. Consequently, they tend to give idealized responses. An ideal response to a visual hallucination suggestion would be an experience that was indistinguishable from an actual perception. Consequently, when asked to describe their experiences, simulators lie as instructed and give idealized hallucination reports that sound like perceptions (e.g., vivid, complete, and solid).

On the basis of this hypothesis, Spanos, de Groot, et al. (1987) demonstrated that the reliable differences in responding between simulators and nonsimulators that Orne (1959, 1979a) had attributed to "trance logic" were more parsimoniously explained in terms of the different demands to which these subjects were exposed. These findings indicate that differences in the behavior of simulators and nonsimulators that were originally attributed to subtle cognitive processes unique to a supposed hypnotic state turn out, instead, to result from subtle differences in the contextual demands to which nonsimulators and simulators are exposed. Rather than supporting the notion that hypnosis is an altered state associated with unique cognitive processes, research on the topic of trance logic has underscored the pervasive and sometimes subtle ways in which situational variables influence the experiences and reports of hypnotic subjects.

SUMMARY

Hypnotic behavior is goal-directed social action and is much more ordinary than it initially appears. Contrary to popular conceptualizations, hypnotic procedures do not greatly enhance responsiveness to suggestion. Nonhypnotic subjects can be induced, with brief instructions, to respond to suggestions in the same way and to the same extent as hypnotic subjects. The available evidence fails to support the common beliefs that hypnotic procedures produce a unique state of consciousness (i.e., a trance state), unique changes in cognitive functioning, or unique changes in physiological responding. On the contrary, the available data indicate that hypnotic and nonhypnotic subjects process information in the same way.

These findings have important implications for theories of MPD because, historically as well as currently, a number of these theories have been based on serious misunderstandings concerning the nature of hypnotic responding. For example, several modern theories (Bliss, 1986; Braun, 1990; Ross, 1989) of MPD are based on the unsupported notions that hypnotic behavior occurs in an altered state of consciousness and that hypnotic and nonhypnotic experiences are processed, and stored in memory, in different ways. These ideas gain legitimacy because, in many professional as well as lay circles, the mythology of hypnosis on which these ideas are based is assumed to be true.

Central to the mythology of hypnosis are the ideas that highly hypnotizable subjects can produce dramatic changes in perception and memory that transcend normal abilities, and that these subjects actually lose voluntary control over their own behavior to dissociated subsystems that are created by suggestions. MPD theorists often assume that these ideas are valid and that they can help explain the loss of control that MPD patients supposedly experience when dissociated alters "take control" or compel patients to behave against their own wishes. These ideas are examined in the next chapter.

3

HIGH HYPNOTIZABILITY AND DRAMATIC BEHAVIORS

The fact that hypnotic procedures are not more effective than various nonhypnotic procedures in enhancing responsiveness to suggestions is now generally accepted even by investigators who are identified with traditional views concerning hypnosis (e.g., Bowers, 1976). Nevertheless, some subjects, regardless of whether they are administered a hypnotic induction procedure, exhibit what appear to be very dramatic responses to suggestions. For instance, some highly hypnotizable subjects report that they lose control over their motor responses and, despite their best efforts, cannot bend their arm or open their eyes, and, as described earlier, some report becoming selectively blind or deaf following suggestions. Obviously, if responses such as these are taken at face value, they indicate that some subjects undergo truly remarkable mental changes following suggestions. As some traditionally minded hypnosis investigators argue, whether a hypnotic induction procedure is required to elicit such responses is of relatively minor importance (Bowers, 1976; Hilgard, 1986). The fact that highly hypnotizable subjects can carry out such amazing feats is evidence that these subjects possess highly unique and unusual abilities.

But should these dramatic-looking responses really be taken at face value? The available research now clearly indicates that the answer is no.

When the seemingly dramatic responses of highly hypnotizable subjects are examined carefully, they turn out to be more mundane then they originally appeared.

NEGATIVE HALLUCINATIONS

Among the most dramatic claims associated with hypnosis are reports of suggestion-induced negative hallucinations: the idea that highly responsive hypnotic subjects can be made to suffer some profound sensory loss (e.g., deafness, blindness) through suggestion. For example, Erickson (1938a, 1938b) contended that hypnotic deafness was indistinguishable from neurologically produced deafness. As evidence, he reported that 6 out of 30 subjects whom he judged to be in "hypnotic trance" failed to respond to deliberately embarrassing remarks, did not raise their voices to overcome extraneous noise, and did not react to unexpected sounds. Relatedly, several investigators (Black & Wigan, 1961; Crawford, MacDonald, & Hilgard, 1979; Korotkin, Pleshkova, & Suslova, 1969) concluded that hypnotic suggestions for deafness actually impaired their subjects' hearing because the subjects reported sounds as less loud after the hypnotic suggestions than before. Similar claims have been made for the reality of hypnotic blindness, on the basis of subjects' reports that they could not see stimuli (Blum, 1975; Zamansky & Bartis, 1985).

The problem with inferring impairments in hearing or vision in these studies is fairly obvious. Suggestions for deafness and blindness tacitly instruct subjects to behave as if they are deaf or blind. Consequently, subjects who hear and see quite well, but are motivated to present themselves as "hypnotized," may report their hearing or vision as impaired or engage in other voluntary behaviors (e.g., consciously suppress startle responses to "unexpected" noises) that convey the impression of deafness or blindness.

Sutcliffe (1961) described this problem more than a generation ago. He labeled investigators who were willing to infer dramatic changes in the perceptions of hypnotic subjects solely on the basis of subjects' verbal reports or other voluntary behaviors as "credulous." He contrasted credulous investigators with "skeptical" investigators who refused to draw inferences about perceptual change on the basis of voluntary responses that could be easily influenced by situational demands independently of any actual changes in perception. Sutcliffe (1961), as well as Pattie (1950) before him and numerous investigators after him (see W. J. Jones & Flynn, 1989, for a review), demonstrated that when perceptual alteration was measured by using objective criteria that subjects could not easily influence voluntarily, the evidence that suggestions produced dramatic perceptual changes all but disappeared.

For example, several studies (Barber & Calverley, 1964b; Kline, Guze, & Haggerty, 1954; Kramer & Tucker, 1967; Scheibe, Gray, & Keim, 1968; Sutcliffe, 1961) examined the reality of hypnotic deafness by using a procedure called delayed auditory feedback (DAF). In the DAF paradigm, subjects wear headphones while they read aloud. Subjects are tape recorded as they read, and their voice is played back to them over the headphones. As long as what subjects are hearing over the headphones corresponds to what they are reading, they read aloud normally. However, when a slight delay is introduced between what subjects are reading and what they are hearing, subjects with normal hearing begin to pause, stammer, and stutter. Deaf subjects, of course, are not affected by DAF. In all of the studies that used this procedure, hypnotic subjects given deafness suggestions stuttered during DAF in the same way as subjects with normal hearing. Thus, despite their claims of being unable to hear, the objective evidence from DAF studies indicates that the hearing of "hypnotically deaf" subjects is unimpaired.

A number of other paradigms for objectively assessing perceptual response have been used to assess not only hypnotic deafness (Pattie, 1950; Spanos, Jones, & Malfara, 1982) but also hypnotic blindness (Miller, Hennessy, & Leibowitz, 1973; Pattie, 1935), hypnotic color blindness (Barber & Deeley, 1961), hypnotic cutaneous anesthesia (Pattie, 1956), and hypnotically altered perception of egocentric distance (MacCraken, Gogel, & Blum, 1980). In each case, the results indicated that hypnotic suggestions for perceptual change did not result in objective evidence of perceptual change—despite subjects' reports to the contrary.

Although the studies cited above indicate that hypnotic suggestions frequently fail to produce sensory impairments, they say little about the variables that do influence subjects to alter their verbal reports following negative hallucination suggestions. It is well-known, however, that subjects in psychology experiments that have nothing to do with hypnosis frequently misdescribe their experiences to conform with normative pressures (Asch, 1952) or to save face (Levy, 1967), and they frequently respond to the requests of authority figures by carrying out behaviors that they find personally distasteful (Milgram, 1974). Consequently, it should not be particularly surprising if hypnotic subjects also sometimes knowingly exaggerate their degree of responding, and misdescribe their subjective experiences, to meet experimental demands.

To examine these ideas, Spanos, Flynn, and Gabora (1989) devised a methodology that provides a relatively unambiguous index of behavioral compliance during negative hallucination responding. Highly hypnotizable subjects were administered a hypnotic induction procedure and were told that, when they opened their eyes, they would see a completely blank piece of paper. In fact, the paper had printed on it a large and easily visible number 8. Subjects were asked to open their eyes and look at the piece of paper. During the 60 seconds that the paper was in front of them they were asked to describe what they saw. If they said the paper was blank, they were asked repeatedly if they were certain that there was nothing on it. Under these circumstances, the large majority of these highly hypnotizable subjects admitted seeing the number 8 on the paper. However, 15 subjects reported on each probe that the piece of paper was completely blank and had nothing on it. The paper was removed from the subjects' view, and the hypnotic procedure and blindness suggestion were canceled. The 15 subjects who consistently claimed blindness for the number 8 were then interviewed by a second experimenter, who administered instructions designed to elicit from subjects a confession that they had, in fact, seen the number 8 on the paper. These subjects were told that people who attempt to fake hypnosis always insist that they are unable to see anything on the paper from the moment that they opened their eyes. However, they were further told that nonfaking subjects see a figure on the paper that gradually fades. Finally, subjects were told that the experimenter was interested in determining how the figure on the paper had faded over the 60-second exposure interval, and they were asked to draw what they had seen during each of the four 15-second segments of that interval.

It is important to keep in mind that the experimenter never told subjects what had been on the piece of paper. Therefore, subjects who drew a number 8 as being present in one of the 15-second segments must have seen that number on the paper during the suggestion period but lied at that time about having done so. Because subjects had been repeatedly asked about what was on the paper as they looked at it, their reports of seeing nothing cannot be explained in terms of retrospective reinterpretation or memory failure (Burgess, Spanos, Ritt, Hordy, & Brooks, 1993).

All but 1 of the 15 subjects who claimed that they saw nothing on the paper during the suggestion period drew an 8 during the interview period. These findings demonstrate that highly hypnotizable subjects who report the perceptual distortions called for by negative hallucination suggestions sometimes purposely exaggerate their reports to meet experimental demands.

Obviously, these findings do not mean that hypnotic responses are always faked or that compliance is an all-or-nothing activity. As pointed out by Wagstaff (1983, 1986), highly hypnotizable hypnotic subjects probably try their best to generate the subjective experiences called for by suggestions. Compliance is most likely to come into play when subjects who have an investment in presenting themselves as deeply hypnotized are unable to generate the experiences and/or behaviors that will sustain that self-presentation. It is in just such situations that people typically cheat or exaggerate in everyday life, and it should therefore come as no surprise that such situations also elicit varying degrees of compliance from hypnotic subjects. In summary, these findings support the hypothesis that compliance is a central component in hypnotic responding (Burgess et al., 1993; Spanos & Coe, 1992; Wagstaff, 1981, 1985).

INVOLUNTARY HYPNOTIC RESPONSES?

Hypnotic subjects sometimes report that their responses to suggestions feel effortless and involuntary (Spanos, Rivers, & Ross, 1977; Weitzenhoffer, 1974). In addition, they sometimes behave as if they are unable to resist the effects of suggestions. For instance, some subjects who are given a suggestion that their arm is stiff and rigid appear to struggle unsuccessfully to bend the arm, and some given suggestions for amnesia report being unable to recall despite trying to do so (Spanos, Cobb, & Gorassini, 1985). Highly hypnotizable subjects are particularly likely to respond in these ways. Traditional theorists argue from such evidence that highly hypnotizable hypnotic subjects lose control over their own responses. According to Hilgard (1977a), for example, "one of the most striking findings of hypnosis is the loss of control over actions normally voluntary" (p. 115). Alternatively, sociocognitive theorists hold that hypnotic subjects retain control of their behavior and guide it in goal-directed fashion to meet situational demands. According to this perspective, one of the central demands of the hypnotic situation is to behave as if one has lost control over suggested responding. Some subjects succeed in meeting this demand by interpreting their goal-directed responses as involuntary happenings (Lynn & Rhue, 1991; Spanos & Gorassini, 1984; Spanos, Rivers, & Ross, 1977).

A number of well-known studies in social psychology (e.g., Bem, 1967) demonstrate that people frequently define their feelings and their actions in terms of the context in which these responses occur. Without realizing it, people are often strongly influenced in how they define their own behavior and the behavior of others by the situation in which the behaviors occur. For instance, in a classic study, Schacter and Singer (1962) found that people who had been given a drug that caused physiological arousal interpreted their symptoms of arousal (e.g., rapid heart beat) as either anger or euphoria depending on the context in which the symptoms were experienced. Similarly, the way in which people interpret the behavior of others is strongly dependent on what they know about the actors involved and the contexts in which the behaviors occur. For instance, if we see A push B, know that A and B are friends who often engage in such "horseplay," and observe the behavior in a context where "horseplay" is considered appropriate (e.g., at the beach), then we are likely to interpret A's push as a friendly gesture. However, if we know that A and B are leaders of rival drug gangs, and the push occurs in a darkened alley, we are likely to apply a more sinister interpretation than "friendly horseplay." In short, almost all behavior is open to a wide range of interpretations. In everyday life, people interpret their own actions and the actions of others in terms of a background of tacit understandings and in terms of the particular understandings that are primed by the context in which the behavior occurs.

People in our culture hold well-developed ideas about hypnosis, and one of these is the belief that hypnotic responses are involuntary occurrences (London, 1961; McConkey, 1986; Spanos, Salas, Bertrand, & Johnston, 1989). In other words, defining a situation as hypnosis primes people to interpret the resultant behavior of hypnotic subjects in terms of tacit understandings concerning involuntary responding. Moreover, the hypnotic situation typically unfolds in a manner that strongly reinforces the tacit understanding that hypnotic responses occur involuntarily.

To illustrate these ideas, Spanos, Salas, et al. (1989) showed subjects videotapes in which a female model slowly moved her arm. Subjects in one group saw the model with her eyes closed and her head bent down on her chest. They also heard a voice tell the woman that she was now deeply hypnotized. Next the voice administered an arm levitation suggestion, and the woman slowly raised her arm. Subjects in another group saw a woman intently reading a book. The woman stopped reading and said "there goes that fly again." Slowly she raised her hand, appeared to be tracking a fly, and finally slammed her hand down on the table and said "got him."

Following their respective video presentations, the subjects were asked to describe everything that had happened in the video and everything they could recall about the woman's behavior. Subjects who saw the hypnosis video almost always described the woman's arm movement as an involuntary occurrence or happening. They wrote sentences such as "her arm went up" and "her arm floated in the air." The wording of these sentences implies that some agency other than the woman was responsible for the arm movement. In other words, they imply that subjects construed the woman's behavior to be an involuntary occurrence.

Subjects who saw the fly-swatting video described the woman's behavior very differently. Now, the woman's behavior was implicitly defined as goal-directed and voluntary. Subjects wrote sentence like "she lifted her arm to hit the fly," which imply that the woman was the agent of her own behavior. In other words, subjects in these two groups defined similar overt behaviors (i.e., the woman lifting her arm) in very different ways depending on the context in which the behavior occurred.

The same cues that led observers of the hypnotic video to define the model's behavior as involuntary are likely to lead hypnotic subjects to define their own overt responses in the same way. Hypnotic subjects, like everyone else, are engaged more or less continuously in using inputs from the social context to interpret, understand, and guide their own behavior. The cues in the hypnotic situation bias subjects to adopt an interpretation of their responses to suggestions as involuntary, and some subjects respond to these cues by adopting that interpretation.

FACTORS THAT LEAD TO INVOLUNTARY RESPONSES

Two questions now arise: What are the variables in the hypnotic situation that lead subjects to adopt involuntariness interpretations, and why do highly hypnotizable subjects apply such interpretations to their own responses more readily than others?

Wording of Suggestions and Involuntariness Interpretations

The most important component of the hypnotic situation for leading subjects to define their responses as involuntary appears to be the wording of suggestions. Recall that suggestions do *not* explicitly instruct subjects to carry out overt behaviors. Instead, suggestions are worded in the passive voice and inform subjects that certain events are happening *to* them. In other words, suggestions invite subjects to adopt and temporarily treat as veridical an "as-if" situation, namely that their own actions are no longer self-initiated or goal-directed.

Spanos and Katsanis (1989) demonstrated the importance of suggestion wording in determining reports of involuntariness by administering a suggestion for pain reduction to highly hypnotizable subjects. Both hypnotic and nonhypnotic subjects in this experiment were administered a cognitive strategy (imagining the hand in a protective glove). However, for half of the hypnotic subjects and for half of the nonhypnotic subjects, the strategy was worded in the passive voice to imply that pain reduction would occur automatically and without effort. For the remaining hypnotic and nonhypnotic subjects, the strategy was actively worded to imply that subjects had to exert voluntary effort to reduce pain. Hypnotic and nonhypnotic subjects reported pain reductions of equivalent magnitude and reported that their pain reductions occurred effortlessly to an equivalent degree. Hypnotic subjects rated themselves as more deeply hypnotized than did nonhypnotic subjects. Importantly, subjects given the passively worded suggestion (both hypnotic and nonhypnotic) rated their pain reductions as much more automatic and effortless than did subjects given the actively worded suggestion (both hypnotic and nonhypnotic).

The failure of Spanos and Katsanis (1989) to find differences in involuntariness ratings for hypnotic and nonhypnotic subjects is strong evidence against the idea that feelings of involuntariness are an intrinsic aspect of hypnotic responding. Instead, whether highly hypnotizable subjects define their responses as events that happened to them involuntarily or as self-generated actions depends on contextual factors such as the wording of suggestions that bias the causal interpretations that they apply to their own behaviors.

Individual Differences in Involuntariness Ratings

Despite the passive wording of hypnotic suggestions and other contextual cues that call for involuntary interpretations of responding, hypnotic subjects frequently fail to define their responses to suggestions as happening involuntarily. In fact, about half of the time that subjects pass suggestions by making the appropriate motor responses, they report that their responses felt more voluntary than involuntary (Spanos, Radtke, et al., 1983).

As indicated earlier, both people observing a hypnotic situation and people participating as subjects in such a situation are exposed to cues that bias them to interpret hypnotic behaviors as involuntary. However, people serving as hypnotic subjects are also exposed to a set of private cues to which external observers do not have access. Subjects, unlike observers, receive cues from their own thoughts and their own bodies concerning the movement of their limbs, and these cues are likely to compete with and contradict external cues that indicate that responses should feel involuntary.

For instance, suppose a subject with her hand in her lap is given a suggestion for arm levitation. If the subject simply waits patiently for her arm to rise by itself, she will fail the suggestion. In other words, the arm will not go up by itself, and unless she lifts it, it will remain in her lap despite the suggestion (Spanos, Burnley, & Cross, 1993). This, of course, is not an uncommon response. In fact, most hypnotic subjects fail most of the suggestions that they are administered (Spanos, Radtke, et al., 1983). On the other hand, if the subject decides to lift her arm, thinks about the fact she is lifting it, and attends to the sensations associated with lifting it, she will pass the suggestion but is likely to interpret her arm movement as a voluntary response. One way out of this dilemma is for the subject to lift her arm without focusing attention on her decision to do so, and instead, shifting her attention to an "as-if" situation that is congruent with the idea that her arm is "really" going up by itself. As mentioned earlier, many suggestions explicitly instruct subjects to carry out imaginings of this kind (e.g., imagine your arm pumped up with air; imagine a magnet pulling your hands apart; imagine that your elbow is caught in a vise that keeps your arm from bending). Subjects who pass suggestions report a wide range of experiences in response to those suggestions. Some subjects simply try to exclude competing thoughts and imagine exactly what the suggestion tells them to. Others use the suggested imaginings as a springboard for more elaborate suggestion-related fantasies, and some ignore the specific imaginary situation contained in the suggestion and create their own "as-if" imaginary situation (Sheehan & McConkey, 1982; Spanos, 1971). A number of studies (reviewed by Spanos & Barber, 1974) have indicated that the extent to which subjects become absorbed in such suggestion-related imaginings correlates with the extent to which they rate their responses to suggestions as feeling involuntary, and also with their level of hypnotizability. Highly hypnotizable subjects become more absorbed in suggestion-related imaginings than do less hypnotizable subjects.

Of course, another way for subjects to deal with demands to define their behavior as involuntary is to exaggerate when asked to rate the extent to which their suggested responses felt involuntary (Wagstaff, 1981). Although the extent to which such exaggeration occurs is unclear, some evidence now indicates that highly hypnotizable subjects sometimes exaggerate the extent to which their responses to suggestion felt involuntary (Spanos, Burgess, Cocco, & Pinch, 1993).

Failing to Resist Suggestions

Challenge suggestions involve two components. The first component informs subjects that a particular response is occurring (e.g., your arm is stiff and rigid, so stiff and rigid that it can't bend). The second component challenges subjects to try and counter this response (e.g., try to bend your arm). Frequently, highly hypnotizable subjects fail to counter the responses called for by challenge suggestions (e.g., they fail to bend their arm), while giving the appearance of trying unsuccessfully to counter them. Taken at face value, such demonstrations support the notions that hypnotic responses are involuntary and that subjects actually lose control over their own behavior. However, as occurs commonly with hypnotic behavior, things are not as they appear, and such demonstrations should not be taken at face value.

When highly hypnotizable hypnotic subjects are challenged to counter a suggested response, it is usually assumed that they interpret the challenge as a serious request and do their best to meet it. Consequently, their failure to counter when challenged (e.g., failure to bend their arm) is typically interpreted as their inability to counter.

The sociocognitive perspective does not begin by assuming that subjects interpret the challenge as a serious request to counter their responses. On the contrary, this perspective contends that highly hypnotizable subjects interpret the challenge as part of a "make believe" scenario in which they are to behave "as if" they are unable to counter the suggested response. One implication of being unable to counter a response involves failing to do so when challenged. By struggling unsuccessfully to counter the suggested response when challenged, subjects add legitimacy to their "as-if" performance (Spanos, Cobb, & Gorassini, 1985).

Early attempts to address the issue of control during hypnosis usually involved instructing subjects preexperimentally to try and prevent (i.e., counter) the occurrence of responses that were to be suggested in a forthcoming session. Results were contradictory. For example, W. R. Wells (1940) reported that his subjects almost always failed to counter suggested responses, whereas P. C. Young (1927) found that they were almost always successful at countering suggestions. Hilgard (1963) found that subjects countered about half of the time. Unfortunately, none of these early studies systematically varied instructions to counter or other contextual variables that might effect subjects' interpretations of test demands.

Spanos, Cobb, and Gorassini (1985) found that highly hypnotizable subjects who were led to believe that "deeply hypnotized" people retained (rather than lost) control over their behavior almost always countered suggested responses when challenged and almost always defined their suggested responses as voluntary rather than involuntary. However, subjects who were led to believe that "deep hypnosis" was associated with losing control almost always failed to counter suggested responses and described their responses as involuntary. Lynn, Nash, Rhue, Frauman, and Sweeney (1984) obtained similar findings in a related experiment.

SUMMARY

The seemingly dramatic behaviors associated with hypnosis, when examined critically, turn out to be much more mundane than they originally appeared. Despite initial appearances, even highly hypnotizable hypnotic subjects do not, in any commonly accepted sense of the terms, become blind or deaf when given negative hallucination suggestions, and they do not lose control over their behavior. On the other hand, hypnotic subjects are quite capable of lying, and they sometimes exaggerate and purposefully misdescribe their experiences to present themselves as meeting suggested demands.

MPD theorists frequently imply that hypnosis is a process that happens to people rather than as something that people do. Instead, many data support the hypothesis that hypnotic behaviors are goal-directed enactments and that highly hypnotizable subjects are cognizing individuals who are attuned to even subtle interpersonal cues and who are invested in meeting the social demands of hypnotic situations to present themselves as "good" subjects (Sarbin & Coe, 1972; Spanos & Coe, 1992). The demands contained in hypnotic suggestions call for particular subjective experiences as well as corresponding overt behaviors. For instance, suggestions for amnesia require not only that subjects fail to report target material but also that they define themselves as having forgotten that material. However, suggested experiences such as temporary forgetting or reduced pain do not occur automatically. Instead, these experiences must be generated by subjects who use their attentional and imaginal abilities in attempting to create these subjective effects.

Hypnotic behavior looks unusual because hypnotic subjects are asked to do unusual things, things that in the normal course of everyday life people are rarely called on to do (e.g., behave as if they cannot bend their arm or as if they cannot see a clearly visible number on a page). However, the ways in which hypnotic subjects carry out these unusual behaviors are mundane and involve the same psychological processes that people use to negotiate social situations in everyday life. Excellent hypnotic subjects choose to become absorbed in suggestions in the same way that many people become absorbed in movies and novels—to the exclusion of other things going on around them. Excellent hypnotic subjects are motivated to uncover and respond in terms of the tacit and sometimes ambiguous rules that constitute the hypnotic interaction in the same way that people who are motivated to do so uncover and respond in terms of the tacit rules that govern other novel social interactions. Excellent hypnotic subjects respond to the requests of a legitimate authority figure (the hypnotist) in the same way that most of us respond to the requests of authority figures in everyday life. Excellent hypnotic subjects sometimes misdescribe their experiences to create the impression they wish to convey, as all of us do in many everyday situations. "Trance states" and unusual cognitive abilities are no more required for an understanding of hypnotic behavior than they are required for an understanding of other social behavior.

4

HYPNOTIC AMNESIA, POSTHYPNOTIC RESPONSE, AND "BRAINWASHING"

HYPNOTIC AMNESIA

Amnesia has long been a hallmark of hypnotic responding, and during the 19th century it was thought to occur spontaneously as a function of the transition from being "hypnotized" to being awake (Sarbin, 1962; Sarbin & Coe, 1972). MPD patients frequently behave as if one or more of their alter identities are amnesic for the memories of other alters. MPD theorists typically describe such amnesia as an involuntary and spontaneous occurrence that is akin to hypnotic amnesia (Bliss, 1986). For example, Bliss (1986) suggested that early trauma produces a hypnoticlike state that terminates in hypnotic amnesia. It is this automatically occurring hypnotic amnesia that supposedly prevents many people from being able to recall early traumas, and it is behind this "amnesic barrier" that alter personalities supposedly develop outside of the awareness of the host personality.

Contrary to such descriptions, however, amnesic displays are not a common accompaniment of hypnotic performances, unless the amnesia has been explicitly suggested (Coe, 1989). Spontaneous amnesia is a rare occurrence, and when it does occur, it may simply reflect subjects' implicit understandings of the hypnotic role. Even highly hypnotizable subjects typically recall the contents of their hypnotic session following its termination, unless they are explicitly suggested to do otherwise. When amnesia is suggested (e.g., "you will be unable to recall anything that happened during the session"), hypnotic subjects proffer a wide range of reports in describing their experiences. Contrary to the way hypnotic amnesia is described in the MPD literature (e.g., Bliss, 1986), many subjects describe their forgetting as an active process that involves self-distraction and other strategies aimed at inhibiting recall (Spanos & Bodorik, 1977). Some hypnotic subjects do report that they were unable to recall target material and that their amnesia felt involuntary. Nevertheless, the available experimental data indicate that even these subjects retain rather than lose control of memory processes and guide their recall in terms of the social demands to which they are exposed (Coe, 1989; Spanos & Coe, 1992). For example, Silva and Kirsch (1987) convinced highly hypnotizable hypnotic subjects who were displaying amnesia that they would be able to recall the "forgotten" information, but only under certain conditions. Almost all subjects behaved in terms of the expectations conveyed to them by recalling and failing to recall "forgotten" material in the appropriate sequences. Relatedly, Coe and Sluis (1989) exposed highly hypnotizable subjects who exhibited posthypnotic amnesia to strong and repeated demands to remember. Under these circumstances, even subjects who had insisted that their amnesia was involuntary showed very substantial recovery of the "forgotten" memories. In fact, even without strong demands to remember, many amnesic subjects recall much of the supposedly forgotten material following simple requests to try and remember more (Dubreuil, Spanos, & Bertrand, 1983).

MPD patients are frequently described as living for years with alter personalities of which they are totally unaware (Kluft, 1985a, 1985b). However, hypnotic amnesia is rarely complete even amongst highly hypnotizable subjects. Moreover, among those few subjects who exhibit total amnesia, more than half report postexperimentally that, during the amnesia test period, they had consciously remembered but failed to report at least some of the target information (Spanos & Bodorik, 1977).

The "memory deficits" displayed by hypnotically amnesic subjects vary dramatically as a function of the expectations to which they are exposed. Thus, depending on the suggestions they are given, these subjects behave as if they have forgotten an entire list or only a subset of the list; all of the concrete words on a list but none of the abstract words, or vice versa; the number 4 while recalling all remaining numbers; and so on (Coe, 1989). Studies have also indicated that hypnotic subjects showed deficits on episodic memory tasks but not on semantic memory tasks (thus exhibiting dissociation between memory systems) or on both episodic and semantic memory tasks (i.e., no dissociation), as a function of subtle experimental demands (Spanos, Radtke, & Dubreuil, 1982). Exhibiting the very wide range of memory performance changes called for in these different experiments requires that hypnotic subjects retain rather than lose control of memory processes and guide their amnesic displays in terms of their understanding of what is called for by the amnesia test situation. For example, if the hypnotic amnesia task involves forgetting all of the words on a list, subjects often attempt to accomplish this task by diverting their attention away from the entire list and from any cues that remind them of the list. Thus, when asked to try and recall the words, these subjects might, instead, focus on how relaxed and heavy their body feels or think about what they will have for dinner later. To the extent that they succeed in deflecting attention away from the task of recalling the words, they define themselves as being amnesic. However, if the amnesia task requires that subjects recall only one portion of a list (e.g., all of the bird words on a list made up of bird, flower, and city name words), the deflection of attention away from the entire list is no longer a useful strategy. Under these circumstances, subjects who display "amnesia" usually segregate the list mentally into to-be-forgotten and to-be-recalled segments. They then tend to focus on and rehearse only the to-be-recalled words as a way of avoiding the to-be-forgotten bird words (Bertrand & Spanos, 1985).

MPD patients also exhibit a wide range of amnesic deficits that are difficult to explain in terms of involuntary memory dysfunction. Some report a one-way amnesia between alter identities, whereas others report a two-way amnesia. When switching alter identities, most such patients retain basic skills like reading and writing. In some early cases, however, these abilities were purportedly lost and had to be relearned by the new identity (Hacking, 1991; Kenny, 1986). In many modern cases, MPD patients switch back and forth between alters (and thereby between sets of supposedly segregated memories) very quickly. However, in a series of 19th-century British cases described by Hacking (1991), these kinds of switches between alters frequently involved a period of transitional sleep. Nineteenth- and early 20th-century MPD patients rarely displayed more than two or three alter identities (Bowman, 1990). Modern patients, on the other hand, display an average of 15 or more alters, and some of these patients exhibit over 100 alters (Ross, Norton, & Fraser, 1989). In other words, the number of "dissociated memory systems" supposedly possessed by MPD patients has grown exponentially since the beginning of the present century. These kinds of differences in the amnesic displays over time and across patients suggest that MPD patients, like hypnotically amnesic subjects, alter their patterns of recall as a function of their understanding of what is expected. As the expectations of therapists concerning the amnesia of their patients change, patients change their amnesic displays to meet the new expectations.

Work with non-MPD psychiatric patients also indicates that psychogenic amnesia is a goal-directed achievement influenced by subjects' understandings and by legitimation received from others, rather than an involuntary happening (Kirshner, 1973). For instance, Parfitt and Gall

(1944) worked with combat veterans whose reports of amnesia prevented their return to active service. Rather than legitimating these amnesic displays, Parfitt and Gall informed the patients that their memory would return and continued to convey this expectation in their interactions with the patients. Parfitt and Gall did not use any treatment to lift patients' amnesia other than telling them that they could remember. Exposure to these consistent demands to recall rather than to continue forgetting led most subjects to recover their memories. On the basis of these and other clinical findings, Kirshner (1973) suggested that psychogenic amnesia can be construed as a transitional social role that is adopted to deal with conflict and stress. Such an analysis may be useful for explaining how hypnotic interventions that legitimate remembering can often induce a "sharing" of memories among the several identities enacted by multiples (Allison & Schwarz, 1980; Bliss, 1980; Ross, 1984). It is now well established that hypnotic procedures do not possess intrinsic properties that enhance recall (M. C. Smith, 1983; Wagstaff, 1989). However, such interventions may provide a legitimating context for redefining the situation as one in which displays of cross-identity remembering are now considered role appropriate.

Braun (1990) has suggested that the segregated memories displayed by different alters reflects state-specific recall. Application of the state specificity idea to the amnesia seen in MPD patients suggests that experiences acquired in one psychological state (i.e., identity A) will not be remembered when the person is in a different state (i.e., identity B). However, these experiences will be easily remembered when the person is again in the first state (i.e., identity A). This formulation cannot account for the one-way amnesia that is commonly reported by MPD patients (e.g., identity A is aware of its own memories and those of identity B, but identity B is aware only of its own memories). In addition, this hypothesis cannot explain cases in which people who display distinct identities show no cross-identity amnesia.

Heterosexual male transvestites in our own culture exemplify such cases. During adolescence, heterosexual transvestites typically cross-dress to heighten sexual pleasure. As they grow older, however, many of these men cross-dress independently of sexual gratification and develop an elaborate "femme" identity. Unlike transsexuals, who often describe themselves as women trapped in a man's body, transvestites view themselves as alternating between a male identity and a female identity. When enacting their femme identity, they typically dress as women, act as women, refer to themselves with a woman's name (their femme name), and interact with others as women (Talamini, 1982). Despite these clear-cut and sustained differences in identity enactments, transvestites do not display between-identity amnesia. While enacting their femme self, they recall and freely discuss their masculine self and vice versa (Docter, 1988). These findings indicate that amnesia between identities does not arise automatically as a function of the differences in psychological functioning that are involved in enacting one identity as opposed to another. Instead, these findings suggest that whether amnesia is associated with alter identity enactments will depend on the expectations and purposes associated with those enactments.

POSTHYPNOTIC RESPONDING

According to some clinical investigators, many MPD patients were abused throughout much of their childhood by satanic cultists. Supposedly, the cultists not only tortured the children in various ways but also hypnotically "programmed" them to respond in particular automatic ways when presented with specific cues. For instance, when asked to divulge the names of the cult members who supposedly tortured them, some MPD patients are described as going into hysterics or becoming unable to speak. Purportedly, these behaviors are "programmed" responses designed to prevent disclosure of the identities of cult members (Fraser, 1990; Mayer, 1991). For instance, one patient in therapy described as follows the manner in which hypnosis was used to "program" her:

> They found I was easy to . . . hypnotize, an open mind. That's when they put the trigger words in. If the words were said then I would cut off completely into a hypnotic state within the coven so that they could use me in rituals, [and so that] out of the coven, if I ever went out, I would not disclose information. (Boyd, 1991, p. 365)

Relatedly, Wong and McKeen (1990) described as follows an MPD patient who had purportedly been satanically abused during childhood:

> It seems that there is a "trigger mechanism" programmed into her; when the cult wants to recall her back to the region where they operate, they send a message that will trigger the recall mechanism and she will be compelled to return to them. The stimulus for this recall mechanism would probably be an innocent appearing phrase in a letter to her; or symbolized in an object which she might receive as a gift. . . . (p. 15)

The implication of such accounts is that hypnotic and other procedures have been used to "implant" a suggestion (e.g., "you will be unable to speak when asked about cult members") that the patient no longer remembers but that continues to automatically elicit the suggested responses whenever the appropriate cue is presented to the patient (e.g., questions about cult members).

Such accounts of "cult programming" are clearly inconsistent with the evidence presented above that indicates that hypnotic subjects retain rather than lose control over memory processes and retain control over even those behaviors they label as involuntary. Moreover, these accounts are also inconsistent with the available evidence concerning posthypnotic responding.

The idea that hypnotic subjects can be transformed into robotlike automata who are automatically compelled to obey suggestions that they do not remember receiving is an old one. In the 19th century, this idea was popularized in du Maurier's (1895/1992) novel *Trilby*, in which a beautiful and innocent young woman is controlled by a scheming and unscrupulous hypnotist named Svengali. In the middle of the 20th century, the idea was repopularized by another novel, *The Manchurian Candidate* (Condon, 1959/1991), which was made into a successful (and very entertaining) motion picture. Moreover, a number of poorly controlled studies were conducted that purportedly supported the validity of automatic posthypnotic responding (Erickson & Erickson, 1941).

An important study by Fisher (1954), however, seriously challenged the idea that posthypnotic responses occurred automatically. Fisher (1954) administered an hypnotic induction procedure to 13 subjects and informed them that after they had been awakened, they would be compelled to scratch their ear whenever they heard the word *psychology*. Following instructions to awaken from hypnosis, the experimenter and his assistant carried out a discussion with subjects in which the word *psychology* was repeatedly mentioned. During this phase of the study, the assistant made it clear that he was keeping track of the frequency with which subjects scratched their ear in response to the cue word. All 13 subjects scratched their ear every time the cue was administered. In the next phase of the experiment, the experimenter and the assistant behaved so as to imply that the experiment was over and that they were no longer interested in posthypnotic responding. Under these circumstances, only 2 subjects responded each time the cue was given, and 9 did not respond to even a single presentation of the cue. In the third phase, the experimenter reminded subjects that the experiment was still going on. Following this reminder, 11 of the subjects scratched their ear when presented with the cue. In a related study, St. Jean (1978) found that almost all subjects stopped responding posthypnotically to a prerecorded auditory stimulus when the experimenter hurriedly left the room to attend to an emergency.

The findings of these two studies are a clear indication that posthypnotic responding does not occur automatically. Instead, its occurrence is determined by subjects' beliefs about what is expected from them. As long as they believe that the experiment is ongoing and that they are still in the role of hypnotic subjects, they behave accordingly and scratch their ear when cued. However, when they interpret the behavior of the experimenter to mean that their role as hypnotic subjects is terminated, they stop emitting posthypnotic responses.

A few of the subjects in both the Fisher (1954) and St. Jean (1978) experiments continued to respond even after it was implied that the experiment was over. On the one hand, this could mean that those subjects remained suspicious that the experiment was still in progress and responded accordingly. On the other, it could be argued that these subjects really were responding automatically to the posthypnotic cue.

Orne et al. (1968) examined these ideas by comparing posthypnotic responding in highly hypnotizable hypnotic subjects and low hypnotizable simulators. All of Orne et al.'s subjects were tested in two sessions that were spaced 2 days apart. In the first session, subjects were told that they would touch their ear whenever they heard the word *experiment*. They were further told that they would continue to respond in this manner until the suggestion was canceled by the hypnotist in the second session. Both hypnotic subjects and simulators exhibited high levels of posthypnotic responding when they were formally tested by the hypnotist in their first and second sessions. Following their first session, subjects were scheduled by the secretary for their next appointment. As a natural part of the scheduling procedure, the secretary used the cue word *experiment* and noted subjects' responses. When subjects arrived for their appointment, they again met and were surreptitiously tested by the secretary. Orne et al. found that 5 of the 17 highly hypnotizable hypnotic subjects, but none of the low hypnotizable simulators, responded to the secretary's presentation of the cue word on both test days.

In the Orne et al. (1968) study, the hypnotic subjects and the simulators were exposed to the same hypnotic testing procedures, and the hypnotist was blind to subjects' hypnosis-simulator status. Because of these factors, Orne et al. contended that the hypnotic subjects and the simulators were exposed to the same experimental demands and therefore developed the same expectations concerning what was role-appropriate hypnotic behavior. Consequently, the failure of any simulators to respond to the secretary's presentation of the cue word was taken to mean that experimental demands had not engendered expectations for such responding in either the simulators or the highly hypnotizable hypnotic subjects. Believing they had ruled out expectations, Orne et al. concluded that, in at least a few subjects, "hypnosis is able to produce an enduring response which is automatically instigated by an appropriate signal" (p. 195).

As was described in the earlier discussion of "trance logic," the assumption that hypnotic subjects and simulators are exposed to the same experimental demands is now known to be inaccurate (de Groot & Gwynn, 1989). The simulation instructions used in Orne's (1979a) laboratory strongly emphasized that simulators were to fool the *hypnotist*. In the Orne et. al. (1968) study, this emphasis may have deflected the attention of simulators away from entertaining the idea that the secretary was part of the experiment. The fact that only a minority of hypnotic subjects responded to the secretary indicates that her presentation of the cue word was relatively subtle. Only the simulators had been explicitly informed that their only task was to fool the hypnotist. Therefore, the simulators may well have been even less likely than the hypnotic subjects to have connected the secretary's use of the cue word with the experiment (Wagstaff, 1981).

To examine further the automaticity hypothesis, Spanos, Menary, Brett, Cross, and Ahmed (1987) presented posthypnotic cues to subjects in a context that was further removed from the experimental situation than had been the case in the Orne et al. (1968) study. In an initial session, highly hypnotizable subjects were given the posthypnotic suggestion to cough whenever they heard the word *psychology*. This suggestion informed subjects that they would continue to make this response in the presence of the cue word until they returned to the laboratory a week later to be tested once again. On the day of the retest, subjects were tested with the cue word in three separate settings that were associated with increasing closeness to the experiment. These three tests were called "informal" tests to differentiate them from the formal testing for posthypnotic responding conducted by the hypnotist in the experimental room. The first and most important informal test occurred in a corridor completely outside the laboratory area. Each subjects was approached by a confederate whom the subjects had never previously met. The confederate posed as a lost student and asked subjects for directions to the psychology department (this department is located two floors above the hypnosis laboratory). After finishing with this confederate, subjects proceeded to the laboratory entrance, where they were met by a second confederate, a graduate student whom they had never met. The graduate student administered the second informal test by asking subjects if they were here for the psychology experiment. Subjects were then escorted to the hypnotist, who carried out the third informal test by casually making the following comment to subjects while walking with them to the experimental room: "I'm glad you could make it for today's psychology experiment."

This experiment also included two groups of low hypnotizable simulators. Those in one group were given standard simulation instructions that emphasized that they were to fool the hypnotist. Those in the other group were given simulation instructions that emphasized that they were to try to fool not only the hypnotist but also anyone else who might be connected with the experiment.

All of the subjects in the Spanos, Menary, et al. (1987) study made the requisite posthypnotic response when they were formally tested by the hypnotist both in their initial session and a week later in their retest session. Consequently, any failure on their part to make the posthypnotic response during the informal tests cannot be explained away by arguing that the tendency to respond posthypnotically had simply decayed with time between the two formal sessions.

None of the highly hypnotizable subjects and none of the simulators made the posthypnotic response to the cue given by the first confederate (i.e., outside the laboratory). Moreover, none of the high hypnotizables and only one simulator (from the modified simulation condition) made the posthypnotic response to the cue given by the graduate student as subjects entered the laboratory. About half of the subjects in each group gave the posthypnotic response when tested informally by the hypnotist as they walked to the experimental room. These findings contradict the notion that posthypnotic responses are involuntary "programmed" behaviors that are elicited whenever subjects are exposed to specific cues. Instead, these findings indicate that posthypnotic responses are carried out only so long as subjects define themselves as participating in a situation that calls for them to adopt the role of hypnotic subject. When the situation changes so that subjects no longer interpret the stimulus cue as relevant to their self-presentation as hypnotic subjects, they stop enacting the posthypnotic response. When the hypnotic role is again made salient to them, subjects again begin to respond to the presentation of cues by carrying out the appropriate posthypnotic behaviors.

BRAINWASHING

Studies dealing with hypnotic amnesia and posthypnotic responding typically involve one or only a few sessions. According to proponents of the satanic cult hypothesis, however, these cults use much more extensive time frames when "programming" and "brainwashing" their victims, and use torture and other forms of physical and psychological coercion along with hypnotic procedures to create human automatons. Supposedly, such long-term programs of brainwashing can produce human robots who respond automatically to posthypnotic cues, develop a slavish loyalty to their torturers, adopt the beliefs of the cult, and exhibit amnesia for whatever the cult leaders wish them to forget.

The term *brainwashing* was first used by Edward Hunter (1951), a journalist and covert Central Intelligence Agency (CIA) employee, to explain the supposed success of the Chinese communists at eliciting false confessions and other forms of cooperation from American prisoners of war during the Korean conflict. According to Hunter (1960), the procedures used by the communists to elicit cooperation were new and highly sinister and could effectively rob people of their will and insidiously transform them into slavish robots:

The intent is to change a mind radically so that its owner becomes a living puppet—a human robot—without the atrocity being visible from the outside. The aim is to create a mechanism in flesh and blood, with new beliefs and new thought processes inserted into a captive body. What that amounts to is the search for a slave race that, unlike the slaves of olden times, can be trusted never to revolt, always to be amenable to orders, like an insect to its instincts. (Hunter, 1960, p. 309)

For a short time during a period of intense anticommunist propaganda during the 1950s, Hunter's (1960) idea that sinister influence procedures can be used to transform victims into human robots appeared to gain at least partial legitimation in some academic circles (Sargent, 1957). However, careful examination of the influence procedures actually used to "brainwash" prisoners yielded a very different picture (Biderman, 1960; Farber, Harlow, & West, 1957; Lifton, 1961; Schein, 1961).

The Chinese communists used a variety of social influence procedures, none of them particularly arcane or previously unknown, to induce cooperation and, sometimes, attitude and belief change. These procedures included control of information (e.g., forced repeated exposure to public propaganda lectures, censoring of mail so that prisoners received only bad news from home), the production of demoralization by generating mistrust among former comrades and disrupting group loyalties, harsh physical treatment followed by small rewards for cooperation, inducing what appeared to be unimportant but public displays of cooperation (e.g., signing a statement that indicated that American society had social problems) and then using the public evidence of cooperation as a means of extracting further concessions, and so forth (Schein, 1961).

Some of the social influence procedures used to induce the signing of false confessions were both subtle and clever. For example, silence in the face of an accusation usually implies agreement with the accusation. Consequently, interrogators were sometimes successful at inducing an uncooperative prisoner to speak by accusing him of things the interrogator knew to be false. Because not answering the false accusation carried the implication that it was probably true, some prisoners spoke up to deny the accusation. In so doing, these prisoners tacitly agreed to discuss rather than remain silent on certain issues. Because discussion and argument normally involve compromise and a conversational give and take, some prisoners were induced in this manner to make compromising statements about their military activities or about their country (Biderman, 1960).

The indoctrination procedures used by the Chinese were probably somewhat effective at inducing long-term changes in beliefs among Chinese political prisoners. Even here, however, the degree to which prisoners maintained their new beliefs was largely determined by whether those beliefs were shared by the social groups they joined after their release from prison (Lifton, 1961). The indoctrination procedures conducted on prisoners of war were, by and large, a failure (Schein, 1961). Despite the massive propaganda efforts made by the Chinese, very few prisoners actually made false confessions, and very few engaged in more than trivial cooperation with the communists (Scheflin & Opton, 1978). Moreover, the little cooperation that did occur appeared to be based primarily on expediency rather than ideological change. At best, only a minuscule proportion of the 3,500 American prisoners of war held in Chinese camps exhibited any evidence of conversion to communist ideology (Lund & Wilson, 1977).

In short, the so-called brainwashing techniques used by communists on political prisoners and prisoners of war were nothing more than a combination of physical coercion and well-known social influence procedures. Many of these procedures are used routinely in various social organizations in our own society. During basic training, for example, the military regularly controls information and attempts to disrupt the recruit's civilian identity and loyalties while developing group cohesion and a new identity built around new loyalties. Similar procedures are often followed to teach new beliefs and attitudes, build new loyalties, and construct new identities when people join psychotherapy and other self-help groups, college fraternities, political campaigns, and convents and other religious groups. Such procedures, particularly when applied to willing volunteers as opposed to unwilling prisoners, are frequently effective in producing belief change and new commitments. Obviously, however, these procedures do not produce robots who respond automatically to prearranged cues and who develop amnesia on command (Bromley & Shupe, 1981; Ofshe, 1992a, 1992b).

The idea that "brainwashing" consists of powerful, sinister techniques that transform people into automata is similar to the traditional notion that hypnosis is a powerful force that can do the same. It should not be surprising, therefore, that these two ideas soon became identified as related to each other. In the 1950s and 1960s, the CIA experimented with drugs, electroshock, and hypnotic procedures in an attempt to develop secret agents who would function as automata. In the fantasy world of Allen Dulles and other high-ranking CIA officials, the goal was to develop agents who could be provided with information and then be made amnesic until presented with a prearranged cue. Thus, should they fall into the wrong hands, the amnesic agents would be unable to divulge their secrets even under torture. Relatedly, these fantasy agents would be "programmed" to assassinate key targets upon presentation of a cue and later have no knowledge of what they had done (Marks, 1979).

The CIA agent-as-robot fantasy was, of course, based on the robot view of brainwashing popularized by Hunter and others during and after the Korean conflict (Hunter, 1960). The CIA did, in fact, fund a wide range of experimentation into the role of drugs and hypnotic procedures at inducing amnesia, antisocial and self-injurious behavior, and so forth. Some of this work was conducted openly in universities and some surreptitiously and unethically on unwilling subjects who were exposed to sometimes brutal and disgusting procedures (Marks, 1979; G. Thomas, 1989). The upshot of all of this work was consistent with what has been learned from the scientific studies of "brainwashing" and the scientific study of hypnotic phenomena—namely, that intact people are not transformed into mindless automata by physical coercion or social influence (Ofshe, 1992a).

Obviously, this conclusion does not mean that people cannot be induced to change their beliefs, make false confessions, or commit antisocial or self-destructive acts. Common observation, coupled with a good deal of experimentation in social psychology, indicates that group pressures toward conformity and normal tendencies to obey legitimate authority can produce frightening levels of behavioral compliance and sometimes substantial attitude and belief change in a great many people (Asch, 1952, 1956; Milgram, 1974; A. G. Miller, 1986; Sherif, 1936). Although hypnotic procedures can be used to produce such change, they are no more effective in this regard than nonhypnotic procedures (Coe, Kobayashi, & Howard, 1973; Orne & Evans, 1965). Moreover, the compliance and belief change generated by even the coercive social influence procedures used on political prisoners does not occur because people have been transformed into unthinking automata who act automatically or who become amnesic for the orders they have been given.

With respect to the satanic cult hypothesis, the evidence from studies of "brainwashing" are clear. Even if satanic cults that kidnapped and tortured victims existed, the available evidence indicates that such cults would be unable to reliably transform their victims into loyal robots who responded automatically to prearranged posthypnotic cues, exhibited amnesia on command, and maintained an abiding loyalty to their torturers even after they had left the cult. The idea that people can be transformed into robots in this manner is a cultural myth that grew out of the Korean conflict and subsequent cold war tensions. The myth was reinforced both by simplistic notions concerning Pavlovian conditioning and by even older cultural myths concerning the coercive "power" of hypnosis. The robot mythology was maintained because it served a number of useful propaganda purposes, and it continues to serve such purposes today for those who use notions like "brainwashing," "mind control," "spot hypnosis," and "cult programming" to explain why people sometimes join new religious movements such as the Unification Church (Moonies) and the Hari Krishna sect (Anthony & Robbins, 1992).

As we shall see in more detail later, there is no good evidence to support belief in the existence of a conspiracy of murdering, child-abusing satanic cultists. However, the idea that such cults exist has come to serve important political and ideological functions for some conservative Christian religious groups. This idea has also gained adherents among mental health professionals within the MPD movement who have been directly or indirectly influenced by the religious mythology of those conservative religious groups. For members of some conservative religious groups, the notion that satanic cults can create human robots functions to personify the power of a mythical enemy who can only be protected against by a redoubling of faith and a recommitment to religious values (Victor, 1993).

A number of psychiatric theorists seemed to advocate what amounts to a person-as-robot view of MPD before the infusion of evangelical Christian thinking into the MPD movement. For instance, the notion of person-as-robot seems to be implied by the following notions, all of which are common among MPD theorists: Alter personalities can be created outside of awareness, such personalities can "take over" a person's functioning, alters can be cued during hypnosis to "come forth" and speak, people are amnesic without knowing why for periods when an alter is "out," alters can create complex plans for future behavior outside of the awareness of the host personality, alters can purposely place the confused host in embarrassing situations, and alters "hold" the painful memories of childhood abuse of which the host personality remains unaware.

Given the prior acceptance of all of these beliefs, the notion that robotlike processes could be initiated in captured victims by organized cultists is a relatively small step. Moreover, it is a step that can be difficult to avoid if the last belief described above is taken seriously. If the alters of MPD patients really "hold" painful abuse memories, and if those alters describe memories of satanic ritual abuse, what then? Either the patients' reports are believed and the satanic conspiracy described is real, or the reports are disbelieved and the notion of alters who "hold" such dissociated memories is called into question. For many MPD theorists, believing the bizarre memory reports of patients has been favored over questioning the validity of those reports and, by implication, the validity of the notion of dissociated alters. In the next chapter, I examine whether such an unwavering belief in the validity of memory reports is warranted by the available evidence.

SUMMARY

MPD theorists may well be correct when they contend that the amnesia of MPD patients resembles hypnotic amnesia. However, the descriptions of hypnotic amnesia given by these theorists are often misleading (e.g., Bliss, 1980, 1986). Contrary to these descriptions, the available data indicate that hypnotic amnesia does not occur spontaneously following the termination of hypnosis. In addition, the recall deficits that follow suggestions for amnesia do not involve an automatic and complete forgetting of events. Instead, hypnotic amnesia (and most likely much of MPD amnesia as well) involves goal-directed enactment aimed at meeting social expectations. Such amnesia is frequently defined by subjects as involving voluntary self-distraction, it is rarely complete even in highly hypnotizable subjects, when it is complete it frequently involves conscious withholding, and it is typically of short duration. Hypnotic subjects retain rather than lose control of memory processes and, in that way, display the particular "memory deficits" called for by the current test situation (Coe, 1989; Spanos, 1986b).

Accounts of "cult programming" are inconsistent with evidence showing that hypnotic subjects retain control over both memory processes and other behaviors they label as involuntary. Although it has been widely believed that hypnotic subjects can be transformed into automata who are compelled to obey suggestions, evidence suggests that posthypnotic responding is shaped by subjects' beliefs about what is expected of them. The notion that people can be transformed into robots by "brainwashing" and related techniques is shown to be a cultural myth.

II

CREATING FALSE
MEMORIES

5

DISTORTIONS OF MEMORY

Patients sometimes enter psychotherapy with no memory of having been sexually abused as children and then, during the course of therapy, begin to remember early abuse. Relatedly, some patients who were aware of having been abused when they entered therapy recall new and more horrendous instances of abuse as therapy progresses. For example, memories of having been abused in satanic cult rituals often come to light for the first time during psychotherapy. Frequently hypnotic regression procedures are used in the recovery of such hidden memories. The recall of previously "hidden memories" occurs in patients with a wide range of diagnoses including MPD, but according to some therapists, MPD patients are especially likely to recall hidden memories of particularly savage and traumatic satanic abuse (Mayer, 1991). Therapists working with patients who recall "hidden memories" usually accept patients' memory reports as valid (Bass & Davis, 1988; Blume, 1990; Fraser, 1990; Fredrickson, 1992) and often provide patients with strong encouragement to try and remember such forgotten traumas. Depending on their theoretical orientation, these therapists argue that either during childhood their patients repressed memories of the abuse they suffered (Fredrickson, 1992; Maltz, 1990) or these memories became "dissociated" from other memories (Bliss, 1986; Fraser, 1990). According to these perspectives, hypnotic regression or other procedures aimed at facilitating recall allow the patient to gain access to long-hidden traumatic experiences.

Critics of these ideas argue that therapeutic procedures like hypnotic regression and guided imagery that are aimed at facilitating recall may, instead, create false memories (Ganaway, 1989; Lindsay & Read, 1994; Loftus, 1993a, 1993b; Lynn & Nash, 1994; Mulhern, 1991a, 1991b; Ofshe, 1992b; Orne, 1979b; Spanos, 1994; Spanos, Burgess, & Burgess, 1994). According to this view, therapists may inadvertently lead patients to generate abuse fantasies that are consistent with what the therapist believes happened to patients during childhood. Patients are likely to construe such fantasies as real memories, and therapists are likely to legitimize these construals. Before discussing these issues, it is worth examining some basic ideas and research concerning human memory.

MEMORY AND ITS DISTORTIONS

Memory as Reconstruction

One view common among many lay people, as well as some professionals, holds that memory works something like a videotape recorder. According to this view, experiences are laid down in memory like images on film, and remembering a particular event involves finding the right segment of film and then playing it back. Of course, some segments of film may be difficult to locate, and others that are particularly frightening might be repressed so that they cannot be played back without some special intervention like hypnosis or psychoanalysis. In some respects, Freud held to such a view of memory. Although he argued that memories could be distorted in various ways, he also frequently compared himself to an archaeologist who could circumvent such distortions to uncover the real memories of childhood that were buried by repression (Spence, 1982). In the 1950s, this videotape view of memory seemed to gain strong support from the work of Wilder Penfield, a neurosurgeon who electrically stimulated the exposed cortex in patients being operated on for intractable epilepsy (Penfield & Roberts, 1959). When Penfield applied a mild electric current to certain portions of the temporal lobe, patients sometimes appeared to vividly recollect long-forgotten memories that unfolded in sequence. To Penfield and Perot (1963), it appeared as if experiences were stored in memory as they occurred, and that even childhood memories could be recalled vividly and in detail, as if the electrical stimulation operated like the playback button on a video recorder.

Criticism of Penfield's work was not long in coming (see Horowitz, 1970, for a review). Essentially, the critics pointed out that the reports proffered by Penfield's patients frequently included many unrealistic elements and much obvious distortion that could not represent accurate memories. Instead of supporting a tape-recorder model of human memory, Penfield's work seemed more consistent with the notion that memory is essentially reconstructive in nature.

The idea that what we remember is a reconstruction of events influenced by such factors as expectations, mood states, information obtained since the original experiences, attitudes, current concerns, and other dynamic psychological factors was first developed by Bartlett (1932). In a series of highly influential studies, Bartlett asked subjects to read a complex but ambiguous story. The best-known of Bartlett's stories was called "The War of the Ghosts" and described how two men, who went down to a river to hunt seals, met a group of warriors on a war party. One man accompanied the warriors, who turned out to be ghosts. This man eventually returned home, described the battle he had participated in, and then died.

Bartlett asked subjects to recall the story at various intervals following their initial reading. As expected, the longer the recall interval, the fewer the number of correct details recalled. Of particular importance, however, was the fact that subjects did not simply recall less information, but they also changed the story in various ways so that it became more congruent with their implicit expectations. For instance, some subjects described the two men as going to the river to fish, a much more common activity in our culture than seal hunting. Sometimes the fact that the warriors were ghosts was eliminated, and they were described instead as Indians. After all, in our culture (as opposed to some others), the idea of battles between ghosts and people makes little intuitive sense, whereas battles between rival Indian tribes is commonly depicted in movies and books. Details that were never in the original story, but that make intuitive sense, were sometimes added, such as reports that the men first became aware of the ghosts by hearing their paddles in the water. The original story made no mention of paddles. In other words, remembering the story was not simply a matter of "playing back" information from the story that was stored in memory. Instead, it involved constructing a story that included some of the elements of the original, but that was also shaped in terms of subjects' implicit understandings and cultural categories. Thus, the story that subjects "remembered" often included details and sequences that were not in the original but that made intuitive sense in terms of subjects' implicit, culturally derived expectations.

Bartlett's (1932) notion that recall is influenced by such factors as expectation and psychological set is now well established (Mandler, 1984; Neisser, 1976), and numerous studies have indicated that variables like expectation can distort as well as facilitate recall. For instance, Brewster and Treyens (1981) had subjects sit in the office of a graduate student for 35 seconds on the pretext of waiting for an experimenter. The experimenter then escorted subjects to a different room and asked them to describe in writing everything that they could remember about the graduate student office in which they had briefly waited. A great many subjects recalled seeing books on the shelves of the office. However, there had been no books in the office. Subjects remembered seeing books that were not there because they were aware that they were describing an academic office, and typically, such offices contain books. Thus, subjects' remembrance of the specific office they were in only a few moments earlier was a reconstruction based, in part, on their implicit (but in this case erroneous) expectation of what such an office is like.

Postevent Information

In the past 20 years, much of the work that has examined factors that produce distortions in memory has been guided by a practical consideration: understanding the nature of the errors made by eyewitnesses to crimes (Loftus, 1979). Eyewitness testimony is very frequently in error, and such errors constitute the single most important reason for the conviction of the innocent for crimes they did not commit (Yant, 1992). Moreover, some of these errors are produced by information that the witnesses received after the crime had occurred (i.e., postevent information). In other words, later information retrospectively distorted the recall of earlier (i.e., the crime) information. A series of studies by Loftus and her associates (reviewed in Loftus, 1979) illustrated this process. In a typical experiment, subjects were shown a series of slides depicting a traffic accident. The critical slide showed a car going through an intersection marked by a stop sign. Later on, after termination of the slide presentation, subjects were asked a series of questions about what they had seen. For half of the subjects, one of these questions asked if subjects had seen the yield sign. Because all subjects had seen a stop sign instead of a yield sign, this question was designed to distort subjects' recall of what they had earlier seen. The remaining subjects were not asked a question about the type of sign they had seen. Still later, subjects in both groups were given a forced-choice recognition test. They were simultaneously shown the slide they had originally seen, which contained a stop sign, and a slide they had never seen that contained a yield sign, and asked to choose the one that they had earlier been shown during the slide presentation. A substantial number of the subjects who had been asked the misleading question chose the slide with the yield sign, whereas almost all of the control subjects chose the slide with the stop sign. In other words, misleading information imparted during questioning about the original slide sequence led subjects to falsely remember events that had never even appeared in the slides. More recently, two studies indicated not only that misleading postevent information created new false memories but that it also impaired the recall of accurate information (R. F. Belli, 1989; Lindsay, 1990).

Postevent information can seriously impair the recall of frightening events as well as mundane ones. Abhold (1993) studied subjects who, 6 years previously, had attended a football game in which one of the players had been very seriously injured. Many of these subjects made serious errors when attempting to recall the 6-year-old event. In addition, when exposed to misleading information about what had happened at the game, many of these subjects incorporated the misleading information into their recall. For example, when given the false suggestion that they had seen blood on the injured player's jersey, more than one quarter of the subjects "remembered" incorrectly that this had been so.

The status of the interviewer can also influence the response of subjects to misleading questions. Smith and Ellsworth (1987) showed subjects a videotape of a robbery and later questioned them about what they had seen. The interrogator was described to subjects either as a novice concerning the crime or as an expert on such films. During the interrogation, the interrogator asked a number of misleading questions. Subjects questioned by the expert recalled more of the incorrect misleading information than those questioned by the novice. Therapists, of course, are experts whose opinions are highly valued by their clients and whose statements about what clients probably experienced during childhood may well shape how clients remember their childhood (Bonanno, 1990).

For our purposes, two consistent sets of findings from the research on eyewitness memory are particularly important. The first set of findings is that the expectations of the interviewer, transmitted through leading questions, are a potent cause of recall error. Leading questions not only increase the likelihood that subjects will answer in line with the question but also tend to impair the recall of accurate information and increase the confidence that subjects place in the validity of their own recall (Loftus, 1979; 1993b).

Accuracy and Confidence in Recall

The second important finding from this literature concerns the relationship between accuracy and confidence in recall. In everyday life, people frequently use the confidence with which a person expresses a recollection as a measure of the accuracy of that recollection. For example, jurors at a trial are likely to be convinced by a witness who points to the accused and in a firm, loud voice states, "That's the man, I'm certain that's him. I'll never forget that face as long as I live." They are much less likely to be convinced by a witness who hesitates and then finally says, "I think that's him, but I can't be certain." Relatedly, many therapists assume that the confidence with which a memory is reported is a good indication of the accuracy of that memory. For example, Yapko (1994b) surveyed a large group of psychotherapists and found that almost one quarter agreed either slightly or strongly with the statement "One's level of certainty about a memory is strongly positively correlated with that memory's accuracy" (p. 232). Despite its intuitive appeal, and despite the opinions of the therapists surveyed by Yapko (1994b), the idea that the confidence placed by a person in his or her memory is a good guide to the accuracy of his or her memory is simply incorrect. On the contrary, a good deal of research now indicates that the relationship between accuracy of recall and confidence in that recall is quite weak. In fact, in some studies, this relationship fails to attain statistical significance (for reviews, see Bothwell, Deffenbacher, & Brigham, 1987; G. L. Wells, 1993; G. L. Wells & Murray, 1984).

In part, the relationship between accuracy and confidence is weak because these two variables are influenced by different factors. For instance, the accuracy with which an eyewitness describes and identifies a target person is influenced by such things as the amount of lighting present, the duration of the exposure, the amount of previous contact with the target, the focus of the subjects' attention during the witnessing incident, the amount of time that intervenes between the event and its recall, and so on. On the other hand, confidence can vary independently of accuracy because of such factors as the amount of time spent silently rehearsing the recall, preparatory information aimed at boosting confidence, expectations about what the target "should" have looked like, the number of times a witness is asked to recall, and so on (Spanos, Quigley, Gwynn, Glatt, & Perlini, 1991; Wells & Murray, 1984). Relatedly, Suengas and Johnson (1988) found that the act of verbally describing an experience made it more difficult for subjects to accurately distinguish between whether their experience was the memory of a real event or an imagined event. The importance of the fact that there is, at best, only a weak relationship between the accuracy of remembrances and the confidence displayed in them is difficult to overemphasize. In many therapeutic contexts, patients are strongly encouraged to generate recollections of having been abused during childhood, to repeatedly verbalize those recollections to the therapist, and to treat those recollections as real and accurate memories (e.g., Bass & Davis, 1988; Blume, 1990). In light of the weak relationship between recall accuracy and confidence, the hazards of such practices should be apparent.

New Information and New Attitudes

It is commonly believed that highly salient and meaningful events are particularly resistant to memory distortion. To examine this idea, Harsch and Neisser (1989; see also Neisser & Harsch, 1992) questioned college students the day after the explosion of the space shuttle *Challenger*, about how they first heard of the event. Three years later, the subjects were questioned once again, and this time they also indicated their level of confidence in the various details of their memory (e.g., where they were, who they were with). When checked against their day-old recall, the subjects' 3-year recall was highly inaccurate. Only a very few subjects were correct about all of the details they remembered, and a full one quarter of the sample was incorrect about every single detail. The degree of confidence that subjects placed in their 3-year-old recall and the vividness with which they recalled were unrelated to their accuracy. Also unrelated to the accuracy of the subjects' delayed recall was the degree of emotion that they had displayed to the original event. Subjects who had initially described themselves as experiencing strong emotions when they heard the news of the explosion (e.g., shocked, horrified, crying) did not recall any more accurately 3 years later than those who had not experienced strong emotions. Although none of the subjects had forgotten that the *Challenger* exploded, three fourths of them could not remember that they had filled out a questionnaire about their memory of this event the day after it had occurred. In short, even memories for highly salient and frightening events like the *Challenger* disaster are subject to alteration and distortion with time. As with relatively mundane events, the confidence that people place in salient and frightening memories is not a good guide to the accuracy of those memories.

Several months after questioning subjects for the second time about the *Challenger* explosion, Neisser and Harsch (1992) asked them to return for a third, two-part session. During the first part of the session, the subjects were again questioned about what they remembered. Next, the subjects were administered an interview aimed at enhancing recall by instructing subjects to try and mentally reinstate the context and emotions they had originally experienced, as well as by administering other cues aimed at enhancing recall. The recall-enhancing procedures used by Neisser and Harsch were similar to those sometimes used by police to facilitate the memories of eyewitnesses to crimes, and by therapists to facilitate the recall of long-forgotten traumatic memories. These recall-enhancing procedures were completely ineffective in enhancing the accuracy of the subjects' recall. In fact, even when the subjects were shown their original report made the day after the explosion, their original memories were not jogged into returning. Instead, the subjects expressed surprise and often indicated that the original record was simply not how they now remembered the event. In summary, the findings of the Neisser and Harsch study indicate that long-delayed recall for even highly salient events is often inaccurate; that the accuracy of such recall is unrelated to the emotionality of the original experience, the vividness with which the experience is recalled, or the degree of confidence placed in the recall; and that procedures aimed at enhancing recall accuracy often fail completely at actually improving recall.

Frequently, the way that people view the past is governed by their current attitudes and views of themselves. Moreover, in an attempt to view themselves as behaving consistently, people sometimes distort their memories of their past behavior to align it with current practice. For instance, Collins, Graham, Hansen, and Johnson (1985) surveyed high school students about their use of alcohol, tobacco, and illegal drugs. The subjects were again surveyed at two later intervals: once a year later and then again two and a half years later. At each of the later intervals, subjects were asked to recall the amount of substance use they had reported on the initial survey, as well as their current substance use. Subjects frequently misremembered the extent to which they had used substances in the past. Moreover, the pattern of memory errors was related to the subjects' current substance use. For example, in subjects whose use of alcohol had changed over the two-and-a-half-year period, recall of how much they drank initially was more closely related to how much they now reported drinking than to how much they had reported drinking on the initial survey. In other words, subjects biased their recall of their earlier drinking habits to bring them into line with their current drinking habits.

Similar biases also occur in the way people recall their earlier attitudes, opinions, and beliefs. For instance, Bem and McConnell (1970) found that college students favored student control over the university curriculum in an initial opinion survey. A week later, students were induced to write an essay favoring the opposite position, and this procedure produced a corresponding change in the subjects' attitudes (they were now less likely to favor student control). Some of these subjects were then asked to recall the opinions that they had endorsed a week earlier during the initial survey. The opinions that subjects recalled expressing during the initial survey were much more closely aligned with their revised (post-essay-writing) opinions than to the opinions they had actually expressed in the previous week.

In a related study, Marcus (1986) assessed the attitudes of a very large group of high school seniors concerning such issues as the equality of women, the legalization of marijuana, and the rights of accused individuals. The subjects were originally assessed in 1965 and were retested in 1973 and again in 1982. In the 1982 assessment, Marcus asked subjects not only to rate their current attitudes but also to indicate how they had responded to each scale in 1973. In the case of almost every dimension, the way subjects remembered having responded in 1973 was more closely related to their 1982 attitudes than to the attitudes they had actually endorsed in 1973. Taken together, the findings from these studies (Bem & McConnell, 1970; Collins et al., 1985; Marcus, 1986) indicate that the manner in which subjects currently view themselves and present themselves to others influences the ways in which they remember their past attitudes, beliefs, and behaviors. In short, people reconstruct their memories of the past to make them congruent with their views of the present.

When people learn new information about a person, they often reorganize what they know about that person's past to make it consistent with the newly acquired information. For example, many people in our culture hold stereotyped views concerning the childhood habits and experiences of homosexuals (M. W. Ross, 1980). Consequently, when we learn that someone we grew up with is gay, we are likely to reorganize what we remember about that person's early life to make it consistent with our stereotypes concerning the upbringing and earlier experiences of gay people. For example, Snyder and Uranowitz (1978) had subjects read a narrative depicting the life of a woman named Betty. After completing the narrative, half of the subjects were told that Betty was homosexual, whereas the remainder were told that she was heterosexual. A week after reading the narrative, the subjects in both groups responded to a series of multiple-choice questions concerning facts in Betty's life. Some of these questions were designed to tap information that was relevant to stereotypes about gay life histories (e.g., questions about heterosexual dating in high school). Subjects who had been told that Betty was homosexual incorrectly "remembered" more information that was congruent with stereotypes about homosexual life histories than did subjects who were told that Betty was heterosexual. Interestingly, the bias toward remembering homosexual life events was equally large regardless of whether subjects had been informed about Betty's sexual orientation immediately after reading her life story or a week later. In short, subjects reorganized the way in which they remembered Betty's past to make it consistent with their views of the kind of past a homosexual female is "supposed" to have. M. W. Ross (1980) provided evidence that suggests that homosexuals also hold stereotyped views concerning the early experiences of gays and that these stereotypes lead them to reconstruct their own past histories in terms of these stereotypes.

New information and changes in priorities and expectations can influence people to reconstruct their biographies and thereby change their remembrances of the past. One potent determinant of the way people view the present is their current mood. The outlook of depressed people, for example, tends to be bleaker and more pessimistic than that of nondepressed people. Importantly, evidence indicates that mood influences people's recall as well as their current outlook. For instance, a number of studies have indicated that negative mood states increase the likelihood that subjects will recall negative information about themselves (e.g., Bower, 1981; Hammen, Marks, deMayo, & Mayol, 1985; Teasdale, Taylor, & Fogarty, 1980). In addition, Lewinsohn and Rosenbaum (1987) found that negative mood influenced how adults recalled the way in which they had been treated as children by their parents. These investigators assessed the extent to which adults in several groups remembered their parents as treating them in an unloving and rejecting manner. Subjects in one group had a history of depression but were not currently depressed. Those in a second group had a history of depression and were currently depressed. A third group of subjects had no history of depression. Currently depressed subjects described their parents as less loving and more rejecting than did subjects who had never been depressed. In earlier studies, findings of this kind had been taken to mean that poor parenting was related to the development of depression in adulthood (e.g., Becker, 1962). However, Lewinsohn and Rosenbaum (1987) also found that currently depressed people rated their parents as more rejecting and less loving than did people with a history of depression who were not currently depressed. In addition, subjects in the latter group did not differ from people who had never been depressed in how they rated their parents. In other words, the subjects' remembrances of their parents were not constant. People with a history of becoming depressed remembered their parents as being either relatively loving and accepting or relatively unloving and rejecting, depending on their mood at the time their memories were assessed.

By and large, people seek psychotherapy because they are depressed or in some other way troubled. The findings of Lewinsohn and Rosenbaum (1987) suggest that the negative remembrances of childhood and parents that patients often express to their therapists may, at least in part, be biased by the patients' current concerns and mood states. Obviously, the accuracy of such remembrances is unlikely to improve if, as commonly occurs, therapists selectively encourage even more negatively toned recollections from their patients (Campbell, 1992).

The purpose of psychotherapy is to change the client for the better, and frequently, people who have completed therapy describe their current levels of behavioral functioning as much more adequate than was their pretherapy behavior (e.g., Bergin, 1971). When therapists and clients use such reports as evidence for the efficacy of psychotherapy, they are, of course, assuming that clients' recollections of their pretherapy behavior are an accurate baseline against which to measure improvement. This assumption, however, may well be in error. Instead, the recollections that clients generate may involve reconstructions that change the past so as to make it congruent with the view of the present that the clients have come to believe or wish to convey.

For instance, Conway and Ross (1984; see also Hirt, 1990) examined the efficacy of a program designed to improve study skills. Initially, subjects were assessed on such dimensions as how effectively they used their study time, their note-taking skills, and so on. Subjects were then randomly assigned to a study skills program or waiting list control condition. Following treatment, subjects in both conditions were again assessed on study skills. In addition, subjects were asked to recall what they had reported about their study skills in the initial session. There were no initial differences in study skills between the groups, and neither group exhibited a significant increment in study skills from the initial assessment session to the final assessment session. Thus, the study program did not produce any noticeable improvement in study skills. Interestingly, however, subjects administered the study skills program remembered their study skills as being significantly worse than they had initially reported them to be. Control subjects, on the other hand, recalled their study skills in more or less the same way that they had initially reported them. In other words, subjects who underwent the study program biased their recall of their initial study skills so as to make their recollections consistent with the idea that the program had helped them.

Because psychotherapy clients frequently develop strong emotional involvements with their therapists (Frank, 1973), findings like those of Conway and Ross (1984) suggest that clients may reconstruct their memories to make them consistent with what they perceive to be the wishes of the therapist or what they believe will win the therapist's approval or sympathy.

Some modern psychoanalysts (e.g., Schwaber, 1983; Spence, 1982) have become acutely aware of the difficulties (some would say impossibility) involved in reconstructing a historically accurate view of the past on the basis of patients' recollections during therapy. Spence (1982), for example, has suggested that memory reconstruction occurs more or less continuously during the course of psychoanalytic treatment:

> Under the press of a strong transference—either positive or negative—what the patient is saying about the past must be translated into what he is demanding of the present. If he needs to be pitied, for example, he might exaggerate the misery of his childhood; if he wants to be praised for being an exceptional analytic patient, he may generate a crystal-clear memory of an infantile event. These reports have nothing much to do with the past as experienced or with other reports of the same event at different times in the analysis. Rather, they are tokens in a conversational exchange designed to win some kind of response from the analyst. As in any bargaining session, truth takes the back seat; to treat these reports as faithful accounts of some earlier time is to overemphasize the historical side of the analytic process and to underplay its conversational overtones. (p. 95)

SUMMARY

A great deal of evidence now indicates that memory is not simply reproductive but instead involves reconstructive elements. Rather than calling up pictures of the past that are accurately imprinted on some kind of mental filmstrip, remembering involves constructing the past on the basis of current beliefs, task demands, expectations, moods, and wishes. What is recalled frequently contains inaccuracies, distortions, and outright fabrications, and the confidence that people place in their recall is not a good indicator of recall accuracy. Recollections are easily and strongly distorted by leading interviews and repeated requests to recall and other situational pressures, as well as by motivational concerns such as the need to view oneself as competent and consistent.

Psychotherapies that emphasize the recall of forgotten childhood events, and that repeatedly press patients to recall such events, are probably maximizing the likelihood of obtaining distorted, inaccurate, and, at times, completely illusory memories. Recently, a number of investigators have suggested that just such processes of memory reconstruction may, at least in part, account for what were probably the most influential cases of reported child sexual abuse in the annals of psychotherapy: the early case reports of Sigmund Freud.

6

THE SEDUCTION THEORY: OLD AND NEW VERSIONS

FREUD'S SEDUCTION THEORY

In 1896, Freud proposed his famous "seduction theory," the idea that hysteria is caused by childhood sexual trauma. According to Freud (1896a), the patients he treated entered therapy with no knowledge that they had been sexually abused in childhood, and in fact, they usually became indignant at the idea that such abuse could have occurred. Nevertheless, as therapy progressed, all of these patients remembered such abuse and frequently "relived" the abusive scenes with great emotion in his office. On the basis of these recovered memories, Freud concluded that hysteria was caused by child sexual abuse (i.e., seduction).

In all of these respects, Freud was similar to those modern psychotherapists (e.g., Blume, 1990; Fredrikson, 1992) who have suggested that large numbers of women who are unhappy, dissatisfied with various aspects of their lives, or exhibiting one or more of a very wide range of symptoms including depression, insomnia, nightmares, eating problems, sexual difficulties, somatic concerns, relationship problems, and so forth were sexually abused as children but have forgotten the abuse. These therapists contend that such symptoms are caused by repressed memories of abuse and that therapy should be aimed at helping these women to recognize the fact that they were abused and to remember the forgotten abuse.

Within 18 months of formulating his seduction theory, Freud abandoned it and claimed that he had been misled by the fantasies of his patients. According to this idea, the scenes of childhood sexual abuse reported by his patients had never really occurred. Instead, these scenes of having been sexually "seduced" in childhood were wish-fulfilling fantasies based on the patients' own repressed sexual impulses (Esterson, 1993). Late in his career, Freud (1933) described his repudiation of the seduction theory as follows:

> In the period in which the main interest was directed to discovering infantile sexual traumas, almost all my women patients told me that they had been seduced by their father. I was driven to recognize in the end that these reports were untrue and so came to understand that hysterical symptoms are derived from phantasies. (p. 120)

One important implication of Freud's repudiation of the seduction theory was a shift in the focus of therapy. Instead of attempting to uncover the memories of real traumas, psychoanalysis was aimed at understanding unconscious impulses and fantasies and the manner in which these were purportedly repressed and related to adult symptoms of psychopathology (Esterson, 1993; Macmillan, 1991).

Most investigators have taken Freud's description concerning the origins and eventual repudiation of the seduction theory at face value (e.g., Gay, 1888; Lasch, 1985). Even investigators (Blamary, 1979; Masson, 1984) who question Freud's stated reasons for repudiating the seduction theory have assumed that, during therapy, Freud's patients actually did more or less spontaneously recall that they had been sexually abused as children. This assumption has led some to argue that Freud was unable to face the implications of his own findings. According to this view, Freud was unwilling to face the awful truth that huge numbers of women had been sexually abused in childhood. In addition, he may have feared that his findings would not gain scientific acceptance because they threatened the patriarchal values and worldview that underlay 19th-century psychiatric thinking. Consequently, Freud abandoned both his theory and the reality of his patients' experiences and instead developed a theory and a therapy that denigrated his patients' experiences as fantasies (Herman, 1992; Masson, 1984). Thus, according to Herman (1992), "[psychoanalysis] was founded in the denial of women's reality" (p. 14).

A number of investigators (Esterson, 1993; Macmillan, 1991; Schatzman, 1992; Schimek, 1987; Toews, 1991), however, now argue that a careful reading of Freud's work suggests that his early patients did *not* spontaneously recall child abuse during therapy. More specifically, it is the contention of these investigators that the abuse memories of Freud's patients did not emerge through free association during therapy, as Freud implied. Instead, these reports of abuse had two sources, (a) expectations forcibly transmitted from Freud to his patients and (b) Freud's belief that he could accurately infer abuse memories in the absence of any direct reports of such abuse from his patients.

Freud believed that hysterical symptoms were connected to the memories that gave rise to those symptoms, through a chain of associated ideas. Thus, his therapeutic technique of free association involved following the chain of associated ideas backward from the associations called up by the symptoms to the supposedly repressed memories that gave rise to the symptoms. Because the complex of associations between symptom and originating memories supposedly formed an unbroken (although sometimes unconscious) chain, it was inevitable that the process of free association would lead back to the causal memories. Moreover, because the train of connections between ideas was supposedly determined entirely by the past experiences of the patient, the process of recollection could not be influenced by the expectations of the therapist (Macmillan, 1991).

Because of his belief that a therapist's expectations could not influence the train of memories recalled during free association, Freud frequently transmitted to his patients directly, repeatedly, and forcibly the idea that they had been sexually abused as children. Pressure such as this was justified, Freud believed, because patients were often resistant to believing that they had been abused, and the overcoming of such resistance was crucial to the success of the treatment. For example,

> [Once certain of a correct diagnosis] we are in a position to translate the symptomatology into aetiology; and we may then boldly demand confirmation of our suspicions from the patient. We must not be led astray by initial denials. If we keep firmly to what we have inferred, we shall in the end conquer every resistance by emphasizing the unshakeable nature of our convictions. (Freud, 1898, p. 269)

When the memories generated by Freud's patients did not fulfill his theoretical expectations, the patients were pressed to recall still earlier events:

> If the first-discovered scene is unsatisfactory, we tell our patients that this experience explains nothing, but behind it there must be hidden a more significant earlier experience. (Freud, 1896a, pp. 195–196)

Patients were not simply instructed to recall earlier events; they were informed repeatedly about the specifics of what they were expected to eventually remember:

> [The patient's attention is directed] to the associative thread which connects the two memories—the one that has been discovered and the one that has still to be discovered. A continuation of the analysis then leads in every instance to the reproduction of new scenes of the character we expect. (Freud, 1896a, p. 196)

Following repeated and sustained pressure of this kind to generate memories of events that Freud was certain his patients must have experienced, the patients often concurred by generating the requisite "memories." For instance,

> Not at all infrequently the patient begins by saying: "it's possible that I thought this, but I can't remember having done so." And it is not until he has been familiar with the hypothesis for some time that he comes to recognize it as well: he remembers—and confirms the fact, too, by subsidiary links—that he really did once have the thought. (Breuer & Freud, 1895/1964, p. 299)

In many cases the patients exposed to such procedures probably came to genuinely believe that they had been abused in childhood. On the other hand, some patients may have simply complied with the interpersonal pressure that Freud exerted and told him what he obviously wanted to hear without actually coming to believe it. For instance, Lowenfeld, a contemporary of Freud, reported the following in 1899:

> By chance, one of the patients on whom Freud used the analytic method came under my observation. The patient told me with certainty that the infantile sexual scene which analysis had apparently uncovered was pure phantasy and had never happened to him. (cited in Masson, 1985, p. 413)

In short, given that Freud explicitly and repeatedly transmitted his expectations to patients in the context of a protracted therapeutic relationship, it is hardly surprising that many of his patients reported early memories of abuse. Many of these patients probably came to believe that they had been abused and eventually "remembered" just those abuse events that Freud had posited. Others may have simply given in to social pressure and reported what Freud wanted to hear. As we shall see in later chapters, patients often follow the leads provided by their therapists and construct fantasies that fit with their therapist's ideas about what must have happened to them. With the legitimation of their therapists, many of these patients come to believe that their fantasies are real memories.

In a good many cases, however, it appears that Freud's patients, despite his strong encouragements to do so, never actually recalled scenes of sexual abuse (Esterson, 1993; Schimek, 1987). In these cases, Freud simply inferred the occurrence of childhood abuse on the basis of his patients' free associations, because it appeared logical to him to do so. For instance,

> Even when everything is finished and the patients have been overborne by the force of logic and have been convinced by the therapeutic effect accompanying the emergence of precisely these ideas—when, I say, the patients themselves accept the fact that they thought this or that, they often add: "But I can't remember having thought it." It is

easy to come to terms with them by telling them that the thoughts were unconscious. (Breuer & Freud, 1895/1964, p. 300)

In other words, Freud assumed that his patients had been abused even when they failed to recall such abuse, because the occurrence of abuse was consistent with his hypotheses at the time (Esterson, 1993; Macmillan, 1991). Freud's theoretical ideas concerning the causes of hysteria gradually changed, and the way in which he reported his patients' memories changed accordingly. The initial seduction theory demanded that his patients had suffered sexual abuse as children, but the identities of the actual abusers were relatively unimportant. However, as Freud came to emphasize the importance of incestuous wishes in the etiology of hysteria, it became important to identify the patients' fathers as their abusers (Macmillan, 1991). Freud's descriptions of his patients' abuse memories changed to fit his changing theoretical ideas. In his first paper on the seduction theory, Freud (1896b, p. 163ff.) described 13 patients. Seven of these had purportedly been sexually abused as children by other children (usually slightly older siblings), and the remainder had supposedly been abused by adults who were not relatives of the child (e.g., nursemaids, tutors). In another paper that included 5 new cases added to the original 13, Freud (1896a, p. 207ff.) described most of the abusers as adults including close relatives. Still later, after having developed the notion of the Oedipus complex, Freud described the father as the seducer in all of these early cases (Freud, 1933). As Macmillan (1991) pointed out,

> That there had been successive transformations of children into adults unrelated to them, of those adults into relatives, and of those relatives into fathers seemed to have been forgotten. Only the image of the fantastic seducer father remained. (p. 210)

As indicated by several investigators, these inconsistencies raise serious questions about the accuracy with which Freud reported his clinical findings (Cioffi, 1974; Macmillan, 1991; Schimek, 1987). More generally, these inconsistencies, along with Freud's methods for discovering repressed "memories" of child sexual abuse, illustrate how the preconceptions held by clinicians can influence the symptoms and memory reports displayed by their patients and, in so doing, generate the evidence used by the clinicians to support their initial preconceptions.

THE SEDUCTION THEORY REVISITED:
INCEST-RESOLUTION THERAPY

Many therapists continue to use the kinds of leading procedures used by Freud to initially obtain support for his seduction theory. In fact, for all intents and purposes, these investigators have revived Freud's seduction theory by suggesting that a very wide and amorphous group of psychological difficulties and problems in living stem from repressed memories of child sexual abuse. For example, Blume (1990) has contended that "half of all incest survivors do not remember that the abuse occurred " (p. 81), and Fredrickson (1992) has claimed that "millions of people have blocked out frightening evidence of abuse, years of their life, or their entire childhood" (p. 15).

Like Freud, incest-resolution therapists frequently press patients to overcome their denial and recover their hidden memories of abuse. The therapeutic procedures used by such therapists vary. Many, for example, are loosely based on 12-step programs borrowed from Alcoholics Anonymous and involve combinations of individual and group therapy approaches. Frequently, these approaches incorporate a wide range of "pop" psychology notions including ideas like codependency, treating the "inner child," and ideas from family systems theory. Common to these approaches, however, is the assumption that unremembered incest is relatively common and manifests itself in a very wide range of relatively common (as well as not-so-common) psychological and physical problems. In addition, it is assumed that the uncovering of repressed memories is crucial to treatment and that resistances and denials by patients that incest occurred are to be expected and overcome (Blume, 1990; Fredrickson, 1992).

For example, many of these ideas are echoed in *The Courage to Heal* (Bass & Davis, 1988), a well-known self-help manual for abused women and for those who believe they may have been abused. The book is frequently recommended to clients by therapists throughout North America. Readers are informed that a third of North American women were sexually abused as children and that many of these women have completely repressed their memories of this abuse. Readers are also provided with numerous relatively common symptoms of distress (e.g., low self-esteem, depression) and informed that these are symptoms of abuse even when the abuse is not remembered. Women who are uncertain as to whether they have been abused are given the following advice: "If you are unable to remember any specific instances like the ones mentioned above but still have a feeling that something abusive happened to you, it probably did" (p. 21). Later, this message is repeated even more forcefully:

> Yet even if your memories are incomplete, even if your family insists nothing ever happened, you still must believe yourself. Even if what you experienced feels too extreme to be possible or too mild to be abuse, even if you think, "I must have made it up," or "No one could have done that to a child," you have to come to terms with the fact that someone did do those things to you. (p. 87)

Like Bass and Davis (1988) it is common for other incest-resolution therapists to avoid expressions of doubt concerning any recovered memory claims made by their patients (Courtois, 1988; Fredrickson, 1992; Olio, 1989). Courtois (1991), not unlike Freud in his "seduction theory" phase, has advocated that "even if abuse is denied, the therapist who continues to have suspicions must ethically continue to explore its possibility and, whether acknowledged or not, connect abuse with its associated symptoms" (p. 54).

Recently, Poole and Lindsay (1993) surveyed a random sample of 200 doctoral-level psychotherapists concerning the frequency with which they used incest-focused memory recovery techniques such as hypnosis, instructions to work at remembering abuse, dream interpretation, and so forth. Of those who returned questionnaires, 74% reported using one or more specific techniques to help clients recover memories of childhood sexual abuse. For example, 38% of the respondents used hypnosis for this purpose, 52% used dream interpretation, and 62% encouraged their patients to work at remembering abuse. These therapists indicated that, on average, they suspected abuse in 26% of their adult female patients who initially denied any abuse. Moreover, they reported that 42% of these initial deniers recovered memories of childhood sexual abuse during therapy.

Not all incest-resolution therapists work extensively with MPD patients, but most therapists who work with MPD patients function, among other things, as incest- (and other sexual abuse) resolution therapists. The notion that hidden memories of sexual abuse are the cause of MPD pervades the field, MPD therapists are particularly likely to use hypnotic and other highly leading procedures both to diagnose MPD and to uncover hidden abuse memories, and MPD patients appear to be particularly likely to remember particularly horrendous childhood abuse with satanic cult involvement (Mulhern, 1991b).

Given that memory reports are known to be malleable and easily influenced by suggestion and expectation, why do many therapists use highly leading and suggestive procedures to recover childhood memories of incest and other forms of sexual abuse from their clients? Most likely because these therapists accept the validity of the assumptions described earlier, namely: (a) Incest is a relatively common occurrence, (b) childhood sexual abuse is typically forgotten, and (c) such abuse is strongly associated with a number of symptoms that allow the abuse to be confidently diagnosed even in the absence of any corresponding conscious memory. The validity of these assumptions will be examined in the next chapter.

SUMMARY

Like many modern psychotherapists, Freud first believed that many women who are unhappy and dissatisfied with their lives or show a wide variety of emotional symptoms were sexually abused as children but had forgotten the abuse. Careful reviews of Freud's work suggest that the abuse memories he elicited were shaped by expectations he forceably transmitted to patients, coupled with his belief that he could validly infer that abuse had occured in the absence of any direct reports from his patients.

Contemporary incest-resolution therapists also press patients to overcome their denial and recover their hidden memories of abuse. Although these therapists may use a wide range of approaches, they share the assumption that unremembered incest is relatively common and manifests itself in a very wide range of psychological and physical symptoms. Their therapeutic focus is on uncovering repressed memories, with the expectation that patients will display resistance and denial that will be overcome by extensive probing and "memory work." The malleability of the resulting memory reports was not recognized by Freud and is not understood by incest-resolution therapists.

7

CHILD SEXUAL ABUSE AND THE FATE OF ABUSE MEMORIES

THE PREVALENCE OF CHILDHOOD SEXUAL ABUSE

Before the 1970s, the issue of childhood sexual abuse was rarely raised, and there appeared to be a general perception that its prevalence was low (e.g., Weinberg, 1955). Since the 1970s, however, both public and research attention have been focused on this topic, and there is now general consensus among most professionals that such abuse is substantially more prevalent than previously believed (Finkelhor, 1979; Herman, 1993; D. Russell, 1988; Stinson & Hendrick, 1992). How prevalent, however, remains controversial (Kutchinsky, 1992). Prevalence rates for childhood sexual abuse are usually determined by obtaining retrospective reports from adults concerning their sexual experience as children (e.g., Finkelhor, Hotaling, Lewis, & Smith, 1990; D. Russell, 1988; Wyatt, 1985). The prevalence rates obtained in this way vary dramatically across different studies. For instance, in a series of studies reviewed by Pope and Hudson (1992), rates of reported child abuse by women ranged from a low of 27% to a high of 62%, and in a sample of 50 consecutive female patients in an urban emergency room, Briere and Zaidi (1989) found that 70% reported a history of child sexual abuse. Although a number of factors probably contribute to the variability found in prevalence estimates of child abuse (e.g., the nature of the populations sampled, the phrasing of questions), the most important of these factors is the breadth with which the term *sexual abuse* is defined in different studies (Peters, Wyatt, & Finkelehor, 1986; Stinson & Hendrick, 1992). Not surprisingly, studies that include noncontact abuse (e.g., seeing someone exhibit their genitals, being the recipient of unwanted sexual remarks) obtain substantially higher prevalence rates than studies that restrict the definition to forced sexual contact. For instance, Peters et al. (1986) cited a study in which a large random sample of women in Los Angeles were asked about forced sexual contact before the age of 16. By this definition, 6% of these women had been sexually abused. On the other hand, Wyatt (1985) included a broad range of contact and noncontact behaviors in her definition of sexual abuse and found that 62% of her sample of Los Angeles women had been abused before the age of 18.

For our purposes, the issue of definition is important because incest-resolution therapists frequently cite evidence to indicate that sexual abuse is relatively common (the one-third figure—mentioned in chapter 6—cited in *The Courage to Heal* [Bass & Davis, 1988] is an example) and then go on to imply from these high figures that incest is probably relatively common. In fact, however, studies that have explicitly questioned respondents about incest indicate that it is substantially less common than many other forms of sexual abuse. For instance, although the Wyatt (1985) study estimated the prevalence rate for sexual abuse among Los Angeles women at 62%, only 1.6% of reported abuse incidents involved sexual contact by fathers. Relatedly, Cole and Putnam (1992) calculated a prevalence rate for incest of 1.4% on the basis of data from Finkelhor et al. (1990). Baker and Duncan (1985) found that only .25% of a large random sample of British subjects reported sexual intercourse with a blood relative, and D. Russell (1988), in a well-known study of women in San Francisco, indicated that less than 5% reported actual or attempted sexual contact by their fathers. Several studies have assessed incest in psychiatric samples. Browning and Boatman (1977) reported a history of incest in 3.8% of child psychiatric patients, and in a study conducted in Ireland, Lukianowicz (1972) found that 4% of female psychiatric patients reported a history of incest.

Even if we take the highest of these figures (D. Russell, 1988) as the best prevalence estimate of remembered incest and assume, as do some incest-resolution therapists, that half of all incest victims have no memory of abuse, the resultant figure for the percentage of actual or attempted father–daughter incest victims is less than 10%. This figure is very substantially less than the one-fourth to one-half prevalence estimates commonly cited by incest-resolution therapists. Moreover, because it is based on the one study with the highest prevalence estimate, and because there appears to be no evidence to support the hypothesis that half of all incest victims forget their abuse, this estimate itself is a good deal higher than warranted by the available data taken as a whole.

In summary, when sexual abuse is broadly defined, estimates of its rate of prevalence tend to be high. However, prevalence rates for incest are always substantially lower than prevalence rates for broadly defined sexual abuse. Although some incest-resolution therapists believe that high proportions of women are incest victims (e.g., Blume, 1990; Fredrickson, 1992), I contend that those figures are debatable. As pointed out by Lindsay and Read (1994), the relatively low base rate for the occurrence of incest indicated by the available empirical data has important implications concerning the likelihood of false diagnoses in incest-resolution therapy. These data suggest that the large majority of women who do not remember incest at the start of therapy may not be incest victims. Consequently, if therapy leads frequently to the recall of incest, many of these incest "memories" are likely to be false.

THE FATE OF CHILDHOOD MEMORIES OF ABUSE AND TRAUMA

Repression

Freud developed the concept of repression near the end of the last century to explain the supposed forgetting of traumatic events that, he believed, lay behind the formation of hysterical symptoms. Freud viewed repression as an alternative to Janet's concept of dissociation (Macmillan. 1991), and in later chapters I will deal with some of the historical and social background that led to the development of this concept. Initially, Freud viewed repression as involving conscious attempts to avoid thinking of unpleasant or frightening events. Eventually, however, he came to conceptualize the process as entirely unconscious. Supposedly, anxiety-provoking thoughts or events would be forgotten without the person's conscious participation. Thus, the person would not only be unaware of the anxiety-provoking thoughts or events, but would also be unaware that he or she had engaged in the process of forgetting those events (Macmillan, 1991).

The concept of repression not only became central to psychoanalytic thinking, when combined with the notion that problems in adulthood stem from experiences in early childhood, it also became an integral part of popular American culture (Torrey, 1992). The notion of repression implies that painful or frightening events are *likely* to be forgotten. Consequently, if someone exhibits psychological problems for which they cannot pinpoint a cause, repressed childhood memory can serve as the obvious explanation. In the 1970s, when attention focused on the victims, symptoms, and treatment of sexual abuse, the themes of repression and childhood etiology were adapted to "explain" how repressed memories of abuse accounted for the unhappiness and dissatisfactions that some women experienced in life.

Given the pervasiveness of the concept of repression, and its un-questioned acceptance in numerous clinical circles, it is of interest to note that over 70 years of empirical research have failed to uncover unambig-uous evidence for the kinds of memory processes posited by this notion (Holmes, 1974, 1990). Consequently, we should be cautious before simply assuming that traumatic events are likely to be forgotten or, when such events are forgotten, that repression serves as a useful explanation for the forgetting.

Infantile Amnesia

Freud (1905) noted that people have difficulty recalling events that occurred when they were young. Modern memory research has confirmed that people are only very rarely able to recall events that occurred before they were 3 or so years old, and quite incapable of recalling events that occurred when they were 1 or 2 (Pillemer & White, 1989). Freud (1905) suggested that the inability to recall early events stemmed from repression, and some modern incest-resolution therapists echo this view by suggesting that memory gaps for the events of childhood are evidence of forgotten childhood sexual abuse (Fredrickson, 1992). In fact, the available evidence indicates that the inability to recall early events has nothing to do with repression or motivated forgetting of any kind. The forgetting of events that occurred before ages 3 or 4 appears to be universal. Such forgetting is labeled *infantile amnesia* and is related both to maturational changes that continue to occur in the nervous system after birth and to developmental changes in cognitive and linguistic functioning that influence how children process, retrieve, and share information (Howe & Courage, 1993; K. Nelson, 1993; Pillemer & White, 1989). Infantile amnesia has even been demonstrated in some animal species (Spear, 1979).

Controversy remains about the earliest age from which people can accurately recall memories (Loftus, 1993a; Usher & Neisser, 1993) Nevertheless, there is no good evidence to suggest that people can recall anything that happened to them before they were 2 or so years of age, and some investigators have suggested that memories from ages that young are likely to be false and the result of stories that people heard later about earlier events (Loftus, 1993a). The phenomenon of infantile amnesia is relevant to the topic of recovered memories in two ways. First, it accounts for why children who were actually abused at very early ages (i.e., before 3 or 4) are unlikely to remember their abuse (Terr, 1988). Second, it suggests that memories recovered in therapy of abuse that supposedly occurred when the person was younger than 3 of so years of age are very likely to be confabulations.

STUDIES OF MEMORIES OF ABUSE

Three types of studies have been conducted to determine what happens to memories of early abuse. The first type simply involves questioning women who report having been abused as children about their memories of the abuse. In the second type of study, attempts are made to corroborate reports of abuse with objective evidence (e.g., court records, diary entries, confessions of the perpetrator), and the third type of study begins with people whose early abuse has been documented and then assesses the memory of those individuals for their abuse.

Uncorroborated Retrospective Reports

Briere and Conte (1989, 1993) asked psychotherapists to administer a questionnaire to those of their clients who had reported a history of forced-contact sexual abuse at or before age 16. The questionnaire asked if, between the time they were first abused and their 18th birthday, there was ever a time when they could not remember the abuse. A substantial 59% of the 450 patients surveyed answered "yes" to this question, and an affirmative answer was more likely when the purported abuse involved violence, occurred relatively early, and persisted for a longer period of time.

Unfortunately, a number of factors make interpretation of these findings difficult. As pointed out by Loftus, Polonsky, and Fullilove (1994), the question asked of patients was ambiguous. What did patients mean when they indicated that there was a time when they could not remember their abuse? Perhaps some meant something like "I knew it happened, but I didn't want to think about it," or "I tried to block it out." On the other hand, others may have meant something like "I had no idea whatsoever that I was ever abused." The latter type of response is consistent with the notion of repression. However, the former responses imply an unwillingness rather than an inability to recall. Because Briere and Conte (1989, 1993) did not question subjects about the meaning of their "yes" responses, it is unclear how many of them were indicating an inability rather than an unwillingness to recall.

An even more important problem with the Briere and Conte (1993) study stems from the fact that all of the subjects were patients in psychotherapy for sexual abuse. Thus, to the extent that they may have been subjected to the kinds of procedures used by incest-resolution therapists, their recovered memories of abuse may have been confabulated. No attempt appears to have been made to obtain independent corroborative evidence for patients' abuse memories. Consequently, it is impossible to determine what proportion of the abuse memories recovered by these patients were accurate recollections as opposed to therapy-induced illusory memories.

Loftus et al. (1994) found that 54% of 105 women who were outpatients at a substance abuse center reported a history of childhood sexual abuse. Among those who reported abuse, most (69%) claimed to have remembered it continuously, 12% claimed to remember parts but not all of the abuse, and 19% claimed that they had forgotten the abuse for a period of time. The 19% forgetting rate obtained by Loftus et al. is of course, a great deal lower than the 59% rate reported by Briere and Conte (1993). Moreover, unlike Briere and Conte (1989, 1993), Loftus et al. found no relationship between reported forgetting of abuse and the violence of the abuse. Loftus et al. also found that abuse memories that had been forgotten for a time were less clear, less pictorial, and recalled as having been less intense than abuse for which subjects had continuous memories.

As Loftus et al. (in press) recognized, their study included many of the shortcomings of the Briere and Conte (1993) study. Once again, it was unclear what was meant by subjects who claimed that they forgot their abuse for a period of time, independent confirmation of the forgotten abuse was not available, and the extent to which the recovered memories of abuse might be confabulated could not be determined.

Attempts to Confirm Abuse Retrospectively

Herman and Schatzow (1987) obtained data from 53 women who participated in therapy groups for incest survivors. All of these patients reported that they either remembered the incest or strongly suspected that it had occurred but could not remember it clearly. Herman and Schatzow classified 26% of these women as exhibiting severe memory deficits, either because they could remember very little of their childhood or because they claimed to have recently recovered previously forgotten memories of abuse. The patients in these therapy groups were encouraged to obtain corroborative evidence of their abuse, and 74% of them claimed to have done so. However, two important points must be made about these findings. Recall that 74% of the patients in these groups did not exhibit evidence of severe memory deficits, the same as the percentage of subjects who claimed to obtain corroboration. Herman and Schatzow did not provide a breakdown of the proportion of the patients without memory deficits and the proportion with severe deficits who provided corroboration. Concerns about therapy-induced false memories usually arise in cases where patients claimed initially that they could not recall abuse and only later recovered memories of abuse. Thus, the critical question "What proportion of the patients *with recovered memories* provided corroboration for their previously forgotten abuse?" was neither addressed nor answered by this study.

A second, and even more important, difficulty with the Herman and Schatzow (1987) study involves the nature of the purported corroboration obtained by patients. This consisted entirely of patients' verbal reports that they had obtained corroboration. For instance, some patients claimed that they confronted their abusers and obtained confessions, one patient claimed to have found a diary in which her (deceased) accuser described abusing her, and so forth. However, none of these claims appear to have been substantiated by the therapists. For instance, it appears that the therapists never actually read the critical diary, contacted the confessing abusers, and so on. In other words, objective corroboration of recovered abuse memories—corroboration that was independent of patients' verbal reports —does not appear to have been obtained in this study.

It is important to keep in mind that the patients in the Herman and Schatzow (1987) study were participating in incest survivor groups. These groups involve patients' discussing their incestuous experiences, encouraging one another to recall such experiences, and validating each others' recovered "memories." A long line of social psychological research indicates that people in groups will often misdescribe their experiences and alter their behavior to conform to group norms and to the expectations of both authority figures and other group members (e.g., Asch, 1952, 1956; for a review, see R. Brown, 1986). Such pressures toward conformity are likely to be particularly strong in small, ongoing, cohesive therapy groups around which patients construct identities as "survivors" (Tavris, 1993). In fact, some patients who participated in such groups have commented on the strong social pressure they felt to generate memory reports of child sexual abuse that they knew were false, to win the approval of therapists and other patients (Whitley, 1992). Similar pressures might also lead patients to generate corroborative evidence if such is called for and rewarded by the group.

In several studies involving adult and adolescent patients diagnosed with MPD or other dissociative disorders, attempts have been made to corroborate reports of childhood sexual abuse (Coons, 1993; Coons & Milstein, 1986). In these cases, the corroborating evidence of child abuse was objective and independent of patients' reports. It consisted of medical and social service records that documented the abuse near the time of its occurrence. Unfortunately, these studies presented no evidence to suggest that the abuse was ever forgotten. It is worth emphasizing once again that there is no serious controversy concerning the validity of continuous memory of abuse. Disputes revolve around memories that were recovered long after the abuse occurred, and usually in the context of psychotherapy. It is not clear that the evidence presented in these studies (Coons, 1993; Coons & Milstein, 1986) relates to this issue.

Memories for Documented Abuse

The best research strategy for assessing what happens to memories of abuse involves the following steps. People who suffered documented (e.g., in court or social service agency records) sexual abuse or other severe trauma during childhood are selected. Sometime after the abuse has come to an end, these people are questioned concerning their memories for the documented abuse. Terr (1988, 1990, 1991), for example, studied children who experienced one or more early traumatic events (e.g., being the victims of a kidnaping). These children suffered a range of symptoms that were probably attributable to the trauma. Nevertheless, those who were over 3 years of age at the time of the traumatic event did not forget the trauma. On the contrary, they often had vivid and generally accurate memories of the events.

Terr (1991) distinguished what she called type I trauma (exposure to a single traumatic event such as rape by a stranger) and type II trauma (exposure to repeated traumas such as the multiple sex acts associated with incest that occurred over a number of years). Terr (1988) argued that it is type I traumatic events that are not forgotten (in children 3 or over) but are, instead, remembered vividly. Terr (1991) contended that children exposed to type II trauma have memories that "appear to be retained in spots, rather than as complete wholes" (p. 14). Such statements imply that early repeated abuse is remembered, but remembered imperfectly. However, Terr (1991) also contended that patients who suffered type II traumas sometimes exhibit massive forgetting for large parts of their childhood or for the entire set of traumatic events. Unfortunately, Terr (1991) provided no empirical evidence of her own for such massive forgetting. In her 1988 report, Terr described five children who were 36 months old or older when they experienced a trauma that she defined as repeated or long in duration. All of these children retained at least some verbal memory for the traumatic events they endured.

Interestingly, Terr's (1991) contention that exposure to repeated negative events produces spotty and incomplete memories is consistent with what is known about memory for repeated nontraumatic events (Hudson & Nelson, 1986; Linton, 1982). Suppose, for example, a child goes to a neighborhood restaurant as part of a semi-regular family ritual between the ages of 4 and 8. As an adult, this person probably remembers that she went regularly to the restaurant with her family. She may also recall a number of unusual or salient events quite clearly, such as the time she was taken ill at the restaurant and had to be taken home early. Nevertheless, most of what occurred on the outings is forgotten, the memories she does retain are fragmented, and events from one outing are likely to blend together in her memory with events from others. In short, she has constructed a schema or script for "childhood trips to the restaurant" that allows her to reconstruct what these trips were generally like. Nevertheless, she is unable to accurately reconstruct all (or even many) of the individual trips or remember most of what occurred on the individual trips.

Thus, the patchy and disjointed quality of the memories associated with type II traumas may have less to do with the traumatic nature of the events recalled than with the repeated nature of those events. If, in our example, we substitute father–daughter incest for the restaurant trips, we might expect the adult victim to have constructed a schema for the former that allows her to reconstruct what these painful episodes were generally like, but in which many details are lost or blended together. Memories of incest, of course, tend to be unpleasant and, therefore, may tend to be consciously avoided and suppressed rather than rehearsed. Memories for restaurant visits, on the other hand, are likely to be pleasant or at least neutral and, therefore, at least occasionally rehearsed. For reasons such as these, one might expect memories of repeated abuse to be even more incomplete than memories for more conventional repeated events.

Suppose, for some reason, that it becomes important for the woman in our restaurant example to spend time remembering these trips and that she tries repeatedly to recall these events. Under these circumstances, she may well recover some previously forgotten memories of her trips. Some of these new memories may be accurate and some may not. Without independent corroboration (e.g., videotapes of the trips), it would be impossible to determine their accuracy. The same may well be true of our hypothetical incest victim. By focusing on her abuse and trying to remember more, she may succeed in generating new memories. Although some of these may well be accurate, others may not, and telling one from the other in the absence of corroboration is likely to be impossible.

Femina, Yeager, and Lewis (1990) interviewed 69 adults who had been severely abused during childhood (documented in social service records, etc.). Eighteen of these subjects (26%) denied or minimized the abuse that was documented in their records. An effort was made to recontact these subjects to clarify the reasons for the discrepancies between their early records and later interviews. Subjects who could be recontacted were given a second interview aimed at developing rapport. All of the reinterviewed subjects who had denied or minimized abuse during the first interview now acknowledged that they remembered the abuse. These subjects claimed that they made their initial denials out of embarrassment, a wish to protect the perpetrator, and so forth. For instance, one woman who, as a child, had been sexually abused by her father and almost drowned by her mother gave as her reason for denying abuse during the first interview as "cuz I wanted to forget. I wanted it to be private. I only cry when I think about it" (p. 229). All of the subjects in the Femina et al. (1990) study would probably be classified under Terr's (1991) schema as suffering type II trauma. Nevertheless, none of these subjects exhibited the kind of complete forgetting postulated by some incest-resolution therapists.

Williams (1993) interviewed 129 women who had documented histories of childhood sexual abuse. The abuse had occurred sometime between early infancy and 12 years of age, and the subjects were interviewed 17 years later to determine whether they recalled the specific abuse incident documented in their records. Thirty-eight percent of these women did not remember the documented abusive incident. As would be expected because of the influence of infantile amnesia, the younger the subject at the time of the abuse, the less likely they were to remember it as an adult. On the other hand, much of the forgetting found in the Williams study cannot be explained in terms of infantile amnesia. For instance, 31% of the subjects who were 7 to 10 years old and 26% of those who were 11 or 12 years old at the time of the abuse were unable to recall the incident as adults. These ages are well beyond the age of offset for infantile amnesia.

It is important to keep in mind that the subjects in the Williams (1993) study were asked to recall a specific incident of abuse that had been documented in their records. Most of the women in this study reported instances of sexual abuse other than the index incident they were explicitly asked to recall, and this was as true for women who were unable to recall the index incident as it was for women who did recall the index incident. In fact, only 12% of the women in the study claimed not to remember any instance of child sexual abuse. It would be interesting to know the age of occurrence of the documented abuse for the 12% that remembered no abuse whatsoever, but this information was not provided.

In summary, most of the women studied by Williams (1993) suffered what Terr (1991) classified as type II trauma, repeated instances of child sexual abuse. The large majority of these women remembered that they had been sexually abused as children, although a substantial minority were unable to recall the specific incident documented in their records. Taken together, the findings of Williams (1993), Femina et al. (1990), and Terr (1988, 1990) indicate that, in the large majority of cases, women who were sexually abused in childhood (after ages 3 or 4) remember that they were abused. When the abuse was recurring or long-lived, such women may often forget specific instances and numerous details. However, forgetting that they had been abused at all appears to be an uncommon occurrence.

As pointed out by Spence (1993), discussions of child abuse and of the fate of memories of such abuse is complicated by the moral outrage that is frequently elicited by this topic. This outrage tends to get projected onto the child. Because we are outraged by the idea of someone sexually fondling a child, we tend to assume that the child experiences the same outrage and revulsion. Consequently, it is assumed either that the abused child will retain a vivid, traumatic memory of the abuse or, alternatively, that he or she will be so overwhelmed by the abuse as to repress all memories of its occurrence. In fact, however, very little information is available concerning how such activities are understood by young children, and undoubtedly their understandings change as they grow and learn to adopt the moral stance of those around them. Although some events may be traumatic, in other cases, events that morally outrage adults may not be construed as traumatic or even as particularly memorable by the child at the time of their occurrence. Consequently, some abuse events that occur during childhood may be forgotten for the same reasons that most other mundane events of childhood are forgotten. From the perspective of the child, there may be little about at least some abusive episodes that are particularly salient or memorable.

SYMPTOMS OF SEXUAL ABUSE

Incest-resolution therapists (Bass & Davis, 1988; Blume, 1990; Fredrickson, 1992) frequently contend that incest and other forms of sexual abuse produce a range of psychological symptoms and that the presence of these symptoms can be used to accurately infer childhood abuse when patients do not remember the abuse and even when they explicitly deny such abuse. It is important to understand that these investigators are not simply postulating that sexual abuse often produces psychological difficulties—a position with which most investigators agree. Instead, incest-resolution therapists go further and imply or suggest that particular symptoms or constellations of symptoms present in adulthood are strongly indicative of childhood sexual abuse. For this reason, self-help books that deal with "repressed memories" frequently contain long lists of symptoms that the authors suggest can be used to infer a history of abuse. The lists are sometimes extensive and include a wide range of behaviors. The more common symptoms include low self-esteem, relationship difficulties, sexual problems, depression, anxiety, phobias, somatic symptoms, nightmares, and panic attacks (Blume, 1990; Fredrickson, 1992).

For instance, a group called Survivors of Incest Anonymous provides a 20-item questionnaire. The questionnaire informs people that "if you have answered 'YES' to three (3) or more of these questions, Survivors of Incest Anonymous can help" (Gavigan, 1992, p. 247). The questions ask about such common problems and concerns as the following:

Do you have problems with self-confidence and self-esteem?
Do you feel you are either passive or aggressive? Do you have problems acting assertively?
Do you feel you have to "control" your emotions?
Do you feel easily intimidated by authority figures?

Have you ever been promiscuous? When you have sex, are you really seeking love, affection and acceptance?
Do you have a problem with alcohol, drugs, food, migraines, or back pain? (Gavigan, 1992, p. 247)

Even this small sample of questions makes it clear that one would probably be hard-pressed to find anyone who could *not* answer yes to three such questions. In short, the symptom lists used by incest-resolution therapists cast a very wide net and create the impression that almost any indication of psychological distress, or any perceived psychological shortcoming, is symptomatic of hidden sexual abuse. Fredrickson (1992) even suggested that fear of the dentist may indicate repressed memories of oral sexual abuse in childhood.

The difference between postulating that abuse may cause later symptoms and postulating that a set of symptoms is a diagnostic criterion for abuse is important. An example can help to clarify this distinction. An elevated temperature is a symptom of appendicitis. However, an elevated temperature, in and of itself, is not a diagnostic criterion of appendicitis because it is also a symptom of a great many other disorders, many of which (like the common cold) occur much more frequently than appendicitis. Consequently, the surgeon who removed someone's appendix simply because the patient had a temperature would be inviting a lawsuit.

It is worth noting that sets of correlated symptoms also need not be uniquely diagnostic of a particular disorder. For instance, people with some forms of cancer may suffer an elevated temperature, a feeling of general malaise, and muscle pain. Nevertheless, the regular co-occurrence of these symptoms in cancer patients cannot be used to differentially diagnose cancer because that co-occurrence is common to numerous disorders that have a substantially higher base rate of occurrence than cancer, like the flu. The same is true for the co-occurrence of such symptoms as depression, low self-esteem, and relationship difficulties. People who are depressed often also experience low self-esteem and problems in ongoing relationships. However, the fact that a person experiences all three characteristics does not mean that these constitute additive evidence that the person was abused. Such co-occurrence can result from any number of problems other than early abuse (e.g., problems at work, financial difficulties, dissatisfaction with what one has accomplished in life, a chronically ill child to care for).

A large number of studies (for reviews, see Beitchman, Zucker, Hood, DaCosta, & Akman, 1991; Beitchman et al., 1992; Kendall-Tackett, Williams, & Finkelhor, 1993) have indicated that people who were sexually abused in childhood frequently exhibit higher levels of distress and psychopathology than people who were not abused. Moreover, people who experienced relatively more severe forms of childhood abuse tend to exhibit higher levels of psychopathology than those who experienced relatively less severe abuse (e.g., Elliott & Briere, 1992). The interpretation of these findings is, however, complicated for a number of reasons.

Despite mean differences in psychopathology between the abused and nonabused, people who were abused in childhood exhibit wide variability in the extent and type of psychological difficulties they later manifest. In fact, Kendall-Tackett et al. (1993) reported that approximately one third of childhood abuse victims were symptom-free as adults. Even when the abuse is severe, some victims appear to manifest few psychological difficulties. For example, Lukianowicz (1972) reported that 23% of father–daughter incest victims suffered no ill effects from their experiences. Moreover, the evidence fails to support the hypothesis that abuse is related to a unique symptom or constellation of symptoms. For instance, although many abused people report low self-esteem and feelings of depression, many other abused people do not report these symptoms. Furthermore, many nonabused people also report low self-esteem and depression. In fact, the large majority of people who report low self-esteem and depression do not report a history of severe child sexual abuse.

People who experienced childhood sexual abuse frequently differ from the nonabused in many ways other than a history of sexual abuse (Alexander & Lupfer, 1987; Harter, Alexander, & Neimeyer, 1988). For example, incest victims often come from families that were dysfunctional in many ways other than in perpetrating incest. When abused and nonabused people are compared on psychopathology or other variables, it is frequently unclear to what extent the differences between these groups in psychological symptomatology are due to the abuse experiences per se, or to the many other demographic and early history variables that differ between these groups (Nash, Hulsey, Sexton, Harralson, & Lambert, 1993a, 1993b). For example, Nash et al. (1993a) examined the relationship between abuse history and numerous indicators of psychopathology while controlling statistically for the perceived dysfunctionality of subjects' early home environment. As in previous studies, abused subjects reported higher levels of psychopathology than the nonabused. However, relationships between abuse and psychopathology were eliminated when family dysfunctionality was controlled. In other words, people who grew up in highly dysfunctional families, whether sexually abused or not, tended to report relatively high degrees of psychopathology.

Studies like that of Nash et al. (1993a), which assess both abuse history and perceived dysfunctionality of family environment on the basis of retrospective reports from the same subjects, are certainly not without interpretive problems of their own (see the exchange between Briere & Elliot, 1993, and Nash et al., 1993b). Nevertheless, the available evidence makes it quite clear that the practice of inferring abuse on the basis of presenting symptoms of distress or psychopathology is empirically unjustified and can only lead to a substantial overdiagnosis of abuse.

SUMMARY

Although incest and other forms of severe childhood sexual abuse are more common than was once believed, I believe that they are not nearly as common as incest-resolution therapists frequently imply. Moreover, the best available evidence indicates that people who were abused after the ages of 3 or 4 years almost always recall the fact that they were abused. If the abuse was long lasting or repetitive, people are likely to forget specific instances, blend together different instances in memory, and in various other ways distort what occurred. Contrary to the claims of incest-resolution therapists, however, they are unlikely to forget completely the fact that they were abused. The available evidence indicates that there is no specific psychological symptom or set of symptoms that can be used to reliably infer a history of abuse. Symptoms such as depression and low self-esteem are not displayed by all women with a history of childhood sexual abuse, and the majority of women who report such symptoms did not suffer severe sexual abuse during childhood. In short, there is no more evidence to support modern "seduction theories" based on the notion of repression than there was to support the original "seduction theory" that Freud quickly abandoned.

All of this has important implications for women who enter therapists' offices feeling depressed and dissatisfied with themselves, but having no memories of childhood sexual abuse. The present analysis suggests that, in the large majority of cases, those women are probably correct when they claim that they were not abused. The indignation they sometimes show when abuse is suggested to them by their therapists is probably not an indication of denial or massive repression. It is much more likely to be an indication of the fact that the therapists' suggestion has no basis in reality. Nevertheless, as was true with Freud's early patients, many modern patients who are treated by incest-resolution therapists come to believe that they were sexually abused as children, despite their initial denials. For those patients who are eventually diagnosed as suffering from MPD (as well as for many who are never given this label), hypnotic memory recovery procedures are frequently the vehicle by which the abuse memories are recovered. These procedures will be discussed in the next chapter.

8

HYPNOSIS, AGE REGRESSION, AND MEMORY

Hypnotic procedures in various forms have been used for many years to facilitate recall. As we shall see in later chapters, hypnotic age regression was used by psychotherapists to uncover purportedly hidden memories long before the current wave of interest in child sexual abuse (Ellenberger, 1970), and many police forces throughout North America continue to use hypnotic procedures to "refresh" the memories of eyewitnesses to crimes (Orne, 1979b; Wagstaff, 1989). The constructive aspects of memory and the manner in which it is influenced by situational variables and expectations should be kept in mind when evaluating the effects of hypnotic procedures on memory.

HYPNOSIS AND EYEWITNESS MEMORY

Early studies that examined the effects of hypnosis on recall frequently used nonsense syllables or other meaningless stimulus materials and were fairly far removed from such practical concerns as facilitating the recall of witnesses to crimes. Nevertheless, despite any good empirical support concerning their efficacy, the idea that hypnotic procedures could greatly enhance accurate recall became well entrenched. Such procedures were used throughout much of the present century (and continue to be used) as an aid to the interrogation of witnesses (Laurence & Perry, 1988). In the 1970s, police departments across North America greatly increased their use of hypnotic procedures to "refresh" the memories of eyewitnesses. A number of investigators began to express concerns that hypnotic interviews might, in fact, lead witnesses to generate false memories, and thereby lead to the conviction of innocent suspects (Diamond, 1980; Orne, 1979b). To examine these ideas, recent studies have focused on how hypnotic and nonhypnotic procedures influence the ability of witnesses to mock crimes to select the "criminal" from a mug-shot lineup or to recall details of the criminal or the crime scene. Of particular interest in many of these studies have been the effects of leading questions both on the accuracy of recall in hypnotic subjects and on the confidence that such subjects place in their inaccurate memories (for reviews, see McConkey, 1992; M. C. Smith, 1983; Wagstaff, 1989).

A study by Spanos, Gwynn, Comer, Baltruweit, & deGroh (1989) illustrates the kind of methodologies used in this area. Subjects high and low in hypnotizability watched a short video that depicted a store robbery and fatal shooting. Following the film, subjects were distracted for several minutes and then wrote descriptions of what they had seen. Several days later, subjects returned to the laboratory and saw a second video in the form of a newsreel. The second video depicted the arrest of a suspect in a recent series of store robberies. The suspect who was arrested was not the robber in the first video. Although the suspect in the second video resembled the robber in the first video in age and general appearance, he also differed from the robber in eight specific characteristics (e.g., the suspect had a tattoo on his arm, the robber did not; the suspect wore wire-rim glasses, the robber did not wear glasses). Several days after the second video, subjects returned once again to the laboratory, where they received one of four interrogations. Each interrogation condition included both high and low hypnotizable subjects.

Subjects in one condition received a hypnotic induction along with instructions to place themselves mentally back at the scene of the crime and imagine the crime unfold on a "mental TV screen." These are the kind of instructions typically used by police when hypnotically interrogating witnesses (Reiser, 1974, 1980). Following these instructions, the subjects were asked a series of leading questions. These questions were designed to lead subjects to attribute characteristics of the suspect seen in the second video (e.g., a tattoo) to the robber seen in the first video. These leading questions instructed subjects to imagine close-ups of the robber and describe what they saw (e.g., "OK, now zoom in closer on his upper arm, can you see the tattoo?").

Subjects in a second condition received the same sequence, with one exception: They were not administered a preliminary hypnotic induction procedure. Subjects in a third condition were administered neither the hypnotic induction nor the mental imagery instructions about reliving the crime on a mental TV set. However, they were asked the same number of leading questions. Finally, control subjects were not administered either a hypnotic induction procedure or imagery instructions or leading questions.

Following these procedures, subjects were shown a mug-shot lineup and asked if they could identify the robber. The lineup included the suspect from the second video but did not include the robber from the first video.

The subjects in the three conditions that were administered leading questions misidentified many more characteristics of the suspect from video 2 as belonging to the robber in video 1 than did the control subjects. The subjects in the three leading-question conditions also chose an incorrect mug shot much more frequently than did control subjects. Highly hypnotizable subjects in the three leading-question conditions misidentified more characteristics and picked an incorrect mug shot more often than low hypnotizables. High hypnotizables also displayed more confidence that their incorrect mug-shot identifications were accurate than did low hypnotizables.

Nothing in the findings of this study suggests that hypnotic interrogations facilitate accurate recall or protect against incorrect recall or incorrect identification. Although hypnotic procedures were no worse in these regards than nonhypnotic procedures, they were certainly no better. Moreover, both the hypnotic and nonhypnotic subjects given leading questions very frequently chose and confidently identified the mug shot of an innocent person, and misattributed many false characteristics to the innocent person.

Other studies in this area have not always produced the same pattern of findings as the Spanos, Gwynn, et al. (1989) experiment. Nevertheless, there is enough consistency in the findings to support the following generalizations. Most of the evidence indicates that hypnotic procedures do not facilitate either accurate recall or accurate recognition. In a few studies, hypnotic subjects recalled more correct information than did nonhypnotic subjects, but in these studies the hypnotic subjects also usually recalled more incorrect information than did the nonhypnotic subjects. These findings do not indicate that hypnotic procedures improve memory. They simply indicate that sometimes such procedures increase the willingness of subjects to recall information about which they are uncertain. Some of the uncertain information that is recalled happens to be correct, but much of it is incorrect (for reviews see McConkey, 1992; M. C. Smith, 1983).

Hypnotic subjects are at least as likely as nonhypnotic subjects to be misled in their recall by leading questions (McConkey, Labelle, Bibb, & Bryant, 1990; Sheehan, Garnett, & Robertson, 1993; Spanos, Gwynn, et al., 1989). Both hypnotic and nonhypnotic subjects are frequently overconfident about the accuracy of what they recall. Although the evidence is mixed, some studies have suggested that hypnotic subjects exhibit even larger overconfidence effects than nonhypnotic subjects. Certainly, however, the evidence does not support the idea that hypnotic procedures reduce overconfidence effects (McConkey, 1992; M. C. Smith, 1983; Wagstaff, 1989).

Highly hypnotizable subjects are no more accurate in their recall and recognition than low hypnotizable subjects. On the other hand, some studies have found that highly hypnotizable subjects exhibit greater levels of overconfidence in their recall than do low hypnotizables (McConkey, 1992; Wagstaff, 1989). Greater overconfidence in high than in low hypnotizables is not always found (e.g., Spanos, Quigley, et al., 1991), and some evidence suggests that the relationship between confidence in incorrect recall and recognition and hypnotizability is mediated by contextually generated expectations (e.g., Gwynn, Spanos, Nancoo, & Chow, 1993). Nevertheless, there is no evidence whatsoever to suggest that high hypnotizability protects subjects from becoming overconfident in their incorrect recall or inaccurate identifications.

In summary, a good deal of evidence indicates that eyewitness recall is frequently inaccurate. Sometimes, in fact, it is spectacularly inaccurate. The bulk of the evidence fails to support the hypothesis that hypnotic procedures do anything to improve memory, and, under at least some circumstances, such procedures may make people overconfident about incorrectly remembered events.

Studies of eyewitness recall typically deal with memories for relatively recent events. In most of these studies, for example, subjects are questioned about mock crimes or other situations that occurred no more than a few weeks previously. However, in most cases, the traumatic events recalled by psychotherapy patients purportedly occurred and were repressed many years before they were again recalled during therapy. In general, memory tends to deteriorate and to involve more distortions as time from the original event increases (Loftus, 1993a; Yarmey, 1990).

Despite the consistent lack of empirical support for the proposition that hypnotic procedures facilitate accurate recall, surveys conducted of clinicians indicate that many of them appear to believe incorrectly that hypnotic age-regression procedures do, in fact, lead to the accurate recall of early memories (Loftus & Loftus, 1980; Yapko, 1994a). For instance, Yapko (1994a) found that 47% of the therapists surveyed agreed to some extent with the statement that "psychotherapists can have greater faith in details of a traumatic event when obtained hypnotically than otherwise" (p. 167), and nearly 54% agreed to some extent with the statement that "hypnosis can be used to recover memories of actual events as far back as birth" (p. 168). In a related study, Rogers and Brodie (1993) found that 70% of the social workers whom they surveyed believed that hypnosis increased the accuracy of recall. Contrary to these opinions, the available evidence fails to support the hypothesis that hypnotic age-regression procedures enhance the accuracy of long-delayed recall.

HYPNOTIC AGE REGRESSION

Hypnotic age-regression instructions inform subjects that they are going back in time, usually to a specific earlier age suggested by the hypnotist. According to the mythology associated with hypnosis, age-regressed subjects, in some real sense, develop the psychological organization of children and accurately "relive" earlier experiences in just the way they originally happened.

These ideas are false. It is now well established that age-regressed subjects do not display the cognitive or emotional characteristics of children in any inerrant fashion. Instead, they play the role of being a child—they behave "as if" they have become a child—and the accuracy with which they play this role depends on the expectations that they hold. To the extent that age-regressed subjects hold beliefs and expectations about childhood that are accurate, their age-regression performances are likely to be accurate. However, to the extent that their expectations and beliefs are inaccurate, their age-regression performances are off the mark (Barber, 1969; M. R. Nash, 1987). For example, O'Connell et al. (1970) compared real 3-year-olds with highly hypnotizable subjects who were age regressed to age 3. When allowed to make mud pies, both the age-regressed and the real 3-year-olds did so with evident pleasure. While their hands were covered in mud, the experimenter offered subjects a lollipop and purposely held it so that subjects would have to reach around his hand to get at the stick. The age-regressed subjects simply grabbed the candy portion of the lollipop with their dirty hands and put the dirty candy in their mouths. The real children were much more sensible. They reached around the experimenter's hand, grabbed the lollipop by the stick and put the clean candy in their mouths. These findings provide an amusing demonstration of how incorrect implicit beliefs about how children behave guide the performance of age-regressed subjects. In addition, the finding that age-regressed subjects were willing to suck on dirty candy indicates something of the lengths to which subjects will go to fulfill their understandings of what constitutes the hypnotic role.

A large number of studies (for reviews, see Barber et al., 1974; M. R. Nash, 1987) have examined the authenticity of hypnotic age regression by using cognitive, perceptual, and intellectual tasks for which there are standardized childhood norms. In a typical experiment, for example, the IQ scores attained by subjects age regressed to age 3 might be compared to the normative IQ scores for 3-year-old children. These studies indicate consistently that the performance of age-regressed subjects differs consistently from the way real children at the specified age perform. On IQ tests, for example, age-regressed subjects typically overestimate the performance of real children and thereby attain much higher IQ scores than do average children of that age (Nash, 1987).

Age-regressed subjects exhibit substantial variability in the extent to which they give convincing performances of childhood. For instance, despite common knowledge about the limited verbal abilities of 5-year-olds, some subjects who claim to be 5 years old when regressed to that age write and spell complex sentences like adults and give their answers in an adult voice. Others are much more convincing; they sound childlike, write in block letters, and exhibit at least the superficial characteristics expected from 5-year-old children. However, convincing performances of age regression are not specific to hypnosis. Both nonhypnotic subjects given age-regression instructions and simulators asked to fake the behavior of children are as likely to give convincing performances of age regression as are hypnotically regressed subjects (e.g., Greenleaf, 1969; O'Connell et al., 1970; Troffer, 1966).

The convincingness of an age-regression performance should not be confused with the authenticity of that performance. The fact that some actors do a better job than others at portraying Henry V tells us absolutely nothing about the real Henry or even about how much the actors know about the real Henry. Similarly, the convincingness of age-regression performances may tell us something about the differential ability of subjects to become absorbed in their role, to vividly imagine themselves as a child, and to give good dramatic performances, but differences in convincingness do not tell us anything about the behavior and cognition of real children. Even the most convincing age-regression performances do not indicate that subjects have, in any meaningful sense, "gone back" to an earlier age. Along these lines, it is worth noting that, in several studies (Kline, 1951; Rubenstein & Newman, 1954), subjects were administered age-progression instructions. Subjects who gave convincing performances of age regression also gave equally convincing performances of themselves as old people. It makes no more sense to argue that age-regressed subjects have "gone back" to being children than to argue that age-progressed subjects have "gone forward" to senility.

An early study by True (1949) appeared to indicate that subjects exhibited substantial increases in accurate recall during hypnotic age regression. True hypnotically age regressed his subjects to three different ages (ages 11, 7, and 4 years), and at each of these ages told them that it was their birthday or Christmas day. Subjects were then asked to name the day of the week. Subjects named the correct day an amazing 81% of the time. Taken at face value, these findings indicate that hypnotic age regression substantially enhances the ability of subjects to accurately recall information from earlier in their lives.

Once again, however, seemingly dramatic findings associated with hypnosis did not bear up to scrutiny. A number of studies failed to replicate True's (1949) findings (Barber, 1961; H. L. Best & Michaels, 1954; Fisher, 1962; Leonard, 1963; Mesel & Ledford, 1959; O'Connell et al., 1970; Reiff & Scheerer, 1959).

Although the reason for True's (1949) original results are not entirely clear, O'Connell et al. (1970) pointed out that the structure of True's experimental methodology left ample opportunity for experimenter bias to influence the results. To be conducted appropriately, the experimenter in the True study should have been unaware at the time of testing of the actual dates on which the birthdays and Christmas fell. By being unaware, the experimenter could not have unwittingly provided subjects with cues as to the correct answers. True, however, was aware of the correct days of the week on which each subject's birthday or Christmas day fell. After subjects were regressed to the appropriate age, True's procedure for determining the day on which the relevant event fell involved asking subjects in progression "Was it Sunday? Was it Monday?" and so on. Obviously, this procedure maximizes the likelihood that changes in the experimenter's tone of voice and inflection when he reached the correct day could have informed subjects as to the correct answer.

The role of misleading information from the hypnotist in influencing subjects' recall of earlier events during age regression has been illustrated in several relatively recent experiments (Laurence & Perry, 1988; Spanos & Bures, 1994; Spanos & McLean, 1986; Weekes, Lynn, Green, & Brentar, 1992). In these studies, subjects were asked to describe a night during the last 2 weeks in which they slept through until morning without awakening. Following their description of such a night, highly hypnotizable hypnotic subjects were age regressed back to that night and asked to "relive" what had happened. During the "reliving" period, the experimenter informed subjects that it was four o'clock in the morning and asked them if they heard the loud noises. Although all of these subjects had previously reported that they had slept through the night undisturbed, some now reported that they had been awakened by loud noises. After termination of the hypnotic procedures, subjects were again asked about the noises, and some of them continued to insist that the noises had actually occurred on the night in question and had not simply resulted from the suggestions of the hypnotist.

Two of these studies (Spanos & Bures, 1994; Weekes et al., 1992) included highly hypnotizable nonhypnotic subjects and low hypnotizable simulators as well as high hypnotizable hypnotic subjects. The nonhypnotic high hynotizables were as likely as the hypnotic subjects to report believing that the noises had really occurred. Simulators were at least as likely, and sometimes more likely, to do the same.

It is important not to exaggerate the ease with which hypnotic and nonhypnotic suggestions can be used to inculcate false memories. For instance, although many of the subjects in the above studies reported believing that the suggested noises had really occurred, these beliefs do not appear to have been particularly strong or stable. For instance, in two of these studies (Spanos & Bures, 1994; Spanos & McLean, 1986), most of the subjects were led to quickly disavow their beliefs in the reality of their false memories when they were exposed to situational demands that put a premium on differentiating fantasies from real memories rather than on confusing fantasies and memories. In another study (McConkey et al., 1990), subjects who claimed in the laboratory that the suggested noises were real changed their minds and reported that the noises were not real when they were questioned later outside of the laboratory. Relatedly, Barnier and McConkey (1992) found that some subjects who reported suggested pseudomemories during an experiment reported postexperimentally that they had done so to comply with experimental demands. Others reported being unsure whether the suggested characteristics they recalled were memories or imaginings, but they had been willing to call them memories during the experiment because the experimenter appeared to believe that they were memories.

In evaluating these findings, it is important to keep in mind that patients undergoing incest-resolution therapy, like the subjects in the above experiments, are, at first, often unsure whether the abuse experiences they uncover are memories or fantasies. It is for this reason that incest-resolution therapists warn patients to expect such uncertainty and attempt to persuade them that such uncertainty does not mean that their memories are false (Fredrickson, 1992).

FACTORS INFLUENCING DESCRIPTIONS OF "MEMORIES" AS REAL

In real-life forensic and clinical situations, people are frequently exposed to very strong demands to give reports that correspond to the expectations of authority figures (e.g., the police during eyewitness interrogations or interrogations aimed at eliciting confessions from suspects, or therapists during age regression aimed at uncovering early trauma). The extent to which subjects in these situations believe their own reports is often impossible to determine. However, it is clear that hypnotic subjects in experiments sometimes purposely misdescribe their experiences (e.g., Spanos & Flynn, 1989), witnesses sometimes lie about what they have seen (Yant, 1992), innocent suspects sometimes confess to crimes that they did not commit (Gudjonsson, 1992), and in some circumstances, patients in psychotherapy purposely misdescribe their behavior (Hoelscher & Lichstein, 1984; Hoelscher, Rosenthal, & Lichstein, 1986).

For example, Hoelscher & Lichstein (1984) used relaxation procedures to treat patients with high levels of anxiety. Part of the treatment program involved home practice. Patients were given relaxation tapes to listen to at home and were asked to record the number of times they had listened to the tapes. However, the tape machines given to the patients included a device that enabled the experimenters to determine how frequently the tapes had actually been played and thereby provided a check on the accuracy of patients' self-reports. Patients' self-reports of home practice were inflated by a whopping 126% over actual practice time. Hoelscher et al. (1986) replicated these findings in a sample of hypertensive patients. The implications of these findings are quite clear: Psychotherapy patients sometimes purposely misdescribe their experiences to convey a positive impression to their therapists.

This same phenomenon sometimes also occurs in therapy aimed at recovering abuse memories. For example, Whitley (1992) described a patient called Brenda who admitted to confabulating memories of abuse in response to persistent pressure for more such memories from her therapist:

> "But [the therapist] kept pressing me for more," said Brenda (not her real name). "But there weren't any more. I wrote more detailed things about my father that didn't happen." While part of her believed what she was writing another part didn't. On a yellow legal pad, Brenda wrote, "I'm making this up. I'm a bad girl, I'm making this up."
>
> [The therapist] refused to believe she was fantasizing. All victims maintained they were making it up, [the therapist] told her. They didn't want to admit it had really happened. (p. 37)

Subjects' own initial beliefs about their memory reports may be less important than the fact that authority figures tend to treat the reports as both believed in and accurate. Once a witness or patient is aware that his false reports are being believed by respected authority figures, it may be particularly difficult for him to recant and tell the truth. In fact, under these circumstances, he may be under great pressure to reorganize his thinking to convince himself that his own lies are really truthful. The following self-description by a patient who recovered "memories" of sexual abuse during hypnotherapy describes both the patient's doubts about the reality of her "memory" and the therapist's attempts to redefine those doubts as evidence that the abuse actually occurred:

> Throughout this experience, my mind kept telling me that I was making up a story. My mind had interjected with such comments during other hypnotherapy experiences also. At times I was aware of my mind

trying out a variety of thoughts and emotions in attempting to make a scene flow. . . . I questioned [my therapist] about this. She told me it was very normal, and that as my subconscious was describing the repressed memories, my conscious mind, still in denial, was coming in and out. (Goldstein & Farmer, 1993, p. 326)

The typical hypnosis or eyewitness memory experiment lasts for one or a few sessions. However, the recovery of abuse "memories" usually occurs over a protracted period of time. Patients who undergo incest-resolution therapy are frequently distressed, insecure people who become dependent on their therapists and on other members of abuse "survivor" networks for social support and for the maintenance of self-esteem (Haaken & Schlaps, 1991). These patients are attuned to what their therapists wish to hear and may be strongly motivated to generate the kinds of "memories" that will win attention and social approval. During such therapy, a number of factors that influence these patients to define their recovered abuse "memories" as real come into play.

One factor that probably helps patients to define their memories as real involves encouraging them to take concrete behavioral steps that heighten their commitment to the reality of their "memories." A simple and relatively subtle means for achieving such commitment involves encouraging patients to write their "memories" down. A number of social psychological experiments (for a review, see Cialdini, 1984) have indicated that people become much more committed to a belief and much less likely to change their beliefs in the face of contradictory evidence when they take the simple step of writing down their beliefs. Writing the beliefs and showing the writings to others (e.g., the therapist) make those beliefs public. Once such a permanent public record is created, people experience pressure to behave (and believe) in a manner consistent with the record they created.

A related procedure for enhancing commitment is to encourage public avowals or descriptions of a belief. Vocalizing a belief in a public forum, like writing down a belief, creates consistency pressures that enhance commitment to the belief. Of course, in addition to creating consistency pressures, groups that provide emotional and social support can also enhance members' commitments to shared beliefs (e.g., each of us was abused) by reinforcing and directly encouraging such beliefs and discouraging contrary beliefs.

All of these procedures for enhancing patients' commitments to the reality of their recovered abuse "memories" are commonly used during incest-resolution therapy. Patients involved in such therapy are routinely encouraged to write down their recovered abuse memories, even when they are unsure that those memories are real. M. Brady (1992), for example, informed patients that "we must break a silence we have kept within ourselves. To do this in writing can be a way to capture our experience, to reel it in from where it has resided in the ocean of our unconscious life" (p. 8). Frequently, these patients also participate in "survivor" groups that encourage them to vocalize recovered "memories" of abuse, and, thereby, to further commit themselves to the reality of such "memories." For example, one "survivor" who eventually rejected the reality of her recovered "memories" described the importance of sharing experiences and affirmation by group members in legitimating recovered memories:

> One woman told me it was therapeutic for her to hear about my repressed memories because she had trouble accepting hers as real, and felt more confident about hers after hearing mine. . . . The similarities [in the reported memories of group members] were mind boggling. There had to be something to the repressed memory theories if all of us were having similar experiences. . . . [After a group member role played a scene in which she improvised a confrontation with her "abuser," the therapist] would ask her if she needed a "reality check" during which the woman could ask any or all of the group members if they thought she was crazy or had looked stupid. Everyone always responded kindly with words of commendation and support, and often disgust for the perpetrator. (Goldstein & Farmer, 1993, pp. 310–311)

A particularly potent tactic for enhancing patients' commitment to their abuse memories involves encouraging them to confront their "abuser." Even though the accused is likely to deny the abuse, the public act of confrontation creates consequences and thereby commits the patient to a course of action based on the premise that the memories are real. The more consequential this course of action (e.g., breaking ties with her parents, causing rifts between believing and nonbelieving siblings), the more difficult it becomes for her to retreat from her belief that her recovered "memories" are real.

Recovered-memory patients who publicly accuse their "abuser" (usually their father) are usually met with denial and indignation. When repeated accusations do not produce a confession, it is common for these patients to break or greatly reduce contact with their families (Goldstein, 1992). One consequence of this reduced contact is to insulate these patients from information and arguments that contradict their beliefs that they were abused. Thus, the only voices these patients are likely to hear reinforce the notion that their recovered "memories" are accurate.

The importance of authoritative pronouncements, coupled with isolation from contrary opinions, in inculcating false memories is illustrated by the false confessions sometimes elicited during police interrogation. Most people who falsely confess to crimes during police interrogation do not believe their confessions. Instead, they falsely confess to eliminate the anxiety and insecurity induced by the interrogation situation (Gudjonsson, 1992). In a number of well-documented cases, however, the suspects, at least temporarily, came to believe in their confessions. In these cases, suspects were typically led to believe that they were unable to remember having committed the crime.

This process is illustrated in the case of 18-year-old Peter Reilly, who returned home to find his mother's mutilated body. During a long and intensive interrogation that included a polygraph examination, Reilly was informed by the police that he had most likely killed his own mother. Reilly's denials were met with repeated statements claiming that the polygraph had indicated that his denials were inaccurate. Reilly was further informed that, because of psychological problems, he could not remember killing his mother. He was also provided with a number of hypothetical scenarios that provided motives for his supposed killing of his mother: "[Your mother] flew off the handle and went at you or something and you had to protect yourself" (Connery, 1977, p. 67).

As the interrogation proceeded, Reilly began to doubt his own memory and to believe the story that was persistently presented to him by the police: namely, that he had killed his mother but, because of a mental block, was unable to remember having done so. Eventually, he confessed and, in his statement to the police, included such vivid details as slashing at his mother's throat with a razor and jumping up and down on her legs.

The available evidence now indicates that Reilly was completely innocent of his mother's murder (Barthel, 1976; Connery, 1977). Moreover, as is common in these cases, Reilly retracted his confession shortly after his interrogation. In other words, beliefs in false confessions tend to be fragile and are maintained by the context of the interrogation situation. The important variables in this context that generate and maintain belief in false memories appear to be (a) presentation of a rationale that explains how suspects committed a crime without knowing it (e.g., memory for the crime was repressed), (b) persistent expressions by authority figures indicating that suspects are guilty, (c) reinforcement of such expressions by selectively presenting evidence that supposedly indicates guilt (e.g., the polygraph is always accurate and it indicates that you did it), (d) isolation of suspects from anyone who might proffer alternative interpretations, and (e) attempts to develop rapport with the suspects and, subsequently, to convince them that they will experience relief following a confession.

The variables important in inducing false memories in the police-interrogation situation are also present in many therapeutic situations, including incest-resolution therapy. Unlike the interrogation situation, however, the therapeutic situation is frequently maintained for a substantial period of time. Moreover, in incest-resolution therapy, clients frequently interact with numerous people in different situations who consistently legitimate the reality of their recovered memories.

Uncertain beliefs tend to increase in strength when they are advocated repeatedly by respected sources and by a number of different sources

(Cacioppo, Claiborn, Petty, & Heesacker, 1991). Of particular importance to the maintenance of a belief is the existence of a reference group central to the person's life that advocates and reinforces that belief. For example, people who undergo even highly emotional conversion experiences at religious revival meetings rarely maintain their new beliefs unless they become immersed in a social group that shares and reinforces the expression of those new beliefs (Argyle, 1958). Relatedly, the thought-reform procedures used to convert Chinese intellectuals to the communist ideology rarely induced lasting changes in belief unless the converts' new beliefs were consistently reinforced by groups they joined after their release from prison (Rickett, 1957).

Incest-resolution therapy, with or without the use of hypnosis and regression techniques, involves reinforcing patients' construals of their recovered "memories" as real rather than fantasies. Not only are patients' "memories" repeatedly legitimated and reinforced by their primary therapists, but they are also reinforced by books like *Courage to Heal* that patients are encouraged to read (Tavris, 1993) and by other patients and professionals with whom patients interact in therapy groups and through the many informal contacts that they establish as they become part of the "incest survivors network."

A number of well-known studies (e.g., Hovland, Janis, & Kelley, 1953; King & Janis, 1956) on attitude and belief change have indicated that people are much more likely to change their ideas in the direction of a message if, instead of simply repeating the message verbatim, they become actively involved in improvising arguments that support the message. When people improvise in support of a particular idea, they focus on personal experiences, and generate arguments, that are tailored to convince themselves that the idea they are supporting is true. Patients who participate in incest-resolution therapy are frequently told that they were probably sexually abused. However, the nature of the specific abuse they must discover for themselves. For patients who had not actually been abused, the "memories" they recover are improvisations. With their therapists' help, these are constructed and shaped by patients until they provide a picture of the past that appears to adequately explain their current distress and problems in living. Actively improvising a picture that makes intuitive sense in terms of patients' personal motives and unique circumstances and experiences probably increases the ease with which the resultant picture is defined as a real memory.

SUMMARY

Hypnotic procedures do not appear to reliably enhance the recovery of accurate memories. Hypnotic subjects are at least as likely as nonhypnotic subjects to make errors in recall, to be misled by leading questions, to confuse imaginings with real memories, and to be overconfident in their recall. In addition, age-regression procedures, whether or not they are associated with hypnotic procedures, do not induce any kind of authentic "reliving" of earlier events. People who are age regressed to childhood do not, in any genuine sense, develop the psychological organization of real children. Instead, they behave in terms of their implicit and explicit expectations concerning childhood. To the extent that these expectations are inaccurate, age-regression performances are correspondingly inaccurate. Although "memories" recovered during age regression may sometimes be vivid and believed in as real, they are by no means necessarily accurate. Misleading questions and suggestions administered during age regression can lead both hypnotic and nonhypnotic subjects to report illusory memories that are described as real. In experimental settings, subjects who generate illusory memories often lose confidence in the reality of their memories when the experiment ends or when they are exposed to demands that lead them to take a critical stance toward their "memories." Similarly, suspects who are led by persistent police interrogation to falsely remember that they have committed a crime typically retract their false confessions once the interrogation ends and they have the opportunity to reevaluate the reality of their "memories" using criteria different from those suggested by the police. Many patients undergoing incest-resolution therapy also initially appear to be uncertain as to whether their recovered "memories" of abuse are illusory or real. Typically, however, these patients are exposed over a protracted period of time to persuasion-inducing procedures that enhance commitment to the reality of their recovered "memories."

9

COMPLEX FALSE MEMORIES, BODY MEMORIES, AND HYPNOSIS

WHY THERAPISTS BELIEVE THE FALSE MEMORIES OF MPD PATIENTS

In the typical eyewitness experiment and even in the "false noises" experiments, the inaccuracies that subjects generate constitute errors and distortions in details. For example, in both real life and in experiments, the typical eyewitness may be wrong about who murdered the grocer during a robbery of the corner store, but he or she is unlikely to fabricate and report having witnessed a robbery and murder that never occurred. On the other hand, MPD patients who recall "hidden" traumatic memories often "remember" complex and detailed scenarios of torture, murder, and human sacrifice conducted by many different people over an extensive period of time.

In an interesting way, the complexity and detail associated with these "remembrances" may lend them an air of credibility. All of us are aware that our memories are fallible for details, and we are all willing to believe that witnesses can make mistakes, misidentify people, and misremember many details. However, it is more difficult to comprehend that people can be led through the use of suggestive therapies to develop complex and often horrendous fantasies and believe that those fantasies are actually memories of things that happened to them many years ago. Common sense suggests that people who proffer such memory reports are liars, psychotic, or telling unpleasant truths. Most of the MPD and other patients who report "hidden memories" of ritual abuse are not psychotic and appear to have no obvious motives to lie. Therefore, because it strains credulity to believe that non-psychotic people could believe in such memories unless they were true, ritual-abuse memory reports may be more difficult to dismiss as memory errors than are simple inaccuracies about detail.

Memories of events long past, such as newly recovered memories of child sexual abuse, can be difficult to confirm with independent evidence. For this reason, many therapists suggest that the internal structure of the memory narratives themselves, along with physiological symptoms that are purportedly related to these narratives, can be used to assess their credibility. Mulhern (1991b) questioned numerous therapists who worked regularly with MPD patients about their reasons for believing that patients' memories of ritual abuse were veridical. These therapists typically described five reasons for believing their patients' narratives. The first of these reasons is that these patients exhibit strong emotional responses when first "recovering" their "hidden memories," and the second is that these memories are vivid, detailed, and coherently organized.

Strong Emotional Responses

A moment's reflection should make it obvious that neither the emotionality with which an event is remembered nor the vividness and detail associated with the memory constitutes good evidence that memories are accurate. With respect to the first reason, for example, eyewitnesses may, with great emotion, misidentify and misdescribe who they saw as they recall the crime they witnessed.

Detailed and Coherent Memories

Good fiction involves narratives that are vivid, detailed, and coherently organized. Who, after all, would bother to read a dull, incoherent, undetailed novel? People frequently spin vivid, coherent, and detailed daydreams (Singer, 1966). Obviously, such characteristics tell us nothing about the veridicality of a remembrance.

In an interesting study, Loftus and Coan (in press) recruited family members to help mislead 5 subjects into falsely believing that they had been lost in a shopping mall when they were 5 years old. For example, a 14-year-old subject named Chris was told (inaccurately) by his brother that he had been lost in a mall and, after a frantic search, had been found walking with an oldish man who had found him crying and walking aimlessly about. Initially, Chris indicated no memory whatsoever for the shopping mall incident. However, on the day Chris was given the false information, he began to "remember" the oldish man, and within 2 weeks he had developed a vivid and detailed "memory" for the entire event. Four other subjects between the ages of 8 and 42 years were similarly misled into developing "memories" of a frightening but completely fictitious event from their childhood. The Loftus and Coan (in press) study demonstrates that vivid, frightening, and detailed false memories can be created by structuring subjects' expectations and then motivating them to search for memories that are congruent with those expectations. This study further demonstrates that hypnotic procedures are not a requirement for achieving such effects.

Spanos, Burgess, Samuel, Blois, and Burgess (1994) used a complex false-feedback procedure to convince subjects that, on the day after their birth, they had probably been in a hospital that hung colored mobiles over the cribs of infants. They were also provided with misinformation that indicated that subjects administered hypnotic (or nonhypnotic) regression procedures can successfully and accurately remember events as far back as birth. Hypnotic and nonhypnotic subjects were then "regressed" back to the day after birth and asked to describe their experiences. The day after birth was chosen as the age to which subjects were regressed because this time period is covered by infantile amnesia and people cannot accurately recall anything that happened to them when they were that young. Consequently, any infancy "memories" reported by these subjects can be confidently described as false memory reports.

Substantial numbers of the hypnotic and nonhypnotic regressed subjects described seeing a mobile hanging over their crib, and even those who failed to recall a mobile reported many other infancy "memories" (e.g., the bars on their cribs, nurses and doctors wearing masks). Importantly, almost half of these subjects described their day-after-birth infancy memories as probably or definitely real memories as opposed to fantasies. Control subjects who had been given no expectations that they would be able to recall infancy memories and no regression procedures were simply instructed to take a minute, think back to the day after their birth, and describe their experiences. Although many of these subjects reported infancy experiences, they almost always described these experiences as fantasies rather than memories.

Along with these experimental studies is clinical evidence that indicates that patients can be influenced to construct vivid, complex, emotionally charged false memories. Van Husen (1988) reported on 48 subjects who had purportedly survived abortion attempts. These subjects were hypnotically regressed back to the period of intrauterine existence, where they "remembered" their experiences in the womb. For instance, these patients "remembered" how, as fetuses, they reacted to abortion attempts with a fear that they would perish. They also "remembered" responding to these attempts by bracing themselves along the wall of the uterus and by reducing their food consumption and mobility. Some of these patients "remembered" that they had a twin that was aborted. These patients were quite definite about knowing the sex of their aborted twin and described with great emotion the loss they experienced when their twin was aborted. The causes for many of the symptoms with which these patients entered therapy (e.g., irrational fears, sleeplessness, paranoid beliefs, procrastination) were supposedly traced back to their traumatic intrauterine experiences.

There is not a scintilla of evidence to suggest that people can remember their experiences as fetuses, and fetuses do not possess the physiological or cognitive capacities required to develop a fear of perishing, become aware of the sex of a co-twin, develop an emotional bond with a co-twin, understand the meaning of an abortion attempt, and so forth. Obviously then, the vivid, coherent, organized, emotionally laden, complex fetal experiences "recovered" by van Husen's (1988) patients were fantasies rather than memories. Characteristics such as the vividness and coherence of experiences simply do not constitute evidence that those experiences are memories rather than fantasies.

Body Memories

The third reason given by therapists for believing the memory reports of their patients is the purported occurrence in these patients of "body memories" before or during the "remembering" of the abuse. Body memories are physiological responses that are supposedly tied to particular early memories. For instance, patients who experience chronic pain or tightness in their arms might eventually "remember" that they were hung up by the wrists during a satanic ritual, or they may experience a reddening of the skin in their neck while "remembering" that a rope had been tied around their neck during such a ritual, or they may develop what looks like a welt raised in the skin on their torso and "remember" that they were whipped on that part of the body by cult members, and so on.

Almost all of the available information concerning body memories is anecdotal. Recently, however, S. E. Smith (1993) reported preliminary results relevant to this topic from a survey of 38 therapists in the Phoenix area who specialized in sexual abuse recovery. On average, the therapists surveyed reported that body memories were experienced by 59% of their clients. A large majority of the therapists (95%) claimed that it was common for memories to surface via body memories, and some therapists reported that 100% of their clients experienced body memories while recovering traumatic memories. When asked how they knew clients were experiencing a body memory, the therapists gave a wide variety of answers that suggested that almost any unexplained twitching, movement, or sensation, particularly when associated with affect, could be considered a body memory. Because body memories supposedly reflect underlying abuse memories, some therapists reported using hypnotic procedures to "track" body memories back to the abuse or satanic cult memories from which they purportedly arose.

A number of difficulties arise with the body-memory criterion. To begin with, a very wide range of different responses are counted as body memories. Some of these phenomena are entirely subjective and dependent on the report of the patient and, therefore, cannot be independently confirmed (e.g., experiencing pain in a part of the body that one "remembers" was subjected to torture). Others consist of physiological responses that are under voluntary control (e.g., tensing of the muscles of the buttocks while "remembering" having been anally raped as a child). Still others involve autonomic physiological responses that some people may be able to bring under indirect control through imagining or that may be generated by expectation and vivid imagery. For instance, Pennebacker (1980) demonstrated that some physiological responses, such as dryness in the throat and stuffiness in the nose, can be brought about simply by thinking about these responses. Relatedly, Coe, Peterson, and Gwynn (1993) recently found that subjects who were informed prehypnotically that hypnosis was associated with such negative symptoms as headache and a stiff neck reported the occurrence of such symptoms following termination of the hypnotic session significantly more often than did hypnotic subjects who were not so informed before hypnosis. Some subjects who possess highly sensitive skin can develop various dermographisms such as wheals following a firm stroking of the skin (T. Lewis, 1927) or localized reddening of the skin following suggestions of having been burned at that spot (M. Ullman, 1947). In very few subjects, expectations and beliefs can produce such autonomic responses as bleeding through the uncut skin (Early & Lifschutz, 1974).

The latter phenomenon was demonstrated in a case of stigmata (Early & Lifschutz, 1974). Stigmata refer to psychologically induced bleeding from those parts of the body from which Jesus supposedly bled during his crucifixion: the hands, feet, and sometimes forehead (produced by the crown of thorns). Typically, this very rare phenomenon occurs at Easter or other religious holidays to highly religious people. A number of such cases have been recorded over the centuries by officials of the Catholic church. Almost all are unreliable because the early biographies of saints in which they are found typically include gross exaggeration and outright fabrication (Bell, 1985). In the few late-19th- and early-20th-century cases that were studied scientifically, fraud and self-induced injury appeared highly likely (Johnson, 1989; Nickell, 1993; Ratnoff, 1969). However, Early and Lifschutz (1974) documented a case of stigmata in a 10-year-old Black Baptist girl. The investigators observed the bleeding firsthand and conducted microscopic examinations of the girl's hands to eliminate physical injury as the cause of the bleeding.

Genuine stigmata are most probably related to a disorder labeled *autoerythrocyte sensitization*, which involves spontaneous hemorrhaging in the absence of current physical trauma (F. H. Gardner & Diamond, 1955; Johnson, 1989). Some evidence suggests that, in predisposed individuals, the hemorrhaging can be induced by suggestion (Agle, Ratnoff, & Wasman, 1967, 1969). For our purposes, cases of stigmata illustrate two important points. First, the fact that most such cases appear to result from self-injury and purposeful fraud underscores the lengths to which people will sometimes go to support a self-presentation that is important to them (in this case a self-presentation as saintly). Second, in the very rare genuine cases like the one reported by Early and Lifschutz (1974), the observed bleeding was not related to memories of early abuse. There is certainly no evidence to suggest, for example, that the patient's bleeding occurred because she had earlier been crucified and bled while recovering this lost memory. Instead, the patient's bleeding (which occurred around Easter) was obviously related to her knowledge of the location of Jesus' supposed wounds, her understanding of the religious meaning of stigmata, and expectations generated by the religious observances surrounding Easter.

People frequently enter psychotherapy with a wide range of somatic symptoms, and this appears to be particularly true for patients who are eventually diagnosed as suffering from MPD (North, Ryall, Ricci, & Wetzel, 1993). In MPD patients, as well as in other patients in whom the therapist suspects hidden memories of abuse, hypnotic and other "memory enhancing" procedures are frequently used to uncover the hidden abuse that purportedly caused the physical symptoms. In other words, the patients' chronic somatic symptoms are sometimes conceptualized by therapists as body memories tied to hidden memories of abuse, and attempts to uncover the abuse are thereby instituted. When such patients "remember" events (e.g., being kicked in the stomach as a child) that seem, intuitively, to correspond to their current somatic symptoms (e.g., tightness and pain in the abdomen), the remembrances are assumed to be both accurate and the cause of the somatic symptoms (S. E. Smith, 1993).

The reasoning that leads to the acceptance of such assumptions is clearly faulty. Even independent verification that the events remembered had actually occurred would not demonstrate that those events had caused the somatic symptoms. Moreover, in a number of cases, the recovered abuse memories that are taken as the cause of somatic symptoms are obviously false. For example, therapists who conduct past-life regression therapy believe that traumas that occurred in previous lives influence the psychological and physical symptoms that patients experience in their current. For instance, Woolger (1987) reported on a patient called Veronica who experienced severe sinusitis. During past-life therapy, Veronica, with great emotion, "remembered" a previous life in which she had been a soldier in World War I who was killed in a mustard gas attack and died sobbing and choking. Supposedly, her sinusitis was caused by this incident from a former life. As her therapist put it, "The tears of her past life had remained lodged, as it were, in her sinuses" (p. 86).

In an even more dramatic case, a patient named Philene suffered chronically from pains in her arms and legs (Lucas, 1987). During a therapy session, Philine began to cry out and sob and then "remembered" a dramatic scene from a past life in which she was tortured by marauding soldiers who cut off her legs (thereby "explaining" the chronic pains in her legs) and dragged her behind a horse until her arms were pulled from their sockets (thereby "explaining" the pain in her arms).

As we shall see in more detail in a later chapter, the available evidence suggests that the past-life "memories" of patients like Veronica and Philine are therapy-induced fantasies rather than evidence of reincarnation. Thus, despite the convictions of both the therapists and patients in these cases, such "memories" cannot possibly be the real explanation of the patients' physical symptoms. Instead, these physical symptoms become conceptualized by both therapists and patients as body memories tied to a past life. With the aid of the regression procedures used in this kind of therapy, patients construct past-life fantasies that are congruent with, and used as explanations for, their somatic symptoms. These fantasies are legitimated by past-life therapists as real memories, and the existence of the somatic symptoms (or their diminution following the recovery of the hidden "memories") is taken as evidence for the reality of the past-life "memories."

Some experimental evidence does indicate that a very few subjects experience a reddening of the skin when remembering earlier incidents in which they were burned (Johnson & Barber, 1976; Spanos, McNeil, Gwynn, & Stam, 1984). In these cases, however, the memories of the burn incident had not been repressed; subjects easily recalled these incidents whenever they chose to do so. Moreover, the occurrence of the skin coloration changes in these cases does not indicate that the details of what subjects remembered and became absorbed in imagining were accurate. Recall that M. Ullman (1947) obtained similar coloration changes in a subject who was asked to simply imagine being burned.

Similarities in Report

The fourth reason given by MPD therapists for believing descriptions of early ritual abuse was based on their belief that similar reports were proffered by patients who had never met one another and who, therefore, could not have influenced one another's reports (Mulhern, 1991b). As Mulhern (1991b) pointed out, however, the fact that patients with similar stories never met does not preclude the possibility that the therapists of those patients were in communication with one another or were exposed to similar training procedures concerning the elicitation of satanic abuse memories. As we shall see in some detail later, widespread communication networks involving MPD patients and therapists have been of great importance in disseminating information about satanic ritual abuse.

The Painfulness of Recovered Abuse Memories

A fifth reason sometimes heard for why therapy-assisted recovered memories of incest are likely to be accurate revolves around the observation that the recovery of these memories is difficult and painful for the patient. According to this line of reasoning, it may be possible to instill false memories for emotionally neutral events. Nevertheless, it is unlikely that people can be convinced that a parent whom they had always loved and felt close to is really a sexual abuser, unless their memories of such abuse are really accurate (Kristiansen, 1994).

As indicated by the past-life regressions and fetal "memories" described above, illusory memories may well be experienced by patients as painful and traumatic. In fact, if the scenes recovered in such therapy were not traumatic, they could not serve as personally satisfying "explanations" for the difficulties that brought the patients into therapy. Similarly, theories that hold that current life difficulties stem from repressed or dissociated childhood memories require that these memories be of a painful and traumatic nature. Thus, to the extent that patients are convinced either before or after entering therapy that their current problems stem from painful hidden memories, they are likely to recover "memories" that are congruent with these expectations, even if these "memories" are experienced as painful.

The argument that patients will be unable to generate false memories of someone they have always loved is interesting because of the implicit view of parent–child relationships on which it is based. Somewhat unexpectedly, this view is similar to the view of parent–child relationships propagated by parents who claim to have been falsely accused on the basis of their grown children's recovered memories (e.g., Goldstein, 1992).

The False Memory Syndrome Foundation is an organization largely made up of parents who claim that they have been falsely accused of sexual abuse by their grown (usually female) children. A typical scenario described in the literature of this organization might be that of a middle-class, intact family. One of the daughters in the family, often a professional woman no longer living at home, becomes depressed or dissatisfied with some aspect of her life and enters psychotherapy. Although the daughter had no memories of abuse when she entered therapy, she soon develops false memories of abuse as a consequence of therapy. As a result of these false memories, the previously intact family is torn asunder. Other siblings take sides with either the accuser or the parents, and the previously close relationship between the accusing daughter and her parents is shattered, often irrevocably (Goldstein, 1992).

Within this scenario both the accusing daughters and the accused parents are seen as victims, and the therapist is cast in the role of the evil destroyer of a tranquil family. In the scenario articulated by incest-resolution therapists, the daughter is again cast as the victim, but it is now the parents (and especially the incest-perpetrating father) who are cast in the role of villain. The therapist is assigned the role of hero, and the victim is not only unaware of incest but also believes the myth that her family was happy and that her relationship with her parents was close and loving. The argument would follow that it is because patients hold these (presumably false) beliefs of loving parents that they cannot be brought to falsely remember scenes of incest.

Surely, however, the view that the typical middle-class female psychotherapy patient came from the kind of family depicted on television shows like *Father Knows Best, Leave it to Beaver,* and *Ozzie and Harriet* or even the view that the typical patient believed she came from such a family is patently false. As pointed out by Haaken (1993), the reality of middle-class family life differs from such stereotypic and patriarchal idealizations. Growing up in a typical family involves experiencing resentments, misunderstandings, conflict and competition, arbitrary and abusive uses of power, emotional blackmail, pettiness, the blurring of parent–child role boundaries, and hostility (often expressed surreptitiously by less-powerful family members). Obviously, normal family life does not involve only such negative characteristics, but that negative characteristics are invariably present can hardly be denied.

In short, women who seek psychotherapy are very unlikely to come from a uniformly tranquil and happy family because such families probably do not exist. Moreover, such women are likely to hold a complex and ambivalent view of their parents that includes resentments, fears, confusion, and guilt as much as it includes feelings of warmth and trust.

Ours is a sexually repressive society, and, as Haaken (1993) pointed out, public attitudes toward sexuality and adult–child sexual relations vacillate between denial and panic. Within our society, incest is considered a fundamental evil, an act almost too horrible to contemplate that involves abrogating all that is decent, violating basic trust, and producing deep-rooted psychological harm. Given this cultural view of incest, allegations based on recovered memories of incest may serve a metaphorical function. These allegations may both express and account for, in powerful, concrete, imagery, the poorly articulated, somewhat amorphous anger, hurt, disappointment, and resentment some women may feel toward their parents and towards themselves when they begin psychotherapy. As described by Haaken (1993), sexual abuse stories have become the officially recognized accounts that both sides can agree are emblematic of trauma itself, eclipsing all other childhood traumas or conflicts in scope and magnitude. Given this context of officially sanctioned stories, victims of various forms of psychological abuse may unconsciously create a sexual abuse narrative in seeking legitimacy for their suffering. (pp. 8–9)

As we have seen, however, it is frequently not patients alone who create the sexual abuse narratives that legitimate their suffering. The scenario of unremembered sexual abuse is commonly presented by incest-resolution therapists to their patients to "explain" the patients' complaints. Once such an explanation has been at least tentatively accepted by the patient, the patient and therapist can use hypnotic or other "memory recovery" procedures to flesh out and individualize an incest narrative that "makes sense" in terms of the patient's unique history and set of complaints.

SUMMARY

Therapists who believe the false memories of MPD patients cite several reasons for their belief, all of which are problematic. Reliance on the strength of patients' emotional responses and the detail and apparent coherance of the memories are misleading because these attributes are also seen in demonstrably false recollections and can readily be created experimentally through the use of suggestion.

There is no good evidence to support the hypothesis that so-called "body memories" accurately reflect "hidden memories" recalled during hypnotic "reliving" or other therapeutic procedures. The term *body memory* refers to a wide variety of responses. In many cases, the responses are private (i.e., pain) and unverifiable. In other cases, the responses are under voluntary control (e.g., muscle tensing) or involve autonomic responses that can be influenced by thinking and vivid imagining (e.g., skin coloration changes associated with imagined injury), by suggestion and expectation (e.g., reports of headache), or by direct voluntary response (e.g., firm stroking of the skin to induce wheals in predisposed people). In a very few people, imagery, suggestions, and expectation may produce dramatic physiological changes (e.g., spontaneous bleeding). Finally, the evidence from past-life regression therapy indicates that people may "remember" abuse events that never happened with great emotion and conviction, and then use these false memories as explanations for their somatic symptoms. Unfortunately, there are no data available concerning the frequency of the various classes of so-called body memories and no good evidence that some of the dramatic examples repeated by MPD therapists are anything more than rumors that are reinforced by repetition. The "body memories" that do occur in MPD patients can be accounted for more parsimoniously in terms of expectation, vivid imagery, implicit suggestion, and in some cases, perhaps by self-induced injury (e.g., Kern, 1994), than in terms of the sudden remembering of previously hidden satanic abuse memories.

Widespread communications networks and other forms of publicity help explain the similarities of accounts of early abuse offered by different patients. In addition, the painfulness of recovered abuse memories does not validate them. Theories that are widely held by MPD and incest-resolution therapists lead them to expect and require early pain and trauma to explain the difficulties that bring patients into therapy.

10

UFO ABDUCTION: AN EXAMPLE OF COMPLEX FALSE MEMORY

Sexual abuse during childhood obviously occurs, and sometimes it occurs in the context of kidnapping and torture by multiple assailants (Lanning, 1989, 1992). Although extremely rare, documented cases of sexual abuse followed by the cannibalism of the young victims are not unheard of (e.g., Heimer, 1971). Such real cases, along with the occurrence of "body memories"; the complexity, vividness, and detail of ritual-abuse "remembrances"; the emotionality and apparent sincerity of the patient when recalling these "memories"; and similar memory reports from patients who do not know one another seem to lend credibility to the ritual abuse "memories" of MPD patients. For these reasons, it is important to note that all of the characteristics used to validate ritual-abuse memory reports are also commonly associated with memory reports that, by any reasonable criterion, are known to be false—reports of having been abducted by aliens and transported into flying saucers.

THE SOCIAL BACKGROUND OF UFO REPORTS

Stories about flying ships of various descriptions that contain intelligent, often humanlike creatures have been reported in numerous cultures and historical periods (Vallee, 1969). In the modern era, with the development of manned flight, the frequency of such stories appears to have increased. Interestingly, the characteristics attributed to such flying ships changed with advances in technology. Typically, these characteristics included technologies that were imaginable as realistic at the time, but not yet attainable (Bullard, 1991). In the early 20th century, science fiction pulp magazines and books, influenced by the earlier work of Jules Verne (e.g., *From Earth to the Moon*, 1873), H. G. Wells (e.g., *War of the Worlds*, 1898), and Edgar Rice Burroughs (e.g., *A Princess of Mars*, 1912), provided a regular diet of stories concerning space ships and alien visitors (Beer, 1988). However, serious, sustained, and widespread interest in UFOs occurred only after the Second World War.

The end of World War II saw the dawning of the atomic age, increases in world tension associated with the cold war, the possibility of nuclear annihilation, and the beginnings of space exploration. In complex ways, both the anxieties and hopes associated with these far-reaching social changes reinforced beliefs in extraterrestrial intelligence (Morris, 1992). Notions about cosmic cataclysms (e.g., Velikovsky, 1950) and the superior weaponry undoubtedly possessed by the mysterious inhabitants of UFOs (e.g., Keyhoe, 1950) served as modern mythologies for the expression of anxieties associated with dangerous increases in world tension and the amazing developments of new technologies. Relatedly, stories of contact between earthlings and friendly godlike space visitors (e.g., Adamski, 1955) served as secular substitutes for religious mythologies by providing hope for the salvation of the human race (Morris, 1992).

The first modern UFO sighting was made in 1947 by a civilian pilot named Kenneth Arnold who was searching from the air for wreckage of a lost plane (Beer, 1988). Arnold's description of unusual lights in the sky as "they flew like a saucer would if you skipped it across water" (Story, 1980, p. 25) introduced into our language the new term "flying saucer." Arnold's sighting created a huge wave of interest in UFOs that, with periods of fluctuating enthusiasm, has continued to the present day.

There is no single cause of UFO sightings (H. Evans, 1988; Klass, 1974; Sheaffer, 1986). Among the more common causes is misidentification of heavenly bodies. For example, the apparent motion of the planet Venus as seen from a moving vehicle accounts for a surprising number of UFO reports. Some sightings can be accounted for by meteors and other occasional but well-known (to astronomers) celestial events, and still others involve the misidentification of airplanes, helicopters, weather balloons, and other man-made skyborne objects (Klass, 1974, 1989). Some UFO sightings, along with accompanying photographs of space ships, have been shown to be frauds (Klass, 1974; Vallee, 1988). Growing evidence suggests that many UFO sightings result from a phenomenon known as "earth lights." Earth lights are patterns of light that appear to change shape and move in erratic patterns. They are found in many parts of the world and have been associated with a variety of mythologies from fairies to UFOs (Devereux, 1992). One hypothesis suggests that earth lights are produced by tectonic strain. According to this notion, the movement of underground rock (i.e., the cause of earthquakes) creates strain in the rock material that in turn leads to the emission of visible radiation that is frequently interpreted by observers as UFOs (Devereux & McCartney, 1982; Persinger, 1980, 1981, 1983; Rutkowski, 1988). Importantly, and in contrast to many reports in the popular media, the evidence does not support the notion that UFO sightings are caused by the appearance of extraterrestrial spacecrafts (H. Evans, 1988; Klass, 1974; Sheaffer, 1986; Vallee, 1988).

CONTACT WITH ALIEN BEINGS

Betty and Barney Hill

Initially, the wave of UFO reports that followed Arnold's sighting consisted of purported sightings of the crafts themselves. By the mid-1960s, however, purportedly true accounts of people who claimed to have been abducted by UFO aliens began to appear. The first and most influential of these accounts involved Betty and Barney Hill, a married couple who claimed that a strange light followed their car as they returned to New Hampshire from a trip to Montreal (Fuller, 1996). Betty had been an avid believer in UFOs before the Hills encountered the light that "followed" their car. The day after the trip, Betty described the incident to her sister, another UFO believer, who suggested that Betty and Barney may have been "irradiated" by the mysterious light (Klass, 1989). Shortly thereafter, Betty began to have nightmares in which the strange light became an alien spaceship into which alien beings abducted her and Barney. While she and Barney were on board, the aliens, who communicated with her telepathically, performed various medical tests, examined Barney's genitals, inserted a long needle into Betty's abdomen, and also showed her a star map. Barney had no dreams of an abduction but was the regular recipient of Betty's stories. Shortly after beginning her recurrent abduction dreams, Betty described her experiences to UFO investigators who suggested that the trip from Montreal to New Hampshire had taken 2 hours longer than expected. The UFO investigators neglected to factor into their timetable the facts that the Hills had stopped their car to look at the strange light, and for an undetermined length of time had also left the main highway and taken various side roads to evade the light. Instead, the idea that "missing time" might portend unremembered abduction by UFOs became a staple feature of UFO abduction accounts (Klass, 1989). Betty sought psychotherapy for her nightmares. She was hypnotically regressed back to the abduction and "relived" it in great detail. Barney was also hypnotically regressed. During the regression, he expressed strong fearful emotions as he "remembered" being abducted for the first time. The details "remembered" by Barney were those he had heard many times previously from his wife. Unlike Betty and Barney, the psychiatrist who performed the hypnotic regressions was certain that the Hills' experience was an elaborate shared fantasy (Klass, 1989).

The story of the Hills' "abduction" received wide notoriety. It was given national attention through a two-part series in *Look* magazine and then in a popular book (Fuller, 1996). Relatedly, uncritical and sensationalistic "documentary style" television shows and movies that featured alien contact became popular, and continue to be popular (Sheaffer, 1986). At the same time, reports of contact and abduction with aliens mushroomed, and such reports appear to be increasing in frequency (Klass, 1989).

Research on UFO Experiences

In a recent study (Spanos, Cross, Dickson, & DuBreuil, 1993), people who claimed to have UFO experiences were administered a semi-standardized interview and a series of objective psychological tests and questionnaires. Two other groups of subjects who had not reported UFO experiences were also administered the tests and questionnaires for comparison purposes. One of the comparison groups consisted of university undergraduates, and the other of people who answered a newspaper ad calling for subjects in a study of personality.

On the basis of their interview testimony, the UFO reporters were divided into two groups. Those in one group simply reported distant lights or shapes in the night sky that appeared to move in erratic patterns and that they interpreted as UFOs. However, the 31 subjects in the second group reported more elaborate experiences that included close contact with alien spaceships or with alien beings and occasionally abduction by aliens. Subjects in the two UFO groups did not differ from those in the comparison groups on such dimensions as hypnotizability or the tendency to engage in fantasy. In addition, the subjects in the UFO groups either did not differ or scored higher than the comparison subjects on measures of psychological well-being and IQ. However, subjects in both UFO groups believed more strongly in the reality of UFOs than did comparison subjects, and those with elaborate UFO experiences also held other esoteric beliefs (e.g., belief in reincarnation) more strongly than comparison subjects.

Subjects who reported elaborate UFO experiences were much more likely to report that their experiences were sleep-related than were those who reported more mundane (i.e., lights in the sky) experiences. Many of the elaborate UFO experiences appeared to be night dreams or hypnogogic imagery. For example,

I went to bed and lay down and felt a tickling up my side. I had a flash, a vision of the following scene. I was standing in the kitchen and I opened the door, and there he stood. A tall alien in a blue and black wet suit. He was skinny, bald, with a narrow head, big eyes and light skin. He scared me profoundly. (Spanos, Cross, et al., 1993, p. 627)

Almost a quarter of the subjects in the elaborate UFO group reported frightening experiences that included full body paralysis and frequently vivid, multisensorial imagery. For example,

I was lying in bed facing the wall, and suddenly my heart started to race. I could feel the presence of three entities standing beside me. I was unable to move my body but could move my eyes. One of the entities, a male, was laughing at me, not verbally but with his mind. (Spanos, Cross, et al., 1993, p. 627)

Experiences of this kind are most probably explicable as sleep paralysis. Sleep paralysis most commonly occurs when people are in the process of falling asleep. While still conscious, they suddenly realize that they are unable to move. Typically, however, they can open and move their eyes. Sleep paralysis is typically associated with extreme fear and a feeling of suffocation, and sometimes it is also associated with complex auditory and visual hallucinations and the sense of a presence (Hufford, 1982; Spanos, McNulty, DuBreuil, Pires, & Burgess, 1994). Frequently, the hallucinations take the form of a monster, person, or animal who appears to press or sit on the person's chest. These experiences can occur while the person's eyes are open, and, under these circumstances, the hallucinatory beings are superimposed on the real background of the room in which the person was sleeping.

Estimates of the frequency of occurrence of sleep paralysis in the population vary widely, but most indicate that it occurs at least once in about 15% to 25% of the population (Bell, 1985; Hufford, 1982; Spanos, McNulty, et al., 1994). The finding that a substantial subset of elaborate UFO experiences are explicable in terms of sleep paralysis indicates that at least some of the psychological symptoms associated with these experiences may be grounded in the physiological changes that underlie sleep paralysis.

Many elaborate UFO experiences were not sleep-related, and some of those who had such experiences, like Betty Hill, reported the experience of "missing time." For example,

I was at home folding diapers. . . . I heard the front door open, looked at my watch which read 7:10 and figured it was my husband coming home from work. I heard footsteps coming up the stairs and, as they reached the top of the stairs, I could see two figures walking in unison so that the footsteps sounded like one set of feet. They were about 5'4", slight, with something over their heads. The next thing I knew I was in the middle of folding a diaper and it was 9:30. I had lost two and a half hours. (Spanos, Cross, et al., 1993, p. 627)

Spanos, Cross, et al. (1993) found that the elaborateness of UFO experiences was positively correlated with questionnaires that assessed the propensity of subjects to have unusual bodily sensation and to be fantasy prone. Hypnotizability, on the other hand, was unrelated to the elaborateness of UFO experiences. Ring and Rosing (1990) also found that people who claimed close contact with UFOs or UFO aliens attained relatively high scores on fantasy proneness.

Even the few examples given above should make it clear that the contents of elaborate UFO experiences were sometimes ambiguous. In other words, stories about small beings with something on their heads, or "entities" who communicate telepathically during sleep paralysis, are open to a wide range of interpretations including ghosts, day or night dreams, intrusive fantasies, screen memories, fairies, mental illness, demonic attack, memories from a past life, witchcraft, and, of course, extraterrestrial aliens. Most likely, subjects in the Spanos, Cross, et al. (1993) study interpreted their unusual experiences in terms of aliens as opposed to the many other possible interpretations because they held strong beliefs and expectations about the existence of aliens who visited earth, and those beliefs made the alien interpretation seem intuitively reasonable. In summary, the findings of this study indicate that elaborate UFO experiences that are described by subjects as memories of real events (as opposed to fantasies) often occur in people without manifest psychopathology and are particularly likely to occur among people who believe in alien visitation and who interpret unusual imaginal experiences in terms of the alien hypothesis.

The Formation of Abduction Memories

People who believe that they might have been abducted by aliens but cannot remember, who dream of aliens, who experience gaps in memory that they are unable to explain, or who experience physical symptoms (e.g., headaches, muscle pain, sleep paralysis) or psychological symptoms (e.g., frightening nightmares, depression, sexual dysfunction) that they learn might be caused by unremembered alien abduction sometimes undergo hypnotic (or nonhypnotic) interviews aimed at uncovering "hidden memories" of their abduction (Hopkins, 1981; Jacobs, 1992; Mack, 1994). Frequently, these interviews include two phases. In the first phase, background information is obtained and clients are asked about unusual, disturbing, or inexplicable events that occurred during their life. These include "missing time" experiences, unusual or bizarre dreams, out-of-body experiences, experiences that suggest hypnogogic imagery or sleep paralysis, scars or bruises for which the cause can no longer be remembered, and recurring physical or psychological problems (e.g., nosebleeds, depression, anxiety attacks, nightmares, gynecological problems). Such events are defined as distorted memories of alien abduction or as physical or psychological symptoms that may have been caused by unremembered abductions (Jacobs, 1992; Jacobs & Hopkins, 1992; Mack, 1994). Of course, making such events salient during an initial interview enhances the likelihood that they will be incorporated into any abduction "memories" that are recalled in phase two.

Phase two typically involves hypnotic or nonhypnotic guided imagery that is used to facilitate recall. Frequently, clients are forewarned that the experience might be frightening, that a number of sessions may be required before they remember being abducted, and that some of their memories may be ambiguous and unclear. Clients are also encouraged to say whatever comes to mind during the regression session without censoring their thoughts (Jacobs, 1992; Jacobs & Hopkins, 1992). After such preliminaries, subjects are administered a hypnotic induction procedure and regressed back to the period immediately preceding the abduction. Frequently, for example, they are regressed back to an episode in which they experienced sleep paralysis during the night. Subjects are then encouraged to "relive" the sleep paralysis episode and use it as a springboard for elaborating an entire abduction sequence. Typically, they are led through the induction in temporal sequence. For instance, subjects may be asked to imagine a movie screen on which they see their abduction displayed and to describe what they see as the sequence progresses. Subjects who have difficulty "remembering" some or all of their abduction are defined as "blocking" and are provided with strategies to facilitate recall. For example, subjects may be asked to imagine a curtain and then to peek behind it to their abduction, or they might be instructed to focus on small segments of a scene to better "remember" specific details (Jacobs, 1992; Jacobs & Hopkins, 1992). Sometimes the questions asked of subjects are highly leading as well as frequently repeated (Klass, 1989). Frequently, subjects are asked numerous specific questions aimed at obtaining a detailed description of events. For instance, Jacobs and Hopkins (1992) provide the following sample questions:

> "Are you in a large room, small room, medium sized room?" "What is the lighting like in the room—is it dim, bright, somewhere in the middle?" "What is your own posture—are you standing, sitting, lying down, crouching, etc. ?" "Where is the position of your arms?" etc. (p. 6)

The following exchange between Edith Fiore (1989), who treats patients who report having been abducted by UFOs, and a patient named Sandi illustrates how therapeutic questioning can lead abductees to provide memory reports that confirm their therapists' expectations:

> Dr. Fiore: When you were being poked everywhere, did they do any kind of vaginal examination?
> Sandi: I don't think they did.
> Dr. Fiore: Now you're going to let yourself know if they put a needle in any part of your body, other than the rectum.
> Sandi: No. They were carrying needles around, big ones, and I was scared for a while they were going to put one in me, but they didn't [Body tenses].
> Dr. Fiore: Now just let yourself relax. At the count of three you're going to remember whether they did put one of those big needles in you. If they did, know that you're safe, and it's all over, isn't it. And if they didn't, you're going to remember that too, at the count of three. One . . . two . . . three.
> Sandi: They did. (Fiore, 1989, p. 26)

In some cases, when patients have not generated abduction imagery, therapists explicitly instruct them to imagine being taken into a flying saucer (Kagan & Summers, 1983). During these procedures, clients may also be introduced to the concept of "body memories." They are informed that their body "retains a sensory memory of things that happened to it during the abduction. The subject's body will be able to remember the touch that it felt even if his eyes were closed" (Jacobs & Hopkins, 1992, p. 7).

Why Similarities in Narratives Exist

The use of these procedures has produced vivid, emotionally toned, and coherent abduction "memories" in large numbers of subjects (Bloecher, Clamar, & Hopkins, 1985; Hopkins, 1981, 1987; Jacobs, 1992; Klass, 1989; Mack, 1994). Moreover, the "memories" reported by different people in different parts of the country exhibit numerous similarities. For instance, abductees commonly report that the abduction occurred at night and that they were paralyzed in their beds by aliens who communicated with them telepathically. Frequently, the aliens are described as short, reptilianlike humanoid creatures with large heads that contain two large eyes, and as having two arms and legs and as walking erect. While paralyzed, abductees often report that they were levitated and transported into a large flying saucer. Here they were typically given a medical examination that contained strong sexual themes. Frequently, for example, women abductees report that various instruments were inserted forcefully and sometimes painfully into their vaginas, and male abductees report instruments inserted into their penises to obtain sperm. Some abductees even report having sexual intercourse with aliens who may or may not take on human shape for this purpose. Abductees also report that the aliens sometimes implanted small objects under their skin (thereby accounting for scars of unknown origin and various aches, pains, and other somatic symptoms that now constitute "body memories") or in various bodily orifices (thereby accounting for nosebleeds, gynecological problems, etc.). Frequently, abductees exhibit strong emotion as they recover these "hidden memories" of alien sexual and physical molestation, and some purportedly exhibit symptoms resembling posttraumatic stress disorder (Jacobs, 1992; Laibow, 1990).

In the past few years, it has become increasingly clear to some UFO abduction advocates that people are often abducted on numerous occasions and that such abductions begin in childhood and even occur across generations in the same families. Consequently, repeated hypnotic sessions are likely to be required to help abductees uncover the "hidden memories" of earlier and earlier traumatic abductions (Hopkins, 1987; Jacobs, 1992). Repeated sessions tend to elicit increasingly elaborate abduction memories. For instance, a number of the abductees who were treated by Mack (1994) with repeated hypnotic regressions described not only long and lurid tales of rape by aliens but also seeing and holding the hybrid alien–human babies that resulted from these sexual encounters. In addition, a number of Mack's (1994) abductees have begun to incorporate other popular "new age" beliefs into their abduction scenarios. For instance, some of them relive past lives while remembering their abductions, and some "discover" that they possess an alien identity. These dual-identity subjects shift back and forth between their human and alien identities during their regressions.

Hypnotic procedures are certainly not a requirement for obtaining detailed abduction reports. Nonhypnotic guided-imagery procedures can serve the same purpose. Priming preliminary interviews, preliminary discussion with the examiner, leading questions, prodding requests for more and more details, encouragement to imaginatively "relive" the abduction in sequence and to circumvent "blocks" in memory, and repeated interviews, whether or not they occur within an hypnotic context, are undoubtedly important in the construction and augmentation of abduction narratives. Moreover, "reliving" these experiences in the presence of an authority (the therapist) who encourages such reports and who treats them as real memories as opposed to fantasy productions undoubtedly augments the client's own tendency to define these experiences as real memories. Our earlier discussions of eyewitness testimony and of false memories elicited during age regression indicated that such variables are of great importance in the elicitation of false memory reports. There is every reason to believe that these variables function in the same way during abduction interviews.

It is important to point out that abduction interviews are not the only cause of abduction narratives or of the similarities in such narratives across clients. For instance, some clients report detailed abduction narratives before they receive treatment. Betty Hill, it will be recalled, had constructed the major components of her abduction narrative before she sought hypnotherapy (Klass, 1989), and most clients seek out UFO abduction therapists because, to varying degrees, they already believe that they were abducted (Jacobs, 1992). The reasons that people hold such beliefs are not hard to fathom. As described earlier, UFO beliefs are an important part of popular contemporary mythology, and abduction stories are becoming an increasingly important part of that mythology. Purportedly true stories of abduction like Whitley Streiber's (1987) *Communion* are found in book racks across North America and have become best-sellers. Stories of alien abduction are commonly found in tabloid newspapers and dramatized in popular television "documentaries." These sources describe the "body memories," nightmares, and other symptoms that purportedly signal the "hidden memories" of an abduction experience, and many provide drawings of the aliens as well. The picture on the cover of Striber's bestseller is typical: a bald, humanoid head with reptilian features and large eyes.

How Abductions are Interpreted

In an interesting study that demonstrated the pervasiveness of the cultural mythology concerning UFO abduction experiences, Lawson (1984) administered a hypnotic induction procedure to subjects who had never had a UFO experience and asked them to imagine being abducted by aliens. These subjects frequently proffered elaborate narratives with numerous similarities to the anecdotal reports in the literature from people who claimed to have actually been abducted. Lawson's subjects were not provided with any information concerning abduction accounts before the experiment and were not selected because of any special interest in UFOs. These subjects simply constructed their imaginary abduction narratives on the basis of their background cultural knowledge concerning UFOs and aliens. People who actually become UFO abductees are typically exposed to substantially more information about the phenomenon than were Lawson's subjects.

Becoming an abductee involves a socialization process that deserves more systematic study than it has thus far received. In general, however, the process appears to begin with people who have experienced unusual or frightening experiences like sleep paralysis or nightmares for which they can find no ready explanation, or who feel dissatisfied with their life and are seeking new answers. Sometimes these people self-diagnose their problems as abduction-related on the basis of the similarities between their experiences and what they have learned through the media about abductions. At other times, they confide in friends who "recognize" their problems as abduction-related. These friends then provide the future abductees with sources of information to support the abduction hypothesis. These include books, access to other abductees with similar experiences, and information about UFO organizations (Jacobs, 1992; Mack, 1994). Through such informal networks, future abductees are selectively exposed to information that supports the abduction hypothesis, and they frequently begin to reorganize their biographies in terms of the abduction hypothesis (e.g., the imaginary companions they had as children were "really" disguised space aliens). Eventually, contacts with the informal UFO network lead to a therapist who specializes in regression work for remembering abduction experiences and to abductee support groups that further legitimate the abduction hypothesis.

SUMMARY

Because there are many cultural sources that provide information about UFO abductions, it is hardly surprising that some people who are exposed to these popular sources, and who have experiences that are congruent with popular conceptions of "hidden abduction memories" (e.g., sleep paralysis, unexplained anxiety and physical symptoms, nightmares), conclude that they were probably abducted. It is also not surprising that such people often seek confirmation of their suspicions by turning to a procedure that, according to popular mythology, uncovers "hidden memories": hypnotic age regression. Finally, it is certainly not surprising that exposure to such confirmatory procedures produces "abduction memories" that are similar across clients by containing the elements that are common to popular and widely accessible abduction accounts.

Growth in the number of people who believe that they were abducted has stimulated growth in the number of professionals who treat such people, both individually and in groups. In addition, abduction survivors frequently befriend one another and also participate in support groups where they share experiences and offer one another mutual support (Jacobs, 1992; Mack, 1994). Such a sharing of "abduction memories" is, of course, likely to enhance the uniformity with which such "memories" are described and understood. Group processes are also likely to provide a framework in which individual experiences can be given broader meaning. For instance, by sharing abduction experiences and contemplating their implications, people can come to understand how their own experiences are part of a larger plan by aliens to obtain human genetic material (thus the probing of genitals during medical examinations by aliens) for the purpose of revitalizing their own dying race (Hopkins, 1987).

Interestingly, the meanings attributed by abductees to their alien experiences, and to some extent the experiences themselves, appear to reflect the interests and hypotheses of their therapists. Hopkins (1987), for example, views the aliens as using humans for their own genetic purposes, and it is this theme that runs consistently through the abduction reports of his subjects. Mack (1994), on the other hand, has a strong personal involvement in the environmentalist movement. Despite being abused in various ways by the aliens, his subjects often come to understand that the aliens actually have a benevolent purpose. They wish to warn humankind about the dangers of pollution and other destructive human activities.

The best available evidence indicates that UFO sightings are not alien spacecraft and that alien abductions do not occur (Klass, 1974, 1989; Littig, 1994; Sheaffer, 1986). Thus, the complex, elaborate, and detailed "hidden memories" of alien abduction that are recalled with great emotion during hypnotherapy; the traumatic "memories" of repeated abductions going back to early childhood; and the "memories" of rape and sexual abuse by aliens that were "hidden" since childhood are all confabulations. None of these are real memories of actual occurrences. Instead, they are fantasies that are believed to be memories both by those who generate them and by those who encourage and legitimate them in therapy. Obviously, some of the events that become woven into abduction narratives are very real. The depression, anxiety, and nightmares that lead people to seek help are real enough, as are the sleep paralysis and out-of-body experiences that become transformed into components of an abduction. The nosebleeds, headaches, and sundry aches and pains that become rechristened as "body memories" are also real. And who has never looked at their watch and discovered that more time than one would have expected has gone by, or driven on a long stretch of isolated highway and suddenly realized that they missed their exit and cannot remember what has transpired over the last 20 miles? Despite the inclusion of such real elements, "abduction memories" are fantasy constructions. However, they are fantasy constructions that are organized around expectations derived from external sources, embedded in a belief system that is congruent with their classification as memories, and legitimated as memories by significant others.

The similarities between UFO abduction "memories" and the "memories" of satanic ritual abuse proffered by MPD patients are obvious. All of the characteristics that MPD therapists use as evidence to validate the satanic abuse memories of their patients are present in the false memories of UFO abduction survivors. In both cases, the "memories" often remained hidden for years; were signaled indirectly through nightmares, physical and psychological symptoms, and "body memories"; and emerged only in the course of hypnotherapy aimed at uncovering those memories. In both cases, the "memories" are complex, vivid, and detailed; contain descriptions of traumatic and repeated sexual abuse that began in childhood; and are recalled during therapy with great emotion. In both cases, the "memories" are proffered by many different patients who report similar incidents despite a lack of direct contact with one another. Recently, Olio (1994) reiterated a claim heard commonly from incest-resolution therapists: namely, that there is no evidence to indicate that suggestions given during psychotherapy can produce false memories of abuse:

> To claim that such suggestions have fundamentally and falsely altered an entire client population's understanding of themselves and their histories seems grossly exaggerated. . . . There is no documentation that these types of suggestion are sufficient to produce both false memories of trauma and the accompanying symptoms characteristic of post-traumatic stress disorder. (p. 442)

Contrary to Olio's (1994) contention, the UFO abduction literature amply documents the suggestions-induced inculcation of false abuse memories in an entire client population. The contents of UFO abduction memories are, of course, different from the content of satanic ritual–abuse memories or the contents of recovered memories of "conventional" incest. Importantly, however, the therapeutic procedures used to uncover the hidden "memories" in all of these cases appear to be fundamentally similar. Because UFO abduction memories are illusory, a great deal of caution should be exercised before accepting the reality of any other memories recovered for the first time during psychotherapy.

11

THE EXPERIMENTAL CREATION OF MULTIPLICITY

Central to the idea of MPD is the notion that two or more centers of consciousness coexist within the same individual and manifest themselves periodically as first one "personality" and then another. During the 19th century, the subjects of the early mesmerists frequently behaved as if they had undergone profound changes in consciousness and in personality, and by the end of the century hypnosis was associated with such notions as dual consciousness, subliminal selves, and eventually multiple personalities (Shorter, 1992). However, by the first quarter of the 20th century, these ideas had gone into sharp decline, and with a few exceptions, experimental work relating hypnosis to ideas of multiplicity ceased until the 1970s. Since then, two lines of experimental research have examined variables that influence the development of multiplicity. The first was initiated by Hilgard (1979) and revolved around his notion of a "hidden observer." The second research line, which I discuss later in this chapter, has dealt with the phenomenon of "past-life hypnotic regression."

HIDDEN-SELF EXPERIMENTS

Hilgard (1979, 1991) conducted a well-known series of studies on hypnotic pain reduction that led to the elicitation of "hidden selves" and reports of hidden pain from normal college students who were high in hypnotizability. In a typical experiment, subjects were exposed to a baseline pain-stimulation trial (e.g., immersion of a hand in ice water for 60 seconds). At preestablished intervals during the trial, subjects verbally rated their pain intensity. Afterwards, subjects were administered a hypnotic-induction procedure and instructions that implied that a hidden part of them would remain aware of pain and other experiences that their "hypnotically analgesic part" would be unaware of. Subjects were given practice in reporting "hidden experiences" in a key-tapping code while reporting verbally on their conscious experiences. Later, subjects were given suggestions for hypnotic analgesia and again had their arm placed in ice water. During this period, they were instructed to give verbal (overt) reports that indicated the degree of pain felt by their "conscious hypnotized part" and hidden reports (numbers tapped out in a key-pressing code) that supposedly reflected the pain felt by their "hidden part." Many of the subjects in these experiments exhibited hypnotic analgesia; that is, they reported low levels of overt pain while their arm was immersed. Frequently, these same subjects also provided evidence of a "hidden self" by reporting (through key pressing) high levels of hidden pain. Verbal accounts obtained from these subjects at the end of the experiment indicated that they experienced having a hidden self that was different from their hypnotized self.

Hilgard (1979, 1991) argued that hidden pain reports do not result from suggestions or from experimental demands. Instead, he hypothesized that hypnotically analgesic subjects experience high levels of hidden pain regardless of whether they are instructed to access such pain. Supposedly, this hidden pain remains separated behind an amnesic barrier unless and until the experimenter obtains hidden reports. According to this view, the explicit hidden-observer instructions used in these experiments did not provide subjects with the idea that they had a hidden self or with the idea that hidden reports and overt reports should be different. Instead, Hilgard (1979) argued that these instructions simply provided a structured setting that allowed a preexisting hidden cognitive subsystem to come to light.

A similar perspective and experimental procedure was used by Watkins and Watkins (1980) in a study of hypnotic deafness. These investigators administered hypnotic suggestions of deafness to highly hypnotizable subjects. After subjects indicated that they could no longer hear, they were informed that "although you are hypnotically deaf, perhaps there is some part of you that is hearing my voice (Watkins & Watkins, 1980, p. 318). If subjects responded affirmatively, their hidden part was addressed directly: "Part, I want to talk to you. Will you please come out. . . . Do you have a particular name that you would like me to call you?" (Watkins & Watkins, p. 9). According to Watkins and Watkins, subjects did not present themselves as possessing hidden selves in order to meet the far-from-subtle role demands that called for such enactments. Instead, Watkins and Watkins, in a manner similar to Hilgard (1979), argued that the explicit instructions to exhibit a hidden self simply called forth hidden selves that were already present but unconscious.

In contrast with the views of Hilgard (1977b, 1979, 1991) and Watkins and Watkins (1980), a sociocognitive perspective on hidden-self experiments suggests that ratings of hidden pain and reports of experiencing a hidden self reflect interpretations that subjects derive from the instructions used in hidden-self studies (Coe & Sarbin, 1977; Spanos, 1982, 1991; Wagstaff, 1981). Two experiments (Spanos, Gwynn, & Stam, 1983; Spanos & Hewitt, 1980) obtained support for these ideas by demonstrating that the direction of hidden reports varied with the expectations conveyed by hidden-self instructions. Spanos and Hewitt (1980) tested two groups of highly hypnotizable subjects in a hypnotic analgesia paradigm. Those in one group were given standard instructions that implied that a hidden part of them would continue to feel high levels of pain while their hypnotized part experienced reduced pain (i.e., "more aware" instructions). However, those in the second group were informed that their hidden part was so deeply hidden that it would be even less aware of what had been experienced than was their hypnotized part. Subjects in these two groups showed "hidden selves" with opposite characteristics. Those given "more aware" instructions reported higher levels of hidden than overt pain, whereas those given "less aware" instructions reported lower levels of hidden than overt pain.

Spanos, Gwynn, et al. (1983) also informed high hypnotizables that they possessed a hidden self that could report on its level of pain. Initially, however, these subjects were given no information about whether their hidden selves should feel more pain, less pain, or the same amount of pain as their hypnotized selves. If hidden-observer instructions simply access a preexisting cognitive subsystem that holds high levels of dissociated pain, information about the direction of hidden relative to overt pain should be unnecessary. Instead, the hidden self should simply report the high levels of pain that "it" experiences whenever it is accessed.

Contrary to the dissociation hypothesis, subjects reported no differences between overt and hidden pain when their instructions failed to indicate that a difference was expected. Later, these same subjects reported more hidden than overt pain and less hidden than overt pain as they were sequentially exposed to instructional demands that called for each pattern of responding. In short, the findings of these two studies indicate that hidden-self responding is goal-directed action that is shaped by the demands conveyed in hidden-observer instructions. The instructions provide subjects with the idea that they possess a hidden second self with particular characteristics, and subjects generate the interpretations, experiences, and behaviors that confirm the expectations conveyed by their instructions.

The creation of hidden selves that respond to instruction by behaving as if they possess information that the person's "normal self" is unaware of has been documented in studies on hypnotic age regression, blindness, eyewitness recall, and amnesia, as well as pain reduction (Spanos, Flynn, & Gwynn, 1988; Spanos, Gwynn, et al., 1989; Spanos & McLean, 1986). Moreover, it is now clear that hypnotic procedures are not required to produce hidden selves. Two studies (Spanos & Bures, 1994; Spanos, de Groot, Tiller, Weekes, & Bertrand, 1985) found that nonhypnotic high hypnotizables who were simply asked to try their best to experience suggested effects reported experiencing hidden selves as frequently as corresponding hypnotic subjects.

Spanos, Radtke, and Bertrand (1984) used a hidden-self paradigm to examine the notion that amnesia is an involuntary happening. This study tested 8 highly hypnotizable subjects who had previously failed to breach suggested amnesia despite repeated exhortations to be honest and to try their best to recall. These subjects had been previously taught a list of three concrete and three abstract words. They were informed that the concrete words were stored in one brain hemisphere and that the abstract words were stored in the other. They were further informed that each hemisphere had a hidden self that remained aware of the information in its own hemisphere but was unaware of the information in the opposite hemisphere. Following a suggestion to forget the word list, all subjects exhibited high levels of amnesia for both the concrete and abstract words. Before canceling the amnesia, the experimenter contacted each subject's two hidden selves in succession. Each "hidden self" recalled all of the words associated with "its" hemisphere but none of the words associated with the opposite hemisphere. In other words, all subjects demonstrated that they could remember the "forgotten" words. They breached amnesia in a two-stage sequence that validated their self-presentations as deeply hypnotized and in possession of hidden selves that contained the specific characteristics described in the instructions they had been administered.

The hidden selves that subjects manifested in the Spanos, Radtke, and Bertrand (1984) study were obviously experimentally induced social constructions. When enacting one self as opposed to the other, subjects responded in terms of instructional demands by behaving as if they could recall only the information supposedly held by that one self. In other words, subjects' recall performance was an integral part of their hidden-self identity enactment and reflected their understandings of situationally generated role demands. The performance of subjects in this study resembles that of MPD patients who regularly manifest alters and whose alters purportedly hold abuse memories out of the awareness of the primary personality. The findings of the Spanos, Radtke, and Bertrand (1984) study are consistent with the hypothesis that the identity enactments and recall performance of MPD alters, like that of experimental subjects who manifest hidden selves, can be understood in terms of contextually generated role enactments.

PAST-LIFE REGRESSION

Some believers in reincarnation hold that people can be hypnotically regressed back beyond their birth to previous lives that they lived in earlier eras. The available evidence, however, provides no support whatsoever for this notion and suggests instead that past-life experiences and enactments are fantasy constructions (R. A. Baker, 1992; Spanos, Menary, Gabora, DuBreuil, & Dewhirst, 1991; I. Wilson, 1987).

Three Cases of Past-Life Regression

The best-known case of past-life regression involved Virginia Tighe, a Colorado homemaker who was hypnotically regressed by her neighbor, a businessman named Morey Bernstein (1956). During the regression, Virginia adopted a personality named Bridey Murphy. Bridey (unlike Virginia) spoke with a brogue, sang Irish folk songs, and claimed to come from Cork, Ireland, in 1806. Over a number of hypnotic sessions, "Bridey" provided numerous vivid details of her life in Ireland. She gave her birth date as December 20, 1798; named her father as a Protestant barrister named Duncan Murphy; described her marriage to Sean Brian Joseph MacCarthy; and spoke with seeming familiarity about Irish jigs, kissing the Blarney stone, and other aspects of Irish life. Bernstein told the story of Virginia (given the pseudonym Ruth Simmons) and Bridey in a best-selling book titled *The Search for Bridey Murphy*. A popular Hollywood movie soon followed.

Although it appears that a great many people were convinced of the reality of reincarnation by Bridey's story, the tale soon began to unravel. A search of records in Ireland failed to uncover any documentary evidence for the existence of Bridey or any of her relatives. A newspaper reporter dug into Virginia's past and discovered that, while she was in her teens, a woman named Bridey Murphy Corkell lived across the street from her. One of the reincarnated Bridey's friends was named Kevin and her husband's first name was Sean (Gaelic for John). It is therefore probably no coincidence that one of Mrs. Corkell's sons was named Kevin and another, on which the young Virginia had a serious crush, was named John. Virginia spent part of her girlhood in the company of an Irish aunt who might well have taught her Irish songs and provided her with other background material out of which to fashion Bridey's life story. In addition, Virginia's childhood friends and teachers remembered her as imaginative and as a talented actress who was interested in dramatics and who enjoyed delivering monologs in a well-practiced Irish brogue (M. Gardner, 1957). Finally, careful examination made it clear that Virginia's performance as an early-19th-century Irish maid was only superficially convincing. Bridey, in fact, exhibited numerous factual errors concerning 19th-century Irish life, customs, and tradition (Ready, 1956). For instance, Bridey claimed to live in a wooden house near Cork. However, the houses in that area are made of stone rather than wood (Ready, 1956). On the other hand, the wooden house described by Bridey resembled the white frame house into which Virginia was born in Madison, Wisconsin (M. Gardner, 1957).

An even more dramatic case than that of Bridey Murphy involved a British homemaker given the pseudonym Jane Evans (Iverson, 1977; Moss & Keeton, 1979). During hypnotic-regression sessions, Jane "relived" six previous lives. In one of these, for example, she was "Livonia," the wife of a tutor to the Roman Legate Constantius. Livonia claimed to live in Eboracum (the Roman name for the British city of York) in the 4th century AD. As Livonia, Jane provided vivid and detailed descriptions of life in Roman Britain. Constantius, of course, was a famous historical personage who went on to become emperor of Rome and who lived in Eboracum during the period specified by Jane. Consultation with historians who specialized in that period indicated that the details of life in Roman Britain provided by Jane, many of which required specialized knowledge of the era, were historically accurate. Records of commoners like Livonia are not available, and therefore her existence as a historical personage could not be directly verified.

Jane's undoing came when a writer familiar with her case discovered a historical novel called *The Living Wood* (de Wohl, 1947) in a secondhand bookshop (Harris, 1986). De Wohl's novel included "Livonia" as a fictitious character, the wife of a tutor to Constantius. All of the accurate historical details reported by Jane were also in the novel, as were many of the specific scenes of daily life and specific interactions between Livonia and others. In short, Jane obviously derived her past-life personality as Livonia from a historical novel that she had previously read (Harris, 1986; Wilson, 1987).

Another English case involved a woman who claimed during hypnotic regression to have been on trial for witchcraft in Chelmsford, England, in 1556. With great emotion, and in what appeared to be fluent archaic English, the woman vividly described her trial. At one point, for example, she appeared to be in great pain, dramatically held out her hands with fingers curled up, and described how she had been forced, at one point during the trial proceedings, to hold a red-hot metal bar.

Outside of the hypnotic proceedings, the woman claimed amnesia for memories of the Chelmsford trial and reported that she knew nothing and had read nothing about the trial. Moreover, examination of the contemporary 16th-century pamphlet that described the trial indicated that the woman's descriptions of events were factually correct.

Despite the evidence that appeared to support the genuineness of the case, an expert in archaic English, who listened to a tape recording of a hypnotic session, quickly determined that the regressed woman was not speaking archaic English. Instead, she was using the kind of English used by moviemakers and writers to convey the flavor of 16th-century English speech. More important was the discovery that the 16th-century pamphlets that described the Chelmsford trial contained a critical misprint. The original pamphlet record of the trial gave as the date 1566. Due to a printing error, copies made from that original gave the date incorrectly as 1556. This incorrect date, which was given by the woman during her regressions, had often been used both by scholars and story writers since the 19th century. In short, despite her denials, the woman had obviously obtained information about the Chelmsford trials from sources that quoted the common but incorrect date (Wilson, 1987).

Despite the historical inaccuracies demonstrated in cases like those of Bridey Murphy, Wambaugh (1979) contended that her past-life subjects almost always provided historically accurate information. However, the historical information that Wambaugh elicited from her regressed subjects was common knowledge (e.g., subjects regressed to prehistoric times reported wearing animal skins) and thereby not evidence of real past-life memories. Spanos, Menary, et al. (1991) administered hypnotic suggestions for past-life regression to college students. Those who reported a past life were asked for the date and place in which they were living and then asked questions that had historically checkable answers (e.g., "is your country at peace or at war"). The historical information supplied by subjects was almost invariably incorrect. For instance, all but one subject were unable to give anything but a very vague description of the currency at use in their lifetime (e.g., "we use coins"). The one subject who correctly described the currency claimed to live in the United States in 1950 and knew that George Washington was on the one dollar bill. Because one dollar bills have not changed in this regard since 1950, this one subject's accurate knowledge of currency is hardly evidence for reincarnation.

The quality of subjects' age-regression performances was unrelated to their accuracy. For instance, one female subject described a past life as Japanese fighter pilot in 1940. Her mannerisms, emotional expression, accent, and tone of voice all changed during her performance, but her knowledge of things Japanese remained woefully inadequate. For instance, she was unable to name the emperor of Japan, and she stated incorrectly that Japan was at peace in 1940.

Other investigators have also demonstrated the serious historical inaccuracies that typify the reports of hypnotic past-life regression subjects. Venn (1986), for example, treated a patient who complained of chest pains and who eventually traced these pains to memories of a former life as a World War I fighter pilot who was shot in the chest during aerial combat.

Venn went to great lengths to check the historical accuracy of his patient's reports. Much of the patient's information was incorrect, and the kinds of errors he made would not be expected from a real World War I pilot. Relatedly, I. Stevenson (1994) described numerous historical errors in the past-life reports of patients treated by regression therapists.

It is worth pointing out that some past-life therapists also advocate hypnotically progressing people into future lives. Under these circumstances, the "progressed" subjects become people who have not yet been born. They report on what life is like in the future with all of the vividness and emotion that accompanies past-life regression (Snow, 1989). Past-life hypnotic regression performances are similar to the performances of hypnotic subjects who regress to an earlier period in their current life. In both cases, subjects are invited to generate and act out "as if" experiences. In one case, it is the experience of becoming another person who lived at an earlier time; in the other, it is to experience one's self at an earlier time. In both cases, subjects who enact these roles convincingly become absorbed in creating a make-believe scenario. In both cases, they use information from a wide range of sources to generate experiences and enact responses that are aimed at convincing some audience (including themselves) that they really are a different person from an earlier age, or themselves at an earlier age. Sometimes, the enactments do convey a sense of emotional conviction. Subjects may appear to become someone other than themselves. Subjects age regressed to childhood may suck their thumb and write in block letters, whereas past-life responders may change their mannerisms, posture, and tone of voice as they move from one "life" to the next. Despite such superficial appearances of convincingness, however, careful analysis usually reveals that subjects' performances are inaccurate in important ways. Typically, these inaccuracies occur because subjects' expectations concerning the behavior of children (in the case of age regression) are inaccurate or their knowledge of history (in the case of past-life regression) is incomplete or erroneous. In short, age-regression performances and past-life enactments are social constructions. Subjects who enact these roles become someone other than themselves only in the sense that they become absorbed in behaving "as if" they are someone other than themselves.

For our purposes, past-life constructions are important because they can shed light on the processes by which people come to treat their fantasies as real and because past-life identities are similar in many respects to the multiple identities of MPD patients. Like the identity enactments of MPD patients, subjects who exhibit past-life identities behave as if they are inhabited by more than one self. Like the alter selves of MPD patients, those exhibited by past-life responders often display moods and personality characteristics that are different from the person's primary self, have a different name than the primary self, and report memories of which the primary self was previously unaware. Just as MPD patients come to believe that their alter identities are real personalities rather than self-generated fantasies, many of the subjects who enact past lives continue to believe in the reality of their past lives after termination of the hypnotic procedures (Venn, 1986).

Experimental Studies of Past-Life Regression

Several studies have examined factors that influence the formation of multiple selves by using the phenomenon of past-life hypnotic regression. Kampman (1976) found that 41% of highly hypnotizable subjects manifested evidence of new identities and called themselves by different names when given hypnotic suggestions to regress beyond their birth and become a different person. Contrary to the notion that the development of multiple identities is a sign of mental illness, Kampman's (1976) past-life responders scored higher on measures of psychological health than did subjects who failed to exhibit a past life.

In a series of experiments, Spanos, Menary, et al. (1991) also obtained past-life identity enactments following hypnotic regression suggestions. Frequently, the past-life identities were quite elaborate. They had their own names and often described their lives in great detail. Subjects who exhibited past-life identities scored higher on measures of hypnotizability and fantasy proneness, but no higher on measures of psychopathology, than those who did not exhibit a past life.

The social nature of past-life identities was demonstrated by showing that the characteristics that subjects attributed to these identities was influenced by expectations transmitted by the experimenter. In one study (Spanos, Menary, et al., 1991, experiment 2), subjects in one condition were informed before hypnotic regression that past-life identities were likely to be of a different sex and race from themselves and also likely to live in an exotic culture. Control subjects were administered the same hypnotic regression procedures but given no prehypnotic information about the characteristics of their past-life identities. Subjects provided with prehypnotic information about the characteristics of their identities were much more likely than controls to incorporate these characteristics into their descriptions of their past-life selves.

A different study (Spanos, Menary et al., 1991, experiment 3) tested the hypothesis that experimenter expectations influence the extent to which past-life identities describe themselves as having been abused during childhood. Past-life regression subjects were informed that their past-life identities would be questioned about their childhoods to obtain information about child-rearing practices in earlier historical times. Those in one condition were further told that children in past eras had frequently been abused, whereas those in the other condition were given no information about abuse. The past-life identities of subjects given abuse information reported significantly higher levels of abuse during childhood than did the past-life identities of control subjects. In summary, these studies indicate that both the personal attributes and memory reports elicited from subjects during past-life identity enactments are influenced by the beliefs and expectations conveyed by the experimenter/hypnotist. When enacting past-life identities, subjects shape the attributes and biographies attributed to these identities to correspond to their understandings of what significant others believe these characteristics to be.

After termination of the hypnotic regression procedure, some subjects who had generated past-life enactments believed that their past-life identities were actual, reincarnated personalities who had lived in earlier eras, whereas others believed that their past-life identities were imaginary creations. Hypnotizability did not predict the extent to which past-life responders assigned credibility to their new identities. On the other hand, the extent to which subjects assigned credibility to their past-life identities correlated significantly with the degree to which they placed credence in reincarnation before the experiment and the extent to which they expected to experience a real past life. In short, the extent to which subjects believed that their past-life identities were real rather than imagined was strongly influenced by the extent to which they held prior beliefs that were congruent with and could easily incorporate the idea of a personal past-life identity.

In a final study, Spanos, Menary, et al. (1991, experiment 4) manipulated prehypnotic information that concerned the reality of past-life identities. Subjects in one condition were informed that past-life identities were interesting fantasies but were certainly not evidence of real past lives. Those in another condition were provided with background information that suggested that reincarnation was a scientifically credible notion and that past-life identities were real people who had lived earlier lives. Subjects in the two conditions were equally likely to enact past-life identities, but those assigned to the imaginary-creation condition assigned significantly less credibility to these identities than did those told that reincarnation was scientifically credible. In short, prior information from authority figures influences not only the characteristics and memories that people attribute to their multiple identities but also the degree to which they come to believe in the reality of these identities.

Taken together, the available experimental data indicate that multiple identities are social creations that can be elicited easily from many normal people and that are determined by the understandings that subjects develop about multiple identities from the information to which they are exposed. When the identity to be constructed is relatively complex, such as in past-life regression studies, subjects draw on information from a wide array of sources outside of the immediate situation (e.g., TV shows, historical novels, aspects of their own past, wish-fulfilling daydreams) to flesh out the newly constructed identity and to provide it with the history and characteristics that are called for by their understanding of the current task demands. For instance, after obtaining past-life enactments, Kampman and Hirvenoja (1978) hypnotized their subjects once again and this time asked them for the sources of their past-life reports. These subjects readily admitted that stories heard as children, books, and events in their own lives were the sources of information used to build their past-life identities.

It is clear from these studies (Kampman, 1976; Spanos, Menary, et al., 1991) that the development of multiple identities is not related to psychopathology and that men are as adept as women at creating such identities. Although none of these studies obtained information about whether subjects had been abused as children, the fact that psychopathology failed to predict either the development of these identities or the extent to which subjects construed them to be real rather than imagined makes it unlikely that early abuse played any role in these regards.

All of the multiple-self experiments either tested only highly hypnotizable subjects or found that the development of secondary selves was correlated significantly with hypnotizability. One interpretation of these findings suggests that hypnotizability or its imaginal correlates may constitute a stable cognitive disposition that predisposes individuals to develop multiple identities when such experiences are called for by contextual demands and when these subjects are motivated to respond to those demands. However, an alternative hypothesis suggests that hypnotizability is correlated with the development of multiple identities because the suggestions that called for the development of multiple identities were administered in a hypnotic context and therefore were likely to call up the same attitudes and expectations as the hypnotizability test situation.

SUMMARY

In summary, the experimental data on the hidden-observer phenomenon indicate that the enactment of hidden or dissociated selves by hypnotic and nonhypnotic subjects involves strategic, rule-governed self-presentation. In the studies discussed here, information about the characteristics of the hidden selves was provided by experimental instructions, and subjects guided their experiences and behaviors in terms of these role prescriptions. The hidden-self role sometimes required amnesia as a component. Under these circumstances, subjects who claimed an inability to remember nonetheless maintained control over their memory processes and guided their recall according to the requirements associated with the particular self being presented.

We have also seen that past-life personalities are an experimentally created form of multiple identity. These identities are contextually generated, rule-governed, goal-directed fantasies. Subjects construct these fantasies to meet the demands of the hypnotic regression situation. The suggestions used in this situation tacitly require that subjects' fantasies be framed as autobiographical historical minidramas that are narrated by a first-person-singular identity other than the subject (i.e., the past-life personality). To meet these demands, subjects tend to choose historical times and places with which they are relatively familiar or in which they have a special interest. Within these constraints, they construct a life story that weaves together plot lines, details, and characters that are derived from a wide range of sources and that are expressed as a first-person report.

The extent to which subjects believe that their past-life fantasies are actual personalities from a previous incarnation depends on several interrelated factors. Of particular importance are subjects' prior beliefs and expectations. Subjects who believe in reincarnation and who expect to experience a real past life are more likely than subjects who do not hold such beliefs to interpret their past-life fantasies as evidence of real prior identities. Also important is the information supplied by the experimenter. Subjects are more likely to believe in the reality of their past-life identities when the experimenter, a knowledgeable authority, informs them that such experiences are real rather than imagined. In short, past-life experiences, like UFO abduction experiences, become socially constituted as real events when subjects possess a conceptual framework for organizing and understanding these experiences as real, and when those experiences are legitimated as real by significant others.

III

MULTIPLE IDENTITIES
IN OTHER CULTURES
AND TIMES

12

CROSS-CULTURAL STUDIES OF SPIRIT POSSESSION

Multiple self-enactments occur in a great many cultures throughout the world, but not in all cultures (Bourguignon, 1976). In many traditional societies, and in some subcultural contexts in our own society, multiple self-enactments take the form of spirit possession. In these cases, it is believed that the human occupant of the body is temporarily displaced by another self or selves that are defined as spirits who temporarily take over control of the body. Frequently, the human self claims amnesia for the periods during which the spirit selves are in control (Bourguignon, 1976; I. M. Lewis, 1987).

The frequency with which possession occurs varies greatly from one society to another. In some societies that hold possession beliefs, only a relatively small percentage of the population is ever defined as actually possessed. For instance, Wijesinghe, Dissanayake, and Mendis (1976) reported an incidence of 0.5% for a semi-urban population in Sri Lanka; Carstairs and Kapur (1976) found a period prevalence rate in a rural population on the west coast of South India of 2.8%; and Venkataramaiah, Mallikarjunaiah, Chandra shekar, Rao, and Reddy (1981) reported a prevalence of 3.7% in a different South Indian rural population. In other societies, the rates of possession are extremely high. For instance, in the villages of the Malagasy speakers of Mayotte, Lambek (1980) reported that 39% of the adult women and 8% of the adult men were considered to be possessed. Relatedly, Harper (1963) reported that 20% of the women amongst the Havik Brahmins in Mysore experienced possession, and Boddy (1988) found that in different years 42% and 47% of ever-married women above the age of 15 in the village of Hofriyat in Northern Sudan had succumbed to possession. When considering only women between the ages of 35 and 55, Boddy reported that 66.6% had experienced possession.

In most traditional societies that hold possession beliefs, possession occurs much more frequently among women than among men. This, however, is not invariably the case, and in some societies possession occurs with equal or almost equal frequency in the two sexes (I. M. Lewis, 1987). If nothing else, the marked differences among societies in rates of possession, coupled with the very high rates of possession in some societies, should make us wary of explanations of multiple identity development that emphasize the importance of stable personality or cognitive characteristics such as high fantasy proneness or high hypnotizability as necessary predisposing factors. Sex ratios and the proportion of community members affected also vary widely in some North American groups that display spirit possession.

GLOSSOLALIA: A NORTH AMERICAN EXAMPLE OF SPIRIT POSSESSION

One relatively common form of possession experience in Western society is religious glossolalia (Hine, 1969). Glossolalia involves vocal utterances that consist of semantically meaningless vowel—consonant combinations that sound like language. These utterances are sometimes mistaken by naive listeners as a foreign language. Glossolalia is frequently performed within certain Christian religious settings. It may be accompanied by dramatic behaviors including convulsions, profuse sweating, eye closure, and an apparent loss of consciousness, but it often occurs in the absence of all such dramatic accompaniments (Spanos & Hewitt, 1979). Whether or not glossolalia is accompanied by dramatic displays appears to be dependent on the expectations of the glossolalics and their audience and the norms of the particular setting in which it is displayed.

Traditionally, glossolalia has been interpreted in Christian religious circles as possession by the Holy Spirit, who supposedly speaks His own language (the glossolalia) through the possessed person. In many religious settings, displays of glossolalia are followed by an "interpretation" of what was spoken. Frequently glossolalics claim amnesia for their utterances, and therefore the interpretation is typically offered by someone else—usually by a church leader who has the "gift" of interpretation. Because glossolalia is, in fact, meaningless, the "interpretation" can include whatever the interpreter wishes. Typically, the interpretation supports the central tenets of the religious community.

Rates of glossolalia differ dramatically across different religious groups as a function of expectations concerning who will and will not manifest the phenomenon. In some congregations, glossolalia is encouraged and occurs in all or almost all members. In other congregations, it is relatively rare (Samarin, 1972). Glossolalia can be easily learned through modeling and practice (Spanos, Cross, Lepage, & Coristine, 1986), and congregations that encourage glossolalia typically provide the novice with much encouragement, coaching, and multiple opportunities to closely observe other glossolalics (Goodman, 1972). Glossolalics do not score higher than nonglossolalics on measures of hypnotizability, imaginative activity, or psychopathology (Neanon & Hair, 1990; Richardson, 1973; Spanos & Hewitt, 1979), and the ability to learn glossolalia is unrelated to either hypnotizability or imaginative activity (Spanos, Cross, et al., 1986). Glossolalia can occur with equal frequency in men and women, and when sex differences do occur, they reflect local custom rather than intrinsic gender differences (Samarin, 1972).

In some religious communities, the first manifestation of glossolalia is interpreted as a sign of salvation that signals full acceptance into the religious group. In describing their conversion, new members typically make a sharp distinction between their new (postconversion) identity and their old life of sin. These individuals frequently reconstruct their biographies so as to accentuate differences between their pre- and postconversion identities. In so doing, they emphasize the role of their glossolalic conversion experience as a marker of what they and their community view as a critical transition point between a discarded sinful identity and a new consecrated identity (Hine, 1970; Malony & Lovekin, 1985).

In short, glossolalia is a form of possession occurring relatively commonly in our own society. It is learned behavior, and whether it occurs alone or in combination with other dramatic behaviors depends on contextual demands and the beliefs and expectations of the speaker and audience. It also varies dramatically in frequency from one community to another as a function of community religious beliefs and expectations. In some communities, glossolalia marks a conversion to a new religious identity, and converts frequently reconstruct the way they organize and describe their past life so that it corresponds to the views held by the community concerning the characteristics of preconversion identities.

The characteristics of possession displays in other cultures also vary greatly both among societies and within societies. Possession is not a unitary phenomenon and differs dramatically depending on the status of the possessed person, the context in which the possession occurs, and the meaning attributed to the possession both by the possessed individual and by his or her audience (I. M. Lewis, 1987).

RITUAL POSSESSION

In a number of societies, spirit possession occurs as part of helping rituals. The medium becomes possessed by a spirit or by successive spirits, and it is the spirits that diagnose the client, prescribe treatments, or offer advice for problems in living. The rituals can be private consultations involving only the medium and client, or public ceremonies that involve one or more mediums and large audiences (Lee, 1989; I. M. Lewis, 1987). The structure of these ritual activities clearly illustrates the social nature of multiple-identity enactments and the dependence of such enactments on social validation. The medium and the audience hold complementary expectations concerning the behaviors that define the medium as possessed by a particular spirit and the behaviors that define members of the audience as validating the spirit presentations. The medium presents as a specific spirit by enacting the particular behavioral displays that the audience identifies with that spirit. The audience, in turn, validates the medium's presentation by responding in a manner that is congruent with the particular spirit identity being presented (Firth, 1967; Krippner, 1989; Lambek, 1988; Lee, 1989).

For instance, the transition from the medium's human personality to that of a spirit is marked by readily identifiable signs (e.g., shaking, eye closure) that the audience has learned to interpret in terms of spirit possession. Similarly, the transition from one spirit identity to another is marked by recognizable changes in behavior such as changes in voice, personality, and dress. In some cultures, particular spirits dance to some tunes but not others, and in other cultures each change in spirit identity is marked by replacing a scarf of one color with a scarf of another. When behaving as a warrior spirit, the medium struts to and fro in an aggressive and threatening manner, and the audience responds accordingly by being quiet and respectful. When presenting as a tiger spirit, the medium may walk on all fours and growl while the audience backs away. When presenting as a risqué spirit, the medium jokes with the audience, which responds with relaxation and laughter (Krippner, 1989; Lambek, 1989; Lee, 1989; Saunders, 1977). The result of these mutually supporting interactions is the construction of spirit possession as a social reality (Schieffelin, 1985).

Oftentimes, ritual possession ceremonies can involve a number of people who are possessed simultaneously (I. M. Lewis, 1987). Furthermore, in some ceremonies, a single spirit can move from possessing one person to possessing another. However, the same spirit cannot possess two people simultaneously. Thus, ceremonies that involve the sequential possession of several people by more than one spirit involve a good deal of coordination among the performances of the various mediums, who must be aware of their own performances as well as those of other mediums to keep their changing roles distinct (Lambeck, 1988; Lee, 1989).

The rule-governed nature of ritual possession is also illustrated by the preparation required for a convincing performance. The required props for differentiating spirit identities must be readily available. For instance, when presenting as a tiger spirit, one medium would bite and suck at the patient's body until he produced from his mouth a black substance that he called black pus and blood. The blood he probably produced by biting his own cheek, and the "black pus" he produced by putting ashes into his mouth before the ceremony and before becoming possessed (Peters, 1981).

Learning the Possessed Role

Becoming a spirit medium usually involves an extensive socialization process, and once an individual becomes a medium, periodic possession may be a lifelong occurrence. In some societies, mediumship runs in families and particular spirits move from possessing a parent to possessing one of his or her children. In other cases, mediums are former patients who apprentice with their healer. Frequently, there are a number of different paths into mediumship within the same society. Regardless of the path taken, however, the medium must learn the rules required to give convincing performances that meet the expectations of clients and other audience members (Krippner, 1989; Morton, 1977; Peters, 1981).

Factors important in the socialization of mediums can be illustrated by examining the "espiritistas" of Puerto Rico. Spirit mediumship became popular in Puerto Rico during the 19th century through the work of a French magnetist who wrote under the pen name of Allen Kardec (1886). Kardec believed that every individual possesses a personal spirit that survives bodily death and that can be reincarnated into a new body to continue its evolutionary development. Evolution of this spirit can also be assisted by the existence of guardian angels. Purportedly, everyone possesses the faculties required to communicate with spirits, but only those who choose to develop these faculties go on to become spirit mediums and learn how to assist others to communicate with the spirit world.

Kardec's work was introduced into Puerto Rico during the latter half of the 19th century, where it spread rapidly. During this time, popular folk healers were being disenfranchised both by the Catholic church and by medical licensing boards established by the Spanish colonial government. Although Kardec's spiritist practices shared a number of similarities with indigenous folk healing practices, the codification of his system in written texts, and his use of the language of science to propagate his ideas, gave his system a legitimacy that the folk practices lacked. Consequently, spirit mediums (called "espiritistas") gradually replaced the indigenous folk healers of Puerto Rico (Koss-Chioino, 1992).

Puerto Rican espiritistas diagnose the causes of illness and other problems in living and then help patients to deal with their physical or emotional problems by coming to terms with the spirit world (Garrison, 1977). Most Puerto Rican spirit mediums are women who grew up in poor families. They usually carry out their work as an avocation and rarely take money for their services. On the other hand, for women with an interest in helping others, mediumship can offer respect and a rise in status among peers, as well as a legitimate means of escaping a homebound existence. Espiritistas are self-selected and frequently claim that they received communications from spirits during childhood. Oftentimes, they describe early illnesses or distressing events such as the death of a parent as triggering their first experience with spirits. However, many of these women had parents or grandparents who practiced as mediums, and others recalled being taken as children to spiritist healing groups ("centros") where relatives worked or presided. In short, future espiritistas are often socialized from childhood not only to believe in spirits but also to interpret illnesses and other distressing personal experiences as involving communications from the spirit world. Moreover, they are frequently exposed from childhood to experienced mediums who model possession behavior. In fact, once a woman decides on a calling as an espiritista, she often apprentices with and learns her trade from a more experienced healer (Harwood, 1977; Koss-Chioino, 1992).

Espiritistas usually describe their own initial possession by spirits as occurring during a period of distress. For instance, Koss-Chioino (1992) described a woman named Rosa who was nervous and had difficulty functioning as a wife and mother. Rosa's husband drank heavily, and his philandering caused her great anguish. During a period of distress, Rosa's husband was told by an espiritista that Rosa suffered from spiritual problems and that she should be brought to a centro to be treated. In short, Rosa's symptoms of distress were defined by significant others (and eventually by her) as symptoms of possession, and her contacts with a medium and other possessed individuals provided her with emotional support as well as a framework for understanding and dealing with her problems. After a period of apprentiship, these contacts also provided her with a new identity as a spirit medium.

Periods of distress are frequently associated with a range of intense and sometimes unpleasant sensations (e.g., racing heart, trembling, faintness, headache, difficulties concentrating). These experiences have the quality of being unbidden and uncontrolled. Consequently, given a belief in spirits that can invade the body, such experiences can be interpreted with relative ease as caused by invading spirits. Once the spirit hypothesis is adopted, the expectations associated with it are likely to lead the distressed person to attribute further aspects of experience and behavior to the invading spirit. The following description of an initiatory illness in a patient (later a healer) named Sara seems to describe such a process:

I was unable to concentrate, and this was made worse by the fact that I was frightened. I started to get as if it were a headache. Then I felt a rush of warmth throughout my body. I seemed to be losing awareness of my surroundings, as if becoming ambivalent and my senses weakened. All of a sudden I felt like something inside me, sort of dissociated with myself, wanted to make me pound my fist on the table and start talking. (Koss-Chioino, 1992, p. 60)

Sara's experience occurred during a healing session, and the medium responded by carrying out various motions that were interpreted as contacting Sara's troubling spirit. Sara came to adopt the following spiritual interpretation for her distressing experiences and for the actions of the medium: "She [the medium] then took the spirit as it were, and it turned out that the spirit wanted to interrupt what the other spirit was talking about" (Koss-Chioino, 1992, p. 61).

In Puerto Rico, and in many other traditional societies that hold possession beliefs (I. M. Lewis, 1987), the aim of spiritual treatment is not to exorcize spirits, but to domesticate and communicate with them. Thus, espiritistas do not stop enacting displays of possession as they learn to deal with their distress. Instead, they learn to display possession in the absence of the symptoms of distress that led initially to their diagnosis as possessed. This process is interpreted by the mediums in terms of their developing abilities to communicate and cooperate with their possessing spirits. Ambiguous sensations, such as chills, that earlier may have been interpreted in terms of distress produced by the invading spirit may still occur. Now, however, such sensations are likely to be interpreted as pleasant accompaniments of possession by familiar spirits. Koss-Chioino (1992) described this process:

After practicing mediumship for a number of years, adepts testify that they are affected very little when their own spirit guides come into their bodies. I have watched them tremble only slightly; their voices change only a bit. They themselves report a feeling of a pleasant chill in their bodies and a gentle cool breeze over their heads and backs. These sensations are described as "refreshing currents," "my body feels lighter," "tranquility," and "well-being." (p. 36)

In summary, espiritistas learn the enactments of multiplicity that they and others in their culture define as becoming possessed. Typically, they are exposed from a young age to others who model such behaviors, and they have learned and take for granted a belief system that includes the existence of spirits that can possess people. When they experience distress, those who eventually become espiritistas are likely to come to the attention of a healer who helps them to interpret their distressing symptoms as indications of possession. Participation in a spiritist treatment group and apprentiship with a healer solidify the initiate's interpretations of her experiences and behaviors in terms of possession, and provide her with multiple opportunities for learning the subtleties and complexities of the possessed role.

Relationships between espiritistas and clients involve a number of components. For instance, the espiritistas may prescribe various herbs and perfumed oils, as well as offer counseling around such matters as marital conflicts. Of particular importance, however, is the ability of the espiritista to take into her own body and display the spirit that is causing problems for the client. The troublesome spirit then acts and speaks through the medium to explain why it is causing pain and distress to the sufferer. Koss-Chioino (1992) believes that this process enables clients to see a display of their own thoughts and feelings and to gain some detachment toward them. It may also allow clients to gain a sense of intimacy with a caring person who, in a particularly concrete and literal sense, shares their distress.

To convincingly enact the role of the client's spirit, the possessed medium must use information she learned about her client before she became possessed. These possession displays can be effective only if geared to the unique problems and concerns of the client, and that, of course, requires the use of specific knowledge about the client that was gained before the actual displays of possession. In other words, despite claiming to be amnesic for the period during which they are possessed, mediums obviously use information acquired while nonpossessed to tailor their possession enactments to the demands of highly specific situations.

Becoming a spirit medium, like becoming a glossolalic, sometimes involves the possessed organizing their biographies to correspond with implicit societal conceptions concerning the meaning of possession. In some societies, for instance, the possession careers or mediums are described in highly stereotyped fashion and include a series of stock background events (e.g., fleeing into the wilderness) that explain why they were singled out by the spirits for possession (Morton, 1977). These descriptions need not be accurate. For instance, despite the emphasis placed by Puerto Rican espiritistas on early illnesses, Koss-Chioino (1992) found that mediums and women in "official" mental health professions (e.g., physicians, social workers) did not differ significantly either in current medical complaints or (after corrected for age) in reports of childhood illnesses.

Investigators of mediums in traditional cultures (Harwood, 1977; Krippner, 1989; Leacock & Leacock, 1972) have often commented that these individuals usually appear to be well adjusted, mentally healthy, and competent. Relatedly, Koss-Chioino (1992) found no differences on indexes of psychological distress between spirit mediums and mental health professionals.

The spirit possession enactments of mediums are responsive to socio-cultural changes within their societies, and in some circumstances possession becomes a vehicle for expressing resistance to externally imposed authority (Stoller, 1989). For instance, during the French colonial period, the native African mediums among the Songhay became possessed by a new group of spirits that aped colonial officials and burlesqued French colonial society with displays of exaggerated and satiric behavior. Later, when French rule was replaced by a puritanical Islamic state, mediums expressed their resistance by enacting scatological and overtly sexual possession displays that violated the official Islamic moral code (Stoller, 1989). The responsiveness of possession displays to cultural changes illustrates the constructive and goal-directed nature of possession and the importance of ongoing situational factors (as opposed to idiosyncratic psychological ones) in determining both the character of possession displays and the historical changes that occur in the nature of those displays.

Peripheral Possession

I. M. Lewis (1987) distinguished between central and peripheral possession. In central possession, the medium is possessed by the major deities of the society, and the possession performances serve to publicly reaffirm and support the central values of the society. Typically, the medium in central possession is a respected member of the community. In contrast, peripheral possession afflicts socially marginal and oppressed members of the community. In this case, the possessing spirits are capricious and often amoral members of the pantheon, and possession is associated with illness or emotional distress.

I. M. Lewis (1987) hypothesized that peripheral possession often constitutes a strategy used by the socially powerless to manipulate and obtain benefits from their social superiors. Typically, peripheral possession occurs to people low in the social hierarchy who are experiencing high levels of psychological or interpersonal stress. Frequently, the stress is manifested in various psychophysiological symptoms (e.g., headaches, stomach pains) that are interpreted as initial manifestations of possession. The spirit who possesses the person makes numerous demands that must be met by the family of the possessed. Moreover, because possession is considered involuntary, the disruptive behavior and unusual demands are attributed to the possessing spirit rather than the possessed person. Frequently, peripheral possession is chronic, and new or recurring stresses lead to a recurrence of symptoms (Saunders, 1977; Ward, 1989).

Many traditional societies are strongly patriarchal, and the women in these societies often have few rights and are hemmed in by many social restrictions. Consequently, in most of these societies, it is women rather then men who resort to peripheral possession as an interpersonal strategy for improving their lot. For example, a woman in an unhappy marriage to an inattentive or brutal husband, who lives in a culture that restricts married women almost exclusively to the home, may become possessed by a spirit who demands an expensive public ceremony that includes rich delicacies, new clothing, and interaction with other women. Moreover, when enacting the spirit role, the woman can voice unflattering and insulting remarks to her husband that would not be tolerated if they were defined as coming from her rather than from her spirit (Constantinides, 1977). Relatedly, in some polygamous societies, women reaching middle age or women who experience a miscarriage frequently become possessed as a means of preventing their husbands from taking a second wife (Boddy, 1988; I. M. Lewis, 1987; Ward, 1982). Possession is a public event, and the norms of the community may demand that the husband abide by the requests of the spirit despite his personal feelings toward his wife and despite the substantial expense involved.

As indicated earlier, in many societies where peripheral possession occurs, the aim of treatment is not to expel the demon but to bring it under control so that the possessed person can learn to live with her spirit. Frequently, this taming process is accomplished by the possessed joining a possession cult or club (I. M. Lewis, 1987). Here, the possessed individual joins with other possessed under the tutelage of a shaman. The shaman is herself possessed but has learned to control her possessing spirits and use them as spiritual advisors. The women in the cult meet regularly to hold feasts and dances in honor of the spirits and to seek spiritual advice from the spirits of the shaman (I. M. Lewis, 1987; Morton, 1977). Frequently, these cult groups foster a high level of cohesiveness among the members and often appear to provide tangible psychological benefits for their adherents (Galanter, 1990; Koss-Chioino, 1992; Morton, 1977).

Rates of peripheral possession are not necessarily static within a culture. In societies that condone possession beliefs, cultural changes that produce increases in stress often produce increased rates of possession (Ackerman & Lee, 1981; Phoon, 1982; Sharp, 1990; Teoh, Soewondo, & Sidharta, 1975). For instance, Sharp noted that changes in the educational system in Northwest Madagascar produced a new population of adolescent female migrants who moved from rural villages to towns to attend school. These schoolgirls frequently experienced severe social dislocation and resultant feelings of anomie as a result of the move from home. As a consequence, many of the schoolgirls experienced a type of violent possession that had not been previously seen in children and that did not occur in those children who remained in their villages. In a number of cases, the possession spread from one child to another, leading to small epidemics of possession that periodically led to school closures.

A similar phenomenon has been described as occurring in female Malaysian factory workers (Ackerman & Lee, 1981; Ong, 1988; Phoon, 1982). These women frequently carry out boring, repetitive work for very low wages under poor working conditions. The antiunion policies of the factories effectively prevent organized protest. Under these circumstances, epidemics of spirit possession that involve convulsions and bizarre behavior become a relatively safe way of venting distress and frustration, obtaining time off from work, and rebelling against authority. Because the spirits rather than the possessed women are blamed for the disturbances, possession displays are a safe, albeit indirect, way of expressing grievances. In a factory studied by Ackerman and Lee (1981), increases in the frequency of possession episodes followed a change from relaxed to stricter management. Moreover, the possession displays occurred only among the Malaysian workers whose cultural background of possession beliefs made such possession an acceptable vehicle for the expression of dissatisfaction. Chinese and Indian workers in the same factory never exhibited displays of possession.

The occurrence of epidemic possession that affects numerous people who are in close proximity within a short period of time cannot be accounted for adequately by theories of multiplicity that emphasize idiosyncratic psychological causes. Obviously, the contagion that occurs in epidemic possession results from social factors, from the common understandings held by participants about what constitute legitimate means of expressing dissatisfaction, and from the effects of observing displays of possession and the consequences of those displays.

SUMMARY

Possession phenomena underscore the rule-governed and social nature of multiple-identity enactments. Enactments of spirit possession are clearly goal-directed, learned patterns of social responding. Possessed individuals enact spirit identities that correspond to their understandings and expectations of possession. Possession enactments are public and involve interaction with an audience that legitimates the enactments. These enactments occur in a wide range of circumstances, are carried out by very different kinds of people, and serve a number of different social functions. Possession is sometimes symptomatic of severe stress and accompanied by symptoms of psychopathology. At other times, however, it is enacted by well-adjusted individuals who report happy lives and do not manifest high levels of psychopathology.

13

HISTORICAL MANIFESTATIONS OF DEMONIC POSSESSION

The idea that demons can enter into people and take over their functioning surfaced in Western European history as an accompaniment of Christianity (Spanos, 1983a). Possession by demons is made explicit in the New Testament, which provides numerous examples of both possession and exorcism. Among the most prominent symptoms displayed by New Testament demoniacs (i.e., possessed persons) were convulsions, sensory and motor deficits, enactment of alternate identities, loss of voluntary control over behavior, increased strength, and amnesia (Catherinet, 1972). In the New Testament, individual demoniacs often displayed only one or a few of these symptoms. By the medieval and late medieval period, however, individual demoniacs consistently displayed all or most of these behaviors. (Oesterreich, 1966). In other words, the hodgepodge of odd behaviors described piecemeal in various parts of the New Testament as symptomatic of possession coalesced into a relatively stereotypic social role that has persisted (with important local variations) down to the present day (Spanos, 1983a).

Historical information concerning the rate of occurrence of possession is sparse. Nevertheless, it seems clear that the rate of possession has varied dramatically in different historical eras (Oesterreich, 1966). Possession and exorcism were frequently used as proselytizing tools to impress and convert unbelievers. Consequently, possession appears to have been a relatively common occurrence in the early church while Christianity struggled for supremacy amongst numerous competing religions. After Christianity became the state religion of the Roman Empire, the frequency of possession and exorcisms appears to have waned.

Beginning in the 11th century with the gradual breakdown of feudalism, Western Europe experienced increased politico-religious turmoil that, in the 16th century, culminated in the Reformation and in the breakup of Western Christianity into competing sects (J. B. Russell, 1980). This period also saw the concomitant development and elaboration of the mythology of Satanism. According to the tenets of this mythology, there existed an international satanic conspiracy bent on destroying Christianity. The agents of this purported conspiracy were witches who were believed to worship Satan and congregate at secret nocturnal meetings where they desecrated the symbols of Christian worship and engaged in cannibalism, murder, and sexual orgies (Cohn, 1975). Modern historical scholarship has led to a rejection of the notions that there actually was a satanic conspiracy and that those accused of witchcraft belonged to a large-scale organized conspiracy of any kind. Instead, the idea of a satanic conspiracy existed only in the imagination. This idea existed first in the imagination of cultural elites who established the administrative machinery and legal categories that made satanic witchcraft a crime and its punishment a possibility. The idea then spread down the social scale to become part of the taken-for-granted belief system of much of the populace (Cohn, 1975; Larner, 1981; J. B. Russell, 1980; Spanos, 1978).

From the 15th through the 17th century, possession and exorcism again became common because possession became associated with witchcraft. It was believed in both Catholic and Protestant countries that witches, through Satan's intercession, could send demons to possess people. However, the indwelling demons could be coerced by authorities to name the witch that sent them. The accused witch could then be arrested, tortured into confessing her involvement in a nonexistent satanic conspiracy, and in many cases executed. Thus, during this period demoniacs frequently functioned as witch finders, and those who controlled the demoniacs had a powerful weapon to use against political, social, or personal rivals (Spanos, 1978).

SOME SYMPTOMS OF POSSESSION

Among the most dramatic manifestations of possession were convulsions. Frequently, these occurred during exorcism procedures and particularly in the period shortly before the expulsion of the demon (McCasland, 1951; Oesterreich, 1966). As described by the *Compendium Maleficarum*, the most authoritative witch-hunting manual of the 17th century, "A man may very surely be known for a demoniac if he is disturbed [i.e., convulses] when the exorcisms are read" (Guazzo, 1608/1970, pp. 168). The following description of a 17th-century nun possessed by the demon Asmodius provides an example:

> Asmodius was not long in manifesting his supreme rage shaking the girl backwards and forwards a number of times and making her strike like a hammer with such great rapidity that her teeth rattled and sound was forced out of her throat. That between these movements her face became completely unrecognizable, her glance furious, her tongue prodigiously large, long and hanging down out of her mouth. (Aubin, 1716, p. 226)

In the highly stratified social world of late medieval and early modern Europe, interactions between members of different social classes typically involved stereotypical displays of diffidence and respect shown by members of lower rank to their superiors (Huizinga, 1954). Demons, however, were believed to be intelligent, well traveled, and often privy to the secret thoughts and wishes of others (Catherinet, 1972). Consequently, evidence of learning or intelligence that was assumed to be above the station of members of lower classes could be taken as indicators of possession:

> An even more certain sign is when a sick man speaks in foreign tongues unknown to him or understands in those tongues; or when, being ignorant, the patients argue about high and difficult questions. . . . It is a manifest sign when an ignorant man speaks literary and grammatical Latin, or if without knowledge of the art he sings musically or says something of which he could never have had any knowledge. (Guazzo, 1608/1970, p. 168)

Purported displays of what today would be called telepathy and clairvoyance were also signs of possession. The following account by Glanville (1689) exemplifies the kinds of evidence used to support such claims. To understand this account, it should be kept in mind that, in the 17th century, demoniacs were often thought to convulse when in the proximity of a witch, even when they were unaware of the witch's presence.

> . . . but when the witch was brought in again . . . although she [the demoniac] could not possibly see her, she would be immediately senseless and like to be strangled, and so would continue till the witch were taken out, and then . . . she would come again to her senses. That afterwards Mr. Greatrix, Mr. Blackwell, and some others, who would needs satisfy themselves in the influence of the witch's presence, tried it and found it several times. Although he did it with all possible privacy, and so as none could think it possible that the maid to know either of the witches coming in or going out. (Glanville, 1689, p. 382)

Amnesia for the events that occurred when the demon controlled the victim's body was a common but not invariable manifestation of possession. For example, the following possessed girl experienced long "ludicrous intervals" in which she appeared to be more intelligent than usual but later manifested amnesia for the events occurring during these intervals:

> Her Apprehension, Understanding and Memory, was riper than ever in her life; and yet, when she was herself, she Could Remember the other accidents of her afflictions but forgot almost everything that passed in these Ludicrous intervals. (Mather, 1693/1914, p. 272)

From episodes of possession that did not involve amnesia, it is clear that demoniacs defined their possession as an event over which they could not exercise volitional control. They described their convulsions, contortions, blaspheming, and other behaviors as being carried out in spite of rather than because of their wishes. Thus, when asked why he did not restrain himself, one demoniac replied as follows:

> I cannot help myself at all, for the demon uses my limbs and organs, my neck, my tongue, and my lungs, whenever he pleases, causing me to speak or to cry out; and I hear the words as if they were spoken by myself, but I am altogether unable to restrain them; and when I try to engage in prayer he attacks me more violently, thrusting out my tongue. (Mather, 1693/1914, pp. 131–132)

Possession was interpreted as involuntary not only by the demoniac but by the society at large. The possessed saw themselves and were seen by others as automatons controlled by a foreign agency that had temporarily set the normal personality in abeyance (Spanos, 1983b).

THE SOCIALIZATION OF DEMONIACS

The idea of possession by demons was taken for granted in late medieval and early modern Europe (Baroja, 1964; K. Thomas, 1971). The major components of the demonic role were well-known, and the more subtle aspects of the role were transmitted through the demoniac's exposure to clerical experts. Demonic possession was used as one explanation for certain physical symptoms or for behavior that was socially disruptive or considered abnormal. As is the case in the contemporary diagnosis of MPD, a very wide range of psychophysiological and behavioral dysfunctions were used as possible signs of possession (Robbins, 1959). Whether these signs led eventually to a diagnosis of possession as opposed to one of many possible naturalistic diagnoses (e.g., melancholy) appears to have been more closely related to the diagnostic biases of the clerical and medical experts who diagnosed the patients than to the quality of the manifest symptomatology (Spanos, 1983a; D. P. Walker, 1981).

During the initial stages of possession, the demoniac's symptoms were often ambiguous. Frequently, these symptoms began to correspond to "official" stereotypes of demonic possession as the demoniac gained information about those stereotypes (Spanos & Gottlieb, 1976; D. P. Walker, 1981). For example, the demonically possessed children who participated in the Salem witch panic initially enacted an array of odd behaviors, such as running about the house, creeping under furniture, and adopting unusual postures. After several weeks of close observation by and interaction with neighbors and clergy who suspected demonic intervention, their symptoms became much more stereotypically diabolical. These symptoms now included convulsions, reports of being bitten and pinched, and "seeing" the specters of witches attack them and others (Spanos, 1983b).

The particular behaviors that constituted possession sometimes varied as a function of local beliefs and practices, and these variations demonstrate the social and rule-governed nature of possession. For instance, both Catholic and Protestant demoniacs regularly convulsed and displayed a variety of sensorimotor deficits. In addition, however, Catholic demoniacs invariably exhibited direct evidence of indwelling demon selves. These demon selves spoke in voices different from that of the possessed person, had their own names, and displayed their own unique demonic personalities. In addition, these demoniacs frequently claimed amnesia for the period during which the demon selves were "in control." In short, Catholic demoniacs displayed behaviors that, today, are considered symptomatic of MPD. These behaviors constituted part of a role enactment that also included convulsions, sensorimotor deficits, and a host of other symptoms that were specific to the religious beliefs of the demoniacs and their exorcists (e.g., screaming as if burned when sprinkled with holy water). Importantly, Protestant demoniacs of the same period, despite being defined as possessed and despite exhibiting convulsions and a host of other symptoms, rarely displayed demon selves (D. P. Walker, 1981).

Variations between Catholics and Protestants in the frequency of demon self enactments reflected the different practices toward the possessed adopted by these religions. Catholic exorcism procedures involved the priest communicating directly with the indwelling demon. During exorcism, the priest made a clear distinction between the possessing demons and the person possessed. When questioning a demon, the exorcist expected to be answered by the demon and not by the person possessed (Oesterreich, 1966). The following firsthand account from a 19th-century Jewish exorcism in Russia demonstrates the manner in which such role expectations could be forcibly conveyed to the demoniac:

> "What is thy name?" the rabbi asked the sick woman in a loud, harsh voice. "Esther," replied the girl softly and faintly, trembling all over. "Silence, though chazufe" (impudent woman) cried the rabbi. "I asked not thee but the dibbuk" (demon). (cited in Oesterreich, 1966, p. 208)

As preliminaries to the exorcism rite, the priest was required to contact and question the demons to obtain their names, number, reasons for possessing the person, hour they entered the body, and length of time they proposed to stay (Kelly, 1974; The Roman Ritual of Exorcism, 1614/1976). During the exorcism, the demons were often questioned repeatedly and at great length about their motives, earthly accomplices, status in the social structure of hell, and so forth (e.g., Michaelis, 1613). In short, Catholic exorcism procedures strongly cued demon self-enactments as a central component of the demonic role. In contrast, Protestants rarely used formal exorcism procedures because direct communication with demons was shunned as sinful (K. Thomas, 1971). In place of exorcism, Protestant demoniacs were treated with prayer and fasting, procedures that were much less likely to elicit demon self-enactments.

Detailed information concerning role prescriptions was conveyed to both Catholic and Protestant demoniacs outside of the exorcism situation. The sources of this information could include explicit coaching by parties who held a vested interest in the demoniacs giving convincing performances, exposure to other more practiced demoniacs, and conversations about the occurrence and timing of symptoms that were held in the demoniac's presence (Harsnett, 1599, 1603; Hutchinson, 1720; K. Thomas, 1971; D. P. Walker, 1981). In short, demonic enactments were rule-governed performances shaped by the social context in which they occurred.

A number of potent social psychological factors converged in leading potential demoniacs to define themselves as possessed. These individuals shared the same belief system as the community that labeled them, and they were therefore likely to interpret their own illness of behavioral deviations in the same terms as their neighbors and clerical superiors (Oesterreich, 1966; K. Thomas, 1971). In some cases, demoniacs were made dependent for the satisfaction of their physical and social needs on those who labeled them. The labelers consistently interpreted the experiences of demoniacs in terms of possession and isolated the demoniacs from others who might offer nondemonic interpretations of these events (Spanos, 1983a).

Denials of being possessed sometimes occurred, but these were routinely construed by authorities as indications of a wily demon attempting to escape divine punishment. Continued refusal to define oneself as possessed and act accordingly frequently led to threats of perpetual damnation and sometimes to punishment administered in the guise of benevolently motivated attempts to free hapless victims from demonic control (Harsnett, 1599; Spanos, 1983a).

Demonic possession was not necessarily a label that individuals avoided. Like sufferers of peripheral possession in other cultures, the demonically possessed could use their enactments strategically. Those who became demoniacs were usually individuals with little social power or status who were hemmed in by numerous social restrictions and had few sanctioned avenues for protesting their dissatisfactions or improving their lot. Given the patriarchal and misogynistic culture of early modern Western Europe, it is not surprising that adult demoniacs were much more frequently women than men (Oesterreich, 1966; Spanos, 1983a). In 16th- and 17th-century France, for example, the most celebrated cases of possession occurred among cloistered nuns (Mandrou, 1968). Usually, becoming a nun was not a chosen profession. Instead, adolescent girls were placed in convents by their families to avoid the financial burden involved in providing a dowry (O'Faolain & Martines, 1973). For someone not committed to a religious career, it could be a very dreary existence: chores, frequent prayer, proper deportment, rigid rules, perhaps some teaching, and no men. Woods (1974) described the physical and social conditions of convents during this period as follows:

> In the sixteenth and seventeenth centuries, it has been computed, a nun could generally stand about ten years of incarceration before it killed her. By the end of that time the lack of exercise and sunlight, the gloom, the damp walls, the loneliness, the monotony and the sheer boredom of a life without any hope of change had planted in her the tuberculosis, the dysentery or one of the various fevers that carried her off. (p. 210)

The unwilling nun had no socially recognized means of protesting against her predicament. However, adopting the demoniac role (the components of which were often well-known by nuns) offered a relatively safe avenue of protest. The nun could express her pent-up frustrations by blaspheming against her family, her superiors, and the Church, and she could carry out provocative sexual displays toward her exorcist. In effect, she could express wishes and feelings that in any other social context were heavily sanctioned, because within the confines of the demoniac role, responsibility for such expression was assigned not to her but to the invading demon. Other advantages associated with the demoniac role included escaping from unpleasant responsibilities (e.g., chores) and becoming the center of attention. The possessed nun gained a good deal of sympathy, concern, and solace from individuals of higher social status (e.g., priests, physicians) who, in other circumstances, paid her little attention. She gained fearful respect as well. She became a seer whose words provided hints about the supernatural, and those she accused of witchcraft might well be arrested and executed. Once a nun became possessed, the advantages of her situation soon became apparent to other nuns, and as a result, French convents were frequently swept by small epidemics of possession affecting numerous nuns (Oesterreich, 1966).

England had no cloistered nuns after the 16th century, but possession occurred among a different socially impotent group: children of both sexes (Robbins, 1959). The advantages of adopting the possessed role in England were similar to those in France: an opportunity to vent frustration, sympathetic concern and attention, a rise in social status to that of a person who was listened to and taken into consideration, and an alleviation of burdensome chores. Small epidemics of possession also occurred in England and later in colonial America as well. The contagion usually spread to siblings or other close associates of the young demoniac, who had an opportunity to observe enactment of the role and its reinforcing consequences (Hole, 1947; Notestein, 1911).

Like peripheral possession in other cultures and MPD in our own, demonic possession was often chronic. Frequently, these individuals were possessed by many demons that had to be individually exorcized over a long period of time. Moreover, even the successful exorcism of all of the demons was no guarantee that they would not return. Thus, once possession had been legitimated, it remained an option that could be used as the situation required (Spanos, 1983b).

THE GOAL-DIRECTED NATURE OF DEMONIC ENACTMENTS

Demonic possession was defined by the society at large as involuntary. Medieval canon law classified possession as a type of demonically induced insanity, and the possessed, like other insane, were not considered responsible for their actions (Pickett, 1952). Typically, possessed individuals accounted for their own deviant behavior by using the same explanations as the rest of their community. They disavowed responsibility for demonic behavior by attributing it to the machinations of indwelling demons. Like spirit-possessed individuals in other cultures and MPD patients in our own, demoniacs enacted complex, goal-directed behavior that was geared to the expectations of significant others, but interpreted this behavior as occurring involuntarily. The goal-directed nature of demonic enactments was sometimes obscured by treating the convulsions, sensorimotor disturbances, and hallucinations that constituted the demonic role as isolated symptoms of disease. However, when demonic enactments are viewed within their social context, their goal-directed nature becomes clear.

Convulsions were among the most dramatic symptoms of possession. They continue to be observed in cross-cultural displays of spirit possession (Jilek, 1989) but are rare in modern MPD cases. Undoubtedly, epileptic convulsions were misinterpreted as possession in some cases. In most instances, however, the convulsions associated with possession were not epileptic (Oesterreich, 1966). Instead, these convulsions were socially cued role enactments (Spanos, 1983a). For instance, demoniacs commonly convulsed on cue when presented with the witch that supposedly caused their possession (e.g., Glanville, 1689). Thus, in an English case Mother Samuel was accused of bewitching the three children of a wealthy landowner. The children usually behaved quite normally. In the presence of Mother Samuel, however, their behavior changed dramatically:

> No sooner had Mother Samuel entered the hall but at one moment the said three children fell down upon the ground strangely tormented . . . their bellies heaving up, their heads and heels still touching the ground as though they had been tumblers. ("The Most Strange and Admirable Discovery of the Witches of Warboys," 1593/1972, p. 246)

In Salem, the demoniacs were responsive to social cues from one another as well as from the accused, and they were therefore able to predict the occurrence of one another's fits. In these cases, one of the demoniacs would cry out that she saw the specter of an accused witch about to attack another demoniac. The other demoniac would then immediately enact a convulsive fit (Spanos, 1983b). The termination as well as the onset of convulsions was also socially cued. It was believed at Salem that the touch of a witch would stop convulsions, and the possessed girls responded to this expectation by ceasing their convulsions when touched by an accused witch but by no one else (Spanos, 1983a).

Symptoms other than convulsions were also socially cued. For example, during the Salem trials, the demoniacs sometimes mimicked the accused. When an accused witch rolled up her eyes, the demoniacs followed suit and cried that their eyes were stuck. When rag puppets supposedly used for black magic were burned in their presence, the demoniacs screamed that they were burned (Spanos & Gottlieb, 1976). Relatedly, Catholic demoniacs cried that they were tortured and burned when sprinkled with holy water or touched with the relics of Catholic saints (Harsnett, 1599; Oesterreich, 1966).

Like the ritual ceremonies conducted by spirit mediums in other cultures, the performances of demoniacs often required forethought and the judicious use of props. For instance, the spitting up of pins or nails that were supposedly used by indwelling demons to torture the demoniac internally was a fairly regular feature of English and Continental possession cases (Notestein, 1911; Oesterreich, 1966). Obviously, the demoniacs had to place the pins in their mouths before their performance in anticipation of spitting them out later. Similarly, the Salem demoniacs produced in court pins that they claimed had been used by specters to pinch them and a piece of cloth that they claimed to have torn from the apron of an attacking specter. Once again, the use of such artifacts in an attempt to bolster the validity of their demonic enactments required planning as well as anticipation of the reaction they would produce in their audience.

In many cases, demoniacs may well have become convinced by their own performances, and by the expressed attitudes and beliefs of others, into believing that they really were possessed. Nevertheless, in at least some cases, there is good evidence to indicate that possession enactments were consciously faked. For instance, a number of 16th-century English demoniacs confessed that they had faked their demonic displays and publicly confirmed their confessions by enacting all of their supposedly involuntary symptoms (Harsnett, 1599, 1603). Relatedly, during the Salem witch trials, Daniel Elliot testified that one of the "afflicted girls" boasted to him about her demonic performances by saying that "she did it for sport; they must have some sport" (Woodward, 1969, vol. 1, p. 115).

THE MANUFACTURE OF POSSESSION: A CASE ILLUSTRATION

The manner in which social factors converged in leading people to define themselves as possessed and learn the components of the possessed role is illustrated by a series of late 16th-century English possession cases described in detail in a long pamphlet written by Samuel Harsnett (1603). Harsnett was an Anglican clergyman involved in the apprehension of Catholic missionaries who operated illegally in England. During the 16th century, Catholicism had been made illegal in England by Henry VIII. The missionaries conducted semipublic exorcisms as a means of propagandizing for their outlawed faith. Harsnett's (1603) pamphlet was based primarily on various documents written by the missionaries and captured with them and on the confessions provided by the demoniacs whom the missionaries exorcised.

The missionary priests sailed to England from France. Public exorcisms require demoniacs, but the missionaries had brought none with them. Consequently, they recruited most of their demoniacs from among the servants of the Catholic sympathizers with whom they resided. These servants did not initially believe themselves to be possessed. They learned to construe themselves in that manner as they became involved in the demonic role.

To understand the success of the missionaries at recruiting demoniacs, it should be kept in mind that servitude in 16th- and 17th-century England did not constitute a job in the modern sense. Servants were indentured to their masters for specified periods of time, and during these periods, the masters exerted substantial legal as well as social control over their charges (K. Thomas, 1971). In short, servants were dependent on their masters for the satisfaction of social and physical needs. They could, for example, be beaten by their masters, isolated from others, captured and returned if they chose to run away, and so on. It is also important to remember that, although maidservants did not usually believe themselves to be possessed, they, like the rest of the population, believed unquestioningly in demons, hellfire, and the possibility of possession.

To begin their recruitment of demoniacs, the missionary priests chose a suitable location: a house that was rumored to be haunted. These rumors were reinforced by the priests, and soon members of the household frightened one another with stories of lurking demons. After being primed in this way, individual servants were exposed to a series of experiences that were designed to foster the belief that they were possessed by demons. For example, one adolescent maidservant, who was startled by a missionary priest as she did the laundry, fell and badly bruised herself. The priest was very solicitous and explained that she had been tripped by a devil because she was washing his holy garments. The priest visited the maid regularly during her recovery, provided much sympathetic concern, and informed her that she was possessed by a demon. Although the maid protested this interpretation, her protests were reinterpreted as a subterfuge of the demon. In the several weeks required for her to recover from her injuries, the missionaries remained friendly but talked continually about her possession, the horrible consequences that might ensue if she did not accept the proper treatment (i.e., exorcism), and of conversion to Catholicism as a necessary precondition to the saving of her soul.

Similar procedures were practiced with other potential demoniacs. At every opportunity, they were informed of their grave plight, and then sympathetically and earnestly offered conversion and exorcism as a cure. They were not allowed to leave the house and were isolated from anyone who might offer a nondemonic interpretation of their situation. Their protestations of not being possessed were reinterpreted as evidence that they really were possessed. Relatedly, attempts to run away or changes in mood or behavior were quickly and consistently interpreted as the workings of an indwelling demon. For example one demoniac complained to a priest about harsh treatment and denied that she was actually possessed. She was treated as follows:

> She began to complain unto him of her hard usage, and told him, that she verilie thought they did her injury, and that she was not troubled with any wicked spirits in her. . . . Whereupon he cast his head aside and looking fullie upon her face under her hat, What (quoth he) is this Sara, or the devil that speaketh these words? No, no, it is not Sara, but the devil. And [Sara] perceiving she could have no other reliefe at his hands, fell a weeping, which weeping also he said was the weeping of the evill spirit. (Harsnett, 1603, pp. 186–187)

The missionaries did not directly instruct potential demoniacs to behave in particular ways. However, in their everyday conversation, they repeatedly described the components of the demonic role in great detail, and in earshot of those they wished to influence. One of the demoniacs described this process to an English tribunal as follows:

> It was the ordinary custom of the Priests to be talking of such, as had
> been possessed beyond the seas, and to tell the manner of their fits,
> and what they spake in them . . . and how when reliques were applied
> unto them, the parties would roare: how they could not abide holy
> water, nor the sight of the sacrament . . . how the devills would com-
> plaine, when the Priests touched the parties, that they burned. . . .
> (Harsnett, 1603, p. 36)

The demoniacs were recruited at different times, and those who had learned the role most proficiently served as role models for others. For example, "They permitted me to have access unto Sara Williams when she was in her fits, and informed me likewise of the manner, how she and others had beene troubled" (Harsnett, 1603, p. 265). Thus, novice demoniacs were given firsthand and repeated opportunities to observe both the modeling of demonic role enactments and the rewards contingent on those enactments.

The major sources of reinforcement for appropriate demonic role enactment were interpersonal. Of particular importance was solicitous attention obtained from those high-status individuals who appeared to have such unlimited control of the demoniacs' lives: the missionary priests themselves. Also gratifying to the demoniacs was a sense of power gained from observing the awe and admiration created in the crowds that attended the exorcisms. After all, the demoniacs were the star attractions in what the audience considered a deadly serious combat between the forces of hell and heaven. For example, one demoniac described his motives as follows: "[It may have been] to gaine to my selfe a little foolish commendation, or admiration, because I saw how [those who] were present at many of my fond speeches, did seeme to wonder at me" (Harsnett, 1603, p. 275).

When some demoniacs continued to resist appropriate role enactments, harsh measures were sometimes used to elicit cooperation. For instance, one demoniac was tied to a chair, forced to drink a concoction that produced nausea, and then forced to breath the fumes of burning brimstone. None of this was presented as punishment meted out to the possessed person. Instead, it was defined as a benefit to the possessed person, and as punishment for the indwelling demon.

The missionaries strived to interpret not only the demoniacs' current behavior as consistent with possession, but their past behavior as well. The demoniacs were questioned repeatedly and at length about character flaws and previous sins and failings, and these were interpreted as evidence that they had really been possessed all along. Thus, the priests led the demoniacs to reconstruct their remembrances of the past so as to be congruent with and "make sense" out of their current status as demon possessed.

Harsnett's (1603) report illustrates the overriding importance of social context in shaping manifestations of demonic possession. The missionary priests held enough social power to control the official definition of the situation, and they defined the situation as involving demonic possession. Alternative construals, including some of those proffered by the demoniacs themselves, were not legitimated. Potential demoniacs were isolated from anyone who might support nondemonic definitions of their behavior, and the demoniacs' own attempts to define themselves as "not possessed" were reinterpreted as signs of possession. The components of the demonic role were taught to novice demoniacs indirectly, through overheard conversation and the observation of role models. The priests made themselves the primary sources of satisfaction for the demoniacs' interpersonal as well as physical needs. Appropriate demonic role enactments were met with solicitous attention from the priests and admiration from audiences. The priests did not explicitly instruct demoniacs how to behave and never rewarded them with tangible or explicit rewards like money or praise for a good performance. To have done so would have encouraged the demoniacs to attribute their enactments to external inducement rather than to an indwelling demon. For the same reason, punishment for inadequate role performance was defined as punishing the demon in an attempt to help the person possessed. Finally, demoniacs were encouraged to reinterpret their previous experiences in a manner consistent with the idea that they were now possessed.

SUMMARY

Historical manifestations of demonic possession resemble historical manifestations of MPD in numerous important respects. For both phenomena, rates of occurrence have varied dramatically from one historical period, and from one locale, to another, and a very wide range of behavioral problems (e.g., depression, erratic behavior) and physiological disturbances (e.g., headaches, vague physical complaints) could be taken as symptoms of the purported underlying disorder. In the case of both phenomena, some experts diagnosed many more cases than others. Moreover, the kinds of symptoms displayed by both MPD patients and demoniacs have varied with the interests of the particular experts who investigated and treated these cases. The more attention paid to the dramatic symptoms displayed by these patients, the more extensive, elaborate, and dramatic the symptomatology has tended to become. Catholic cases of demonic possession, like cases of MPD, involved the regular enactment of alternate selves. In the Catholic possession cases, these multiple self-enactments were closely tied to highly leading diagnostic and treatment procedures (i.e., exorcisms) that cued and reinforced displays of multiplicity. As we shall see, displays of multiplicity by MPD patients are also often cued and reinforced by the procedures purportedly used to diagnose and treat that condition.

In cases of demonic possession, and also in cases of cross-cultural spirit possession, those who defined themselves as possessed often reorganized their biographies to make them consistent with their current identity as possessed. Both the biographies and the current behavior of demoniacs were consistently defined and interpreted in terms of possession by high-status others who limited the demoniacs' exposure to alternative interpretations, provided exposure to demonic role models, and reinforced through repetition and reward demonic interpretations. As indicated in earlier chapters, such variables appear to be important in leading patients who undergo incest-resolution therapy to define their recovered "memories" as real. As we shall see, these variables are also important in enabling MPD patients to define their experiences in the terms suggested by their therapists.

14

THE SOCIAL FUNCTIONS OF POSSESSION

The role of demonic possession was maintained over a number of centuries because it provided theories both of deviant personal behavior and of complex sociopolitical events that were consistent with dominant religious mythologies. The status of demoniac became associated with a number of important social functions. The notion provided a culturally consistent explanation for various physical disorders and for otherwise inexplicable propriety norm violations. When coupled with exorcism procedures, the role provided a way to reintegrate deviants into the community, served as a device for proselytizing, and in numerous ways bolstered the religious and moral values of the community. As is true in some cases of peripheral possession, the role also provided a means for allowing, while simultaneously controlling, some expressions of personal and social dissatisfaction. In addition, from the 15th to the 18th centuries, the role was exploited in order to control personal, political, or ideological enemies by having demoniacs label them as witches (Spanos, 1983b).

THE USE OF DEMONIC POSSESSION IN RELIGIOUS PROSELYTIZING

In the early years of the Christian tradition, exorcisms tended to be relatively unstructured and unelaborated ceremonies that consisted primarily of commanding the demons to depart in the name of Jesus. With time, the procedure became longer and more complex, and eventually it became standardized. Prayers were added, the indwelling demons were addressed directly to gain certain information, and the use of consecrated objects and holy water became common. By the late Middle Ages, the procedure had become quite elaborate and involved numerous prayers and adjurations and sometimes even violent cursing of the demons by the exorcist. Exorcisms sometimes lasted months or even years. Frequently, these were performed publicly, sometimes with groups of demoniacs at once (Kelly, 1974; Oesterreich, 1966). For instance, it has been estimated that on one day as many as 7,000 people attended a public exorcism in Loudon, France, during the 17th century (Baskin, 1974). Every exorcism represented a dramatic moral confrontation between the power of God and that of the Devil. Consequently, successful exorcisms illustrated the power of the church, affirmed its values, and helped to maintain its authority.

The successful exorcism of those possessed was a powerful tool for converting unbelievers as well as redoubling the faith of believers. For example, the writers of the New Testament not only portrayed Jesus as casting out demons but described the demons as recognizing Jesus as the son of God and as acknowledging their submission to his greater power. These stories cannot be read as history (Spanos & Chaves, 1991). Instead, I believe they are propaganda vignettes generated by a young religion that was in competition for converts against more established belief systems. Relatedly, many early Christians contended that demons could be driven out only in the name of Jesus and used their success at exorcism as proof of the validity of their doctrines (Kelly, 1974; Oesterreich, 1966).

Christianity became the state religion of Rome in the 4th century CE, and with its firm establishment the frequency of exorcisms appears to have decreased (Oesterreich, 1966). Nevertheless, tales of exorcism and possession continued to serve pedagogical purposes. Instructional tracts used in the training of clerics included many stories of Christian saints casting out demons who had been impervious to the techniques of non-Christian exorcists. Frequently, these same tracts also described possession as just punishment for the sin of pride (Kelly, 1974). During the Reformation and Counter-Reformation movements of the 16th and 17th centuries, possession and exorcism again became important tools for winning religious converts. In an age where distinctions between church and state were not as sharply drawn as they are today, religious conversion often meant political conversion as well. For an example of the political uses of possession and exorcism, we turn once again to 16th-century England.

Possession as Propaganda in England

England was newly Protestant during the latter half of the 16th century, and the head of the English (Anglican) church was the monarch,

Elizabeth I. England had been Catholic until Elizabeth's father (Henry VIII) severed connections with Rome earlier in the century. Established ideas do not always change quickly. Many Englishmen, some who were wealthy and powerful, continued to abide by Catholicism in private and hoped for the eventual restoration of their religion in England (K. Thomas, 1971).

The Anglican church attempted to adopt a middle-of-the-road position between what it considered to be the abuses of Catholicism, on the one hand, and radical Puritanism, on the other. Thus, the Anglicans deemphasized the marvelous, eliminated indulgences, closed the monasteries, discouraged the veneration of saints, and all but eliminated the practice of exorcism. Demonic possession and exorcism were considered to be Catholic and Puritan tricks aimed at beguiling the ignorant. Possession by demons was not denied as a theoretical possibility, but specific instances of possession were regularly interpreted in terms of deliberate fakery (Notestein, 1911; K. Thomas, 1971). The propaganda value of exorcism was clearly appreciated by the Anglicans, who did their best to track down and punish Catholic and Puritan exorcists who operated illegally in England.

England's most serious military threat at this time was from Spain and her ally France, and a Spanish invasion was expected imminently. (It was attempted in 1588, and led to the destruction of the Spanish Armada). England's enemies hoped to aid the coming invasion by enhancing pro-Catholic sentiments among the English populace. It was hoped that if such sentiments grew sufficiently strong, an invasion might set off popular rebellions within England that would aid the Catholic cause. To realize this purpose, Catholic missionaries were landed in England with the intent of converting as much of the populous as possible. The missionaries were housed and plied their trade in the homes of wealthy Catholic sympathizers in the areas of Buckinghamshire and Middlesex from 1585 to 1586 (Law, 1894; Notestein, 1911). The major tool of the missionaries for effecting conversions was semipublic displays of successful exorcisms. These were the missionary priests pursued by Harsnett (1603), whose procedures for manufacturing demonic possession were described in the last chapter. The missionaries capitalized on the Anglican policy of disallowing exorcisms by declaring that the Anglicans had fallen away from the true faith and, therefore, did not have the power to cast out demons. The missionaries, on the other hand, used successful exorcisms to demonstrate the validity of their own doctrines.

The demoniacs who were recruited and shaped by the missionary priests carried out enactments that were clearly geared toward supporting the religious values of the Catholic church. For instance, as representatives of Satan, they claimed to hate the Catholic church but to love Protestants. They were unaffected by Anglican prayer books but screamed as if burned when touched by the relics of Catholic saints. The missionaries contended that demons were forced to speak the truth when confronted by representatives of the true faith. Following this, the demoniacs affirmed the truth of the doctrine of transubstantiation and the falseness of Protestant doctrines (Harsnett, 1603).

Possession as Propaganda in France

Possession and exorcism were used as propaganda in France as well as England. For instance, during the second half of the 16th century, while France was beset by civil strife between Catholics and French Protestants (Huguenots), there occurred a series of possession cases that were used as propaganda for the Catholic cause (Walker, 1981). During exorcisms, the demoniacs in these cases frequently affirmed the truth of Catholicism and spoke of loving Calvin and Huguenots (e.g., Michaelis, 1613). The Catholic doctrine of transubstantiation, the belief that the consecrated host actually becomes the blood and body of Christ, came to play a prominent role in the exorcisms because that doctrine was rejected as magical superstition by the Huguenots (Walker, 1981). Historically, the host had not played as prominent a role in Catholic exorcisms as other artifacts such as relics and holy water. Now, however, it was brought to the fore, and demonstrations of its power in subduing demons became a vehicle for supporting Catholic doctrine and denigrating Huguenot heresies. For example, during public exorcisms at Laon in 1566, Nicole Obry was possessed by more than 30 demons, the most important of whom was Beelzebub. Traditional artifacts of exorcism like the sign of the cross and relics could hurt and anger Beelzebub, but not subdue him. Upon being shown the host, however, Beelzebub was rendered temporarily impotent. Nicole's convulsions would cease, and Beelzebub would retire temporarily into her left arm. Following the convulsions, Nicole remained rigid and seemingly insensible, and she revived only when a consecrated wafer was placed on her lips. Beelzebub also spoke directly through Nicole. At these times, he acknowledged that the Huguenots were inspired by the devil and that the consecrated wafer really did contain the blood and body of Christ (Walker, 1981).

Changing political considerations demand changes in how former enemies are portrayed. In 1598, Henry IV issued the Edict of Nantes in an attempt to end the religious wars between Catholics and Protestants. The edict guaranteed the free exercise of Protestantism throughout most towns in France, freedom for the Protestant press, and the right of Huguenots to hold public office. Although the Pope condemned the edict, the Parliament of Paris reluctantly gave it official registration in 1599 (Durant & Durant, 1961). The edict was unpopular with Catholics throughout France and generated resistance in numerous guises.

In this context, a traveling demoniac named Marthe Brossier, through her possessing demons, again began spewing anti-Huguenot propaganda during exorcisms. Marthe and her family moved from town to town putting on displays of public exorcism for which they appear to have been well rewarded financially. Marthe was well aware of the career of Nicole Obry and modeled her possession displays on those of Nicole. Like Nicole, Marthe was possessed by the Huguenot-loving Beelzebub, and her public exorcisms drew large crowds and reinforced already strong anti-Huguenot feeling. However, anti-Huguenot possession displays that once received encouragement, or at least toleration, at the highest political levels were now a political embarrassment. Consequently, the Bishop of Paris arranged for a committee of theologians and physicians to test the reality of Marthe's possession (Walker, 1981).

Tests of the reality of demonic possession varied in stringency (Robbins, 1959). Some, like discriminating between consecrated and unconsecrated wafers, or between holy water and untreated well water, were essentially impossible to pass consistently if administered fairly and honestly. Others, like convulsing at the sign of the cross, or displaying insensibility when pricked with a needle, were under voluntary control and, therefore, easier to pass. Thus, the means to either legitimate or discredit the reality of any particular possession case were always at hand. The care and stringency with which these tests were applied depended in large part on the outcome desired by those who used the tests and the lengths to which they were willing to go (e.g., coaching demoniacs, providing obvious cues about what was and was not real holy water) to attain desired outcomes (Spanos, 1983b).

Henri IV was concerned by the anti-Huguenot feeling stirred during Marthe's exorcisms. Dutifully, the commission arranged by the Bishop of Paris, after determining, for example, that Marthe's demons could not understand either Greek or Latin, concluded that Marthe was a fraud. However, the Capucins, whose brothers exorcized Marthe and who had a vested interest in the continuation of her possession, summoned a commission of their own that declared Marthe's possession genuine. Her public exorcisms resumed. At the behest of the king, Parliament ordered the exorcisms stopped. Marthe was imprisoned for a short time, and her book describing the possession of Nicole Obry was taken from her. After her release, she was escorted back to her home town, where officials were assigned to prevent her from traveling (Walker, 1981).

It is worth noting that possession displays were used for propaganda purposes by Protestants as well as by Catholics. Puritan demoniacs in both England and Colonial America ranted against Calvin and claimed an affinity for the Pope, Quakers, and Anglicans (Harsnett, 1599; Mather, 1693/1914). Demoniacs in Boston, Salem, and England also affirmed Puritan doctrines by claiming an inability to read the writings of Calvin (indicating that demons could not abide sacred writings). However, these same demoniacs read the sacred writings of Catholics, Anglicans, and Quakers with ease (Calif, 1700/1914; Mather, 1693/1914; K. Thomas, 1971).

WITCHCRAFT ACCUSATIONS AND POSSESSION

Beliefs concerning sorcery—the idea that magical means can be used to injure others—had been a regular part of village life in Western Europe since antiquity and long antedated the Christian concept of the devil (Russell, 1980; Spanos, 1978). By the 15th century, however, the notion of sorcery had become closely identified with the Christian idea of demonic witchcraft. Moreover, the notion of demonic possession, which evolved independently of the idea of witchcraft, became associated with witchcraft in the 15th century. From the 15th through the 17th centuries, demonic possession was often viewed as a species of bewitchment; that is, witches were viewed as people who, with the devil's help, could direct demons to possess (i.e., bewitch) people. Nevertheless, the possessing demons knew the identity of the witch who had sent them, and the demons could be coerced by clerical authority to name the offending witch. When the accusations of demoniacs were legitimated by authorities, the persons named as witches might be subject to arrest and even execution. Consequently, demonic enactment took on an additional political dimension as a vehicle for discrediting economic, personal, or political rivals by causing them to be labeled as witches.

Colonial American Witch Hunts

On October 30, 1671, 16-year-old Elizabeth Knapp of Groton, Massachusetts, began to behave strangely. Initially, she complained of unusual sensations in her limbs and of difficulty breathing, but by the next day her behavior had become frighteningly bizarre. She was described as follows:

> . . . sometimes weeping, sometimes laughing, and [making] many foolish and apish gestures. In the evening, going into the cellar, she shrieked suddenly; and being inquired of the cause, she answered that she saw two persons in the cellar; where upon some went down with her to search, but found none. . . . [Later that evening she was] suddenly thrown down into the midst of the floor with violence, and taken with a violent fit . . . and with much ado was she kept out of the fire from destroying herself. After which time she was followed with fits, from thence till the Sabbath Day, in which she was violent in bodily motions, leapings, strainings, and strange agitations, scarce to be held

in bounds, by the strength of three or four—violent also in roarings and screamings, representing a dark resemblance of hellish torments. . . . (Willard, 1683, pp. 176–177)

There was no doubt in the mind of Samuel Willard, the town pastor in whose home Elizabeth lived as a servant, that she was demonically possessed and tormented by Satan. Moreover, as frequently occurred in 17th-century Colonial American possession cases, Elizabeth accused a neighbor of bewitching her. According to Willard (1683),

Either she [the neighbor] or the Devil in her likeness and habit, particularly her riding hood, had come down the chimney [and] stricken her that night [when] she was first taken violently. (p. 177)

To test the validity of Elizabeth's accusation, the accused neighbor was brought to the Willard home. Elizabeth was believed to be blind during her fits. Consequently, her ability to recognize the accused neighbor by her touch alone constituted evidence of a preternatural connection between them:

For although her [Elizabeth's] eyes were (as it were) sealed up (as they were always, or for the most part, in those fits, and so continue in them all to this day), she yet knew her [the accused's] very touch from any other, though no voice were uttered, and discovered it evidently by her gestures, so powerful were Satan's suggestions in her. (Willard, 1683, p. 177)

In 1692, two decades after the events at Groton, two girls aged 9 and 11, who lived in the home of the town pastor in Salem Village, Massachusetts, also began to behave strangely and soon displayed many of the symptoms that had been earlier exhibited by Elizabeth Knapp. Within a short period, the two Salem girls were joined in their fits and torments by several others. Accusations of bewitchment based on seeing the "shapes" of the accused soon followed, and these led to the arrests that culminated in the famous Salem witchcraft panic. Before it ended, the Salem panic had become the largest witchcraft scare in Colonial America. Hundreds of suspected witches were arrested, and 19 of those convicted were executed. The major source of evidence in almost all of these cases was the same as that given by Elizabeth Knapp: reports from the afflicted indicating that they saw the specters (thus the term *spectral evidence*) of the accused tormenting them and others.

Unlike what happened at Salem, however, no witchcraft panic occurred in Groton, Massachusetts, as a result of Elizabeth Knapp's accusations. Samuel Willard, the minister at Groton, refused to legitimate Elizabeth's accusations. Instead, he informed Elizabeth and the rest of his parish that the devil was "the Father of lies" and could not be trusted. After dutiful prayer, Elizabeth acknowledged her errors and retracted her accusations (Willard, 1683). A similar event occurred in Boston in 1693 during the possession of 17-year-old Margaret Rule. Margaret, like both Elizabeth and the afflicted girls at Salem, saw the specters of several people engaged in various nefarious activities. She accused these individuals of witchcraft and gave their names to her minister. The minister, however, refused to proceed with accusations based on such spectral evidence (Calif, 1700/ 1914).

When examined together, the Groton and Boston cases, on one hand, and the Salem case, on the other, begin to illustrate how social and political consideration could influence both the witchcraft accusations of demoniacs and the manner in which those accusations were treated by the wider community. Witchcraft accusations by the possessed were not necessarily believed and automatically acted on by those who held social power. Moreover, without legitimation by authorities, accusations did not generate formal court proceedings. However, the rules for granting legitimation to accusations were ambiguous. For example, reports of spectral attack given by possessed adolescents could be either believed, as was done at Salem, or dismissed as the product of "the Father of lies," as was done at Groton. Precisely because they were ambiguous, those rules could be applied and interpreted selectively to meet the vested interests of varied groups who held social power.

These considerations suggest that an adequate account of why witchcraft accusations were sometimes legitimated and sometimes not cannot be obtained by focusing on the psychology of the possessed individuals. What is required instead is an examination of the broader social context in which those accusations were made, and an understanding of the beliefs and motives of those who held the power required to transform the reported imaginings of the possessed into the social reality of formal witchcraft accusations (Demos, 1982; Spanos, 1983a). For example, an adequate understanding of the events at Salem requires a careful analysis of Salem Village as a community and of the social, political, and economic factors that produced dissention between competing groups within the community. Such an analysis has been provided by Boyer and Nissenbaum (1974).

Boyer and Nissenbaum (1974) pointed out that Salem Village was not an independent political entity in 1692. Instead, it was part of Salem Town. The village did not have an independent local government; it paid its taxes to the town, its constables were chosen by the town, and its legal disputes were settled in the town by magistrates who were not part of the local community. Some in the village and many in the town had vested economic interests in maintaining the status quo. On the other hand, many of the villagers saw their economic and political futures best served by establishing Salem Village as an independent political entity, a full-fledged town with its own church and local government. The lack of a local government or a court system responsive to local needs made the settling of legal disputes between villagers a bitter and protracted process. As pointed out by Boyer and Nissenbaum (1974),

> What made Salem Village disputes so notorious, and ultimately so destructive, was the fact that structural defects in its organization rendered the Village almost helpless in coping with whatever disputes might arise. . . . Given the ineffectiveness of the Village's institutional structures, private grievances and disputes escalated with a rapidity which must have startled even those embroiled in them, until the entire community, willy nilly, was drawn in. (pp. 51–52)

The Puritans had emigrated from England to America to establish a theocracy. The church was the hub of Puritan communities and was as much a political as a religious institution. In such communities, the establishment of a church was the first step toward political autonomy (Boyer & Nissenbaum, 1974). Salem Village established its own church after a protracted struggle. Nevertheless, conflicts about whether to separate completely from Salem Town or maintain political ties to it remained heated. These conflicts were expressed in disputes about the village minister (for example, who should pay his salary, how he should be selected, who should be allowed to join the church). Those who lived relatively far from Salem Town usually had a vested interest in political autonomy and supported the minister. Those who lived close to Salem Town and who had vested economic interests in maintaining strong connections with the town opposed the minister. Early in 1692, as conflicts surrounding the minister grew more intense, and threats to depose him escalated, the two children living in his home began to display the first signs of demonic "affliction." Accusations of witchcraft soon followed, and the pattern of those accusations mirrored the economic/geographical factionalism that characterized village politics. Members of the faction that supported the minister and favored political autonomy for the village accused members of the opposing faction of witchcraft (Boyer & Nissenbaum, 1974). Although the demoniacs were the vehicles through which the accusations were made, the legitimation of those accusations, at least initially, was in the hands of community leaders who held vested interests in allowing the accusations to be treated as serious evidence of witchcraft.

The characteristics of those initially accused of witchcraft by the afflicted girls were congruent with long-standing community conceptions of the kind of person who might be a witch. Thus, the first to be accused was a poor woman of no fixed address who smoked a pipe and begged for a living. However, by the time the trial court met for its initial session, over 70 people had been arrested. The collective fear of witches was now acute, and public pressure to convict was strong. In addition, the accusations had already been legitimated during pretrial judicial examinations. Consequently, it is not surprising that the court legitimated the accusations further by beginning to convict the accused (Weisman, 1984). Gradually, the afflicted girls began to accuse people who did not conform to the popular stereotype of a witch. However, because the court had legitimated earlier accusations by the afflicted, there was little it could do but continue its policy. For the same reason, the court had a vested interest in validating the legal standing of "spectral evidence" despite the reservations of some prominent clergy. Without the admissibility of spectral evidence, the large majority of witchcraft cases could not have been prosecuted.

In summary, locally generated factional conflicts that stemmed from differences about whether Salem Village should become an independent political entity led the court to side with one faction in that dispute and initially validate the status of the afflicted adolescents as witch finders. Having done so, the court had little choice but to maintain the afflicted in that status. To have done otherwise would have meant discrediting their earlier decisions as well as those of the pretrial magistrates. However, maintaining the legitimation of the afflicted required the adoption of judicial procedures (i.e., the admission of spectral evidence) that had the effect of expanding rather than limiting further accusations. All of these events were consistent with and interpreted in terms of the apocalyptic fantasies of the Puritan clergy (Spanos, 1985; Weisman, 1984).

The Salem trials were eventually ended by sociopolitical counterpressures that led to the dissolution of the trial court. As more and more socially prominent people were threatened with accusation, steps were taken to apply political pressure that would end the trials. Finally, following the accusation that his wife was a witch, the royal governor lost patience with the legal proceeding, disbanded the original court, and appointed a new court that acquitted all defendants (Boyer & Nissenbaum, 1974; Weisman, 1984).

The Urban Grandier Case in France

The importance of vested sociopolitical interests in the legitimation of witchcraft accusations brought by the possessed is clear in Continental as well as in Colonial possession cases. For example, in what is arguably Europe's most famous witchcraft case, demonically possessed nuns from the Ursuline convent in Loudon, France, accused Urbain Grandier of witchcraft in 1633 (Baskin, 1974; Huxley, 1952; Robbins, 1959). Grandier, a popular but rakish priest, was suspected of fathering the child of the local prosecutor and openly consorted with one of his young penitents. More important to his eventual fate, he also alienated a number of clerical superiors, including the powerful Cardinal Richelieu.

Grandier had petitioned for the position of confessor to the Ursuline nuns, but the position went instead to one of his enemies, Father Mignon. Mignon heard and probably encouraged numerous confessions from his penitents that involved Grandier appearing to them in the night. Other symptoms of possession soon followed, and eventually all of the nuns in the convent exhibited full-blown and dramatic displays of demonic possession. The mother superior, Sister Jeanne des Anges, was possessed by two demons. While being interrogated by Mignon during an exorcism, one of Sister Jeanne's demons claimed that he had been sent to possess the nun by Grandier (Huxley, 1952).

Grandier, however, also had supporters, and the outcome of the exorcism was simply a prohibition by the archbishop against further exorcisms. Not to be outdone, Grandier's enemies appealed to friends of Cardinal Richelieu, who soon arranged for a commission to investigate charges that Grandier was a witch. The exorcisms were resumed and carried out publicly and with much fanfare to huge audiences. Demons speaking through the nuns again accused Grandier of witchcraft. In addition, Grandier's cause was not helped when several of his rejected mistresses were recruited to the fray and accused him of numerous sexual improprieties that he had purportedly carried out in church.

Grandier was eventually tortured, found guilty of sorcery, and burned alive at the stake. Clearly, however, this train of events did not occur simply because he was accused by a group of lowly nuns of bewitching them. It was Grandier's personal and political enemies both within and outside the church who legitimated (and most likely initially suggested) the accusations made by the demoniacs. In fact, during Grandier's trial, Sister Jeanne and other nuns attempted to retract their earlier statements against the priest. They confessed to an ecclesiastical court that their earlier testimony had been dictated to them by some of Grandier's clerical enemies. The nuns were informed by the court that it was the demons rather than themselves who made these confessions to save one of their servants. Grandier's trial continued to its grim conclusion (Huxley, 1952; Robbins, 1959).

SUMMARY

Both witchcraft trials and the use of possession in proselytizing served important social functions. Possession and exorcism functioned as ideological tools used to affirm parochial religious values and win converts while debasing competing religious beliefs. Relatedly, possession displays were strategic enactments that varied as a function of the expectations and demands of different exorcists and different audiences. As in cross-cultural manifestations of spirit possession, a major feature of the demonic role involved conveying the impression that behaviors were no longer governed by the actor. However, conveying this impression convincingly required that demoniacs retain behavioral control and gear their enactments to

contextual demands in a manner consistent with their audience's conception of what constituted possession. Demonic performances were orches-
trated (probably with varying degrees of conscious intent) by those who
held power over the demoniacs for the purpose of affecting the attitudes
and beliefs of potential converts and to denigrate competing belief systems.
Political elites were well aware of the propaganda value of possession and
exorcism, and exploited them to political advantage. When political re-
alities changed, those who had earlier fostered a credulous acceptance of
possession were quite prepared to arrange conditions that would lead to its
discreditation when doing so was deemed politically advantageous. Taken
together, these considerations suggest that viewing demonic enactments in
terms of individual psychopathology is to seriously distort their meaning.

Relatedly, witchcraft trials that were based on the accusations of the
demonically possessed should not be seen as the more or less automatic
responses of credulous bureaucrats. Instead, such accusations must be understood within a social nexus and in relation to a host of sociopolitical
interests. Whether or not the accusations of demoniacs were believed or
defused depended on interactions among a number of factors that included
the nature of the personal and social conflicts that led to the accusations;
the reputation and social standing of the accused in the community; and
the economic, social, and political advantages and disadvantages that
might be expected from the legitimation of the accusations.

The satanic mythology that constituted the ideological prop supporting both witchcraft accusations and demonic enactments became increasingly less influential with the waning of the 17th century. Interestingly,
however, this mythology has been reinvigorated in late 20th-century North
America, with the rise in economic and political power of the religious
right. One manifestation of this reinvigorated mythology has involved re-
legitimating the idea of ritual sexual abuse carried out by a powerful but
secret Satan-worshiping cult (J. Victor, 1993). Just as the demonically possessed came to be conceptualized as victims of Satan and his servants in
the 15th century, MPD patients have come increasingly to be seen as satanic cult victims in the late 20th century. The association between demonic possession and witchcraft served a number of social, political, and
ideological purposes. Such purposes should be kept in mind when, in later
chapters, we examine the association between MPD and recovered "memories" of satanic ritual abuse.

15

FROM POSSESSION TO DUAL CONSCIOUSNESS

Demonic possession remained a fairly common occurrence throughout the 18th century. Even in the early 19th century, such cases occurred frequently enough for Esquirol (1838/1963) to classify them as a type of demonomania and devote a chapter to them in his famous *Des Malades Mentales*. Interpretations of possession, however, were changing. During the 18th century, religious interpretations continued to be considered seriously in some intellectual circles (Leventhal, 1976; Wilkins, 1974). For instance, as late as 1749, a German nun was burned as a witch for causing the possession of her sister nuns, and in 1731 the exorcism of Catherine Cadiere, a possessed French nun who claimed that she was seduced by her exorcist, drew large crowds and much scandal (Robbins, 1959). Nevertheless, purely medical explanations for possession became increasingly prominent as the 18th century progressed (Diethelm, 1970; Tourney, 1972), and this naturalistic view had gained general acceptance in intellectual circles by the beginning of the 19th century.

The gradual conceptual shift from possession to natural disease that occurred from the 16th through part of the 19th centuries was associated with delimited changes in patients' role performance. As patients as well as physicians began defining behavioral deviance as a purely medical issue, role behaviors that were incompatible with notions of natural disease became less prominent (e.g., displaying demon selves, vomiting pins, defining oneself as possessed). Role behaviors that could be more easily conceptualized in terms of natural disease (e.g., convulsions, anxiety, vague physical complaints, temporary sensory and motor disturbances, temporary amnesia) continued to be enacted as a more or less recognizable syndrome throughout the 19th century that was commonly labeled as hysteria (Janet, 1925; Shorter, 1992).

Throughout the 18th century, somnambulism, catalepsy, and ecstasies continued to occur in religious contexts, but increasingly, these and related phenomena were given naturalistic explanations. For instance, between 1728 and 1732, about 600 alleged miracles occurred at a Parisian cemetery (Garrett, 1975; R. A. Knox, 1950). The behavior of the participants at these "miracles" included convulsions, analgesia, reported amnesia, and indications of preternatural knowledge. The participants, known as "convulsionnaries," were usually women. Huge audiences went to watch the convulsionaries perform and participated in the procedures by stroking or hitting them to stop the convulsions (Garrett, 1975; Hecker, 1837/1970). Popular interpretation of these phenomena revolved around notions of divine intervention or demonic possession (Garrett, 1975; Wilkins, 1973). Among most of the medical community and the intelligentsia, however, naturalistic interpretations in terms of hysteria or faulty imagination clearly predominated. Thus, the catalepsies, somnambulisms, amnesias, and convulsions that had earlier been diagnosed as possession were increasingly defined by medical and intellectual elites in terms of medical disease regardless of whether they occurred in religious or secular contexts (Wilkins, 1972).

The conceptual shift from supernatural to naturalistic explanations of possession was dramatized most clearly in the 18th-century confrontation between John Joseph Gassner and Franz Anton Mesmer. Gassner was a Catholic priest from Swabia who believed in demonic possession and had, in fact, cured himself through exorcism. He also exorcized thousands of others in Swabia, Switzerland, and Tyrol (Ellenberger, 1970; Hartshorn, 1879). His procedures were as follows:

> Gassner regarded faith as an essential condition to be cured . . . he almost always touched the affected part. Sometimes he rubbed his hand upon his [the patient's] waist or neck, but it was not always the case. Gassner had the power by his will, to make the pulse of his patients vary. . . . He paralyzed their limbs; caused them to weep, to laugh, soothed or agitated them simply by expressing his order in Latin, or rather mentally. (Hartshorn, 1879, p. 304)

Despite his widespread popularity, Gassner was out of step with Enlightenment thinking, and in 1775, Prince Max Joseph of Bavaria appointed a commission of inquiry into his practices. Mesmer (1779/1948) had developed a new theory of disease and its cure, "animal magnetism," and was invited to watch Gassner's performances. Briefly, Mesmer believed that a "subtle fluid" permeated the entire universe, including the human body. Disease resulted from an obstruction or disharmony of this fluid within the body, and cure of disease was effected by redistributing and harmonizing the flow of fluid. Redistribution of fluid in the sick could be brought about by the transmission of magnetic fluid from the therapist (magnetizer) to the sick. Using magnetism, Mesmer replicated all of the behaviors displayed by Gassner's demoniacs and concluded that Gassner's demonstrations could be explained in naturalistic terms; according to Mesmer, Gassner had unwittingly magnetized his patients (Ellenberger, 1970).

FROM EXORCISM TO MAGNETISM

The techniques used by the magnetizers to cure their patients quickly became standardized. Before deciding on a career in medicine, Mesmer had trained for the priesthood (Podmore, 1909), and in numerous respects his magnetic procedures resembled the procedures used by Catholic exorcists. Like earlier exorcists who frequently made use of a laying on of hands to effect a cure (e.g., Harsnett, 1599), magnetists used long stroking motions (called "passes") close to the patient's body to direct healing magnetic fluid from their own bodies into those of their patients (Binet & Fere, 1888; Deleuze, 1825/1879). Catholic exorcists made extensive use of holy water, relics, and other consecrated objects, whereas magnetists used objects into which they had directed magnetic fluid. For example, patients might be instructed to drink magnetized water between therapy sessions or to hold a magnetized handkerchief over a painful or diseased area of the body (Deleuze, 1825/1879; Grimes, 1845).

The role of exorcist involved the development of an appropriate attitude toward oneself as well as the procedure of exorcism. Exorcists construed their activity as involving moral confrontations between good and evil that required strong faith in God and in the procedures of exorcism. Also required was the leading of a moral life and spiritual cleansing before exorcism (The Roman Ritual of Exorcism, 1614/1976). If exorcists failed to meet these requirements, not only might the procedure fail, but they themselves might become possessed by the demons they attempted to cast out. Possession of an exorcist was, in fact, a not uncommon occurrence, and it was usually explained in terms of pride on the part of the priest or his failure to gird himself with the proper degree of faith and moral purity (Huxley, 1952; Spanos & Gottlieb, 1979).

In their initial theoretical formulations, the magnetists viewed themselves as repositories of an impersonal fluid that could be directed into the bodies of their patients through the use of passes. This mechanical conception was, however, quickly modified, and the magnetizer's personal characteristics and attitudes became seen as crucial to the success of the treatment. Puysegur (1784/1820), for example, stressed the importance of the magnetist's will and faith in effecting a cure. Passes without appropriate willing and faith he considered useless. Like exorcists, the magnetists often construed their activities in moral terms. Disease was a moral evil and health a moral good. Virtue was necessary for the maintenance of health, and vice could produce disharmony and disease. Magnetizers were pledged not only to treat sickness but to prevent injustice and promote honesty and correct conduct (Bergasse, 1785/1970). Engaged in a moral confrontation with the evil of disease, the magnetist would be victorious only if he first girded himself with the appropriate moral stance (Darnton, 1970; Deleuze, 1825/1879).

Inappropriate magnetizing, like inappropriate exorcism, could produce harmful effects not only in the patient but in the magnetizer as well. Thus, the magnetizer who used incorrect techniques, or who was morally or physically unfit to magnetize, might develop symptoms of the patient's disorder (Deleuze, 1825/1879; Newman, 1847). For instance, Deleuze (1825/1879) warned novice magnetizers that "you may experience a feeling of pain or a difficulty in the internal organs of your body, corresponding with those which are affected in your patient" (p. 262).

In summary, there were important similarities between the roles of exorcist and magnetist. In both cases, the treatments were construed as involving moral confrontations. Evil could be conquered in such confrontations only if the representative of good (exorcist or magnetist) was morally purified, possessed abundant faith in his procedures, and maintained a firm control over himself and the situation. Moral failings in exorcists or magnetists could lead to their developing the symptoms of their patients. These considerations suggest that the exorcist–demoniac role served as a template from which the magnetizer–magnetized subject role was constructed (Spanos & Gottlieb, 1979).

By the early 19th century, the social role of the magnetized subject had also become fairly well demarcated. Its enactment consisted of a set of unusual behaviors that were elicited within the social context of a relationship between magnetizer and patient. These unusual behaviors were, in large measure, secularized versions of the behaviors that had earlier constituted the demonically possessed role. Included were convulsions, analgesia, heightened intelligence, clairvoyance, amnesia, catalepsy, and increased and decreased sensory abilities. It is important to keep in mind that, at least initially, these behaviors did not occur together in a syndrome because they were suggested to patients by their magnetizers. As described above, in the 18th century, this constellation of behaviors, when occurring in women, were considered symptomatic of hysteria (Cheyne, 1742; Raulin, 1758; Veith, 1965; Whytt, 1767). For instance, Mesmer's first patients often exhibited convulsions, catalepsy, paralyses, and various sensory deficits before he met them. Instead of suggesting these behaviors, Mesmer attempted to control and regulate the timing of their occurrence and eventual disappearance. There is little evidence to indicate that amnesia, intellectual enhancements, and purported displays of clairvoyance occurred initially because of suggestions given by the magnetizers. Instead, some evidence indicates that displays of amnesia occurred but went largely unnoticed in Mesmer's pupils (Podmore, 1902). Similarly, Puysegur (1784/1820), far from suggesting amnesia and intellectual enhancements to patients, appeared to be astonished at their initial occurrence (Binet & Fere, 1888). Magnetized patients, like modern hypnotic subjects, were of course attuned to the interests and expectations of their magnetizers. Consequently, particular aspects of the hysterical constellation could be deemphasized or much elaborated depending on interactions between subjects' understandings of what was sought or required by the magnetizer and the concern, interest, and curiosity displayed by magnetizers in what their patients displayed.

Of particular interest to magnetizers were the cognitive changes displayed by their patients. In 1784, Puysegur, a disciple of Mesmer, magnetized a servant named Victor to treat a bronchial ailment. Instead of convulsing, however, Victor appeared to undergo a fundamental alteration in experience. He appeared to be much more intelligent than usual, was able to converse knowledgeably about topics that Puysegur assumed Victor knew nothing about, and even seemed to possess the ability to read Puysegur's mind. Nevertheless, after termination of the magnetic session, Victor claimed to recall nothing of what had transpired. However, when later remagnetized, Victor recalled all that had occurred in his previous magnetic session. The cognitive symptoms that magnetism appeared to bring about were labeled *artificial somnambulism* (Ellenberger, 1970). As described in the last two chapters, a century before Puysegur, all of the symptoms of artificial somnambulism were well-known symptoms of demonic possession.

In the 18th century, the term *somnambulism* had two meanings. One type of somnambulism, sleepwalking, had been well-known since antiquity. Physicians were aware that sleepwalkers sometimes perform complex activities while asleep, with no memory of what occurred after awakening. Another type of somnambulism was similar in some respects to displays earlier seen in demoniacs and also involved the enactment of complex activities for which the patient later claimed amnesia. This second type of somnambulism was thought to occur spontaneously (as opposed to "artificially induced," as in Victor's case) and sometimes appeared to involve two distinct states of consciousness separated by a period of sleep or convulsions. While in their "second states," these patients often appeared to be happier, more outgoing, and more intelligent than usual. They also often appeared to be clairvoyant; exhibited enhancements in abilities (e.g., sang more beautifully); and displayed a variety of symptoms that came and went including blindness, paralyses, and anesthesia. Reported amnesia between the two states was also a common occurrence (Crabtree, 1992; Hacking, 1991; Shorter, 1992). In several of these cases, after a long period of sleep or apparent coma, patients not only displayed amnesia for their earlier life but also behaved as if they could no longer remember basic skills such as reading or writing and underwent retraining for these skills (E. T. Carlson, 1981; Hacking, 1991; Shorter, 1992). In a number of these "dual consciousness" cases, there is evidence to suggest that the patients were treated with magnetism and that, therefore, their symptom displays may have been shaped by their therapists to an unknown degree. In other cases, the patients appeared to be displaying their symptoms in the absence of magnetic or other potentially suggestive treatments (Hacking, 1991). On the other hand, the odd constellation of symptoms exhibited by these patients (e.g., dual consciousness separated by transitional periods of sleep, correctly predicting one's future convulsive attacks, sensory and motor dysfunctions that appeared in one "state" and not the other, amnesia between "states"), which had earlier been seen in cases of demonic possession, suggests that these displays reflected patients' implicit, socially generated conceptions of what were considered "appropriate" ways of becoming ill and expressing dissatisfactions.

The artificial somnambulism associated with magnetism, like "spontaneous" somnambulism, also seemed to imply the existence of a second consciousness. While magnetized, the subject appeared to live a different life, with its own continuity that was separate from the subject's ordinary existence (Crabtree, 1992). From the perspective of an exorcist, of course, somnambulism would obviously be a manifestation of an indwelling demon whose intelligence and personality were separate from, and sometimes displaced, those of the person possessed. From the perspective of magnetists and later hypnotists, who adopted a worldview that excluded supernatural elements, the existence of a foreign consciousness injected from the outside was not an acceptable theoretical tenet. Instead, these investigators explained somnambulism by positing two consciousnesses within the same person. One of these was the ordinary consciousness of waking life. The other was a subterranean consciousness that manifested itself in magnetism or in diseased states (Decker, 1986; Ellenberger, 1970).

As described by Shorter (1992), in a number of late 18th- and early 19th-century cases of magnetic somnambulism, the "second states" of patients were given their own names, and while in these "states" the patients acted in ways and displayed characteristics that differed dramatically from their normal, nonmagnetized personalities. The best known of these early "second state" cases was a patient of Charles Despine named Estelle (Ellenberger, 1970; Shorter, 1992). Estelle entered Despine's clinic in 1836 at age 11. At that time, she was described as a spoiled child who exhibited complete paraplegia and suffered from a host of other psychophysiological symptoms. After 5 months of uneventful hydrotherapy, Despine was told by Estelle's mother that the girl was being comforted by a choir of angels each evening. For Despine, this meant that Estelle suffered from ecstasy, a disorder that was treatable by magnetism. He began to magnetize Estelle, and soon she developed a second state in which she appeared much healthier and purportedly displayed a range of psychic abilities and unusual sensory phenomena. For instance, she purportedly experienced a transposition of her senses that enabled her to read with her fingertips.

Displays of unusual sensory abilities like reading with the fingertips or with the pit of the stomach were not uncommon in early 19th-century cases of magnetism and were consistent with contemporary notions concerning the functioning of the nervous system (Dingwall, 1968; Shorter, 1992). Obviously, reading with the fingertips or stomach is impossible. How then did the magnetized subjects of the day accomplish such feats? The answer is simple enough: The subjects cheated, and the doctors who tested for these phenomena often did so in such a sloppy and informal manner that the cheating went undetected (Dingwall, 1968; Gauld, 1992; Podmore, 1902). Such phenomena indicate once again the extent to which patients are sometimes willing to use trickery to impress and meet the expectations of their therapists. They also illustrate the rather profound levels of credulity sometimes displayed by therapists to reports and displays from patients that are both interesting and consistent with the therapists' theoretical assumptions.

During her magnetic condition, a comforting angel named Angeline appeared to Estelle. Angeline engaged Estelle in conversation and also directed her treatment. The prescribed treatment was much to Estelle's liking. For instance, with respect to diet, Angeline prohibited foods that Estelle didn't like and ordered that Estelle should be allowed anything that she liked. Within a short time, Estelle began to spontaneously enter her magnetic condition and alternated each 12 hours between her original sickly personality and her outgoing, active, magnetic personality (Ellenberger, 1970). Soon Despine "discovered" double existences in others of his patients, one of whom displayed six separate states (Shorter, 1992). Although Despine was particularly impressed by Estelle's purported sensory feats and bizarre symptoms, the behaviors that most intrigued later investigators were her display of what would later be labeled multiple personality. During the last quarter of the 19th century, when the first wave of multiple-personality cases began to build, Estelle's case was resurrected and used as evidence for the prior existence of multiple personality as a distinct syndrome (Ellenberger, 1970). Therefore, it is worth noting Shorter's (1992) description of the context in which Estelle's symptoms of multiplicity first arose:

The context of Estelle's multiple personality disorder was, therefore the theater of florid magnetism and catalepsy then prevailing at [Despine's clinic]. Many of the other patients were producing bizarre symptoms: it must have seemed to an intelligent young girl rather the order of the day that she bring forth some of her own. (p. 161)

Cases like those of Estelle, which involved the manifesting of what would later be called a secondary personality during magnetism, were relatively common in the early 19th century. However, in many such cases the secondary personality continued to be conceptualized as a supernatural entity such as a demon, ghost, or angel, rather than a naturalistic second consciousness.

The transition from demonic to naturalistic explanations of magnetic behavior involved various attempts to combine these alternative frames of reference. For instance, Mesmer's conceptions of disease, cure, and magnetic fluid were completely naturalistic. Nevertheless, notions of magnetism and somnambulism were quickly integrated into supernaturalistic frames of reference. Two such instances included the association of magnetism and spiritism, and the notion of demonico-magnetic affections.

Belief in communication with the spirit world was widespread in Paris during the second half of the 18th century. Séances and mediums were common, and magnetism quickly became associated with the spiritism movement. Somnambulism was soon conceptualized as a state that allowed for direct contact with the spirit world (Gauld, 1992; Segouin, 1853; Thouret, 1784). Magnetism began to be increasingly used as a procedure for divination and spirit communication, somnambules became professionalized as mediums, and before the end of the century this spiritualist form of magnetism had spread throughout Europe (Darnton, 1970; Ellenberger, 1970; Gauld, 1992).

The magnetic relationship that emerged in the late 18th century as a secularized version of the exorcist–demoniac relationship was, by the early 19th century, partially reincorporated into a supernaturalistic framework. The magnetized patient, initially conceptualized as ill rather than possessed, was, within a few years, reconceptualized by many as possessed —usually by good spirits, angels, or departed relatives—but possessed nonetheless (Spanos & Gottlieb, 1979).

In the early 19th century, Justin Kerner (1834), a German physician and romantic poet, developed the notion of demonico-magnetic affections. Kerner believed that individuals, sometimes unbeknownst to themselves, could be possessed by demons. His treatment for such individuals was a mixture of exorcism and magnetism. The first step involved the individual becoming aware of the fact that his or her affliction was demonic in nature.

Once the patient recognized the existence of the demon within, its expulsion by means of a magnetic exorcism could proceed. Occasionally, as in the following case, the procedure failed:

As for the action of the magnetic passes which I only tried upon her two or three times, the demon tried to neutralize them immediately by counter passes made with the girl's hand. (Kerner, 1834, p. 40)

In summary, the association of magnetism with spirit possession and mediumship and the development of the concept of demonico-magnetic affections indicate that in the early 19th century the paradigm shift from supernaturalistic to naturalistic explanations for unusual behaviors was still not completed, even for some physicians. More important for an understanding of MPD, the occurrence of these phenomena indicates that displays of multiple identity in association with magnetism were fairly common during this period. The step from displaying a spirit or demon during magnetic sessions to displaying a secular alternate personality was not a large one.

FROM MAGNETISM TO HYPNOSIS

By the middle of the 19th century, both possession and magnetism were frequently interpreted by the medical mainstream in terms of hysteria (Drinka, 1984; Ellenberger, 1970). With increases in scientific knowledge, explanations of behavior and physiological functioning in terms of magnetic fluids that flowed from one person to the next fell increasingly out of favor. Scientific and medical thinking during this period were influenced by a rise in the popularity and status of neurology. One important consequence of this change in the scientific zeitgeist was the replacement of both spiritual and "fluidist" hypotheses of magnetic phenomena with hypotheses based on contemporary notions of neurological functioning (Shorter, 1992). The replacement of these older hypotheses was gradual. In one form or another, for example, "fluidist" ideas persisted in some circles beyond the end of the 19th century (Podmore, 1902). Even more important, spiritualist ideas again became prominent around the middle of the 19th century as part of a reaction against scientific materialism. As we shall later see, the spiritist movement played a prominent role in the evolution of multiple personality as a distinct disorder (Decker, 1986; Kenny, 1981). Nevertheless, it was scientific materialism and contemporary neurology that provided the mainstream understandings for hysteria and that ushered in the change from magnetism to hypnosis.

The best-known neurological alternative to the fluidist hypothesis of magnetic phenomena was Braid's (1843/1960) notion of "neurohypnology." Misled by the lethargic appearance of his patients, Braid initially accounted for magnetic phenomena in terms of spreading neural inhibition induced by sustained visual attention and eye muscle fatigue. Supposedly, the spreading of this neural inhibition backwards from the optic nerves into the brain produced a state akin to sleep in which the phenomenon of magnetism (now relabeled *hypnosis*) occurred. By 1847, Braid (1855/1970) had substantially modified his physiological speculations concerning neurohypnology and developed the concept of *monoideism*. Monoideism was based on the idea that William James (1890) was to later label as *ideo-motor action*. According to this notion, ideas that remain uncontradicted by other ideas lead automatically to the corresponding behavior. For instance, suppose the hypnotist communicates to his subject the idea that her arm should become stiff and rigid. The subject in turn focuses her attention on the idea of her arm becoming stiff, to the exclusion of all competing ideas. According to the monoideism hypothesis, the idea of stiffness will be translated into the corresponding behavior, and the subject's arm will automatically stiffen.

As we saw in chapter 3, hypnotic behaviors, despite external appearances, do not occur automatically, and cannot be adequately explained in terms of ideo-motor action. Nevertheless, Braid's notion of monoideism was an important advance over earlier theorizing because it provided an explanation for the observation that the behavior of magnetic and hypnotic subjects was influenced by expectations transmitted by their therapists. Moreover, because this hypothesis was also consistent with the mechanistic ideas that underlay contemporary neurological thinking about behavior, it became highly influential. The notion of monoideism strongly influenced the work of Bernheim and other members of the so-called Nancy school, who made ideo-motor action the central tenet in their theory of "suggestion" (Spanos & Chaves, 1991). Thus, for Bernheim (1886/1900), the suggestions of the hypnotist were translated by the patient into representations or ideas that led automatically to corresponding behaviors. Because the elicitation of the behaviors was automatic, they were experienced as unwilled. Thus, the hypnotic subject was still conceptualized as an automaton. Now, however, the automaton was driven by the suggestions of the hypnotist:

> In hypnotism the subject's condition is such that the idea suggested imposes itself with greater or less force upon the mind, and induces the corresponding action by means of a kind of cerebral automatism. (Bernheim, 1886/1900, p. 28)

HYSTERIA, HYPNOSIS, AND CHARCOT

Jean Martin Charcot was one of the most important figures in French neurology in the latter half of the 19th century. After establishing his reputation in neurology, he developed an interest in the role of psychological influences on neurological disorders and, more specifically, an interest in hysteria and its differentiation from epilepsy. At the Salpetrière, a combination chronic care hospital and poor house, Charcot housed together on the same ward women who suffered from epilepsy and those who were diagnosed as hysterics. Consequently, the hysterics had ample opportunity to learn firsthand the components of a good convulsion, as well as other neurological symptoms associated with epilepsy (Drinka, 1984; Ellenberger, 1970).

In many respects, patients labeled as hysterics in the 18th, 19th, and early 20th centuries shared many similarities with earlier demoniacs. They tended to be unhappy women who were socialized into viewing themselves as weak and passive. They were dissatisfied with their lives, socially and economically powerless, hemmed in by numerous social restrictions, and without access to a means of voicing or even conceptualizing their dissatisfactions outside of adopting the role of a sick person (Smith-Rosenberg, 1972). Such a description was particularly true for the poor, uneducated women from lower-class backgrounds who made up the bulk of the hysterics housed at the Salpetrière and who often lived at the hospital for long periods of time (Ellenberger, 1970). Once these women were hospitalized, the social structure of the institution functioned to shape, reward, and maintain skillful and often highly elaborate enactments of the hysterical role. These women, both dependent on and in awe of Charcot and his associates, were attuned to the many cues provided by Charcot's staff concerning the behaviors expected of them. Charcot's staff and students were afraid of displeasing or contradicting him. Therefore, with varying degrees of subtlety, they shaped patients to display the constellation of symptoms that Charcot believed were the intrinsic components of hysteria and of hypnosis as well. The patients, often anxious to please and desirous of being the center of attention, guided their role enactments in terms of the cues provided by the staff.

Charcot prided himself on scientific objectivity and careful observation of symptoms in individual patients. However, for him, objectivity meant observation and recording of discrete behavior with little reference to the social context in which the behavior occurred. Unlike Braid and Bernheim, Charcot never appreciated the profound role played by therapists' expectations in influencing the beliefs and behaviors of their patients (Shorter, 1992; Spanos & Gottlieb, 1979). As Ellenberger (1970) stated it, "a peculiar atmosphere of mutual suggestion developed between Charcot, his collaborators and his patients" (p. 98).

Charcot believed that hysteria was an inherited neurological disease, but that psychological traumas could "shock" the inherently weak nervous system of these patients and thereby generate or exacerbate specific symptoms. Hysteria, he believed, included chronic neurological symptoms such as visual-field deficits, contractures and hemianesthesia, and acute symptoms such as convulsive fits that, in advanced cases, included a highly elaborate display of interrelated symptoms labeled *grand hysteria* (Owen,

1971). The convulsive attacks associated with grand hysteria included three and sometimes four stages. The epileptoid stage came first and usually began with the patient falling backwards and supposedly losing consciousness. Soon the patient entered a tonic phase during which the arms ands legs oscillated violently. This was followed by relaxation. Next came the stage of clownism characterized by bizarre twisting, turning, and acrobatic movements that sometimes culminated in an *arc-de-cercle*, a position in which the patient arched her back upwards and supported herself on her head and heels. The third stage, labeled *passionate attitudes*, was characterized by frightening visions and an odd mimicry during which the patient struck unusual postures such as prayer, anger, or crucifixion. For instance, if during this stage the hypnotist curled the patient's fingers into a fist, the patient was likely to display the corresponding emotion and behave as though she were angry. On the other hand, if her hands were placed into a praying position, the patient was likely to develop a beatific expression. Sometimes a fourth stage characterized by confusion and seeming delirium also occurred (Owen, 1971; Shorter, 1992).

Charcot believed that pressure applied to the ovarian region and to various other points on the body (called hysterogenic points) could elicit full-blown attacks of grand hysteria or could terminate such attacks once they had begun. One of his interns even developed an "ovarian compressor," a kind of girdle worn by patients to suppress hysterical fits (Drinka, 1984; Shorter, 1992).

Charcot experimented with a variety of treatments for hysteria including electricity, magnets, and hypnosis. For instance, he came to believe (and regularly demonstrated in his patients) that hysterical symptoms could be moved with a magnet from one side of the body to the other. It was further believed that hypnotized patients found one pole of a magnet to be pleasing and the other pole frightening. E. Hart (1898), for example, described a demonstration of this phenomenon performed by Luys, a colleague of Charcot's:

> Dr. Luys took into his hand a bar magnet and handed it to the hypnotized Mervel [the patient]. "What do you see," he said, "from the pole?" Presently Mervel's features which up to that moment had been expressive only of stupor, became animated and smiling; he caressesed the end of the magnet with both hands. "Ah," he said with delight, and like a child playing with some beautiful new toy, "see the blue flames; it's blue, the flames are playing about, it is the color of the sky—the color of heaven." Then the bar was reversed, and the opposite end was shown. "Ah," he said, "that's red." His features contracted, his brows were knit, his face was expressive of horror and fright. "Take it away," he said, "it's red; I don't like it, it hurts me." . . . These phenomena, Dr. Luys explained to me, were constant,

and were related to the attractive and repulsive poles of the magnet respectively, and to the colored flames which highly sensitive subjects in the somnambulistic state saw emanating from them. (pp. 60–61)

E. Hart (1898) was skeptical of such demonstrations and went on to show that such displays were due to patients' expectations and desires to please the doctors rather than to any intrinsic effects produced by the magnets themselves. He concluded as follows:

> The whole of these phenomena in all of these patients and subjects were, as might be expected, frauds, impostures, and simulation, originating no doubt, in suggestions made to them, lectures given before them, documents communicated to them, and verbal conspiracies hatched in the waiting-room, carried out in the wards, and cleverly worked up by practice to an extraordinary degree of perfection. (p. 62)

For Charcot, hypnosis, like hysteria, was an indication of a weak nervous system, and he argued that only hysterics could be hypnotized. Grand hypnotism, he believed, included three stages—lethargy, catalepsy, and somnambulism—each with its distinctive symptoms. The behaviors associated with these stages, he argued, did not result from suggestion. Instead, they flowed automatically from changes in the nervous system associated with hypnosis. Some of Charcot's former students and others sympathetic with his views replicated displays of grand hypnotism in their own hospitals. Charcot gave lecture–demonstrations concerning hypnosis and hysteria that featured his star patients enacting their dramatic displays. Many of these lecture–demonstrations were open to reporters and other members of the public. Charcot's ideas became a part of the public domain, and displays of grand hypnotism became the rage among the literary and intellectual elites of Paris. Displays of hysteria and grand hypnotism began to appear not only in hospitals other than the Salpetrière but in theaters and salons as well. A number of popular novels included characters and story plots based on Charcot's idea (Shorter, 1992).

Bernheim (1886/1900), on the other hand, pointed out that none of the many patients that he and his colleagues treated at Nancy displayed such symptoms, and other investigators pointed to the atmosphere of collusion and suggestion that characterized the Salpetrière. For instance, one investigator "had personally observed the patients agreeing on their roles with each other a week in advance" (Shorter, 1992, p. 183). Relatedly, Dingwall (1968, p. 256) described how one of Charcot's most famous hysterical patients confessed not only to faking her performances at the Salpetrière but also to enjoying duping and making fools of the doctors who were taken in by her performances. After observing a number of the weekly public demonstrations of hypnosis given by Charcot, Munthe (1929) concluded as follows:

Many of [Charcot's hypnotic subjects] were mere frauds, knowing quite well what they were expected to do, delighted to perform their various tricks in public, cheating both doctors and audience with the amazing cunning of the hysteriques. The were always eager to "piquer une at-taque" of Charcot's classic grande hysterie, arc-en-ciel and all, or to exhibit his famous three stages of hypnotism: lethargy, catalepsy, som-nambulism, all invented by the Master and hardly ever observed out-side the Salpetrière. (pp. 302–303)

Charcot died unexpectedly in 1893, and by that time medical opinion concerning his ideas about hysteria and hypnosis was, for the most part, negative. By and large, Bernheim's doctrine of suggestion carried the day, and there was general agreement that the bizarre antics played out by patients at the Salpetrière, and at other institutions touched by Charcot's influence, resulted from inadvertent suggestion, surreptitious training, and expectation. The men who gained administrative power at the Salpetrière following Charcot's death were not sympathetic toward his ideas. Rein-forcement and encouragement to patients for enacting the bizarre syn-dromes that constituted grand hysteria and grand hypnotism ceased, and displays of these behaviors rapidly diminished and eventually disappeared altogether (Ellenberger, 1970; Shorter, 1992). Nevertheless, Guillain (1959), as a young medical student at the Salpetrière, described how some of the old hysterical women, hospitalized since the days of Charcot, could be induced for monetary remuneration to enact the hysterical attacks of earlier years.

SUMMARY

For our purposes, three aspects of Charcot's involvement with hysteria and hypnosis are particularly relevant. First, this episode illustrates once again the very strong influence that therapists exert over the beliefs and enactment of their patients. Many of Charcot's star patients were most probably faking at least some aspects of their performances. On the other hand, many of these patients undoubtedly believed themselves to be suf-fering from a disorder labeled as hysteria and defined their own bizarre performances to themselves in the same way that the doctors defined their performances. Like modern hypnotic subjects who use their attentional and imaginal abilities to develop experiences that are congruent with the be-haviors they enact, many of Charcot's subjects probably used the same abilities to convince themselves as well as their doctors that they really experienced the subjective components of the symptoms they so skillfully enacted under his tutelage.

The second important lesson of this historical episode is its illustra-tion of the extent to which therapists can allow themselves to be fooled by performances that they themselves are responsible for creating in their patients. By focusing exclusively on what his patients did, and ignoring the context in which they did it, Charcot was misled into believing that socially created enactments and experiences were really the symptoms of a functional neurological disorder. Moreover, Charcot was misled in this way despite the fact that cues communicated by him during his own interactions with his patients were one of the major sources of information used by them to generate their enactments. At least in part, Charcot was misled because of his own theoretical formulations. Because he assumed that hysterical symptoms were the expression of an innate neurological weakness, he failed to attend to the very obvious social contingencies that guided his patients' enactments.

Finally, this episode illustrates the importance of professional status in legitimating socially generated enactments as symptoms of disease. Not surprisingly, Charcot greatly influenced the opinions and attitudes displayed by his students and close colleagues toward hysteria and hypnosis. However, Charcot's influence extended well beyond the Salpetrière. Following his clinical demonstrations and public presentations, both grand hysteria and grand hypnotism were seen at hospitals in various parts of Europe and were transmitted to the general public in the form of newspaper stories, plays, and novels (Shorter, 1992). Thus, within a relatively short period of time, complex sets of behaviors that were obviously contextually generated social products entered the public consciousness as the automatically occurring symptoms of a strange disease.

When looked at from the distance of a century, it is easy to see that grand hysteria and grand hypnosis were contextually supported social products that were shaped by the diagnostic and therapeutic practices of the attending physicians and that were legitimated as "real diseases" by the authority and reputation of Charcot. All of this should be kept in mind when examining MPD. Like Charcot's grand hysteria, MPD is a contextually supported social product that is shaped by diagnostic practices and legitimated as a "real disease" by psychiatric authority.

16

FROM DUAL CONSCIOUSNESS TO MULTIPLE PERSONALITY

As described earlier, cases in which patients appeared to display and alternate between more than one consciousness were reported during the first half of the 19th century, and many of these cases were associated with magnetism and magnetic spiritism. In the last quarter of the 19th century, particularly in France and the United States, "dual consciousness" began to be relabeled as multiple personality, and the number of such cases increased dramatically. A number of factors played a role in the development of these trends. One of these factors was the use of multiple personality by positivist philosophers to discredit rival philosophical positions (Hacking, 1992; Sutcliffe & Jones, 1962). Another was a renewed interest in spiritism that began to develop around mid-century and that reflected a reaction against Darwinism and the materialism on which it was based (Decker, 1986; Ellenberger, 1970).

POSITIVIST PHILOSOPHY

As described by Hacking (1986, 1992), positivist psychologists in the late 19th century were intent on establishing a materialist basis for the soul. The neo-Kantians, against whom the positivists struggled, maintained notions of a transcendental unity of apperception, and transcendental self and will. According to these views, the self or "I" referred to in such statements as "I think" was a necessary requirement for objective thought, perception, and freedom of will. Personality was attributed to a soul, and the soul was considered indivisible. The existence of persons with two or more personalities, two or more distinct, thinking "I's" with amnesia for one another, challenged the notion of a single, transcendental consciousness and was thereby used as support for the positivist alternative (Roth, 1989).

When these philosophical disputes became heated in the last quarter of the 19th century, Eugene Azam, a surgeon from Bordeaux with an interest in hypnosis, resurrected an old case of double consciousness with amnesia that he had treated with hypnosis 15 years previously. The case involved a teenage girl named Felida who passed back and forth between a depressed, neurotic personality who displayed the usual symptoms of hysteria to a cheerful, lively second state. Unfortunately, little information is available concerning the conditions under which Felida began to display her second personality. Typically, however, the switch from one personality to another involved Felida falling into a deep sleep from which she purportedly could not be awakened and that lasted for 2 or 3 minutes (Roth, 1989). As we saw earlier, the interspersion of sleep during the transition between personalities was a common characteristic of mid-19th-century cases of dual consciousness. The presence of this characteristic in Felida's case suggests that her other symptoms may also have been shaped by prevailing popular notions concerning displays of dual consciousness.

Shortly after Azam's publication of this case, other investigators began "recognizing" the same pattern of symptoms in their own earlier patients (Hacking, 1986, 1992). Thereafter, Janet (1907, 1925) and others used hypnotic procedures to "discover" and name hidden personalities in their hysterical patients. The highly leading character of these hypnotic interviews is illustrated by Janet's (1886) interaction with a 19-year-old female hysteric called "L" (i.e., Lucy). L displayed all of the dramatic symptoms of grand hysteria and was also an excellent hypnotic subject. During the cataleptic stage of grand hypnotism, she exhibited the mimicry that characterized passionate attitudes. For instance, when Janet closed her fingers into a fist, L's demeanor took on the appearance of rage and her arm struck out. In short, L was a well-trained hypnotic subject who was attuned to the expectations of the doctors who tested her. While in catalepsy, L supposedly could not hear or speak. She could, however, write. During her fourth hypnotic session with Janet, the following exchange occurred:

Q: [From Janet:] Do you hear me?
A: [She wrote:] No.
Q: But in order to answer you have to be able to hear.

A: Yes, absolutely.
Q: So somebody's got to be hearing me, right?
A: Yes.
Q: Who's that?
A: Somebody other than L.
Q: Good! Another person. Shall we call her Blanche?
A: OK, Blanche.
Q: Well . . . Blanche, do you hear me?
A: Yes. (Janet, 1886, p. 589)

As this exchange makes clear, "Blanche" was a social creation generated by L in response to Janet's (1886) leading interrogation. In another case, a hysteric treated by Janet had been earlier trained to exhibit double consciousness and secondary personality by magnetists who used her as a medium in public demonstrations of somnambulism (Owen, 1971). In short, the cases of multiple personality "discovered" by Janet and other French psychiatrists at the end of the 19th century did not arise *sui generis* in a social vacuum. Like the grand hysteria with which they were often associated, these cases reflected an interaction between shaping provided by therapists and patients who were both eager to please and often already well acquainted with the process of molding symptoms to meet the expectations of their doctors (Shorter, 1992).

Janet was, of course, associated with Charcot and the Salpetrière. Following Charcot's death, the new administrators at the Salpetrière were hostile to Janet's ideas. Both hysteria and hypnosis came increasingly to be explained in terms of suggestion and malingering in mainstream French psychiatry, and by the end of the century cases of multiple personality, like cases of grand hysteria, were on the decline in France (Hacking, 1992; Shorter, 1992).

Despite the waning influence of his ideas in France, Janet (1907) had a strong, albeit temporary influence on thinking about multiple personality in the United States. Early in the 20th century, he gave a series of invited lectures at Harvard University. There he alluded to the importance of multiple personality in the struggle between positivist and theological worldviews by describing Asam's famous patient Felida:

Allow me to make you acquainted with Felida. She is a very remarkable personage who has played a rather important part in the history of ideas. . . . Her history was the great argument of which the positivist psychologists made use at the time of the heroic struggles against the spiritualistic dogmatism of Cousin's school. But for Felida, it is not certain that there would be a professorship at the Collège de France and that I should be here speaking to you on the mental state of hystericals. (p. 78)

SPIRITISM AND MULTIPLE PERSONALITY

As indicated earlier, by the latter half of the 19th century, materialism had become the dominant scientific ideology, and in biology the materialist ideology was reflected in the Darwinian revolution (Kenny, 1981; Webb, 1974). The Darwinian theory of evolution held that humans were descended from earlier animals. One implication of these ideas was that the nervous system, like other organ systems, exhibited evolutionary continuity, and another was that consciousness and other psychological characteristics were epiphenomenal reflections of neurological functioning. Within this system, there was no room for a transcendent soul that survived death.

For many philosophers and scientists, as well as lay people, these ideas were extremely troubling, challenging as they did fundamental, widely accepted, and often taken-for-granted notions concerning religion and the existence of an afterlife (R. L. Moore, 1977; Webb, 1974). One reaction to the unsettling nature of these materialistic claims, and to the loss of prestige and authority suffered by traditional religious institutions in the 19th century, was an upsurge in the popularity of spiritism that began around the middle of the century.

In 1848, the Hydesville, New York, home of John and Margaret Fox and their two daughters was troubled by strange rapping noises. It soon became clear to Mr. and Mrs. Fox that the rappings stemmed from some disincarnate intelligence and that their daughters, ages 11 and 13, served as mediums for this intelligence. It was soon discovered that the disincarnate intelligence was the spirit of a deceased person and that questions asked of the spirit through one of the Fox sisters would receive an answer in a preestablished code of rappings. News of the rappings spread rapidly, and soon the Fox sisters were giving public demonstrations of their mediumistic talents to huge and enthusiastic audiences. New mediums quickly modeled themselves on the Fox sisters, and within a few years spiritism became immensely popular not only in America but in Europe as well (Brandon, 1984; Podmore, 1902). Eventually, the Fox sisters were exposed as frauds, and one of them confessed in some detail how they created the rapping sounds by "cracking" their fingers and toes. Neither the exposure nor the confession had a noticeable impact on the spread of spiritism, one of the most prominent social movements to occur in America in the decade before the Civil War (Brandon, 1984; R. L. Moore, 1977).

The cumbersome practice of communicating with spirits through rappings soon gave way to the direct possession of the medium by a spirit. The process became quickly standardized and usually involved the medium becoming possessed by a spirit guide or control. The spirit guide functioned as an intermediary to the spirit world. During a seance it was the spirit guide speaking through the medium who made contacts in the spirit world with the particular spirits with whom the sitter wished to communicate.

Frequently, 19th-century spirit guides were American Indians. As in cross-cultural displays of possession, where different mediums are possessed by the same spirit, many 19th-century mediums used the same relatively small coterie of Indian spirit guides (Brandon, 1984; R. L. Moore, 1977). The historical reasons that spirit guides were Indians is not entirely clear, although Brandon (1984) suggested that the practice might have been related to the possession by Indian spirits that was common in Shaker communities in the first half of the 19th century.

Mediumship clearly involved the creation of multiple identities. Moreover, like many instances of cross-cultural possession, and many modern cases of MPD, the regular and repeated possession of the medium often continued throughout his or her life. Typically, possession involved mediums taking on the mannerisms, personality, and vocal inflections of the particular spirit who possessed them, and following possession episodes the mediums usually claimed amnesia for the experience. Sometimes possessing spirits wrote rather than spoke messages for which the medium claimed amnesia, and this practice of "automatic writing" was later incorporated into the hypnotic performances of MPD patients.

Mediumship became a profession that was sometimes lucrative, and for women it offered a rare opportunity for social mobility and financial independence outside of marriage (R. L. Moore, 1977). Of course, successful mediumship required that the medium provide the sitter with a convincing display of possession, and this in turn required the medium to obtain all possible information about the sitter and the sitter's earthly relationship with the deceased who was to be contacted in the spirit world. Obtaining such information involved such techniques as "reading" the sitter's verbal and nonverbal responses to ambiguous communications, in order to gradually develop an increasingly full and accurate picture of the deceased that could then be fed back to the sitter. Frequently, sitters who traveled in the same social circles used the same spirit medium, and this afforded the medium an opportunity to obtain information and gossip about her other clients and their deceased friends and relatives (Kenny, 1981). Also involved were more clearly fraudulent practices such as using confederates to obtain information about clients or the circulating of information about common clients by cooperating mediums (Brandon, 1984).

As the 19th century progressed, manifestations of "physical mediumship" became increasingly prominent. Physical mediumship involved some material manifestation of the spirit that proved the spirit's existence. For example, the medium might be tied up and placed in a box in a corner of a darkened séance room. After a few minutes, while sitters sat holding hands around a table, a luminous figure would emerge from the box, walk about the room, and perhaps touch one or more of the sitters. The figure would then return to the box. Later, when the lights were turned on, the sitters would find the medium still tied up in the box. Supposedly, the efforts of the medium allowed the spirit to materialize by developing an ectoplasmic body that was visible to the sitters during the séance. With the invention and popularization of photography, spirit photographs also became popular (Brandon, 1984).

Ectoplasmic spirit bodies, spirit photographs, and other physical manifestations of mediumship were, of course, fraudulent (Brandon, 1984; T. H. Hall, 1984). These manifestations could occur only because the mediums were aware of the effects they wished to achieve and arranged the props, confederates, and complex sequences required to create the desired impressions. For instance, mediums sometimes provided one another with the written recipes required to create a luminous, diaphorous impression while role-playing a materialized spirit. One such recipe required 22 yards of gauzy, white silk that was to be washed in a prescribed manner and then treated with various oils, varnish, and luminous paint (Brandon, 1984). In short, physical mediumship illustrates very clearly the goal-directed and rule-guided nature of mediumistic performances. These performances could be brought about only through coordination and planning that occurred well before the actual performance. Physical mediums and mental mediums (those through whom spirits spoke) were, of course, often the same people. One does not have to posit arcane or complex unconscious mental processes to account for how mediums manifested the spirit identities required during séances. These individuals enacted their spirit roles in the same way that actors enact their stage roles. Did these mediums become convinced by their own enactments and actually believe themselves to be possessed? Perhaps some did hold such beliefs at least part of the time, but the manifestations of physical mediumship certainly suggest that many mediums were quite willing to purposefully deceive their audiences and were well aware of their own participation in these deceptions.

As indicated above, the spiritualist movement that flowered in the second half of the 19th century had numerous antecedents including the earlier spiritualist ideas associated with Mesmerism, Swedenborgianism, and various other religious sects popular in the first half of that century (Gauld, 1992; R. L. Moore, 1977; Shortt, 1984; Webb, 1974). Moreover, this movement became quickly allied with a wide range of other social movements. In Britain, for example, spiritism became associated with Owenite socialism, and in the United States the movement was allied with the women's rights, abolition, utopian socialism, and other radical social movements (Kerr, 1972; R. L. Moore, 1977; Shortt, 1984; Webb, 1974).

Although spiritism was, at least in part, a reaction against the materialism that dominated scientific thinking, it gained much of its appeal through claims of a scientific basis. Unlike traditional religions that based their doctrines on revelation and ancient authority, the adherents of spiritism claimed to offer scientific proof (the materializations and discourses of departed spirits) of the survival of bodily death and of the moral coherence of the universe (Hynes, 1968).

For advocates of scientific materialism, the proofs offered by spiritism were branded as bogus, and the mediums themselves were dismissed as either charlatans or mentally deranged (Shortt, 1984). For other investigators, however, the demonstrations of spiritism offered at least the possibility that the dogma of materialism might be overthrown. Some of these investigators, like Henry Sidgwick, Edmund Gurney, and Fredrick Myers, had grown up in religious households. They struggled to retain some semblance of religious belief, but their exposure to science left them racked with religious doubts (Webb, 1974). In 1882, Sidgwick, Gurney, and Myers, along with others, established in Britain the Society for Psychical Research (SPR). The purpose of the SPR was to examine with scientific rigor those phenomena that appeared to challenge materialist assumptions. As described by Brandon (1984),

> Thus the SPR was from the first involved in the quest for a peculiarly ninteenth-century grail: positive and intellectually acceptable proof of immortality cleared of any association with fraud or humbug. Spiritism seemed to offer a path to this goal; it was therefore hard to resist, even though humbug, fraud and triviality were associated with a good deal of spiritism. (p. 88)

The establishment of the SPR coincided with a broader neoromantic rebellion against materialism and its emphasis on manifest appearances (Decker, 1986; Ellenberger, 1970; Webb, 1974). Within the Catholic church, this rebellion was manifested as a renewed emphasis on the miraculous, which included the legitimation of apparitions of the Virgin Mary and subsequent miraculous healings, stigmatics who bled on holy days, nuns who purportedly lived for long periods eating nothing but an occasional communion wafer, and a reemphasis on such mystical dogma as the Virgin Mary's bodily assumption into heaven (Drinka, 1984; Zimdars-Swartz, 1991). Outside of the Catholic church came a renewed interest in Eastern religions and mystical traditions and the establishment of underground religions that emphasized magical beliefs and practices. Jewish mystical writings and study of the Cabala also gained a new popularity. Philosophers, poets, novelists, and artists like Nietzsche, Dostoevsky, and Verlaine emphasized the irrational and the hidden meanings behind external appearances. Occult movements like Theosophy, the Rosecrucians, and the Order of the Golden Dawn, which claimed to possess hidden truths, flourished (Webb, 1974).

For the neoromanticists, phenomena like automatisms, mysticism, amnesia, somnambulism and multiple personality implied unconscious functioning, self-deception, and a hidden reality beneath manifest appearances. Consequently, these phenomena seemed to underscore the limitations of materialist philosophy. The neoromantic reaction against materialism helped to spawn a popular literature that focused on hypnosis and multiple personality. Thus, George Du Maurier's (1894) *Trilby* introduced the evil Svengali who hypnotically controlled the mind of the innocent heroine, and the topic of multiple personality was treated in such works as Oscar Wilde's (1890) *The Picture of Dorian Grey*, Paul Lindau's (1893) *The Other*, and most famous of all, Robert Louis Stevenson's (1886) *The Strange Case of Dr. Jekyll and Mr. Hyde*. All of these works focused on antimaterialist themes emphasized by the neoromaticists—the role of the irrational in human activity, and a hidden aspect of mental functioning that could be influenced by hypnosis, or that manifested itself in terms of a second personality with motives and desires that were hidden from normal awareness.

The phenomena investigated by the SPR, like those emphasized by the neoromaticists, were those that seemed to challenge the assumptions of materialism. Included were purported displays of telepathy and clairvoyance as well as spirit mediumship, automatic writing, hypnosis, and multiple personality. These phenomena were, of course, interrelated and often displayed by the same subjects. As indicated above, mesmerism and later hypnosis had long been associated with mediumship as well as with purported displays of unusual sensory and cognitive feats including telepathy and clairvoyance. In addition, the similarities between mediumship and cases of multiple personality were obvious. Both were associated with hypnosis, and in both cases the subjects were often diagnosed as hysterics, displayed personalities other than their own, and later claimed amnesia for the performances of their alter personalities.

To account for these interrelated phenomena, F. W. H. Myers (1903/1975) developed the notion of the subliminal self. According to Myers (1903/1975), the subliminal self was a region of the mind below normal consciousness. Not only did the subliminal self have an existence separate from normal consciousness, but it also survived bodily death. The inferior functions of the subliminal self included the amnesias and automatisms associated with psychopathology. However, its superior functions included creativity and were manifested in works of genius that involved an uprush of sentiments and feelings from below normal consciousness. Purportedly, hypnosis and suggestion produced their effects by influencing the subliminal region, and through this region communication with spirits of the dead was also sometimes possible.

For F. W. H. Myers (1903/1975), phenomena like multiple personality, spirit possession, and religious ecstasy fell on a continuum that reflected the extent to which the subliminal self intruded into waking life. Myers's (1903/1975) views received a sympathetic hearing from none other than William James (1909), the preeminent figure in late 19th- and early

20th-century American psychology. James viewed hysterics as incipient mediums who were subject to pathological dissociations and multiple personality and who were particularly likely to have their subliminal regions open to spirit influences (Kenny, 1981). James (1909) and other turn-of-the-century psychical researchers (e.g., Flournoy, 1900; Podmore, 1902) were well aware that the spirit personalities exhibited by mediums were influenced by tacit understandings, social expectation, and sometimes outright fraud. Nevertheless, for James and others, the important issue was whether test situations could be created that would enable actual spirit communications to be reliably differentiated from artificial social creations (R. L. Moore, 1977).

Doris

Because multiple personality and mediumship were seen as related, the possibility of spirit influence was raised in cases of MPD as well as in cases of mediumship. For example, one of the most extensively documented early 20th-century cases of MPD involved an imaginative adolescent patient of W. F. Prince (1915, 1916) given the pseudonym Doris. Prince was an Episcopal rector who took Doris into his home after the death of her mother. Prince had an interest in multiple personality before meeting Doris, kept psychological works on MPD around the house, and probably discussed them in Doris's presence. Moreover, Doris had become aware of the literature on MPD before revealing her alter personalities to Prince (Kenny, 1981).

Doris often took afternoon naps in Prince's home, and Prince became aware of her multiplicity by conversing with her while she was supposedly asleep. The extensive mutual shaping carried out between Prince and Doris that led to the "discovery" of her several personalities has been documented by Kenny (1981) and will not be detailed here. Prince's (1916) original description of Doris was entirely naturalistic. However, both Prince and Doris came increasingly to be influenced by the work of J. H. Hyslop (1918), a philosopher from Columbia University who argued that many people thought to be insane were actually the recipients of intruding spirits (Powell, 1980). Hyslop visited Prince early in the development of Doris's multiple identities, and during this time one of her personalities began to display apparent clairvoyance and other indications of spirit infestation (Kenny, 1981). Both Hyslop and Prince became convinced that Doris's case could be accounted for adequately only in terms of the spiritist hypothesis, and Hyslop (1917) even took Doris to consult with a medium who called up the spirits of William James and other departed psychical researchers as case consultants. Doris manifested evidence of "spirit infestation" for the rest of her life, and Hyslop used her case repeatedly in his attempts to overthrow materialism (Powell, 1980).

Miss Beauchamp

The best-known turn-of-the-century American case of multiple personality by far was Morton Prince's (1905/1920) famous Miss Beauchamp. M. Prince (1905) (no relation to W. F. Prince of the Doris case) offered a completely naturalistic account of his famous patient and, in fact, appears to have prevented some of his more spiritualistically oriented colleagues from investigating paranormal abilities in Miss Beauchamp (Hyslop, 1917). Nevertheless, both M. Prince and his patient were enmeshed in social circles where mediums and spiritism were taken quite seriously, and both found it natural to use the imagery of possession and exorcism when describing Miss Beauchamp's experiences. For example, M. Prince (1905/1920) pointed out that Miss Beauchamp "regarded herself as 'possessed' in much the same sense as it is said in the Bible that a person is 'possessed'" (p. 119). Despite Prince's own naturalistic account of his patient, other investigators were inclined to view the Beauchamp case in terms of spirit possession. William McDougall (1920), for example, James' successor at Harvard, believed that one of Miss Beauchamp's personalities was a spiritual being. He spelled out the implications of the Beauchamp case and cases of spirit mediumship as follows:

> If a number of cases of the type of Sally Beauchamp were to be described by other equally credible observers, I think that the weight of their testimony would be irresistible. This conclusion would give strong support to the spiritist explanation of such cases as Mrs. Piper [a well-known Boston spirit medium studied by William James], and would go far to justify the belief in the survival of human personality after the death of the body. (McDougall, 1907, p. 430)

McDougall's equating of multiple personality and spirit mediumship as twin phenomena for shedding light on the survival of bodily death illustrates the role played by cases of MPD in the struggle conducted by a relatively small but influential group of scientists against the materialistic underpinnings of turn-of-the-century science. Ultimately, these scientists were unsuccessful. Materialism carried the day to such an extent[1] that, from a late 20th-century perspective, it is difficult to comprehend the seriousness

---

[1] *A note on contemporary North American spiritism*: Although less common than previously, spirit mediums continue to operate in many North American cities. Biscop (1981, 1985) conducted a long-term participant observation study of a spiritist church in Canada and documented the process by which novices were socialized into the role of medium. Part of the socialization process involved formal teaching, but much of it involved repeated opportunities to observe more experienced mediums, coupled with encouragement in small group settings where novices were informed that mediumship takes time, and where they were provided with helpful feedback for improving their performance. Mediumship may also involve learning how to "read" the client to obtain information about the deceased that can then be fed back to the client as proof of the deceased's survival.

Biscop conducted interviews with six North American mediums and questioned them at length about their backgrounds. Most reported relatively happy childhoods and in marked contrast to modern MPD patients only one reported that she had been sexually abused as a child.

with which highly respected turn-of-the-century investigators studied spirit mediums and psychiatric patients as a means of demonstrating the existence of an afterlife. The incredulity of modern investigators in this regard was prophesied by G. Stanley Hall (1918) as scientific interest in the study of mediumship and multiple personality together went into decline:

> Psychic researchers to-day represent the last potent stand of about all the old superstitions of the past, against which science has contended. The next generation will be hardly able to believe that prominent men in this wasted their energies chasing such a will-of-the wisp as the veracity of messages of the reality of a post-mortem existence, which they can no more prove than dreams of levitation prove that man can hover in the air at will. (p. 154)

SUMMARY

The rise in prominence of the multiple personality diagnosis in the last quarter of the 19th century had multiple causes. One of these was the use of the diagnosis by positivist investigators to discredit competing philosophical positions. Paradoxically, another was the use of the diagnosis by those who struggled against scientific materialism and its implication of a world without transcendental meaning. In France, the multiple personality diagnosis gained much of its prominence through the work of Janet. Janet, however, was associated with Charcot and thereby, rightly or wrongly, with the excesses of the Salpetrière in the matters of hysteria and hypnosis. Following Charcot's death, the new administrators of the Salpetrière distanced themselves as best they could from Charcot's work on hysteria. Displays of grand hysteria by patients were discouraged and quickly ceased to occur. Hysteria, hypnotic phenomena, and by extension multiple personality were explained in terms of suggestion, and Janet's ideas were given no official support. By the end of the century, the diagnosis of MPD had again become rare in France (Decker, 1986).

In the United States, Janet's ideas about dissociation and Myers's ideas about a subliminal self were used together in the study of hysteria, hypnosis, multiple personality, and spirit mediumship. At the beginning of the 20th century, these phenomena were seen by several prominent investigators as falling on a continuum and as providing evidence for the existence of a nonmaterial consciousness that survived death. Fraud, suggestion, and interpersonal shaping by interested investigators were identified by critics of both mediumship and multiple personality as variables that accounted adequately for these phenomena. Proponents argued in turn that such accounts were inadequate. Never far from the surface in these controversies were the implications of these phenomena for the assumptions underlying scientific materialism. With the death of William James in 1910, the antimaterialists lost their most respected academic voice, and within academic psychology, J. B. Watson (1913) soon initiated the behaviorist revolution that relegated consciousness as irrelevant to scientific investigation. Materialist assumptions became as intrenched in psychology and psychiatry as in the "hard" sciences of physics and chemistry. Scientific interest in both MPD and mediumship had waned by the beginning of the second quarter of the 20th century, and this waning of interest was closely related to the largely undisputed acceptance of scientific materialism as the worldview underlying mainstream medicine, psychiatry, and psychology.

17

THE HISTORY OF DISSOCIATION

In the second half of the 19th century, railroads cut across the faces of both Europe and America. Rail travel became a common, although sometimes dangerous, undertaking. Railway accidents were much more common than today, and the injuries that resulted from these accidents had important ramifications for the emerging discipline of psychiatry (Drinka, 1984). Victims of railway accidents were often quick to sue the railroads for damages, and consequently, insurance companies took an interest in determining whether the symptoms that followed an accident reflected actual physical injury, were produced by "psychological shocks" such as fear engendered by the accident, or were due simply to malingering. The neurologists of the day disagreed on the issue of whether ideas associated with some frightening experience could produce physical symptoms. Charcot, however, lent his considerable prestige to the hypothesis that traumatic emotional "shocks" to the nervous system could give rise to mental events that, in turn, produced hysterical symptoms (Drinka, 1984; Sulloway, 1979).

TRAUMATIC HYSTERIA

Along with his diagnosis of grand hysteria, Charcot also espoused the notion of traumatic hysteria. The symptoms of traumatic hysteria were similar to those of grand hysteria in including such manifestations as anesthesias, paralyses, and disturbances of the senses. Unlike the symptoms of grand hysteria, however, those of traumatic hysteria followed closely on a specifiable trauma (e.g., a railway accident). Nevertheless, the trauma suffered by the patient was not seen as directly producing the symptoms. Instead, the trauma was thought to give rise to an overpowering idea, and the idea then expressed itself in a corresponding physical symptom. Charcot (1889) gave as an example a patient who lost consciousness after being struck by a laundry wagon. The patient woke several days later to find himself in the hospital. He remembered nothing of the accident but was told by others what had happened. The patient came to believe (inaccurately) that the wheels of the van had run over his legs, and, as a result of this vivid but inaccurate idea, he developed a paralysis of the legs.

Janet (1920) summarized Charcot's ideas about the psychological origins of traumatic hysteria as follows:

> Charcot, studying the paralyses, had shown that the disease is not produced by a real accident, but by the idea of this accident. It is not necessary that the carriage wheel should really have passed over the patient; it is enough if he has the idea that the wheel passed over his legs. (p. 324)

The mechanism by which the frightening idea was transformed into a physical symptom Charcot (1889) labeled *realization*. Realization was hypothesized as occurring unconsciously. Moreover, the traumatic idea that was realized in hysterical symptoms was itself isolated from other ideas in consciousness. Charcot believed that the emotion or "nervous shock" that occurred at the time of a trauma created a hypnoticlike condition. He further believed that hypnosis was a state different from normal consciousness, and that the ideas that occurred during hypnosis remained isolated from the ideas of normal consciousness. Thus, the ideas that occurred during a trauma-induced hypnotic-like state were isolated from normal consciousness, and therefore, neither these isolated ideas nor the physical symptoms to which they automatically gave rise were influenced by the will of the patient or by the ideas and memories associated with normal consciousness.

Charcot (1889) supported his ideas concerning traumatic hysteria by demonstrating that hysterical symptoms could be produced through suggestion in hypnotic patients. He assumed that hypnotically suggested symptoms of, say, motor paralysis or sensory loss were equivalent to hysterical symptoms of motor paralysis and sensory loss. Moreover, he held that the cause of the symptoms in both hypnosis and traumatic hysteria was the same: ideas occurring in a hypnotic condition that were separated from normal consciousness and, because of their isolation, realized in corresponding physical symptoms. In hypnosis, the ideas giving rise to the symptoms were suggested by the hypnotist. In traumatic hysteria, the traumatic event led to the emotion that produced the hypnoticlike state and also operated much like a suggestion. The traumatic event led to the idea (of, say, paralysis) that in turn produced the corresponding symptom.

For a time, Charcot's (1889) ideas concerning traumatic hysteria were extremely influential. Not only did they form the basis for Janet's (1907, 1925) notion of dissociation, but they also influenced Breuer's very similar ideas concerning symptom formation in hypnoid (i.e., hypnoticlike) states (Macmillan, 1991). Breuer was, of course, Freud's early collaborator and senior author of their joint monograph "Studies on Hysteria" (Breuer & Freud, 1895/1964). Like Charcot, Breuer believed that the memories of earlier perceptions that occurred in hypnoid states could be compared to parasites that were dissociated from normal consciousness and that manifested themselves in terms of periodic hallucinations, contortions, and other hysterical symptoms.

Janet (1907, 1925) elaborated Charcot's ideas into the concept of dissociation: the notion that, in hysterically predisposed people, interrelated sets of ideas sometimes split off (become dissociated from) the larger interrelated set of ideas that constitute normal consciousness. According to Janet, the root cause of dissociation was an inherent weakness in the nervous system of hysterics that led to a narrowing or restriction in consciousness. Supposedly, traumatic events narrowed consciousness still further, and the frightening perceptions and memories associated with the trauma were thereby excluded from the dominant consciousness. These split-off ideas then formed a second consciousness. The manifestations of this second consciousness were experienced by the dominant consciousness as involuntary symptoms. Moreover, the two consciousnesses could be active simultaneously. Therefore, it was possible for an observer to communicate with both of them simultaneously and through independent channels. For instance, the hypnotist might question one consciousness directly while the second consciousness, through the medium of automatic writing, expressed different thoughts. By extension, this idea also led to the notion that one or more "hidden consciousnesses" could acquire information independently of the dominant consciousness. For instance, "Sally," one of the alter personalities of M. Prince's (1905/1920) famous Miss Beauchaump, often claimed to be co-conscious with Miss Beauchaump's primary personality. Thus, while the primary personality engaged in one complex task (e.g., composing a letter), "Sally" claimed that she was often engaged in some quite different task. Some modern MPD proponents appear to take this notion of simultaneously operating consciousnesses seriously. For instance, such investigators occasionally communicate with all of a patient's alter personalities simultaneously by addressing "everyone inside" (Kluft, 1992). Because modern MPD patients purportedly possess an average of 15 or so personalities, this procedure is premised on the idea that the information transmitted by the therapist of such a patient is being simultaneously processed and understood by 15 or so independent cognitive systems or states.

Although Freud flirted with the idea of hypnoid states as causes of hysterical symptoms, he eventually abandoned that notion along with Janet's notion of dissociation. Despite Freud's rejection, the idea common to Charcot, Janet, and Breuer that trauma gives rise to a hypnoid state that isolates or dissociates the traumatic memories from normal consciousness is of more than historical interest. After a long period of neglect that spanned most of the present century, this notion has been resurrected by modern MPD theorists to serve as an explanation for the forgetting of early memories of abuse and for the genesis of alter personalities. Consequently, it is worth a brief digression to review how modern evidence concerning hypnosis and hysteria bears on the validity of this idea.

EXAMINING THE HYPNOID-STATE HYPOTHESIS

The hypnoid-state hypothesis is based on the following ideas: (a) Hypnosis is a distinct and identifiable state of consciousness that differs from normal consciousness. (b) The memories that are formed in hypnotic states are isolated from information in normal consciousness. This idea has three implications. First, the termination of the hypnotic state will lead automatically to amnesia; once the person has regained normal consciousness, he or she will be unable to recall the events associated with hypnosis. Second, the dissociated memories will not be influenced by what occurs in normal consciousness. Third, information can be processed by two or more consciousnesses (i.e., alters) simultaneously and without interference. (c) Traumatic events induce a hypnoid state that, in turn, is associated with massive forgetting of the traumatic events when the person returns to normal consciousness. (d) The sensory losses, motor paralyses, and other symptoms induced by suggestion during hypnosis and by trauma in hysteria are equivalent. Moreover, these are, in fact, real perceptual and motor incapacities over which subjects can exercise little if any control.

Some of the evidence relating to the validity of these propositions was reviewed in chapters 2, 3, and 4. As described in those chapters, there is no good evidence to support the hypothesis that hypnotic responding involves a distinct altered state of consciousness (e.g., Barber et al., 1974; Fellows, 1986). Of particular importance to modern conceptions of MPD, however, is the notion that memories occurring in "hypnoid states" remain segregated from other information in memory.

The Segregation of "Dissociated Memories"

Contrary to the theorizing of some modern MPD proponents, it is well-known that the termination of hypnotic procedures rarely results in reports of having forgotten the hypnotic events (i.e., amnesia), unless the amnesia is directly suggested (Barber, 1969). Moreover, even when amnesia is suggested and subjects claim an inability to recall, the hypnotic memories do not remain isolated from nonhypnotic memories. As pointed out in chapter 4, by exposing subjects who report posthypnotic amnesia to expectations or social pressure to recall, amnesia can be breached without rehypnotizing the subjects (Coe, 1989). It is worth adding that this is not a new finding. Bernheim was well aware that previously hypnotized subjects could be induced to recall their purportedly forgotten hypnotic memories. In fact, Bernheim demonstrated this phenomenon to Freud during a visit by Freud to Bernheim's clinic at Nancy. Bernheim's demonstration was one of the reasons that Freud abandoned the hypnoid-state hypothesis of hysterical symptom formation (Macmillan, 1991). The fact that subjects can recall purportedly dissociated memories without the use of hypnotic procedures runs counter to the idea that the dissociated memories are isolated from the memory processes that occur outside of hypnotic situations.

The idea that memories acquired during a hypnotic session remain segregated from other information in memory was first tested experimentally over 60 years ago by Hull (1933) and his students. Hull concluded that hypnotic memories are not segregated from nonhypnotic ones. Instead, hypnotic memories influence and are influenced by other information stored in memory. Hull's experimental work was one of the reasons given by later investigators (R. W. White, 1941) for rejecting dissociation as an explanation of hypnotic responding.

Although Hull's (1933) experimental procedures can be criticized on a number of methodological grounds, a large number of more recent (and often more methodologically sophisticated) studies have confirmed his findings (see Coe, 1989, for a review). Most of these studies have used proactive and retroactive interference procedures to assess the isolation of hypnotic memories. A hypothetical example can illustrate the logic behind these studies.

Suppose one group of subjects is presented with a word list that consists of city names (list B) . Subjects in a second group are presented with a different list of city names (list A). Later, subjects in the second group are presented with list B. Finally, subjects in both groups are asked to recall the city names on list B. Subjects in the first group (who were presented only with list B) exhibit better recall of this list than subjects in the second group (who were presented with list A before list B). Subjects in the second group exhibit a decrement in recall because the city names presented on list A interfere with their ability to recall the city names on list B. This phenomenon is labeled *proactive interference*.

Now, suppose we also have a third group of highly hypnotizable hypnotic subjects. These subjects are also presented with two lists of city names. However, the first list (list A) is presented during a hypnotic session, and subjects are given suggestions to be amnesic for the list. Following termination of the hypnotic procedures (while still amnesic for list A), subjects are presented with list B and then asked to recall it. If list A, for which the subjects are purportedly amnesic, is really dissociated from other memorial processes, these subjects should be able to recall list B without showing evidence of proactive interference. In fact, studies using this general paradigm indicate that even highly hypnotizable hypnotic subjects who claim amnesia for the first list exhibit as much proactive interference as they would have in the absence of hypnotic amnesia (e.g., Dillon & Spanos, 1983). Other studies using the related phenomenon of retroactive interference have consistently obtained similar results (Coe, 1989). In short, the empirical evidence is clear and consistent. Events covered by hypnotic amnesia are not isolated from other events in memory. Instead, these events interfere with other information and are interfered with by other information in memory. Among other things, these findings clearly contradict the notion that memories of early abuse can be recalled accurately and in pristine form because hypnoidal isolation prevents them from being interfered with by other memories.

The memory interference studies just discussed were conducted with college students, and it is always possible to argue that the dissociations that segregate the memories of MPD or other patients are more extreme and perhaps even qualitatively different from the hypnotic amnesia effects obtained in laboratory settings. Consequently, it is important to note that a few studies have assessed the extent to which the several personalities of MPD patients compartmentalize information and exhibit between-personality interference effects. The findings of these studies (Ludwig, Brandsma, Wilbur, Bendfeldt, & Jameson, 1972; Nissen, Ross, Willingham, Mackenzie & Schacter, 1988; Silberman, Putnam, Weingartner, Braun, & Post, 1985) are consistent with the hypnotic amnesia studies conducted on college students. They indicate that, in MPD patients who exhibit alter personalities that are purportedly mutually amnesic, information acquired by one alter influences the memory of other alters. For instance, Silberman et al. (1985) taught MPD patients lists of related words to assess the effects of retroactive and proactive interference. In one condition, the same alter learned two related lists, and in another condition one alter learned one list while a different alter learned the related list. If alter personalities actually process and store information in segregated cognitive systems, these patients should have exhibited greater within-alter interference than between-alter interference. The reverse was the case. The list learned by one alter interfered substantially with the ability of the other alter to learn the related list, and subjects exhibited even more between-subject interference than within-subject interference. Similar findings were obtained in normal controls who were instructed to pretend having an alter personality.

Nissen et al. (1988) tested the alter personalities of a single MPD patient using a wide variety of memory tasks aimed at assessing both implicit and explicit aspects of memory functioning. Once again, mutually amnesic alters were tested to assess the extent to which learning by one alter influenced (by either facilitation or interference) the performance of another alter. Despite claims by the alters of being amnesic for the experiences of other alters, this subject exhibited substantial between-alter influence on both explicit and implicit memory tasks. For instance, exposing briefly presented word stimuli to one alter in a perceptual identification task produced a priming effect when testing an alter personality. Taken together, the findings of these studies clearly contradict the hypothesis that the memories associated with different alter personalities are isolated and segregated from the memories of other alters.

Interestingly, Nissen et al.'s (1988) patient exhibited a lack of influence between alters on some tasks, particularly tasks that involved semantically rich and complex materials. For instance, one alter was shown a picture and then read an ambiguous statement that described the picture. Another alter, who was not shown the picture, then heard, and was asked to interpret, the ambiguous statement. The interpretation given by the second alter was not consistent with the picture shown to the first alter. Nissen et al. (1988) suggested that the seeming independence between the performances of the alters on tasks such as this indicated that the performance of their patient was not due to faking. It might be more accurate to conclude that such a performance could be due to faking but could also be due to other factors.

For instance, from a sociocognitive perspective, MPD patients may be seen as becoming absorbed in enacting the role of first one alter and then another (Spanos, 1994). This perspective suggests that absorption in the role of alter A may prime the patient to selectively attend to information and recall events that are congruent with that role. However, a "personality switch" that resulted in absorption in the role of alter B would prime different patterns of attending and recall.

A stage actor who becomes immersed in his character tries to see the world the way his character would see it. The actor attempts to feel what his character would feel and to take on the mind-sets that his character would likely develop in different situations. A sociocognitive hypothesis suggests that a similar process may sometimes occur with MPD patients. For instance, if alter A is a "protector personality," the patient may adopt the role of acting tough, becoming sensitive to slights, reacting to such slights with hostility, and so forth. When enacting alter B, the patient may behave timidly, interpret situations as would a frightened person, and so on. If alter A has read an ambiguous passage, it is not surprising that she may interpret it quite differently than she did as alter B when she was shown a picture that corresponded to the passage.

A good deal of evidence (e.g., Brewster & Treyens, 1981; Mandler, 1984) suggests that changes in psychological set influence the performance of normal college students on perceptual and memory tasks. In one study (R. C. Anderson & Pichert, 1978), for example, subjects read a detailed room-by-room written description of a house and its contents. Subjects were instructed to read the description from the perspective of a prospective home buyer. Following a 12-minute distraction task, subjects recalled all they could about the house and its contents. Following another distraction task, half of the subjects then recalled once again in the same way. The other half, however, were asked to recall while taking on the perspective of a burglar rather than a home buyer. On the second recall trial, subjects in the burglar condition recalled significantly more new facts about the house than those in the home buyer condition. Moreover, the new facts recalled by those who took the burglar perspective tended to include information that would be of particular relevance to a burglar (e.g., recall of a coin collection) but relatively unimportant to a prospective home buyer. In other words, a change in psychological set that influenced what subjects deemed important about a situation influenced their recall of that situation.

Nissen et al. (1988) pointed out that their patient exhibited between-personality compartmentalization when the testing materials used "might be interpreted in different ways by different people—or different personalities" (p. 130). The findings of R. C. Anderson and Pichert (1978) suggest that analogous processes to those shown by Nissen et al.'s patient occur in normal people who adopt different psychological sets to the same task. Such findings are quite interesting, but they do not imply the kind of segregation of ideas or isolation of cognitive systems associated historically with the notions of dissociation and MPD.

Simultaneous Performance

Certainly people can perform two relatively simple or overlearned tasks simultaneously and with relatively little interference. For example, most of us have had the experience of daydreaming while driving along a stretch of highway. Such activity obviously involves processing and reacting to perceptual information about the road ahead while simultaneously thinking about something else. However, when attentional demands become more stringent—for example, when we enter busy city traffic—we must choose between daydreaming and driving, or risk an accident.

The available evidence does not indicate that people who develop alter selves are better than anyone else at attending simultaneously to several sources of stimulation. For instance, both MPD patients and subjects who exhibit "hidden observers" or "past life" personalities in experimental situations often score high on tests of hypnotizability. Some investigators (e.g., Putnam, 1993) have even suggested that high hypnotizability involves an ability to dissociate. Nevertheless, highly hypnotizable subjects are no more successful at dividing attention between two tasks than low hypnotizables (Stava & Jaffa, 1988). Relatedly, in two studies (V. J. Knox, Crutchfield, and Hilgard, 1975; J. H. Stevenson, 1976), highly hypnotizable hypnotic subjects who engaged consciously in one task were also given suggestions to simultaneously but unconsciously engage in another. Contrary to the descriptions of co-consciousness given in the MPD literature, carrying out the two tasks simultaneously caused interference despite subjects' reports of being amnesic for their "dissociated" activities. Spanos and Hewitt (1980) asked the overt and hidden "parts" of their hypnotic subjects to simultaneously give numerical estimates of the degree of pain they experienced. Overt reports were given verbally while hidden reports were tapped out on a key press device. Instead of reporting simultaneously, almost all of the subjects reported successively. They first gave overt verbal reports and then tapped out their hidden reports. This pattern of reporting is much more consistent with the idea that subjects quickly shifted attention back and forth between overt and hidden tasks than with the notion that they simultaneously divided attention between the tasks.

It is at least within the realm of plausibility to suggest that some MPD patients may sometimes carry out two overlearned tasks and later attribute the performance of the two tasks to different alters. However, the wisdom of arguing that each personality independently processes information in cases where 15 or more alters are addressed simultaneously seems questionable.

The Effects of Trauma on Memory

A number of studies (for reviews, see Cardeña & Spiegel, 1993; McFarlane, 1988) have assessed the psychological sequelae exhibited by subjects who were exposed to severely traumatic events (e.g., floods, combat, serious accidents, being held hostage). People exhibit wide individual differences in their responses to such experiences, and some suffer a number of debilitating and sometimes long-lasting symptoms. Moreover, these symptoms sometimes include distorted memories for the events and an inability to recall some aspects of the trauma. What rarely if ever occurs, however, is the kind of wholesale forgetting of the entire traumatic episode that is posited to occur as a result of trauma-induced hypnoid or dissociated states. For instance, combat veterans (e.g., Feinstein, 1989) and survivors of hostage takings (e.g., Hillman, 1981) may suffer debilitating symptoms for the rest of their lives and may sometimes have distorted and incomplete memories for their traumatic experiences. Nevertheless, they do not forget the fact that they were in combat or that they had been held hostage.

The Equivalence of Hypnotic and Hysterical Symptoms

As indicated by studies that made use of such indirect perceptual testing procedures as delayed auditory feedback (e.g., Sutcliffe, 1960) and by studies that assessed compliant responding to suggestions for perceptual change (e.g., Burgess et al., 1993), the available evidence now indicates that the so-called sensory deficits exhibited by hypnotic subjects consist primarily of reporting biases rather than perceptual changes. Moreover, any actual perceptual changes that are associated with hypnotic suggestions appear to be brought about by subjects' active use of cognitive and behavioral strategies (e.g., distraction, unfocusing the eyes) rather than occurring automatically. Thus, if hypnotic and hysterical sensory and motor "deficits" really are equivalent, it is because the hysterical "deficits," like those associated with hypnosis, reflect goal-directed enactments aimed at fostering a particular self-presentation (L. P. Ullman & Krasner, 1969).

Although relatively little experimental work has tested the sensory deficits of hysterical patients, what there is is consistent with the view that the symptoms manifested by these patients involve goal-directed enactment. For instance, J. P. Brady and Lind (1961) tested a patient who claimed hysterical blindness in a paradigm that required the subject to choose between two visual stimuli on each of a series of trials. A person who was actually unable to see would be expected by chance to choose correctly about half of the time. However, the hysterical subject chose correctly significantly *less* often than would be expected by chance. In other words, the patient appeared to actively avoid choosing the correct stimulus so as to reinforce her self-presentation as unable to see. Obviously, avoidance of this kind indicates that the patient could see the stimulus.

The notion that hysterical symptoms reflect role enactment and self-presentational concerns rather than ideas isolated from normal consciousness is also supported by findings that indicate that hysterical symptoms can be eliminated by eliminating the interpersonal reinforcements that maintain those symptoms (Kass, Silvers, & Abroms, 1972). For instance, Goldblatt and Munitz (1976) described a 27-year-old man diagnosed with hysterical paralysis of the legs. No attempt was made to uncover unconscious causes of the paralyses. Instead, the treatment included rearranging the patient's environment so that continued displays of paralysis produced various negative consequences (e.g., exposure to a noxious placebo treatment, loss of social reinforcement). At the same time, the patient was provided with a face-saving way of giving up his symptoms without having to define those symptoms as faked or nongenuine. Within a week of this treatment regimen, the patient was cured. He not only walked normally but also did cartwheels to demonstrate his complete recovery. A number of other reports (e.g., Davis & Wagstaff, 1991; Dickes, 1974; Kass et al., 1972) also indicate that behavioral treatments can be effective in eliminating hysterical symptoms.

Perhaps the strongest evidence for the role of interpersonal reinforcement in the maintenance of hysterical symptoms comes not from modern behavioral case reports and clinical studies but from the historical record. Recall that within a short period of time after Charcot's death, hysterical patients, who had for years been exhibiting the florid symptoms of grand hysteria, stopped enacting such displays. When the new administration at the Salpetrière deemed that florid hysterical symptoms were to be ignored or actively discouraged, displays of grand hysteria quickly disappeared.

In summary, the available evidence does not support the usefulness of concepts like hypnoid states or dissociated ideas as explanations for hypnotic phenomena, the formation and maintenance of hysterical symptoms, the amnesia reported by MPD patients, or psychological reactions to trauma. On the other hand, both historical considerations and modern studies suggest that hysterical symptoms (and as we shall see, MPD symptoms as well) can be usefully understood as resulting from a complex negotiation process in which patients lay claim to a fictive illness and doctors validate and shape the manifestations of the "illness" on the basis of their own understandings of the situation. This negotiation process involves patients' background beliefs about illness and their understanding concerning the use of illness language and illness presentations as ways of communicating dissatisfactions and attaining succor. These factors in turn interact with and are changed by the beliefs of doctors and others concerning the causes and symptoms of hysteria. These beliefs are transmitted to patients during the processes of diagnosis and treatment, and over time, patients and doctors come to share a set of common understanding concerning the causes, symptoms, and treatment of the patients' "disease" (R. Rabkin, 1964; Szasz, 1961; D. C. Taylor, 1986; L. P. Ullman & Krasner, 1969).

JANET'S NOTION OF DISSOCIATION

Janet (1889) developed a psychotherapeutic procedure based on his notion of dissociation. For Janet, multiple personality and traumatic hysteria both resulted from the dissociation of ideas. The elaboration of dissociated ideas into an alter personality simply indicated the dissociation of a larger and more complex set of ideas than was the case for other hysterical symptoms. Consequently, Janet used the same basic treatment methods for many of his hysterical patients, including those who exhibited full-blown alter personalities. First the patient underwent hypnosis to discover the supposed dissociated traumatic memories that were maintaining the symptoms. Once the traumatic situation was discovered, Janet might use suggestions to change the patient's traumatic memories into benign ones.

One of Janet's (1889) cases, for example, involved a woman named Marie who suffered recurring hysterical crises, body contortions, and delirium following the onset of her menstrual periods. During hypnotic treatment, Janet asked her to describe her first menstruation. Marie recalled that her first period at age 13 had been unexpected and that because of her shame she had tried to stop the bleeding by immersing herself in cold water. The menstrual flow stopped, but she suffered severe shivering and later an attack of delirium. These symptoms, purportedly without conscious memory of the self-immersion, reoccurred following her later periods. To rid Marie of her symptoms, Janet (1889) hypnotically age regressed her and suggested a new memory as follows:

> It was necessary to bring her back by suggestion to the age of thirteen years, to put her back into the initial conditions of the delirium, and then to convince her that her period had lasted three days and had not been interrupted by any unfortunate accident. Now, when this was done, the succeeding period arrived on the due date and lasted for three days, without bringing with it any pain, any convulsion nor any delirium. (pp. 438–439)

Another of Janet's (1889) cases, a patient diagnosed with multiple personality, suffered from hallucinatory terrors. The patient was called L (Lucy), and during hypnotic treatment Janet traced these symptoms to an event that occurred when Lucy was 9 years old. At that age she had been frightened by two men who jumped out at her from behind a curtain as a practical joke. It was this event that purportedly led to the formation of the patient's secondary personality. In this case, Janet made no attempt to change the patient's memory. Instead, he simply commanded the secondary personality to no longer experience hallucinatory attacks.

It is worth recalling that I first described Lucy in chapter 16. She was the well-trained hysteric who manifested Charcot's symptoms of grand hypnosis and whose first manifestation of a secondary personality occurred only after it had been suggested in a highly leading hypnotic interview conducted by Janet. We should be cautious, therefore, before following Janet in attributing the beginnings of the secondary personality to events that occurred when Lucy was 9 years old.

The last of Janet's (1925) cases that we will examine is that of another multiple personality patient. Achilles was a 33-year-old man who manifested a secondary demonic personality and believed himself to be possessed by the devil. During a hypnotic interview, the patient confessed that he had been unfaithful to his wife while on a business trip 6 months earlier. Shortly thereafter, he began to dream about the devil and soon defined himself as being possessed. Janet treated the patient successfully by assuring him during a hypnotic session of his wife's forgiveness.

Janet's treatment procedures and the results he obtained are important because they influenced the psychotherapeutic procedures used by Freud and helped to establish the still commonly voiced idea that psychological problems in adulthood can be treated successfully by uncovering the "hidden" memories and ideas that supposedly caused the symptoms. Moreover, Janet's use of hypnotic regression to uncover the traumatic memories "held" by alter personalities has served as a model for modern MPD advocates who continue to use hypnotic-regression procedures for the same purpose. Given the appeal of Janet's case histories to modern MPD theorists, it is instructive to examine once again the three cases described above.

Modern MPD theorists emphasize the importance of early abuse, particularly sexual abuse, in the genesis of MPD. The case histories of modern MPD patients are replete with descriptions of the horrendous abuse—violent incestuous rape, physical torture, satanic ritual abuse—that purportedly led to dissociation and the development of alter personalities. It is interesting to note, therefore, that none of the "dissociated memories" recovered by Janet's three patients involved child sexual abuse. The dissociated alter personality manifested by Achilles purportedly developed in adulthood as a result of guilt stemming from an extramarital affair. Marie's trauma was self-inflicted (immersion in cold water at age 13 in an attempt to stop menstruation), and Lucy's alter personality purportedly began its development after Lucy was frightened at age 9 by two men who jumped out from behind a curtain.

Janet was not unusual in failing to uncover child sexual abuse as the cause of his patients' alter personalities. The other early 20th-century psychotherapist most famous for his MPD cases was Morton Prince. His best-known patient, Miss Beauchaump, purportedly began developing her first alter personality after a minor but upsetting interaction with a male friend. At the time, Miss Beauchaump was not a child, but an 18-year-old woman training to become a nurse (M. Prince, 1905/1920). Another of M. Prince's (1908) patients, known as B.C.A., purportedly began developing her first alter personality during adulthood following her husband's death.

In summary, the kinds of events to which Janet and Prince attributed the genesis of multiple personality were very different from the early and horrendous sexual and physical traumas that modern MPD patients routinely "remember" in therapy as causing the formation of their alter personalities. These findings are, of course, consistent with the hypothesis that the preconceptions held by therapists concerning the causes of MPD may influence patients to generate memory reports that conform to their therapist's hypothesis concerning the etiology of their difficulties.

Janet's treatment procedures appeared to be effective. He reported that his patients were relieved of their symptoms when he uncovered the memories that purportedly lay behind the symptoms and then altered or banished the offending memories with suggestion. In the absence of controlled studies, however, anecdotal reports of successful therapy like those given by Janet are of little value in determining whether the treatment procedures were actually effective. Moreover, even if we assume that a treatment was effective in the sense that some aspects of the treatment were related to a diminution of the patient's symptomatology, the effective components may not have been those that the therapist considers crucial.

Janet's treatment (like some modern psychotherapies) was based on the assumption that symptom reduction was produced by the uncovering and banishment of actual memories that were maintaining the symptoms. However, Bernheim (1886/1900) also reported the successful hypnotic treatment of hysterical and other symptoms but made no attempt to uncover hidden memories. Bernheim simply administered direct suggestions for therapeutic improvement. As we saw in earlier chapters, past-life regression therapists and UFO abductions therapists report improvement in their patients even though the "memories" recovered during these therapies appear to be patently false. Relatedly, it is worth recalling that shamans in other cultures often appear to reduce the distress of their clients by helping them to "tame" their spirits and that, historically, exorcists sometimes appeared to do the same by casting out demons. Behavioral procedures aimed at changing reinforcement contingencies without uncovering hidden memories also appear to alter hysterical and other symptoms. More generally, the vast literature on the effectiveness of psychotherapy appears to indicate that a very wide array of treatment procedures (including placebos) that are based on different principles and assumptions can be effective in treating a wide range of problems (e.g., Dawes, 1994; Frank, 1973; Torrey, 1986). Consequently, it is important not to assume that a particular theory of symptom formation is valid simply because treatment procedures based on the theory appear to achieve some success.

THE DECLINE OF DISSOCIATION

Freud was hostile to Janet and his ideas, and, at least in part, Freud's hostility stemmed from his sensitivity concerning priority of scientific discovery. Janet's ideas concerning dissociation and the recovery of hidden memories were published before Breuer and Freud's similar notions, and Freud was ever sensitive to the suggestion that his ideas about repression and symptom formation were but a restatement and extension of what Janet had published previously (Ellenberger, 1970; Sulloway, 1979). It is perhaps not surprising then that Freud did not diagnose multiple personality in any of his patients or that his followers came to view the symptoms of MPD as artifacts produced by incompetent therapeutic interventions.

Even before World War I, Freud's ideas had made remarkable headway, particularly in the United States and particularly in such East Coast enclaves of the intellectual, medical, and scientific establishments as Boston and, especially, New York (Gach, 1980; Torrey, 1992). Here, Freud's ideas competed with, and by the early 1920s largely displaced, notions concerning dissociation and multiple personality (Kenny, 1986; Marx, 1970). Neither Janet, Prince, nor other advocates of dissociation and MPD established a school or recruited disciples to propagate their ideas (Ellenberger, 1970; Hale, 1975). Freud, on the other hand, quickly surrounded himself with a core of loyal followers who established psychoanalytic institutes throughout Europe and in major American cities and who propagated psychoanalytic ideas with a religiouslike zeal (Gach, 1980; Grosskurth, 1991).

Psychoanalysts, and investigators sympathetic to psychoanalytic ideas, attacked both the theoretical adequacy of the concept of dissociation and the therapeutic practices that led to manifestations of MPD. For instance, in several papers, B. Hart (1910, 1926), a prominent early 20th-century psychiatrist, contrasted Freud's ideas with those of Janet and concluded that the notion of dissociation was based on a spatial metaphor that encouraged the misleading (in his opinion) belief that separate personality states could exist simultaneously but independently within the same person. Hart described an MPD patient of his own in whom the manifestations of a secondary personality were related not to earlier traumatic events but to the patient's attempts to avoid dealing with issues raised in the therapy. In other words, Hart conceptualized the patient's manifestation of an alter as a strategic attempt to manipulate the therapist by avoiding discussion of issues deemed important by the therapist. Hart also noted that the patterns of interactions between himself and the various personalities of the patient required some higher-order understanding and coordination of personality manifestations on the patient's part that could not be adequately conceptualized by simply positing two independent agencies within the same person. At the end of his presentation, Hart raised the question of why psychoanalysts so rarely concerned themselves with the phenomena of MPD.

Hart's (1926) paper was discussed by several commentators. Ernest Jones, a prominent psychoanalyst and later Freud's biographer, answered Hart's question by stating that psychoanalysts simply did not come across cases of MPD. The reason for this lack of cases he explained as follows:

> It cannot be mere chance, and I am inclined to think that the main explanation is the artificial nature of most, perhaps all, cases of multiple personality. (Jones, in Hart, 1926, p. 257)

To varying degrees, the other three commentators on Hart's (1926) paper (Brown, Glover, and Mitchell) agreed with Jones that cases of MPD reflected artifacts that resulted from the hypnotic procedures used to diagnose and treat these patients. Brown even indicated that drama and melodrama were of importance to the genesis of MPD and suggested that "the psychology of acting will probably give considerable help in the ultimate solution of this problem" (Brown, in Hart, 1926, p. 260).

By the time Hart (1926) wrote his paper, the battle between psychoanalysis and the dissociationists was largely over; cases of MPD were in decline, and among psychopathologists, Freudian ideas had, by and large, won the day. Prince was well aware of this situation and, according to Murray (1956), wrote somewhat bitterly in a letter of 1928 that "Freudian psychology had flooded the field like a full rising tide, and the rest of us were left submerged like clams buried in the sands at low water" (p. 293).

Two decades after psychoanalysis had largely displaced the ideas of Janet and M. Prince, and at a time when cases of MPD were rarely seen, McCurdy (1941) returned to Prince's Miss Beauchamp to explain the case in terms of the psychoanalytic notion of transference. McCurdy (1941) pointed out that Prince was the "gravitational center" (p. 36) of Miss Beauchamp's world. Prince saw her in therapy for 7 years. Often they saw each other on a daily basis and, in addition to this, also wrote each other regular notes and letters. Miss Beauchamp developed a strong emotional attachment to Prince, and as one personality and then another, alternately teased and flirted with him, attempted (perhaps with some success) to make him jealous, and opposed his interference in her life. Prince, in turn, developed strong paternalistic feelings toward his patient, involved himself in numerous aspects of her life, and responded to each of her personality displays with different emotions. Rather than viewing Miss Beauchamp's changing behaviors as separate "personalities," McCurdy (1941) argued that they could be better described as personifications of the different attitudes that she developed toward Prince during the course of treatment.

Indeed, her relationship with him is a far better reference point for judging her personality changes than is the "real, original, or normal self" that Prince assumed. When she was submissive to him, she was BI; when flippant and flirtatious, BIII; when rebellious, BIV. Prince reacted with considerable emotion to these various attitudes toward himself. He was gentle with BI, amused with BIII, and severe with BIV.

SUMMARY

Psychoanalysis gained much prominence in the early 20th century and was effective in largely shutting out competing theoretical ideas and therapeutic approaches. Following Freud's lead, psychoanalysts rejected the concept of dissociation with its implication of two simultaneously existing states of consciousness. From a psychoanalytic perspective, cases of multiple personality were accounted for in several ways: as complex sets of repressed ideas that alternately became conscious, as artifacts of suggestive therapy, and as manifestations of therapeutic transference reactions that were shaped into alternate personalities that expressed patients' contradictory and changing attitudes toward their therapists. Psychoanalysts did not encourage patients to personify their conflicting attitudes and beliefs as alter selves and implied that such practices constituted poor therapy. Consequently, the patients of psychoanalysts, and others influenced by psychoanalytic ideas, rarely manifested MPD.

IV

THE THEORY OF MULTIPLE PERSONALITY DISORDER

18

MULTIPLE PERSONALITY DISORDER AND SOCIAL LEARNING

As we have seen, toward the end of the 19th century, multiple personality was considered a species of hysteria and had become an established and, at least in France and in America, a relatively common disorder. During this same period, Freud developed the hypothesis that hysteria was invariably caused by child sexual abuse. However, as we have seen, investigators like Janet and Prince, who diagnosed and treated MPD patients with relative frequency, did not regularly discover child sexual abuse as a cause of their patients' symptoms. On the other hand, Freud diagnosed none of his hysterics as suffering from MPD but, during his seduction theory period, "discovered" child sexual abuse in every one of his cases. Modern investigators who frequently diagnose MPD have borrowed Janet's use of leading hypnotic interviews and age-regression procedures to diagnose and treat MPD and adopted Freud's seduction theory as the cause of MPD. The result, as we shall see in the following chapters, is a modern "epidemic" of MPD patients whose alters are often first discovered during hypnotic therapy and whose "dissociative splits" are usually traced to memories of childhood sexual abuse that emerge during such therapy.

PREVALENCE OF MPD AND MPD ALTERS

As we saw in earlier chapters, by the end of the first two decades of the 20th century, the number of MPD cases had dropped substantially, and from the 1920s to 1970, only a handful were reported worldwide. Since 1970, the number of cases reported has increased astronomically, and thousands have now been reported (Boor, 1982; Putnam, 1989). Interestingly, historical changes have occurred not only in the prevalence of MPD but also in the number of personalities supposedly displayed by MPD patients.

The Number of Alters per Patient

As indicated in chapter 4, the number of different personalities per MPD patient has shown a substantial increase since the 19th century. During the 19th century, most cases involved only two personalities (Bowman, 1990). Since 1944, however, almost all cases have involved three or more personalities (Boor, 1982). Modern cases average from 6 to 16 personalities per patient (Coons et al., 1988; Kluft, 1984; C. A. Ross, Norton, & Wozney, 1989). For instance, Kluft (1982) reported that 44% of 54 MPD patients each had more that 10 personalities and 7 of these patients had more than 20 personalities each. Dell and Eisenhower (1990) studied adolescent multiples and reported a mean of 24.1 alter personalities per patient. C. A. Ross, Norton, and Fraser (1989) reported on an MPD patient with 300 alters; and Spencer (1989), in an autobiographical account, claimed to have 400 personalities. On the basis of studies cited in Dell and Eisenhower (1990), North, Ryall, Ricci, and Wetzel (1993) plotted the mean number of MPD alters per patient as a function of year, between 1979 and 1990. In 1979, the average MPD patient manifested just under 10 personalities; by 1989, the mean number was approximately 13 personalities; and in 1990, MPD patients displayed an average of just under 25 personalities per patient.

The increases over time in the number of alters per MPD patient is reminiscent of the increases in the number of demon selves that were commonly manifested in demoniacs who were exposed to a protracted series of exorcisms during periods of peak interest in demonic possession (Harsnett, 1599; Huxley, 1952). Also related are the increases over the years in the number of UFO abductions "remembered" per patient by those who have undergone hypnotic interviews aimed at uncovering such memories. The number of demon selves per demoniac appeared to increase as a function of the length of exorcism procedures and the need for new and exciting demonic manifestations that were required to hold the attention of exorcists and other audience members (Spanos, 1983a). Relatedly, the UFO abduction reports that first occurred in the 1960s (e.g., Fuller, 1996), began with cases in which people were abducted only once. By the late 1980s, however, it became increasingly common to "discover" (through repeated hypnotic sessions) that patients had been abducted on numerous occasions, beginning in early childhood (Hopkins, 1987; Jacobs, 1992; Mack, 1994). A single abduction had become mundane. Generating the sustained attention of therapists appeared to require repeated and more elaborate abductions.

Increases in the number of alters per MPD patient are most likely due to the same factors that explain increases in the number of demon selves and increases in the number of UFO abductions per abductee: Expectations transmitted to patients, and the selective reinforcement of increasingly dramatic displays that, in MPD patients, frequently translates into an increase in the number of alters and (as we shall see below) an increase in the extent of abuse "remembered" by those alters.

Prevalence of MPD

Bliss, Larson, and Nakashima (1983) reported that 60% of the 45 patients admitted to a single inpatient ward with auditory hallucinations were actually suffering from MPD. Bliss (1984b) also diagnosed MPD or probable MPD in 63% of a series of selected Briquet syndrome (i.e., hysteria) patients. Bliss and Larson (1985) diagnosed MPD in 21% of 33 male sex offenders and probable MPD in another 18%. Bliss and Jeppsen (1985) reported that approximately 8 out of 50 (16%) sequentially admitted inpatients on an acute psychiatric ward and 9 out of 100 (9%) private psychiatric outpatients suffered from MPD. C. A. Ross, Anderson, Fleisher, and Norton (1991) diagnosed 3.3% of a sample of 299 psychiatric inpatients as suffering from MPD. C. A. Ross (1991) reported that he and his colleagues had diagnosed MPD in 17% of a sample of adolescent psychiatric patients, 14% of a sample of substance abusers, and 5% of a psychiatric inpatient sample. Ross, Anderson, Heber, and Norton (1990) reported that 5% of a sample of prostitutes and 35% of exotic dancers suffered from MPD.

Despite the high rates of occurrence found in these studies and the high rates reported more informally by numerous clinicians who are strong supporters of the MPD diagnosis, some studies report very low rates of occurrence. Thus, Merskey and Buhrich (1975) found no MPD among 89 patients diagnosed with dissociative or conversion disorders, a population that, according to MPD theorists, is likely to yield particularly high rates of MPD. In addition, a number of highly experienced clinicians with many years of practice report never having seen a case of MPD (Chordoff, 1987; Merskey, 1992; Tozman & Pabis, 1989). For instance, Tozman and Pabis (1989) claimed that "as [psychiatric] practitioners with thousands of patients seen over 40 people years, we report that we have never seen a legitimate case of multiple personality disorder (MPD)" (p. 708). Relatedly, Simpson (1989) contended that

> the distribution of MPD cases is bizarre. There is no normal distribution of cases. I've never met a clinician who, over any significant period of time, has seen just one case. The vast majority of talented, sensitive, observant clinicians have never seen a case at all. A very small number of clinicians report the great majority of case reports. (p. 565)

At the present time, MPD appears to be a culture-bound syndrome. The explosion of cases since 1970 has thus far remained largely restricted to North America. The diagnosis is very rarely made in modern France, despite its turn-of-the-century prominence as a center for the study of MPD. It is also very rare in Great Britain (Aldridge-Morris, 1989; Fahy, 1988), Russia (R. M. Allison, 1991), and India (Adityhanjee & Khandelwal, 1989), and a recent survey in Japan failed to uncover even a single case (Takahashi, 1990).

Modestin (1992) surveyed all of the psychiatrists in Switzerland concerning the frequency with which they had seen patients with MPD. Depending on how it was calculated, the prevalence rate ranged between .5% and 1.0%. More interesting, Modestin noted that 90% of the respondents had never seen a case of MPD, whereas three psychiatrists had each seen more than 20 MPD patients. From the data presented in this article, it appears that 66% of the MPD diagnoses were made by only 6 out of 655 (.09%) psychiatrists. Unlike North American samples in which women are at least three times more likely than men to receive an MPD diagnosis, Modestin found that 51% of the MPD diagnoses were given to men. Modestin's (1992) findings are clearly consistent with Simpson's (1989) contentions that the very large majority of clinicians do not diagnose cases as MPD and that a small number of clinicians account for the overwhelming number of these diagnoses.

The historical changes in the prevalence rates of MPD, the substantial national differences in prevalence and in gender ratios, and the large differences in the frequency with which different clinicians make the diagnosis are difficult to account for parsimoniously in terms of a disease perspective. They are, however, reminiscent of the historical changes in prevalence of demonic possession, the large cross-cultural differences in prevalence of spirit possession, and the large differences in rates of glossolalia seen among different churches in North America. In short, the prevalence data for MPD suggest that MPD, like possession phenomena, is a social creation that varies in frequency as a function of the expectations for its occurrence that are transmitted to patients. A particularly important source of such expectations are therapists committed to the MPD diagnosis, but other sources (e.g., media) have become increasingly important as information about MPD has infused into the wider culture.

An alternative to the social-creation hypothesis holds that the incidence of MPD has not really increased. According to this view, MPD was previously (and often continues to be) misdiagnosed as schizophrenia, psychopathy, and various other disorders (R. B. Allison & Schwarz, 1980; Rosenbaum, 1980; C. A. Ross, Norton, & Wozney, 1989). Purportedly, the current increased incidence for the disorder is apparent rather than real and reflects the fact that actual MPD cases are incorrectly diagnosed less frequently than previously. This account is also sometimes used to explain national differences in MPD rates (Altrocchi, 1992). According to this view, psychiatrists in other countries have not yet developed the diagnostic acumen required to recognize MPD.

A major problem with this account is that the symptoms of MPD are, in fact, quite distinctive. A patient who calls herself Mary on one day and Jane on another, and who behaves very differently as Mary than as Jane, is unlikely to go unrecognized as a candidate for an MPD diagnosis by even an inexperienced clinician. To deal with this difficulty, proponents of the disease model argue that such patients are skilled at hiding their multiplicity and reveal it only when those with acumen enough to correctly interpret the subtle signs use diagnostic procedures that bring forth the multiple identities. In fact, the proponents of the MPD diagnosis agree that the large majority of patients who eventually receive this diagnosis do not enter therapy complaining about multiple personalities, do not exhibit clear-cut evidence of multiplicity, and do not know that they possess alter identities (Wilbur, 1984). MPD has been portrayed as a "hidden syndrome" in which 80% or more of such patients were unaware of the existence of alters before entering treatment with the therapist who uncovered their multiplicity (Kluft, 1985b). Looked at from a sociocognitive perspective, these data suggest instead that the procedures used to diagnose MPD often create rather than discover multiplicity.

TEACHING MULTIPLICITY

Proponents of the MPD diagnosis have described a very large and diverse number of signs that supposedly might indicate this disorder and that can be used to justify probing for confirmation. A few of these signs include depression, somatoform symptoms, headaches, periods of missing time, impaired concentration, hallucinations, sexual dysfunctions, fatigue, and drug abuse (Coons, Bowman, & Milstein, 1988; C. A. Ross, Norton & Wozney, 1989). There are many more. Even this truncated list makes it clear that a very large set of presenting symptoms can be used as possible indicators of MPD.

Once the diagnosis is suspected, it is common practice to ask leading and explicit questions in an attempt to confirm it. Putnam (1989), for example, asks such questions as "Do you ever feel as if you are not alone, as if there is someone else or some other part watching you?" (p. 90). Others apply much stronger pressure. Merskey (1992) recently reviewed a large number of MPD cases from the 20th century and earlier that provided information about treatment procedures and symptomatology. His review included three well-known cases, those of Sally Beauchamp (M. Prince, 1905/1920), *The Three Faces of Eve* (Thigpen & Cleckly, 1957), and *Sybil* (Schreiber, 1973), as well as many lesser known ones. Merskey (1992) found that highly leading and suggestive procedures have long been routine in the diagnosis of MPD.

Perhaps the most common procedure to elicit evidence of multiplicity is the use of hypnotic interviews during which alter personalities are explicitly suggested and explicitly asked to "come forth" and talk with the therapist (R. B. Allison & Schwarz, 1980; Bliss, 1986; Brandsma & Ludwig, 1974). Wilbur (1984) described the process: "The patient is hypnotized and each alternate, in turn, is asked to tell what precipitated it into the life of the birth personality" (p. 28). Bliss (1986) elaborated on the procedure:

> I then suggest that the [hypnotized] patient look into the back of his or her mind to see if there is anyone or anything there. If anything or a person is identified I want to know what or who it might be. [Once an alter has been identified] I then make a rapid survey by asking the personality . . . if she has a name; how long she has been there; the patient's age when she [the alter] came; whether the patient knows her; whether she ever takes over the body; whether she ever directs or influences the patient when the patient has the body; her mission or function; and whether there are other people back there. (pp. 196–197)

The nature of these procedures could result in the erroneous discovery that there often are "other people back there." The flavor of such interviews is conveyed in the following excerpt. The therapist in this case suspected that his patient (named Ned) was a multiple, and before administering a hypnotic induction taught him a finger signaling code for answering yes, no, or stop during the hypnotic interview (Mayer, 1991).

> I was careful to phrase it [the question that follows] impersonally so as not to offend the alternate personalities I suspected dwelled within the young man before me.
> "Are there other people living in Ned's body?"

His right index finger went up.
"Are there more than two?"
His right index finger went up again.
"Are there more than ten?"
The right index finger went up once more.
"More than twenty?"
Again the answer was positive. (Mayer, 1991, p. 36)

Why Mayer (1991) decided to stop at 20 is never specified, but from even this short excerpt one could reasonably conclude that he expected the patient to display alter personalities, transmitted this expectation to the patient, and explicitly defined such alters to the patient as "people other than Ned."

Below is another verbatim excerpt from a hypnotic interview, this time with a suspected multiple named Ken Bianchi. Bianchi had been charged with murder and was interviewed in a forensic context. The interview was videotaped. Following a hypnotic induction procedure, the clinician proceeded as follows:

And I've talked a bit to Ken but I think that perhaps there might be another part of Ken that I haven't talked to. . . . And I would like to communicate with that other part. And I would like that other part to come to talk to me. . . . And when you're here, lift the left hand off the chair to signal to me that you are here. Would you please come, part, so I can talk to you? . . . Part, would you come and lift Ken's hand to indicate to me that you are here? . . . Would you talk with me, part, by saying, "I'm here." (Schwarz, 1981, p. 138)

Following the last question, Bianchi (B) answered "yes" and the clinician (C) initiated the following exchange:

C. Part, are you the same thing as Ken or are you different in any way?
B. I'm not him.
C. You're not him. Who are you? Do you have a name?
B. I'm not Ken.
C. You're not him? Okay. Who are you? Tell me about yourself. Do you have a name I can call you by?
B. Steve. You can call me Steve. (Schwarz, 1981, p. 139)

While enacting the identity of "Steve," Bianchi admitted that he had murdered numerous women. He also indicated that Ken knew nothing of his (Steve's) existence and nothing about the murders. Following termination of the hypnotic procedures, Ken displayed "spontaneous amnesia" for the portion of the interview that involved "Steve" (Schwarz, 1981). Importantly, the clinician who conducted the hypnotic interview with Bianchi pointed out that he did nothing unusual in this case and used such interview procedures regularly to diagnose MPD (Watkins, 1984). In other words, leading hypnotic interviews that repeatedly inform the patient that he or she has other parts that can be addressed and communicated with as if they were separate people are used routinely when diagnosing modern cases of MPD, just as they were when diagnosing turn-of-the-century cases.

Spanos, Weekes, and Bertrand (1985) used the hypnotic interview used with Bianchi to test the hypothesis that such procedures can provide even naive subjects with the information required to enact multiple identities. The subjects were college students asked to pretend that they were in Bianchi's situation and had been accused of committing a series of murders. As in the Bianchi case, they were also informed that the evidence against them was strong and that they had been remanded for a psychiatric interview. Subjects were told nothing about multiple personality. They were simply instructed to use whatever background information they possessed and whatever they could glean from their interview to behave the way they believed an accused in that situation would behave.

Subjects in one group were administered an interview modeled closely on the one used with Bianchi. Role-playing control subjects were also interviewed. These subjects were told that personality was complex and involved walled off thoughts and feelings, but the interviewing "psychiatrist" never informed the controls that they possessed another part that could be communicated with directly.

Most of the role players given the Bianchi interview enacted symptoms of MPD by (a) adopting a different name, (b) referring to their primary personality in the third person, and (c) displaying amnesia for their alter personalities after termination of the hypnotic interview. None of the role-playing controls displayed any of these symptoms.

In a second session, the "psychiatrist" again contacted the alter personalities of the role-playing multiples. These subjects maintained their role successfully in the second session by exhibiting marked and consistent differences between their primary and alter personalities on a variety of psychological tests. Role-playing controls performed similarly on the two administrations of the tests.

For example, during the second session, a sentence-completion test was administered to the alter and primary personalities of each role-playing multiple. Because subjects had been instructed to play the role of an accused murderer, they usually enacted a violent, sociopathic alter personality who admitted the murders and a pleasant but somewhat befuddled primary personality who claimed to know nothing about the murders. Subjects consistently expressed these personality differences when completing sentences. Below are some examples. Subjects always responded to the sentence stems first as the alter personality (AP) and then as the primary personality (PP):

AP: *My mother is* a scum bag just like yours.

PP: *My mother is* a clean, very good woman.

AP: *When I get angry* I like to physically hurt people.

PP: *When I get angry* my mind seems to go blank and I can't remember what I've done. The only way I know is by people telling me. (Spanos, Weekes, & Bertrand, 1985, p. 371).

Importantly, the role-playing multiples responded differently than controls on nonsuggested and relatively subtle indicators of multiple identity, as well as on more obvious indicators. For instance, when enacting their alter personality, subjects typically referred to the primary personality in the third person (e.g., "he's a jerk") rather than in the first person, although they had never been instructed to do so. Relatedly, these subjects displayed amnesia "spontaneously" at the end of their first session. Then, in their second session, they validated their amnesic displays by taking significantly longer than nonmultiple controls to read test instructions that had earlier been administered to the primary personality. Findings such as these indicated that the diagnostic interview administered to these subjects did not simply teach them a set of behavioral responses. Instead, it taught subjects the basic rules required to enact the multiple personality role and to adapt that role to changing contextual requirements.

The rules for enacting the MPD role conveyed by this and similar interviews are as follows: (a) Behave as if you are two (or more) separate people who inhabit the same body. (b) Act as if the you I have been addressing thus far is one of those people and as if the you I have been talking to is unaware of the other coinhabitants. (c) When I provide a signal for contacting another coinhabitant, act as though you are another person. To the extent that patients behave in terms of these rules, the "classic" symptoms of MPD follow by implication and do not have to be individually taught through direct instruction or further suggestion. Thus, it follows from these rules that identity B will discuss identity A in the third person, that identity A will disavow activities attributed to identity B and will exhibit amnesia for the period of B's "takeover," and that the two identities will perform differently on psychological tests.

A replication of this study by Rabinowitz (1989) yielded similar findings. In addition, Spanos, Weekes, Menary, and Bertrand (1986) extended the findings of Spanos, Weekes, and Bertrand (1985) and Rabinowitz (1989) by exposing role-playing multiples to interviews that focused on their childhood experiences. The task of the role players was not, of course, to describe their actual childhoods but instead to use cues gleaned from the interviews to present themselves as might actual patients. Like the histories given by actual MPD patients, the role-playing multiples gave negatively toned descriptions of childhood, described their parents as punitive and rejecting, described an early onset (before age 10) for their alter personalities, and described their alters as "taking over" to handle difficult situations and express strong emotions. The findings of these studies are straightforward. They demonstrate that the interviewing procedures used routinely to diagnose MPD convey all of the information required to allow even psychiatrically unsophisticated subjects to enact the cardinal symptoms of multiplicity. All of the subjects in these studies had been explicitly asked to fake their responses, and consequently, while they displayed the behavioral symptoms of MPD, none came to actually construe themselves as possessing multiple identities. For this reason, it can be argued that people who were not faking would be unlikely to develop multiple identities following exposure to even leading hypnotic interviews. This argument is contradicted by the ample evidence described in earlier chapters that demonstrated that hypnotic procedures that were even less leading than the one used with Bianchi led regularly to enactments of hidden selves and past-life personalities in normal college students who were not faking their performances and who often reported following the hypnotic session that their alter personalities were experienced as real (Spanos & Hewitt, 1980; Spanos, Menary, Gabora, et al., 1991). The effects that leading diagnostic and therapeutic interviews aimed at uncovering MPD are likely to have on many psychotherapy patients were described by Simpson (1989) as follows:

> Procedures regularly followed, such as naming the alternative "personalities" and having long, carefully recorded conversations with them, serve to preserve and reify these otherwise transient situations, locking them into publicly shared "reality". Any "as-if" quality to the original experience is stamped out. The inevitable audio and videotaping provides a handy record of the nuances of the successful performance, and an aid-memoire for both participants to enable the maintenance of a consistent portrayal. (p. 565)

Hypnotic interviews used to diagnose MPD are highly reminiscent of the Catholic exorcism procedures discussed earlier in this book. They have, of course, been secularized to meet the materialist assumptions of 20th-century psychiatry, but the major components are the same. The hypnotist has replaced the priest, and he or she searches out and obtains the names of alters rather than demons. The priest "discovered" when the demons entered the body; the hypnotist "discovers" when each alter split from the "birth personality." The priest "discovered" why each demon entered the person; the hypnotist "discovers" the supposed trauma that led to the formation of each alter. The priest "discovered" the number of indwelling demons; the hypnotist "discovers" the number of alters, and so on. Exorcisms led regularly to the production of multiple indwelling demons, and hypnotic interviews appear to produce their secular counterparts: multiple indwelling personalities.

Several investigators (Putnam, Guroff, Silberman, Barban, & Post, 1986; C. A. Ross, 1989) have pointed out that many patients are diagnosed as suffering from MPD without being subjected to hypnotic interviews. On this basis, it is sometimes concluded that hypnosis does not cause MPD and, therefore, that MPD cannot be explained as an iatrogenic phenomenon. The first of these conclusions is quite correct, but the second is not. As indicated in earlier chapters, hypnotic procedures do *not* contain intrinsic properties that enhance responsiveness to suggestion, facilitate the development of alter personalities, or generate complex behavioral responses of any kind. Instead, hypnotic procedures influence behavior indirectly by altering subjects' motivations, expectations, and interpretations. Whether diagnostic interviews or other procedures facilitate the development of alter personalities will depend on the extent to which those procedures provide cues for such enactments, create expectations that legitimate such enactments, and provide reinforcements for the manifestation of such enactments. In contemporary psychiatric settings, such procedures are often conducted in a hypnotic context. As the literature on exorcism, spirit possession, and glossolalia indicates, however, a variety of procedures conducted in nonhypnotic contexts can be equally effective in serving the same purpose. One does not require hypnotic procedures to conduct leading interviews that cue and thereby generate enactments of multiplicity. Consequently, the fact that enactments of MPD sometimes occur in contexts that are not defined as hypnotic is largely irrelevant to the issue of whether such enactments are iatrogenically generated.

The Role of the Media

Information about MPD is widespread in our culture, and the major components of the role are now well-known to the general public (North et al., 1993). Popular TV shows and movies like *Sybil* and *The Three Faces of Eve*, along with popular biographies like *The Five of Me* (Hawksworth & Schwarz, 1977) and *The Minds of Billy Milligan* (Keyes, 1981), provide extensive information about the symptoms of MPD, and MPD patients, along with their psychiatrists, are sometimes even featured on popular TV talk shows. All of these sources typically depict MPD patients in a sympathetic light, as people with highly dramatic symptoms who, with the help of devoted and empathic therapists, surmount numerous obstacles to eventually gain self-esteem, dignity, health, happiness, and much sympathetic attention from high-status others. In short, the idea of being a multiple, like the idea of suffering from peripheral possession or demonic possession, may provide some people with a viable and face-saving way to account for personal problems as well as a dramatic means for gaining concern and attention from significant others.

The role of the media in fostering MPD was evident in a report by Gruenwald (1971) that concerned a 17-year-old hospitalized female patient. This patient's first enactment of an alter personality occurred the day after seeing the movie *The Three Faces of Eve* on television. Relatedly, Fahy, Abas, and Brown (1989) reported on a patient who presented with symptoms of MPD and who had seen the movie *The Three Faces of Eve* and read the book *Sybil* (Schreiber, 1973).

North et al. (1993) analyzed all available full-length biographies of MPD patients. Included in their analyses were such famous cases as those of Eve (Thigpen & Cleckley, 1957), Sybil (Schreiber, 1973), Miss Beauchaump (M. Prince, 1905/1920), and Ken Bianchi (O'Brien, 1985; Schwarz, 1981), along with 16 others. North et al. (1993) found that most of these patients had been exposed to media depictions of MPD or to other sources of cultural information about the diagnosis. For instance, 53% of these patients had read books or articles, attended lectures, or watched movies by or about MPD patients. Some of these patients were exposed to information about MPD in professional settings. Thus, 17% of these patients had trained in the mental health field, 17% aspired to become mental health professionals, and 28% had extensive psychiatric or medical knowledge. In short, the notion of MPD, and the symptoms associated with this disorder, are well-known in our culture. Moreover, many of the patients who eventually receive this diagnosis appear to have become well acquainted with the requirements of the MPD patient role, and the rewards associated with that role, through the media depictions of MPD common in our culture, as well as through technical information associated with training or interest in the mental health professions.

Thigpen and Cleckley (1957), the authors of *The Three Faces of Eve*, commented on the attractions of attaining an MPD diagnosis. Following publication of their famous book, they were frequently contacted by people who sought legitimation for their self-diagnosis of multiplicity:

> We have had long distance telephone calls from persons announcing themselves as multiple personalities—one went so far as to have each personality introduce itself and speak in a different voice. Similarly, we have had photographs of the different personalities of someone claiming the disorder, and one woman changed handwriting styles from paragraph to paragraph in letters to us (we had reported that Eve had changed writing styles) as if to say "can't you see I have a multiple personality just like Eve?" [Many of these patients] appeared to be motivated (either consciously or unconsciously) by a desire to draw attention to themselves. Certainly a diagnosis of multiple personality attracts a good deal more attention than most other diagnoses. Some patients appear to be motivated by secondary gain associated with avoiding responsibility for certain actions. (pp. 63–64)

The Role of the Therapist

Given the attractions of the MPD diagnosis and the widespread knowledge of its symptoms, it is not surprising that patients sometimes present with such symptoms in the absence of cuing from therapists. Nevertheless, most people are unlikely to sustain enactment of such a role in the absence of legitimation. In the case of Gruenwald's (1971) adolescent patient, for example, the initial enactment of an alter personality may have been tacitly legitimated by the therapist, who reportedly agreed to call the patient by a new name when she displayed her alter personality. The patient went on to display symptoms of MPD chronically. Alternatively, the therapist who treated the case described by Fahy et al. (1988) directed attention away from the patient's alters and focused on her other problems in living. In the absence of the therapist's legitimation, the patient's MPD enactments went into sharp decline.

Simpson (1989) forcefully emphasized the role of therapist legitimation in both the generation and the maintenance of MPD symptomatology:

> My hypothesis is that MPD is an iatrogenic, largely culture-bound disorder, with some resemblances to folie a deux, arising when a bright, suggestible patient meets a bright, suggestible physician convinced that MPD is an important diagnosis. Selective reinforcement of symptoms, unconscious and conscious, progressively shapes the symptoms and behavior of the patient, and the depiction of MPD is elaborated and reinforced. Patients usually show clear primary or secondary gain, but this is often not noted or acknowledged by their therapists, whose own secondary (and maybe primary?) gains are similarly covert. (p. 565)

The importance of interpersonal legitimation in the maintenance of alter identity enactments was demonstrated by Kohlenberg (1973). Kohlenberg commented on how the psychiatric staff of a ward that housed a multiple was sensitized to his three different personality enactments and interacted with each personality in a different manner. To demonstrate the importance of contextual variables in maintaining multiple identity enactments, baseline rates of occurrence were assessed for the behaviors associated with each of the patient's three personalities. Afterwards, the behaviors associated with only one of the personalities was selectively reinforced. The behaviors associated with the reinforced personality showed a dramatic increase in frequency. In later extinction trials, the frequency of occurrence of these behaviors decreased to baseline levels.

Most therapists who treat large numbers of MPD patients deemphasize the role of interview procedures or other iatrogenic elements in the genesis and maintenance of MPD enactments (e.g., Kluft, 1992). Ganaway (1989, 1992, 1995), however, is an exception. Ganaway (1995) is a psychiatrist and director of a dissociative disorders clinic where he has treated over

300 MPD patients. Many of these patients were diagnosed and treated for MPD before arriving at Ganaway's clinic. Ganaway (1994) has become increasingly critical of the MPD diagnosis and of the related notion that early trauma in some relatively direct way induces multiplicity. Instead, he has come to emphasize the role of therapist expectations and the dynamics of the therapeutic relationship in the genesis of MPD.

In many ways, Ganaway's (1992, 1995) analysis of the therapeutic interactions that lead to the development of MPD is similar to McCurdy's (1941) emphasis on the role of therapist–patient transference in the MPD symptomatology displayed by Miss Beauchamp during her treatment by Morton Prince. Ganaway (1995) pointed out that many of the patients who eventually receive an MPD diagnosis are fragile, depressed women who fear abandonment and the withdrawal of nurturing and who (like Miss Beauchaump) develop a strong emotional bond with their therapist. For such patients, the MPD diagnosis may serve as an explanation for their ambivalent feelings, unexplained dysphoria, and inconsistent actions, and may also become a vehicle for eliciting their therapist's attention and concern:

> The patient then may reconstruct through fantasy, confabulation, distortion, and other mental mechanisms entire portions of his or her life history in accordance with the established stereotype for the multiple personality syndrome, which necessarily anticipates the discovery of extensive hidden abuse memories. Through projective identification the patient may attempt to turn the therapist into the ideal nurturing, protecting and accepting mother who will never abandon the patient as long as the patient has one more trauma memory to uncover or one more hidden personality to reveal. (Ganaway, 1995)

The therapist's active role in encouraging and validating the patient's displays of MPD symptomatology is not ignored by Ganaway (1995):

> The therapist's need for empathic mirroring by the patient may result in subtle encouragement of the development in these suggestible patients of stereotypical MPD symptoms and the reporting of false or distorted life experiences to validate the therapist's preconceived beliefs in the high incidence and prevalence of undiagnosed cases of MPD. . . . Therapist fascination for and indulgence in the phenomenology of multiplicity, especially the dramatic identity alterations, inevitably leads to reification of the personality parts and their perceived separateness . . . in the context of a mutual deception between the needy, dependent patient and an accommodating, sometimes also needy therapist.

Like Ganaway (1992, 1995), Simpson (1989) and Sutcliffe and Jones (1962) also emphasized the role of the therapeutic interaction in leading to ever more elaborate displays of MPD symptomatology by needy and suggestible patients. Simpson (1989), for example, pointed out that

> the extent of the [MPD] patient's pathology is proportional to [the] amount and intensity [of their psychotherapy], and shows the most evolved and disturbed anomalies in the most intensively studied cases. It appears to be the norm that further "personalities," often more entertaining and rewarding for the audience, emerge in therapy. (p. 565)

Ganaway (1992) contended that, before coming to his clinic, many of his MPD patients had been reinforced by their previous therapists to exhibit increasingly expansive symptomatology, a multiplication of personalities, and the recovery of increasingly bizarre and horrendous memories of abuse. However, by focusing attention on patients' strengths and on their realistic concerns, while at the same time deemphasizing their MPD symptomatology, Ganaway (1992) succeeded in producing a diminution in such symptomatology:

> The expansiveness encountered by a previous therapist often has curtailed itself when the newly referred patient realizes that my focus is not on the incessant uncovering and identifying of new personality parts to account for all aberrant, inappropriate, or intolerable thoughts, emotions, impulses and behaviors. . . . At this point, more often than not, the patient appears to settle down to the process of working through his or her feelings, reclaiming disowned aspects of the self, and moving past previously pervasive expectation of perpetual victimization. (pp. 203–204)

Currently, the legitimation of MPD often involves a social dimension that transcends the patient–therapist interactions that occur in the consulting room. In some respects, advocacy of the MPD diagnosis has taken on the characteristics of a social movement (Mulhern, 1991b). MPD patients, along with therapists, participate regularly in MPD workshops and conferences, and both patients and therapists frequently have access to national newsletters that provide updated information about the syndrome. Along with their individual therapy, many patients participate in MPD self-help and therapy groups that provide ongoing legitimation for their multiple self enactments. One highly vocal subset of patients have asserted their right to remain multiples (Mulhern, 1991b, 1994). Some therapists use MPD patients as cotherapists to help convince skeptical new patients that their MPD diagnosis is accurate. Relatedly, Kluft (1989) indicated that a high proportion of MPD patients report plans to become psychotherapists. In fact, according to some estimates, 17% or more of the therapists treating MPD are themselves patients or former patients diagnosed with MPD or other dissociative disorders (N. E. Perry, 1992). These therapists, who help to socialize new patient recruits into the MPD role, are reminiscent of those in traditional cultures who, after their own possession, join and sometimes become leaders of the possession cults that shape and legitimate the spirit possession enactments of new members.

SUMMARY

The importance of psychotherapy and therapy-related social supports in the genesis and maintenance of MPD would be hard to overemphasize. Therapists are, after all, typically viewed by their clients as competent experts whose opinions are highly valued and whose suggestions are treated seriously. In addition, psychotherapy clients are often insecure, unhappy people with a strong investment in winning the concern, interest, and approval of their therapist. This is likely to be particularly true of polysymptomatic, chronically disturbed women with a long history of psychiatric involvement, who are typically diagnosed as MPD sufferers. Given these circumstances, mutual shaping between therapists "on the lookout" for signs of MPD and clients involved in creating an impression that will elicit approval is likely to lead to enactments of multiple personality that confirm the initial suspicions of the therapist and, in turn, lead the therapist to encourage and validate more elaborate displays of the disorder (Sutcliffe & Jones, 1962). In addition, the newsletters, therapy groups, workshops, and informal interactions with other multiples that have become an important part of the social life of many MPD patients serve to continually shape and legitimate multiple self enactments.

This analysis does not imply that MPD patients are typically faking their multiplicity. Instead, it suggests that some patients may come to adopt a view of themselves that is congruent with the view conveyed to them by their therapist. Adoption of this view involves clients coming to construe their various "symptoms" (e.g., mood swings, shameful or unrepresentative behaviors, ambivalent feelings, hostile fantasies, forgetfulness, guilt-inducing sexual feelings, bad habits) as the results of personified alter selves. In our culture, it is common for people to describe uncharacteristic or ambivalent feelings and behaviors metaphorically as resulting from different parts of themselves (e.g., "one part of me wanted to do it but another part said no," "I don't know what came over me," "I'm of two minds about the issue"). A sociocognitive analysis suggests that the development of MPD involves a reification of such metaphors that leads both the client and the therapist to construe the client as possessing multiple selves.

19

CORRELATES OF MULTIPLE PERSONALITY DISORDER

PHYSIOLOGICAL CORRELATES OF MPD

The idea that MPD involves many people who in some literal sense reside within the same body is the view most commonly propagated in the popular media, and as we have seen throughout this book, it is not far from the view held by some professionals. It is probably this idea and its implications that have been the main impetus for studies aimed at establishing distinct physiological differences among the alter personalities of MPD patients.

A large number of anecdotal reports as well as some more systematically conducted studies have claimed that different alters of the same patients exhibit different handwriting styles (Coons, 1984; W. S. Taylor & Martin, 1944; Thigpen & Cleckley, 1957), different voice qualities (Coons, 1980; Putnam, 1984), handedness changes, heart rate changes, different allergic responses, different responses to medication (Putnam, 1984; Putnam et al., 1986), the development of hives in one personality and their disappearance in another (Coons, 1984), different patterns of EEG response (Ludwig et al., 1972), changes in respiration rate (Bahnson & Smith, 1975; Larmore, Ludwig, & Cain, 1977), alter-specific patterns of visual evoked potential responding (Braun, 1983; Larmore et al., 1977) and galvanic skin response (GSR) responding (Brende, 1984; Ludwig et al., 1972), alter-specific right–left asymmetries in autonomic responses (Brende, 1984; Gott, Everett, & Whipple, 1984), and numerous other alter-specific physiological responses (for critical reviews, see P. Brown, 1994; S. D. Miller & Triggiano, 1992; North et al., 1993).

Some of the response patterns described above are under voluntary control and therefore change on these dimensions during the enactment of different alters generates little surprise. Anyone can easily manipulate their handwriting style, rate of respiration, and voice quality, and many right-handers can act as if they are left-handed if they choose to do so. In a great many other cases, the alter-specific physiological changes were described in anecdotal reports of clinical observation. Under these circumstances, the reliability of the observations is unknown, and appropriate methodological procedures and safeguards were not instituted. Consequently, in these cases, no firm conclusions about alter-specific physiological changes are possible (P. Brown, 1994; S. D. Miller & Triggiano, 1992)

Alter-specific changes in EEG, visual evoked potential responding, heart rate, GSR, blood pressure, the effects of medication, and other autonomic responses seem dramatic because those responses are usually assumed to be outside of normal volitional control, highly stable, and largely uninfluenced by mundane psychological factors. In fact, however, many autonomic responses (e.g., heart rate, EEG activity, GSR, visual evoked responding) show marked variability within the same person as a function of many psychological variables (e.g., changes in mood state, expectations). For example, significant changes in heart rate, blood pressure, EEG activity, GSR, and muscle tension frequently accompany enhancements in relaxation (Edmonston, 1981, 1991). Changes in muscle tension also discriminate between depressed and nondepressed moods (Greden, Genero, Price, Feinberg, & Levine, 1986), some of the autonomic changes reported among the alters of MPD patients are characteristic of changes in degree of anxiety (Zahn, 1986), and anyone who has worked in an inpatient psychiatric service well knows that the amount of medication required to calm patients or help them sleep varies as a function of how agitated and upset the patients are at the time. EEG alpha activity is profoundly influenced by eye movements (for reviews, see Mulholland & Peper, 1971; Perlini & Spanos, 1991; Plotkin, 1979). For instance, when people keep their eyes relatively still and stare into space without focusing, they generate much more occipital EEG alpha activity than when they make coordinated and convergent eye movements (e.g., as when counting the objects in the room). Self-observation makes it obvious that physiological responses such as heart rate, sweating palms (which influence GSR responding), respiratory changes, degree of muscle tension, and a flushed face are related to changes in mood (just remember the last time you became really angry), and a large number of studies indicate that physiological changes on these dimensions can be induced when subjects simply imagine different moods (for a review, see Sheikh & Kunzendorf, 1984). In predisposed individuals, stress-induced emotional disturbance or strong negative moods can induce asthma attacks (Hyland, 1990; Kleeman, 1967), and, as we saw in chapter 9, expectations and suggestions sometimes coupled with mechanical stimulation can occasionally produce a variety of dermatological changes including weals and hives, as well as localized changes in blood flow that manifest as temperature and coloration changes in the limbs (Johnson, 1989; Sarbin & Slage, 1972). Given all of this, the idea of alter-specific differences in physiological responding loses much of its mystery. It no longer seems particularly surprising, for example, that some MPD patients may well show very different patterns of physiological arousal and different patterns of EEG activity when they become involved in enacting, say, an angry, potentially violent suspicious personality who vigilantly scans the environment as opposed to a quiet, calm, "bookish" personality who enjoys pleasant daydreams.

A number of controlled studies assessing alter-specific physiological changes have begun to appear. Despite earlier reports of consistent between-personality differences in lateralized autonomic asymmetries (Brende, 1984; Gott et al., 1984), Putnam, Zahn, and Post (1990) found no consistent differences in electrodermal laterality in a sample of 9 MPD patients. Eight of these 9 MPD patients did manifest distinct patterns of physiological responding while enacting different alters. However, 3 out of 5 non-MPD control subjects instructed to role-play different personalities did the same. Coons, Milstein, and Marley (1982) compared EEG differences across the alters of two MPD patients and a control subject who simulated alter personalities. The control subject exhibited larger between-alter EEG differences than did either of the MPD patients. Coons et al. (1982) concluded as follows about their own study and others attempting to demonstrate between-alter EEG differences:

> We conclude that the most likely explanation for the differences found in the frequency analysis involves changes in intensity of concentration, mood, and degree of muscle relaxation, and duration of recording involved in such studies. It is not as if each personality is a different individual with a different brain. Instead, to put it simply, the EEG changes reflect changes in emotional state. (p. 825)

Two studies (S. D. Miller, 1989; S. D. Miller, Blackburn, Scholes, White, & Mamalis, 1991) reported significantly more variability within MPD patients than within simulators on several dimensions related to vision, including visual acuity, eye muscle balance, and visual fields. However, at least two qualifications are needed here. As pointed out earlier, simulators simply attempt to fake overt behavior. Consequently, any physiological changes produced by the cognitive or emotional alterations that are generated by becoming absorbed or subjectively involved in role enactment are unlikely to be manifested by simulators. The second qualification, noted by S. D. Miller and Triggiano (1992), suggests that the between-group differences obtained in these studies were more likely due to MPD patients exhibiting more variability than controls in opthalmalogical responding than to consistent between-alter differences in opthalmalogical responding among the MPD subjects.

As will be discussed later in this chapter, MPD patients differ markedly from nonpsychiatric controls on a very wide range of psychophysiological and psychiatric symptoms. For example, MPD patients are much more likely than nonpsychiatric control subjects to be diagnosed as exhibiting a wide array of conversion symptoms (North et al., 1993). Several studies indicate that patients diagnosed as suffering from conversion symptoms are significantly more likely than those given other psychiatric diagnoses to eventually be diagnosed as suffering from real, and sometimes even fatal, neurological diseases (Slater & Glithero, 1965; G. C. Watson & Buranen, 1979; Whitlock, 1967). If more MPD patients than nonpsychiatric controls suffer from undiagnosed neurological disorders, the finding that MPD patients exhibit more variability than controls on such neurologically related variables as eye muscle balance and visual acuity would not be surprising. In short, MPD patients and the nonpsychiatric subjects who typically serve as simulating controls in the kinds of experiments described above probably differ from one another on a large number of psychological and psychophysiological dimensions. Some of these differences might produce different patterns of sensory and perceptual responding (independently of any consistent between-alter physiological differences; North et al., 1993).

Several studies (Braun, 1983; Larmore et al., 1977; Ludwig et al., 1972; Pitblado & Cohen, 1984) reported between-alter differences in visual evoked potential responding in MPD patients. However, none of these studies included non-MPD controls. This is an important limitation, because a number of studies (reviewed by Perlini, Spanos, & Jones, in press) have indicated that expectations and suggestion can produce significant changes in the late components of the visual evoked potential. In addition, numerous artifacts that can be difficult to control (e.g., eye movements) can produce substantial and systematic changes in visual evoked potential responding. For example, a subject who looked intently at the light source when enacting one personality, and who unfocused her eyes when enacting a different personality, might well exhibit sustained and substantial between-alter evoked potential differences. Putnam (1982) reported larger between-alter visual evoked response differences in 11 MPD patients than in simulators. In a later paper, however, Putnam (1984) himself noted that "these findings may be the result of a systematic artifact generated by some of the alternate personalities of the multiple patients and not by the simulating controls" (pp. 35–36).

No psychophysiologist would be surprised to find massive differences on a wide range of physiological responses such as EEG, GSR, heart rate, blood pressure, muscle tension, and so forth before and after a person ran up a flight of stairs, before and during an abrasive interview designed to make people angry, before and after a person learned he or she had won the lottery, or while a person was relaxing at the beach as opposed to taking a difficult exam. Activities that engage cognitive emotional and motoric processes are associated with changes on a wide range of psychophysiological response systems, and activities that require different patterns of cognitive–emotional responding are likely to produce different patterns of psychophysiological responding. From a sociocognitive perspective, enacting alter personalities is something that MPD patients are well practiced at doing, rather than something that happens to them. To the extent that involvement in the enactment of personality A requires the calling up of different moods, different interpretations of social situations, different levels of vigilance toward others, and the enactment of different emotional nuances than does the enactment of personality B, we might expect different patterns of psychophysiological responding to accompany the enactments of personalities A and B.

HYPNOTIZABILITY, DISSOCIATIVE CAPACITY, AND MPD

MPD patients frequently attain high scores on standardized hypnotizability scales (Bliss, 1980, 1984a, 1984b, 1986; Bliss & Jeppsen, 1985; Bliss & Larson, 1985). This finding is frequently interpreted by MPD proponents in terms of the hypothesis that hypnotizability scores reflect individual differences in the capacity for dissociation (Bliss, 1986; Putnam, 1993). One variation of this hypothesis holds that children with a high potential for dissociation are likely to become highly hypnotizable adults. Moreover, when exposed to early trauma, these individuals are likely to develop dissociative symptoms, including the development of alters. A variation of this hypothesis suggests that early trauma enhances the capacity to dissociate and thereby leads to both high hypnotizability and MPD. Both versions of this hypothesis predict strong correlations between measures of dissociation and hypnotizability, and the notion that early trauma (particularly sexual trauma) facilitates dissociation predicts that people who report a history of such trauma should score higher than those who do not on measures of dissociation and hypnotizability.

To test the hypothesis that the capacity to dissociate correlates strongly with hypnotizabililty, Stava and Jaffa (1988) developed several objective indexes of dissociative capacity (e.g., degree of success at dividing attention and performing two tasks simultaneously). None of these dissociative indexes correlated significantly with hypnotizability. E. M. Bernstein and Putnam (1986) developed a questionnaire index of dissociation called the Dissociative Experiences Scale (DES). Putnam (1989) and Frischholz et al. (1992) reported that the DES correlated significantly with hypnotizability. However, two studies (Nadon, Hoyt, Register, & Kihlstrom, 1991; Spanos, Arango, & de Groot, 1993) found that DES scores correlated significantly with hypnotizability only when both indexes were assessed in the same context. When the DES was administered in a context that subjects did not associate with their hypnotizability testing, it failed to correlate significantly with hynotizability. Even when tested in the same context, correlations between DES scores and hypnotizabilty, although statistically significant, were relatively weak. For instance, in the Spanos et al. (1993) study, the in-context correlation between DES scores and a behavioral index of hypnotizability was only .23. Relatedly, the correlations between DES and hypnotizability scores, although statistically significant, were minuscule in both the Nadon et al. (1991) study ($r = .14$) and the Frischholz et al. (1992) study ($r = .12$). Segal and Lynn (1993) found no significant relationship between DES scores and hypnotizability. The findings of these studies indicate a lack of any intrinsic relationship between the DES and hypnotizabilty. Whether these dimensions are found to be significantly related appears to be dependent on expectations generated by testing both dimensions in the same context. Moreover, even when significant correlations between these variables are obtained, they are too small to be of any practical or theoretical significance.

The concept of dissociation is thought by MPD theorists to be particularly important for explaining amnesic phenomena. As pointed out in chapter 4, a number of investigators consider both the amnesia displayed by MPD patients and hypnotic amnesia to reflect the same underlying dissociative process. It is worth noting, therefore, that Frischholz et al. (1992) assessed the degree of hypnotic amnesia displayed by subjects in response to the amnesia item on a standardized hypnotizability scale. The correlation between the number of items recalled during the amnesia period and DES scores was only $-.19$. Moreover, the correlation between DES scores and reversible recall (considered a more sensitive measure of hypnotic amnesia than number of items recalled during the suggestion) was a nonsignificant .08. In short, the processes involved in hypnotic amnesia are largely unrelated to whatever is measured by the DES.

Early Trauma

If early abuse facilitates the use of dissociation as a characteristic cognitive style, and if both DES scores and hypnotizability reflect such a cognitive style, abuse history should correlate strongly with both DES scores and hypnotizability. In addition, because women are much more likely than men to report a history of early sexual abuse, DES scores and hypnotizability should be significantly higher in women than in men.

Several studies have indicated that hypnotizability correlated significantly with severity of childhood punishment and with child abuse (J. R. Hilgard, 1970; M. R. Nash & Lynn, 1986; M. R. Nash, Lynn, & Givens, 1984). However, more recent studies have failed to replicate this relationship (DiTomasso & Routh, 1993; Nash et al., 1993a). Several studies also reported significant relationships between a history of child abuse and DES scores (Chu & Dill, 1990; DiTomasso & Routh, 1993, Nash et al., 1993a). However, the correlations between these variables were often of small magnitude. For instance, DiTomasso and Routh (1993) reported that DES scores correlated only .21 with sexual abuse history and .18 with physical abuse history. In addition, Nash et al. (1993a) found that the relationship between DES scores and reported abuse history fell to nonsignificance after controlling for dysfunctional family environment. In two recent studies, Council (1993a, 1993b) found that the magnitude of the relationship between reported abuse history and DES scores was dependent on whether the DES was administered before or after subjects reported on their abuse history. These findings raise the possibility that the relationship between abuse history and dissociation is an expectancy-mediated artifact.

Most studies report no differences between the sexes in hypnotizabilty (for a review, see de Groh, 1989). Relatedly, the available data also indicate that men and women attain similar scores on the DES (C. A. Ross, Joshi, & Currie, 1990; Sanders, McRoberts, & Tollefson, 1989).

In North American studies, women are assigned the MPD diagnosis much more frequently than men, whereas the one Swiss study (Modestin, 1992) found that men were assigned the diagnosis slightly more frequently than women. Given the consistent failure to find gender differences in hypnotizability, these cross-cultural gender differences in rates of MPD indicate that the relationship between MPD and hypnotizabilty must be moderated by variables other than gender. The hypothesis that this moderator is early child abuse requires that child abuse occur at least three times more frequently in women than in men in North America, but with about equal frequency in men and women in Switzerland. This hypothesis further suggests that the combination of high hypnotizability and early child abuse is much more common in North America, where MPD is relatively common, than in, say, Great Britain and in other societies with very low rates of MPD. The available evidence does not indicate that high hypnotizability is more common in North America than in Great Britain, nor does the evidence indicate very low rates of child abuse in Great Britain (La Fontaine, 1990). For example, C. L. Nash and West (1985) found that 48% of the women they surveyed in the British city of Cambridge reported having been subjected to some form of sexual abuse as children, a figure similar to the prevalence rates obtained in many North American studies.

In summary, the available findings fail to support the hypotheses that hypnotizability is strongly related to measures of dissociation or that there are substantial sex differences in hypnotizability and dissociation. Data concerning relationships between abuse history, on the one hand, and hypnotizability and dissociation, on the other, are, at best, mixed. Replication failures are common, findings that appear to support a relationship between these variables may be artifacts of the testing context or of other uncontrolled variables, and the significant relationships that are obtained between these variables are often too small to be of much theoretical or practical significance. National differences in rates of MPD are not associated with corresponding national differences in hypnotizability, and gender differences in MPD are not mirrored by similar gender differences either in hypnotizability or in DES scores.

Dissociative Cognitive Style

In two studies (E. M. Bernstein & Putnam, 1986; Ross, Heber, et al., 1989), MPD patients attained high scores on the DES and higher scores than normals, alcoholics, neurological patients, schizophrenics, and agoraphobics. These findings are usually interpreted to mean that (a) the DES assesses stable individual differences on a relatively specific cognitive style or capacity labeled as dissociation, (b) MPD patients make much more extensive use of this cognitive style than others, and (c) the symptoms of MPD (e.g., creation of alters, inter-alter amnesia) stem from the extensive use of this cognitive style by people who become multiples. As we shall see, however, these ideas are not without difficulties, and alternative interpretations of these findings are possible.

The DES instructs subjects to indicate the extent to which they have had experiences like the following:

> Some people sometimes find that they are approached by people that they do not know who call them by another name or insist that they have met them before.
>
> Some people find that in one situation they may act so differently compared with another situation that they feel almost as if they were two different people.

Obviously, patients who have defined themselves as suffering from MPD are much more likely than patients diagnosed in other ways to endorse such items. Adopting a self-definition as a multiple means that items of this kind must be endorsed to validate that self-construal and to maintain a public self-presentation that is consistent with that self-definition. Thus, regardless of any hypothesized underlying cognitive style, MPD patients could hardly present themselves as such unless they strongly endorsed such items.

Antens, Frischholz, Braun, et al. (1991) compared the DES responses of MPD patients and two groups of control subjects who were instructed to fake MPD. Those in one faking group were familiar with MPD and those in the other were naive in this regard. Subjects in both of the faking groups attained somewhat higher DES scores than the real MPD patients, although there was substantial overlap between the fakers and MPD patients.

The similarity in performance between MPD patients and fakers found by Antens et al. (1991) demonstrates that the DES is face obvious. The fact that fakers attained somewhat higher DES scores than actual MPD patients is not surprising. As pointed out in chapter 2, people instructed to fake hypnosis frequently respond more strongly to suggestions than non-faking high hypnotizables, because fakers are unconstrained by demands to report honestly about their experiences and instead generate ideal responses. Thus, the results of the Antens et al. (1991) study indicate that the strong endorsement of most or all DES items is what most people expect of the prototypical MPD patient. It is hardly surprising, therefore, that most MPD patients hold the same expectations, but temper somewhat the endorsement of relevant items in terms of the constraints produced by implicit demands for honesty.

Tillman, Nash, and Lerner (1994) pointed out that the DES often correlates highly with other questionnaire indexes of psychopathology. MPD patients are usually chronically disturbed, polysymptomatic women with a very wide range of psychiatric complaints. Such people are likely to attain relatively high scores on almost any self-report index that includes descriptions of psychopathology. Consequently, high DES scores may tell us less about the specific cognitive propensities of MPD patients than about the general tendency of these patients to describe themselves as suffering from a wide range of psychopathological symptoms.

Some evidence indicates that the DES, particularly when administered to clinical samples, is not unidimensional (E. B. Carlson et al., 1991; Frischholz et al., 1992). Later, we will examine how one dimension of the scale—the propensity to become absorbed in imaginative experiences —may be related to MPD.

A particularly obvious shortcoming of the hypothesis that a dissociative cognitive style moderates the relationship between MPD and hypnotizability is the failure of this hypothesis to address the fact that hypnotizability scales measure responsiveness to social communications: the extent to which people construct the experiences and generate the behaviors that are tacitly requested by the suggestions. When hypnotizability is conceptualized as an asocial cognitive capacity for dissociation, an obvious question remains unasked: What are the suggestions (i.e., tacit social communications) that lead to multiple identity enactments?

Recall that hypnotic suggestions are communications that call for the construction of "as if" situations. Thus, suggestions for arm levitation, age regression, and amnesia are, in effect, tacit requests to use imaginative and other cognitive abilities to behave as if one's arm is rising by itself, as if one has reverted to childhood, and as if one is unable to remember. Behaving as if an imaginary scenario is true involves creating the requisite subjective experiences as well as generating the requisite behaviors (Sarbin & Coe, 1972; Spanos, Rivers, & Ross, 1977). The hypnotic interview procedures typically used to "call up" alter personalities, like hypnotic suggestions for age regression, and amnesia, are requests to construct an "as if" scenario. In the case of diagnostic interviews that address alter personalities, subjects are tacitly invited to behave and experience as if they possessed alter identities.

Hypnotizability as Trait

One hypothesis that does not require any particular relationship between child abuse and MPD and that does not ignore the social nature of the suggestive process holds that multiplicity frequently stems from the cuing contained in the kinds of leading questions and interviews described in earlier chapters. This hypothesis further holds that hypnotizability is a stable traitlike characteristic and that high hypnotizables constitute only about 10% of the population. Because high hypnotizables are more suggestible than moderate or low hypnotizables, it is the highs who are particularly likely to respond to the strong cuing for MPD contained in interviews designed to diagnose this disorder (Ganaway, 1989; Mulhern, 1991b).

According to this hypothesis, only a small proportion of people possess the cognitive skills required to generate the "as if" experiences and behaviors called for by suggestions for amnesia, hallucination, and so on, and it is these people who also possess the cognitive skills required to generate the experience of an alter identity when tacitly instructed to do so in a hypnotic interview. This hypothesis accounts for why MPD patients typically score as high hypnotizables. Moreover, it can account for different cross-national gender ratios and cross-national incidence rates by suggesting that these reflect the expectations of therapists who use leading hypnotic procedures. Those who believe MPD is relatively common will use such procedures frequently, those who believe it is more common in women than men will use such procedures more frequently with women than with men, and so on. However, the stable trait hypothesis cannot account parsimoniously for the very high rates of multiple identity enactment seen in some traditional cultures (e.g., 47% of the women in some villages; Boddy,

1988) or for the very high rates of demonic possession seen in some group possession cases where, for example, all or almost all of the nuns in a particular convent displayed possession simultaneously (Huxley, 1952). This hypothesis also has difficulty with the findings that glossolalics do not uniformly exhibit high hypnotizability (Spanos & Hewitt, 1979), that in some congregations glossolalia occurs in all or almost all members (Goodman, 1972), and that people who report contact with UFO aliens do not score particularly high on measures of hypnotizability.

Hypnotizability and Context

An alternative to the stable trait hypothesis suggests that a great many people who do not typically attain high hypnotizability scores possess the cognitive abilities required to enact the "as if" scenarios contained in hypnotic suggestions and in hypnotic interviews that call for multiplicity (Spanos, 1986a). According to this hypothesis, many people fail to respond to hypnotic suggestions either because they have negative attitudes and expectations concerning such responding or because they misinterpret what is called for by these suggestions and therefore do not use the cognitive abilities they possess to generate the requisite experiences. A number of recent studies have obtained support for these ideas by demonstrating that short training procedures aimed at altering subjects' interpretations and attitudes, and sometimes even very brief instructions aimed at changing interpretations alone, produced large gains in hypnotizability. Many subjects who previously scored as low hypnotizables attained high levels of hypnotizability following such interventions (e.g., Gorassini, Sowerby, Creighton, & Fry, 1991; Spanos, Gabora, Jarrett, & Gwynn, 1989; Spanos, Lush, & Gwynn, 1989). In short, hypnotizability is not as immutable as some earlier theorizing indicated (e.g., C. W. Perry, 1977), and a much greater proportion of people than indicated by conventional hypnotizability testing possess the cognitive abilities required to experience the "as if" scenarios traditionally associated with hypnotic suggestions.

Several studies have indicated that relationships between hypnotizability and the degree to which subjects are led by leading questions, or the extent to which they respond to nonhypnotic suggestions, is context dependent (Gwynn et al., 1993; Spanos, Kennedy & Gwynn, 1984; Spanos, Quigley, et al., 1991). In these studies, hypnotizability correlated significantly with suggestibility and with response to leading questions only when subjects connected their hypnotizability with their performance in these other situations.

The leading questions and leading interviews used to diagnose MPD are very frequently conducted in a hypnotic context, and the psychotherapeutic procedures used with these patients to search for more and more alters, integrate alters, and so forth almost always make use of hypnotic procedures. In other words, almost all MPD patients have been subjected repeatedly to hypnotic procedures and have responded repeatedly to these procedures by displaying alter personalities. Given this, MPD patients are very likely to construe themselves as highly hypnotizable subjects who are motivated to respond as directed to communications delivered in a hypnotic context and who expect to respond in this manner. Consequently, when they are tested on standardized hypnotizabilty scales, they are likely to respond in terms of the motivations and expectations derived from their earlier hypnotic experiences and, therefore, attain high hypnotizability scores.

As pointed out in chapter 2, faking high levels of hypnotizability is a simple matter. To the extent that MPD patients construed high hypnotizability as central to their self-presentations, it would be an easy matter for those who were unable to generate the requisite subjective experiences to fake high hypnotizability.

The above discussion should not be taken to imply that relatively stable cognitive propensities play no role in hypnotizability or, alternatively, that contextual demands are the only determinants of hypnotizability. Although substantial proportions of people may possess the imaginative and other cognitive abilities and role skills required to enact the "as if" behaviors called for by hypnotic suggestions, some people may find such enactments much easier and more "natural" than do others.

Fantasy Proneness

A substantial number of studies have reported positive correlations between hypnotizability and various measures of imaginativeness or fantasy proneness (for a review, see de Groh, 1989). The relationships between these variables are not as strong as sometimes implied, and for at least some measures of imaginativeness, relationships with hypnotizability appear to be expectancy-mediated artifacts (Kirsch & Council, 1989). Nevertheless, a good deal of data suggest that many highly hypnotizable subjects can be described as having rich fantasy lives. Along related lines, Sarbin and Lim (1963) found that hypnotizability correlated with subjects' ability to improvise effectively during pantomime role playing; several studies (Coe, 1964; Coe, Buckner, Howard, & Kobayashi, 1972) indicated that people with a background in dramatic acting scored higher in hynotizability than people without such backgrounds; and several studies (Council & Huff, 1990; S. A. Myers & Austrin, 1985; P. L. Nelson, 1989; Wilson & Barber, 1981) indicated that hypnotizability, fantasy proneness, and other measures of imaginative involvement correlated with the extent to which people believe that they have had occult and paranormal experiences.

Although the DES is usually conceptualized as an index of dissociation, a factor analytic study of this scale suggested that one of its major components assesses the tendency to become absorbed in imaginative activity (Carlson et al., 1991). The DES correlates to a moderate degree with various indexes of fantasy proneness and imaginative activity (Frischholz et al., 1992; Nadon et al., 1991; Norton, Ross, & Novotny, 1990; Segal & Lynn, 1993). Like other measures of fantasy proneness, the DES also correlates with the extent to which people believe they have had psychic experiences (Richards, 1991).

Several investigators have hypothesized that MPD patients are likely to be fantasy-prone individuals (Lynn, Rhue, & Green, 1988; Putnam, 1989; W. C. Young, 1988), and some clinical reports describe such patients as highly imaginative people with rich fantasy lives who have spent much time covertly rehearsing and becoming absorbed in a range of "make believe" activities (e.g., Keyes, 1981; Schreiber, 1973). Many MPD patients are also described as theatrical and attention seeking and as having a flair for dramatic presentations (North et al., 1993). As indicated above, these patients also exhibit high hypnotizability and high DES scores. In addition, two studies (Ross, Heber, Norton, & Anderson, 1989a; Stern, 1984) indicated that MPD patients frequently report experiencing a wide range of occult and paranormal experiences. Taken together, these findings suggest that at least a subset of MPD patients can be described as highly imaginative individuals with a tolerance for unusual or exotic beliefs and a flair for the dramatic that enables them to become absorbed with relative ease in "make believe" activities and roles. Given appropriate motivations, such people might be particularly adept at enacting multiple identities when contextual inducements call for such enactments.

PSYCHOLOGICAL CORRELATES OF MPD

At various places throughout this book, MPD patients have been described as chronically disturbed, unhappy, polysymptomatic (usually female) people who are emotionally needy and who use displays of physical and psychological symptoms as a means of conveying their distress and gaining and maintaining the attention of their therapists and others. A number of studies that have examined the characteristic psychological and interactional styles of MPD patients have generated findings that are consistent with this general formulation. For instance, after reviewing published studies and conducting their own analysis of full-length biographies of MPD patients, North et al. (1993) concluded that the three psychiatric diagnoses most strongly and consistently applied to MPD patients were borderline personality disorder, somatoform disorder (also called Briquet's syndrome and hysteria), and antisocial personality disorder (also called sociopathy or psychopathy). As we shall see, each of these diagnoses is consistent with the clinical picture described above.

Borderline Personality and MPD

In a number of clinical studies, large proportions of the MPD patients were diagnosed as meeting clinical criteria for borderline personality disorder (Armstrong & Loewenstein, 1990; Horevitz & Braun, 1984; Kluft, 1982; Rivera, 1991). Among other things, borderlines are described as unstable people who display sudden mood shifts; rapid, marked changes in attitude; impulsivity; and sudden, inappropriate anger. People who receive this diagnosis are described as behaving in these ways on a chronic basis. When provided with the idea of MPD, such people may find it particularly easy to conceptualize their rapid shifts in mood and behavior as stemming from different selves that are at war with one another.

Some investigators (e.g., Kluft, 1985a) contend that borderline personality is distinct from MPD because MPD patients frequently enact symptoms that are not characteristic of borderline personality and because some MPD patients do not exhibit borderline symptoms. It is worth keeping in mind that the diagnostic controversies in this area frequently result from the tendency of psychiatric investigators to reify diagnostic categories and treat them as if they referred to objective and distinct disease entities. Instead, it may be more useful to treat these diagnostic categories as referring to interactional styles that specify some of the relatively stable cognitive, emotional, and behavioral patterns of responding that characterize the ways in which some people typically interact in their dealings with others. From this perspective, it is unnecessary to pigeonhole people into one diagnostic category as opposed to another. For example, the fact that many MPD patients chronically display somatoform symptoms as well as a borderline style of interacting need not create any diagnostic dilemma. It simply indicates that many MPD patients, along with displaying chronic emotional lability, impulsivity, and rapid changes in attitude, also complain chronically about suffering from a wide range of physical symptoms. Relatedly, the fact that not all MPD patients display borderline symptoms should also not surprise us. As we have seen throughout this book, given the appropriate contextual cues, people may enact displays of multiplicity for a wide range of reasons and in a wide variety of situations. The fact that a history of borderline symptomatology may be one avenue for facilitating the adoption and maintenance of multiplicity displays in certain North American clinical contexts certainly does not imply that, in psychiatric contexts, only people with borderline symptomatology will have the ability and motivation to enact MPD when cued to do so.

Somatoform Disorder

As we saw when describing the 19th-century patients treated by Charcot and Janet, the term *hysteria* has long been associated with the display of fictive illnesses. In other words, this diagnosis was applied to people who chronically displayed neurological and other physical symptoms in the absence of evidence of underlying physiological pathology. Classic examples of such displays have included the conversion symptoms enacted so prominently at the Salpetrière: symptoms of uniocular blindness, hysterical convulsions, hemi-anesthesia, limb paralyses that were reversible with hypnosis, and so on. Patients who chronically display somatic symptoms of this kind are currently labeled as suffering from somatoform disorder or (depending on the stringency of the diagnostic criteria used) Briquet's syndrome (Guze, 1970, 1975; North et al., 1993; Perly & Guze, 1962).

MPD patients frequently exhibit a very wide range of chronic somatic symptoms (Bliss, 1980; Coons, 1980; North et al., 1993; Putnam et al., 1986; Ross, Heber, Norton, & Anderson, 1989b) and more such symptoms than patients in most other diagnostic categories. In other words, MPD patients typically meet the clinical criteria for Briquet's syndrome or somatoform disorder (North et al., 1993). Patients given these diagnoses are typically described as overly dramatic and expert at manipulatively using symptoms displays to gain attention from others. For example, according to Kass, Silvers, and Abroms (1972), these patients

> adopt the classical hysterical behaviors to dominate and control relationships that are experienced basically as precarious and untrustworthy. . . . The physician is particularly vulnerable to the hysterical appeal. He is invited to rescue a woman in distress because only he "really knows and understands," but he is frustrated at every turn with increased demands and covert refusals to cooperate. (p. 42)

Relatedly, Murphy (1982) pointed out that

> a dramatic and complicated medical history is characteristically presented by most hysterics. . . . Hysterics frequently present their complaints in a dramatic and florid style. . . . Some hysterics employ indirect, seductive, or manipulative behavior to secure desired medication or attention. (pp. 2559–2562)

It is worth keeping in mind that people diagnosed as borderline personalities and those labeled as suffering from somatoform disorder (or Briquet's syndrome) frequently display a substantial overlap in symptomatology. For example, North et al. (1993) combined Minnesota Multiphasic Personality Inventory (MMPI) data across a large number of studies for patients diagnosed with borderline personality disorder, Briquet's syndrome, and MPD. Mean MMPI profiles for patients in these three diagnostic groups were then superimposed on the same graph. The results were striking and indicated very similar profiles for the three groups, with markedly elevated scores on most clinical scales. The patients in these three groups also exhibited a similar pattern of responding—an inverted V pattern—

across the three MMPI validity scales (L, F, K). This pattern of responding on the MMPI validity scales is usually interpreted as indicating a tendency not only to report but to emphasize and exaggerate psychopathology (Bliss, 1984a, 1984b; Coons, 1984; North et al., 1993). In short, people diagnosed with somatoform disorder or with borderline personality disorder have learned to use the sick role as a means of expressing distress and manipulating others into attending to their emotional needs. Such people often excel at exhibiting symptoms in a dramatic and attention-getting manner and are skilled at modifying old symptoms and adopting new ones to maintain the interest and emotional commitment of their therapists. Once again, it is easy to see how such people would be both strongly motivated to respond to even subtle cues for displays of MPD and particularly skilled at enacting the symptoms of multiplicity called for by those cues. A century ago it was patients, who today would most likely be diagnosed with somatoform disorder or Briquet's syndrome, who learned to display the complex and intricate symptomatology of grand hysteria and grand hypnosis from the cues given by Charcot and his pupils. Today, patients with similar social skills, inclinations for dramatic role enactment, and motivations for using the sick role to meet their emotional and interpersonal needs appear equally adept at learning to define themselves and present themselves as suffering from MPD.

The notion that needy, polysymptomatic patients learn to display the symptoms of MPD with the instigation and legitimation of their therapists has also been conveyed forcefully by Simpson (1989):

> There is no convincing evidence that MPD is a naturally occurring condition, let alone a distinct diagnosis. It is a symptom complex that may be superimposed on other psychopathologies, consequent upon the unfortunate matching of a susceptible patient with a susceptible therapist and trainer. The diagnosis is dysfunctional, focusing attention selectively in a way that will almost invariably worsen the condition, rather than improving it. It occurs in the context of the availability of lengthy psychotherapy. Where the health system or health insurance does not sponsor this indulgence, the condition simply does not occur. (p. 565)

Antisocial Personality and MPD

A history of criminality and antisocial behavior has also been noted in substantial proportions of MPD patients (Allison, 1981; Bliss, 1986; Coons et al., 1988; Fink, 1991; North et al., 1993; Putnam et al., 1986; Rivera, 1991). Although such a history is clearly more common in male than in female MPD patients, it is far from uncommon in the female patients. Antisocial personalities are adept at altering their self-presentations for the purpose of manipulating others. Given that they see it in their best interests to do so, such people may be particularly adept at enacting displays of multiplicity.

Taken together, the symptoms associated with the diagnoses of borderline personality, somatoform disorder, and antisocial personality describe chronically manipulative, emotionally labile, needy persons who possesses a flair for the dramatic and who, over a long socialization process, have learned to strategically display a wide range of psychological and physical symptoms to express distress and obtain nurturing and sympathetic attention from significant others. For many of these people, adoption and maintenance of the sick role constitutes a kind of career to which they devote substantial time and emotional resources. When such people are exposed to general cultural information about a dramatic and attention-getting malady like MPD or to diagnostic interviews that cue and reinforce displays of multiplicity, they are particularly likely to add these behaviors to their already extensive symptom repertoires and exploit the potential of these symptoms for impressing and manipulating significant others.

SUMMARY

In short, there may be numerous cognitive propensities and interactional styles that influence the ease with which individuals carry out multiplicity enactments. On the other hand, motivational and contextual demand variables will undoubtedly interact with, and may at times even override, the effects of such individual difference variables. In addition, it is important to keep in mind that individual difference variables that might facilitate multiple identity enactments in one cultural context may be unimportant or even a hindrance to such enactments in other cultures. For example, borderline characteristics might facilitate a self-definition of multiplicity when multiplicity is defined as a pathology and when erratic and unpredictable behaviors are congruent with the multiple identity role. However, the same characteristics might well hinder displays of multiplicity in a shaman who is required to display restraint and good judgement and whose multiple identity enactments entail regular conformance with ritual requirements.

Hypnotic interviewing is the ritual commonly used in our culture to teach, elicit, and legitimate displays of multiplicity. Other cultures with different worldviews use different rituals for generating such displays. Cross-cultural differences in the rates with which multiplicity is displayed are very large, and in some cultures substantial proportions of the population display multiplicity at some point in their lives. These considerations suggest that the cognitive abilities required to experience and enact multiplicity are fairly common and that the frequency of such enactments is limited at least as much and perhaps more by contextual considerations (e.g., the practices of different therapists, the opportunity to observe more practiced demoniacs, the meanings assigned by different congregations to glossolalia) as by stable individual differences in cognitive abilities.

20

CHILD ABUSE AND MULTIPLE PERSONALITY DISORDER

Most studies find that MPD patients report extremely high rates of childhood sexual or physical abuse (Bucky & Dallenberg, 1992; Coons et al., 1988; Ross, Miller, et al., 1991; Ross, Norton, & Wozney, 1989). These findings are the major source of empirical support for the hypothesis that MPD results from early trauma. As described earlier, however, data obtained from North American spirit mediums as well as from experimental subjects who report past-life identities indicate that multiplicity can occur in the absence of early child abuse. In addition, the correlational nature of the MPD–child abuse findings precludes their establishing a causal relationship between abuse and MPD. Moreover, the frequent reports of child abuse from MPD patients can be accounted for without positing that abuse causes MPD.

As described in chapter 7, when sexual abuse is defined broadly, the sexual abuse of children is a relatively common occurrence in our culture, and such abuse occurs more frequently in girls than in boys (Finkelhor, 1987). The short-term and long-term effects of child sexual abuse on psychological functioning are by no means clear because of serious methodological problems in the studies that have addressed these issues (Beitchman et al., 1991, 1992). Nevertheless, people who were abused as children often report a range of psychiatric problems and undoubtedly come to the attention of mental health professionals at least as frequently and probably more frequently than the nonabused. In this regard, it is useful to recall Briere and Zaidi's (1989) finding that 70% of consecutive female emergency room admissions to an urban psychiatric facility reported a history of child abuse. In patients given the diagnosis of Briquet's syndrome, the rate is even higher. For instance, North et al. (1993) cited findings from an unpublished study that indicated that over 92.2% of Briquet's syndrome patients reported a history of abuse. Consequently, the high rate of abuse in MPD patients can be partly explained by the fact that a substantial proportion of chronically disturbed people who seek psychiatric help (particularly women) are likely to report a history of child abuse. In addition, because some clinicians consider a history of abuse to be a possible sign of MPD, they may be more likely to expose abused than nonabused patients to leading hypnotic interviews and other "diagnostic" procedures that generate displays of multiplicity. To the extent that this pattern occurs, the idea that early abuse is associated with MPD becomes a self-fulfilling prophecy.

Some patients who receive an MPD diagnosis do not remember having been abused in childhood until their multiplicity is "discovered" in therapy. In these cases, the patient's alter personalities report abuse that had purportedly been dissociated from the memory of the presenting personality. Under these circumstances, there is reason to believe that such newly "remembered" abuse is frequently confabulated. In other words, patients who develop the expectation that they must have been abused may construct fantasies of such abuse. Given their expectations, and the validation of these fantasies as actual memories by their therapists, these fantasies are experienced as real memories of abuse. As described in chapters 5, 6, and 7, it is important to keep the fallibility of memory in mind when examining reports of child abuse that emerge for the first time during therapy (Wakefield & Underwager, 1992).

DEVELOPMENT OF THE CONNECTION BETWEEN CHILD ABUSE AND MPD

The strong connection between child abuse and MPD is of recent origin. As we saw, cases reported by Janet, Prince, and other clinicians in the early part of the 20th century and before were much less likely than modern cases to be associated with reports of child abuse (Bowman, 1990; Kenny, 1986). Moreover, the abuse that was reported in these early cases lacked the lurid ritualistic elements that are becoming an increasingly prominent characteristic of the abuse memories proffered by modern MPD patients. An association between MPD and child abuse first came to prominence in the 1970s with the concurrent rise in public interest in child sexual abuse. In the early 1970s, the book *Sybil* (Schreiber, 1973) described the sadistic childhood abuse purportedly suffered by an MPD patient. A number of investigators have suggested that Sybil's MPD symptoms resulted from the expectations of her therapist transmitted through highly leading procedures during an extended course of psychotherapy. Abse (1987), for example, argued that Sybil's alter personalities "seem to have come about from iatrogenic suggestions in the course of therapeutic action" (p. 239), and G. Victor (1975) contended that the book-length case history read like a fairy tale. Victor also noted that, throughout much of the book, the patient denied that she had alter personalities and accepted this view only after much prodding and argument from the therapist. The resultant belief of both the patient and the therapist, that Sybil suffered from MPD, G. Victor (1975) labeled a shared delusion, a *folie à deux*. There is reason to suggest that at least some of the horrendous abuse "memories" described by Sybil were simply fantasies. For instance, Sybil gave extensive descriptions of physical and sexual abuse that she "remembered" suffering as early as 6 months of age. As indicated earlier, infantile amnesia prevents the remembering of autobiographical memories from such a young age, and there is no evidence to indicate that hypnotic or any other memory-recovery procedures can retrieve such early memories.

Despite these contrary interpretations, the book and later television movie were exceedingly popular, and Sybil, even more than Eve (Thigpen & Cleckley, 1957) in the previous decade, became a model of the MPD survivor that greatly influenced the expectations of therapists and patients alike (Ganaway, 1994; Putnam, 1989). Consequently, when MPD patients claim that they cannot remember having been abused, therapists tend to disbelieve them (Bliss, 1986). Instead, therapists may prod them repeatedly in an attempt to unearth such memories. When patients believe they may be fantasizing rather than remembering abuse, their uncertainty may be presented to them as evidence that they are unwilling to face the fact of their abuse. In short, some MPD therapists, like incest-resolution therapists more generally, appear to frequently use leading and suggestive procedures to elicit abuse memories from their patients (Mulhern, 1991a).

Some Problems With the Child-Abuse–MPD Connection

The notion that MPD is caused by child abuse, and particularly by childhood sexual abuse, requires that the relationship between MPD and reported child abuse remain strong despite national boundaries and other differences in the populations from which MPD patients are sampled. However, some evidence suggests national differences in the incidence of abuse reports among MPD patients. C. A. Ross, Norton, and Fraser (1989) found that a sample of American psychiatrists reported a much higher prevalence of child sexual abuse in their MPD patients (81.2%) than did Canadian psychiatrists (45.5%). Relatedly, C. A. Ross (1991) reported that subjects drawn from a nonclinical population and diagnosed with MPD reported much lower rates of child abuse than MPD patients drawn from clinical populations. The findings of these studies challenge the idea of a causal relationship between child abuse and MPD.

Studies of the sexual abuse of children (reviewed by Wakefield & Underwager, 1991) have indicated that the abusers are very unlikely to be women and that this is particularly true when the victim is female. Some studies of hospitalized adolescents who had been sexually abused as children reported that the perpetrators were never female (Emslie & Rosenfeld, 1983; Sansonnet-Hayden, Haley, Marriage, & Fine, 1987). Given the consistency of these findings, those reported by C. A. Ross, Miller, et al. (1991) for MPD patients raise suspicions about validity. These investigators reported that 15.7% of their MPD patients had been sexually abused by their mothers, 2.9% had been so abused by their stepmothers, 10.8% by other female relatives, and 21.6% by other women. Unfortunately, Ross, Miller, et al. did not provide the total percentage of patients abused by a woman, but that total must obviously be quite substantial and well above what would be expected on the basis of other studies of child abuse. Ross, Miller, et al. also reported on the age of earliest sexual abuse for their subjects. A substantial 26.6% reported being sexually abused before age 3, and 10.6% reported being sexually abused before their first birthday. The fact that these ages are much younger than the age at which abuse typically begins (see Wakefield & Underwager, 1992) is problematic. More troubling is that these data were based entirely on the retrospective reports of the patients. Nothing is said in the article about corroboration, and one is left wondering how these patients were able to remember what happened to them before the age of 1 or 2 years.

Reports of MPD patients recovering "memories" of abuse or other traumatic events from very young ages are relatively common. As pointed out earlier, Sybil recovered traumatic "memories" from as young as 6 months of age. Relatedly, Dell and Eisenhower (1990) reported that 8 out of 11 adolescent multiples "remembered" alters that developed at age 3, and 2 of these patients "remembered" the development of alters at 1 year and one and a half years of age. Given that recall from ages as young or younger than 2 years is extremely unlikely because of infantile amnesia, the very early abuse "memories" of MPD patients, like fetal "memories," past-life "memories," and UFO abduction memories, are most likely fantasy constructions rather than remembrances. The strongest evidence for confabulation in the childhood abuse reports of MPD patients, however, comes from the increasingly frequent reports of ritual satanic abuse given by these patients.

A number of years after the publication of *Sybil*, a book titled *Michelle Remembers* (M. Smith & Pazder, 1980) reported on ritual satanic tortures that a woman had purportedly experienced during childhood and then forgotten until they were recovered during therapy. Under the guidance of Laurence Pazder (her psychiatrist and later her husband), Michelle "remembered" that her parents apparently belonged to a satanic cult, she had seen the ritual sacrifice of both children and adults, she was forced to eat the burnt remains of one victim, she was tied up and bitten by small red spiders that were made to crawl over her body, and she was sometimes kept naked in a cage filled with snakes.

I could find no corroborating evidence in M. Smith and Pazder (1980) for the reality of Michelle's remembrances. If for no other reason, skepticism appears warranted by the fact that some of these "memories" involve Michelle's encounters with supernatural beings. In fact, both of Michelle's two sisters (who are never mentioned in the book) and her father have denied all of her allegations (Grescoe, 1980). Interestingly, Pazder had practiced medicine in West Africa in the early 1960s, where he developed an interest in ceremonial magic and acquired an extensive collection of photographs of such ceremonies. During this period, there was widespread concern in Africa over secret societies and their supposed practices of cannibalism and blood sacrifice (Parrinder, 1963; Scobie, 1965). Although Pazder denied that his African experiences influenced Michelle's remembrances, the satanic cult described by Michelle shares numerous similarities with the African "leopard societies" referred to by Pazder (Jenkins & Maier-Katkin, 1991).

Michelle's story was disseminated to a huge audience. Even before the publication of her book, her story was described in *People* magazine, and a version was soon published in the *National Inquirer*. In addition, both she and Pazder have appeared on numerous radio and television shows and frequently speak as experts at conferences on satanic ritual abuse (J. Victor, 1993).

Michelle Remembers (M. Smith & Pazder, 1980) provided a model for the numerous accounts of recovered memories of ritual satanic abuse that followed. For example, a best-selling paperback by Spencer (1989) described an MPD patient who purportedly possessed several hundred alter personalities and whose therapy-induced recovered "memories" of torture, sacrifice, and participation in a black mass resemble the "memories" described by Michelle. Another best-seller (Peterson, Gooch, & Freeman, 1987) described a woman named Nancy with 56 personalities who "remembered" she had been satanically abused only after reading a Steven King novel about satanism. Nancy had also read *Sybil* and for a time was treated by Sybil's psychiatrist.

Lauren Stratford (1988) published her account of childhood satanic abuse in a book titled *Satan's Underground*. Along with the usual stories of human sacrifice and cannibalism, Stratford popularized the idea that cultists force young women to serve as "breeders" of babies who are then taken from them and sacrificed at ritual ceremonies. Stratford was featured on several television shows devoted to the topic of abuse, including the Geraldo Rivera special on the topic that attracted one of the largest audiences in television history (J. Victor, 1993).

Stratford's (1988) is the only account of a ritual abuse survivor that has been subjected to a thorough and independent investigation. A team of investigative journalists (Passantino, Passantino, & Trott, 1990) questioned Stratford's friends and neighbors about her purported early pregnancies and other events described in her book. For instance, none of her friends, relatives, or teachers recalled seeing her pregnant during her teens or early twenties even though she claimed to have given birth to three children (as a cult breeder) during this period. Relatedly, several witnesses reported seeing her engage in self-mutilation, the products of which she later used as evidence of the torture inflicted by the cult. Although Stratford (1988) claimed that she was able to escape from a satanic pornography ring only after her father died in 1983, Passantino et al. (1990) discovered that her father had, in fact, died in 1965. As a result of Passantino et al.'s (1990) expose, *Satan's Underground* was withdrawn from sale by the publisher (J. Victor, 1993).

Michelle's story, along with the similar accounts by Stratford (1988), Spencer (1989), and others that soon followed, became a part of the dogma used by some branches of the Christian fundamentalist movement that became increasingly prominent in many facets of American social and political life during the 1980s. This movement reinvigorated the mythology of satanism. Like its 16th- and 17th-century predecessor, this reinvigorated mythology holds that there exists a powerful but secret international satanic conspiracy that carries out heinous crimes. These crimes purportedly include the kidnapping, torture, and sexual abuse of countless children as well as murder, forced pregnancies, and cannibalism (Bromley, 1991; Hicks, 1991; Lyons, 1988).

Large numbers of therapists who identified themselves as active Christians joined the MPD movement in the 1980s (Mulhern, 1995), and soon accounts like those of Michelle began to be reported by the alters of MPD patients during therapy (Cozolino, 1989; Fraser, 1990; Friesen, 1991, 1992; Gould & Cozolino, 1992; Shaffer & Cozolino, 1992; Young et al., 1991). Some Christian therapists conceptualize their diagnostic task as determining which of a patient's alters are dissociated personality fragments and which are actually possessing evil demons. If the alter is determined to be a dissociated personality fragment, secular treatment is called for. However, if the alter is determined to be a possessing demon, the appropriate treatment involves exorcism or prayer (Friesen, 1991, 1992; T. B. White, 1990).

MPD patients often come from extremely strict, highly religious families (Coons, 1980; Saltman & Solomon, 1982), and such religious training may predispose people to make sharp distinctions between good and bad "parts" of themselves that can be easily conceptualized as alter personalities. In addition, a fundamentalist religious upbringing may make it particularly easy for patients to conceptualize "bad parts" as indwelling demons, if they are reinforced for doing so by their families, religious communities, or Christian therapists. In fact, Ross, Norton, and Wozney (1989) reported that 28.6% of a series of MPD patients identified at least one of their alters as a demon.

By the mid-1980s, 25% of MPD patients in therapy had recovered memories of ritual satanic abuse, and by 1992 the percentage of patients recovering such memories was as high as 50% in some treatment facilities (Mulhern, 1995).

The "memories" of satanic ritual abuse that first began surfacing in the 1980s were in patients who were in their thirties or forties at the time. According to these patients, the abuse purportedly occurred when they were 4 or 5 years of age (or even younger). Thousands of patients throughout North America have now reported such abuse (Bottoms, Shaver, & Goodman, 1991). Therefore, if the ritual satanic crimes "remembered" by MPD patients actually occurred, it would necessitate the existence of a monumental criminal conspiracy that has been in existence for well over 50 years and that has been responsible for the murder of many thousands of people (J. Best, 1990, 1991; Hicks, 1991). As pointed out by Jenkins and Maier-Katkin (1991), this would mean that, from before the Eisenhower era to the present, a sophisticated and highly organized cult of secret satanists has operated undisturbed and without detection throughout North America. Despite kidnapping and killing literally thousands of people every year for over five decades, despite countless rapes and forced pregnancies, despite bizarre ceremonies attended by large groups of people, we could find no evidence that anyone outside of the organization became aware of its existence. The number of people supposedly murdered by satanic cults is truly staggering. Using the estimate of 10,000 murders per year—a figure considered conservative by many cult believers—Bromley (1991) calculated that

> the period covered by current survivors' claims would have produced 400,000 victims, a total rivaling of 517,347 war-related deaths from World War II, Korea, and Vietnam combined. Yet not a single casualty of the satanic cult network has been discovered. (p. 62)

Historically, radical groups and secret organizations have been subject to defection schism and internal conflict (Bromley, 1991). Amazingly, however, no one in the huge satanic organization has defected. No one, because they were drunk, or in love, or feeling guilty over participation in mass murder, or merely boastful, betrayed any secrets of the organization to outsiders who then informed authorities. No member, out of spite or jealousy, even made an anonymous phone call to the police or to a newspaper about the activities of rival members. According to the accounts of some abuse survivors, there is nowhere to defect to, and no authorities to inform, because the cult has penetrated the highest levels of society and its top echelon consists of politicians, physicians, lawyers, judges, and police chiefs (Hicks, 1991). As stated by Jenkins and Maier-Katkin (1991), believing such things "calls less for a suspension of disbelief than a complete rewriting of the history of the United States and Canada" (p. 136).

In this context, it is important to point out that law enforcement agencies throughout North America have investigated numerous allegations of satanic abuse made by MPD patients but have been unable to substantiate the existence of the requisite criminal conspiracy (Lanning, 1989). It is worth emphasizing that criminal conspiracies are very difficult to hide. This, of course, is particularly true when large numbers of conspirators are involved and the crimes involved include murder, enforced pregnancy, and cannibalism, which leave physical evidence that is difficult to eliminate (Kern, 1994; Lanning, 1989). Consequently, the repeated failure of law enforcement agencies to obtain support for the satanic abuse allegations of MPD patients, coupled with the major implausibilities that must be assumed before such stories can be believed, is very strong evidence that the vast majority of these allegations are false and that the "memories" on which they are based are fantasies rather than remembrances of actual events (Hicks, 1991). Like the satanic conspiracy of the 16th and 17th centuries, the modern conspiracy appears to exist only in the imaginations of its propagators.

Satanic Abuse "Memories" and Psychotherapy

Bottoms et al. (1991) surveyed psychotherapists across the United States about the frequency with which they had seen patients who reported ritual abuse memories. Seventy percent of the therapists who responded reported that they had never seen such patients. On the other hand, 2% of the sample (16 therapists) accounted for the majority of such patients. Each of these therapists reported seeing over 100 ritual abuse victims, and one reported seeing approximately 2,000 such cases.

In a related study, Bucky and Dallenberg (1992) surveyed different types of psychotherapists (e.g., psychiatrists, psychologists, social workers, clergy) in the San Diego area concerning their experience with patients who reported symptoms of satanic ritual abuse. Between 67% and 70% of the therapists (depending on therapist type) reported never treating a patient with ritual abuse memories. However, four therapists had each seen 11 or more such patients, and six therapists had each seen more than 50 (the highest allowable number that could be reported on the questionnaire). Taken together, the pattern of findings obtained by Bottoms et al. (1991) and Bucky and Dallenberg (1992) suggests that therapists who regularly obtain such reports may play an active role in shaping the ritual abuse "memories" of their patients.

Findings reported by Shaffer and Cozolino (1992) also point to the importance of therapeutic intervention in generating "memories" of satanic abuse. Shaffer and Cozolino reported on 19 women and 1 man who "remembered" during therapy that they had been satanically abused during childhood. Most of these subjects (75%) reported that the abuse began before they were 5 years of age and had continued into adolescence. Some reported that the abuse began shortly after birth. All of these patients "remembered" that they had witnessed the sacrificial killing of animals, infants, and children or adults; some "remembered" seeing displays of cannibalism and sex with corpses; and most reported that they had been victims of sadistic sexual abuse by multiple perpetrators.

Importantly, patients were unaware of their satanic "memories" before they entered therapy. Their reasons for beginning therapy stemmed from feelings of depression and anxiety and (unspecified) dissociative symptoms. The primary focus of the therapy was on the recovery of memories. Some therapists may have conveyed their expectations that patients would uncover memories of abuse, and their belief that these recovered abuse memories were real. The usual sequence of memory recovery for these patients progressed from "remembering" abuse by acquaintances, to abuse by family members, and finally to ritual satanic abuse by multiple perpetrators of both sexes.

The process of recovering such painful "memories" may not have been without negative consequences for these patients. Some were overwhelmed by feelings of shame and guilt and experienced panic and depression in response to their newly surfacing "memories." All reported suicidal ideation, half reported suicide attempts, and over half were hospitalized during some period of their time in psychotherapy (Shaffer & Cozolino, 1992).

As indicated earlier, therapy-induced "memories" of ritual abuse at the hands of satanic cultists appear to be confabulations. Moreover, because patients almost always begin therapy without such "memories," the satanic content of the "memories" may stem from expectations and beliefs of the therapists that are conveyed during the therapeutic process. In addition, of course, patients may be primed to generate such "memories," and define them as real, on the basis of their background religious beliefs, media presentations, and so forth.

Interestingly, therapists who regularly uncover satanic abuse "memories" often portray themselves as playing little or no active role in shaping their patients' reports. Instead, patients are described as first becoming aware of satanic memories in dreams or flashbacks or as the result of some cue that "triggers" the memory (Shaffer & Cozolino, 1992). However, Shaffer and Cozolino's description of ritual abuse reports "emerging" as part of a progressive sequence of increasingly bizarre and horrific memories of abuse is consistent with Ganaway's (1992) contention that the memories of MPD patients become increasingly expansive to meet the tacit requirements of the memory recovery therapy in which they are engaged. Obviously, such an analysis does not require that therapists provide patients with all of the specific details that come to constitute their "memories." As pointed out by J. Victor (1993), patients can obtain details about satanic rituals from a wide variety of sources including horror movies, tabloid newspaper articles about satanism, popular biographical and autobiographical accounts by survivors, folklore, and so on. With the help of their therapists, such information could be woven by patients into an autobiographical narrative that contains recovered memories of such abuse as a central element. The active role of therapists in shaping such narratives is suggested by Mulhern's (1991a) observations of therapy conducted with satanic abuse survivors. For instance, Mulhern (1991a) provided the following description of the hypnotic procedures sometimes used to elicit satanic ritual abuse "memories" in MPD patients:

> During hypnotic interviews clinicians explicitly described satanic ritual scenes or displayed pictures of satanic symbols to a patient; then addressed "all parts of the patient's mind" or "everyone inside," requesting that any part who recognized the satanic material so indicate either by a nod of the head or by prearranged yes, no and stop ideomotor signals . . . is it possible that these clinicians never paused to consider just what kind of message a patient would receive from a clinician who is holding up snapshots and asking if the patient can identify people as leaders of a group of cannibalistic devil worshipers. (p. 610)

Reports obtained by investigative journalists (Taylor, 1992; Whitley, 1992) from "survivors" who had disavowed their therapy-induced ritual abuse "memories" also point to the active role played by some therapists in the construction of such memories. For instance, one such former patient claimed that

> [the therapist] kept telling me the only way I'd ever get out [of the hospital] was if I began having flashbacks and memories of the abuse. . . . [The therapist] insisted constantly that my father was one of the perpetrators because my dad is a Shriner, and [the therapist] believed that anyone in the Shriners was in a cult. (Whitley, 1992, p. 38)

Rather than telling her story to a journalist, Mel Gavigan (1992) provided a first-person account of how she came to define herself as a ritual-abuse survivor and MPD patient. Gavigan claimed that she had no memories of being abused as a child until she was hospitalized for depression in 1989. Following this hospitalization, she remained in therapy for several years and during this time became aware that she was a multiple, recovered florid memories of satanic abuse, and brought a lawsuit for abuse against her father. During a later hospitalization, Gavigan began to reinterpret her experiences as fantasies rather than as memories and eventually disavowed all of her abuse memories, as well as the existence of her alter personalities. She also dropped the lawsuit against her father. Throughout her account, Gavigan asserted the role of her therapists in inculcating and legitimating her fantasies of having been abused:

> While hospitalized for the depression I was asked by several hospital workers if I had ever been touched sexually in my childhood. Although I could not remember anything I felt pressured to come up with some "answers" for my condition that would be acceptable. . . . My psychologist kept asking about my childhood and he seemed insistent that I had been sexually abused as a child. I tried to be very cooperative. . . . I continued to wrack my brain to try to remember being sexually abused. . . . I was constantly beset by doubts about my experience. It felt that I was "making it up," but it said in *Courage to Heal* that the memories often feel that way. . . . I went to both a hypnotherapist and a clinical psychologist at the same time. . . . Both of the therapists encouraged and pushed me to "remember" more and more. . . . I also started, at this time, to have "memories" of satanic ritual abuse that were always accepted by my therapists and that I was never asked to question. As a result I came up with many more visualizations and some graphic and detailed sexual abuse stories which started to involve murder, The "memories" became increasingly more shocking and violent . . . with the enthusiastic encouragement of my hypnotherapist, I began showing signs of MPD. . . . In the hypnosis sessions, the therapist would have me "relive" the rape but all the while it never felt real. . . . He would ask me if there were any other "people" there with me, and then he would have me identify and name the other "parts" of me. Afterwards, when I went home I would draw them for him. Meanwhile I read books such as *Courage to Heal* and books on MPD. (pp. 246–247)

Coleman (1992) reviewed court documents and interviewed a ritual abuse and MPD "survivor" in connection with the patient's civil suit against a cousin who she claimed was one of her principal abusers. Coleman's reconstruction of this case illustrates how a wide range of factors including the media, information from friends, and interactions with therapists can lead to the generation and elaboration of abuse memories. The patient (called Mrs. Susan Smith by Coleman) suffered from bulimia. She suspected her cousin of abusing his own daughter but had not considered that she herself might have been abused until her general practitioner informed her that 100% of her bulimic patients eventually discovered that they had been sexually abused. Later, Mrs. Smith watched an Oprah Winfrey television show on the topic of abuse and began to feel that she too might have been abused. A friend undergoing psychotherapy confided to Mrs. Smith that she had begun to recover memories of abuse. With this friend's encouragement, Mrs. Smith decided to enter therapy herself to remember the abuse that she was increasingly certain she had experienced.

On the basis of his access to the testimony of Mrs. Smith's therapists, as well as from direct statements from Mrs. Smith, Coleman (1992) concluded that the therapists actively encouraged Mrs. Smith's belief that she had been abused, pressed her to work at recovering more and more abuse memories, and consistently validated her "memories" as real. When Mrs. Smith voiced doubts about the veracity of her "memories," the therapists purportedly worked to actively persuade her of their reality. Mrs. Smith received much positive attention both for the recovery of abuse "memories" and for her emerging identity as an abuse "survivor." For instance after recovering a "memory" of a man urinating into her mouth, Mrs. Smith wrote,

> The more I discovered about what I've been through the more I wonder how I ever survived. . . . You're so strong Susan, so wonderful. You're capable of whatever you believe in. You're ok Susan Smith. You're strong, you're a survivor, and a winner, you're going straight to the top, head of the class. You're OK, you're a winner. I'm really truly beginning to like myself and I really like that—all these years I hated myself. (Coleman, 1992, p. 174)

Under the guidance of her therapists, Mrs. Smith's "memories" became increasingly elaborate and increasingly horrendous. "Memories" of multiple perpetrators and multiple victims were recovered, and after experiences of "flashes" of white candles came "memories" of satanic ritual abuse. In therapy, Mrs. Smith also "discovered" that she possessed numerous alter personalities.

Mrs. Smith "remembered" that numerous other children with whom she had grown up had also been abused. The police interviewed all of the supposed victims named by Mrs. Smith. None of them corroborated her allegations. Mrs. Smith's therapists were not deterred by these multiple failures at corroboration. One of them wrote,

> It is highly likely that most or all of the children that Susan remembers . . . will be unable to remember these experiences. This does not mean

they did not occur any more than Susan's former amnesia means that these events had not happened to her. (Coleman, 1992, p. 173)

Coleman's (1992) account of Mrs. Smith and Gavigan's (1992) autobiographical account contain a great many similarities. Both patients went from no memories of abuse to suspicions of abuse and then entered psychotherapy. During the course of therapy, the suspicions of both patients were purportedly validated by their therapists, and with much encouragement both patients "remembered" more and more instances of abuse and more and more florid abuse. With the encouragement of their therapists, both patients also developed alter personalities and defined themselves as suffering from MPD. The course of therapy in both of these cases was consistent with Ganaway's (1992, 1995) contention that patients' confabulated memories of abuse become increasingly expansive as a result of the tacit (and in these cases explicit) encouragement and approval received from their therapists.

The remark by Mrs. Smith's therapist that the failure of the police to corroborate Mrs. Smith's allegations stemmed from the fact that all of the other victims also forgot that they had been abused is reminiscent of other incredible claims in this area, for instance, the claim that most people fail to observe the alters of MPD patients because these patients are experts at hiding their multiplicity, or the claim that objective evidence for the existence of a large-scale satanic cult is never forthcoming because the cultists are devilishly clever at hiding their tracks or because they run the police forces that investigate the crimes. Post hoc rationalizations of this kind may explain how proponents maintain their beliefs in the face of contradictory evidence. However, to people who are not already believers, the elaboration of nondisconfirmable rationalizations suggests the development of an ideological or religious system rather than attempts at scientific understanding.

As reported by Shaffer and Cozolino (1992), MPD and other patients who report ritual abuse frequently participate in various forms of group therapy along with their individual therapy. Reports obtained from former patients who participated in groups aimed at recovering abuse memories led Whitley (1992) to emphasize the role of contagion in the construction of such "memories." For instance, when one woman recovered a particular type of abuse memory, it was common for another patient to "say the same thing, just changing the 'facts' slightly" (Whitley, 1992). The patients interviewed by Whitley received their treatment in Texas. However, another former patient from Toronto, who was interviewed by a different journalist (Taylor, 1992), gave a similar description of the role played by contagion and the importance of therapist approval in the generation and augmentation of abuse memories:

It gets contagious. This one says she remembers something, then this one. The stories got grosser and grosser and you had a tiny roomful of girls screaming and raging and bawling. If you didn't have any memories, you didn't get any attention. (p. C1)

Some patients report memory fragments or dreams with satanic content and only afterward are exposed to hypnotic interviews aimed at confirming such abuse. However, because many MPD patients are enmeshed in a social network where they hear about satanic abuse from other patients, therapists, and shared newsletters and where they or their fellow patients attend workshops devoted to such abuse, "spontaneous" dreams and memories of this kind are hardly surprising and do not provide serious evidence of actual ritual abuse. In this context, it is worth recalling the ease with which highly hypnotizable college students were induced to enact past-life personalities who "remembered" that they had been abused as children, when the expectation of such abuse had been conveyed to them before their hypnotic regression (Spanos, Menary, et al., 1991). Also relevant is E. F. Loftus and Coan's (in press) finding that people were easily induced to falsely remember that they had been lost in a shopping mall during childhood and the reports of glossolalics in some congregations and spirit mediums in some cultures who reorganize their biographies to bring them into line with cultural expectations concerning the past histories of possessed people.

A Case Example of Satanic Ritual Abuse Memory

The importance of leading interrogations and official legitimation in obtaining "memories" of ritual abuse was underscored in the case of Paul Ingram, a police officer in Olympia, Washington, who confessed to raping and ritually abusing his own children while participating in a satanic cult (Ofshe, 1992b; Wright, 1994). The Ingram family belonged to a fundamentalist Christian church. During a religious retreat for young people that centered on issues of sexual abuse, Ingram's eldest daughter, Ericka, recovered "memories" of having been sexually abused by her father. The "memories" developed after a guest speaker at the retreat, a charismatic Christian who believed that she possessed the gifts of healing and discernment, stood over Ericka and announced to the group that Ericka had been sexually molested by her father. The speaker encouraged Ericka to obtain therapy to recover her abuse memories. Shortly after the meeting, Ericka accused her father and brothers of having sexually molested her since her early childhood. Later, Ingram's younger daughter made similar accusations and added that she had been molested not only by Ingram but also by a group of his friends who met periodically at the Ingram home to play poker (Wright, 1994).

Ingram initially denied all charges, but became convinced by his fundamentalist minister that his daughters would not lie and that the devil may have hidden from him the memories of his sinful acts. The events to which he confessed were purportedly further legitimated as memories rather than fantasies by a psychologist who worked with the police department, as well as by the interrogating officers. Ingram's confessions became increasingly elaborate, and following assurances from the minister that God would allow only true thoughts to come into his memory, Ingram began to recover "memories" of participating in satanic ritual abuse. Neither daughter had mentioned satanic abuse until they heard about this aspect of their father's confession from the minister. Shortly thereafter, both daughters recovered satanic abuse "memories," complete with human sacrifices, enforced pregnancies, and abortions. Ingram's "memories" had not included child sacrifice. Ericka, however, had read *Satan's Underground*, which includes such descriptions, and the entire Ingram family had watched a Geraldo Rivera special on satanic abuse (Wright, 1994).

Following a highly leading police interrogation, one of Ingram's sons also began to recover "memories" of sexual abuse. These "memories" included images of his mother being raped by members of the cult. Soon the daughters implicated their mother as a cult member and an abuser. Ingram's wife, Sandy, was shattered by the breakup of her family and by accusations that she simply could not fathom. She remembered none of the horrendous abuse that her husband and children claimed had occurred for years in her own home, literally right under her own nose. Sandy sought out the minister for support. Instead, he validated the reality of her daughters' "memories" and informed Sandy that she was 80% evil for allowing her daughters to be abused. Later, the minister informed Sandy that she was still 20% good and that her good part could come to the aid of her family. Once again, he encouraged her to search her memory for evidence that would corroborate the testimony of her daughters.

Everyone of importance in Sandy's social world—the police, her minister, her friends, her children, and her husband—validated a reality that she had purportedly participated in but could not remember. Moreover, by failing to remember, Sandy believed that she was contributing to the suffering that her children were obviously experiencing. Finally, Sandy succumbed. Like her daughters and son, she began to "remember" the abuse described by her children (Wright, 1994).

None of the satanic elements of Paul Ingram's story or the stories told by his children could be confirmed by police investigation. For example, Ericka drew a map that located the supposed grave sites of sacrificed children. Extensive search and digging revealed no evidence to corroborate her claims. Although both daughters claimed to have been scarred as a result of ritual torture, medical examination failed to uncover any scars. Ericka claimed that she had been made pregnant while a sophomore in high school and that the fetus had been aborted with a coat hanger. A gynecological examination provided no evidence of an earlier pregnancy and no evidence of sexual abuse or a forced abortion. Julie, Ingram's younger daughter, claimed that she received a threatening letter from her father. However, the letter turned out to be written in Julie's own handwriting (Wright, 1994).

At the behest of the prosecution, Ingram was interviewed by Richard Ofshe (1992b), a sociologist who has extensively studied persuasive communication in cult groups. Although the police and prosecutors were convinced that they had uncovered a murdering satanic cult, Ofshe (1992b) concluded, instead, that Ingram had falsely confessed to events that had never occurred. Many of the events to which Ingram confessed were suggested to him by the police officers and psychologist who interrogated him, and the stories told by his daughters contained numerous and marked inconsistencies. To assess the hypothesis that Ingram's recovered "memories" resulted from suggestion and legitimation from authorities, Ofshe (1992b) constructed a set of abuse events involving Ingram that the police agreed had not occurred. Ofshe then interrogated Ingram with the leading questions and guided fantasy procedures used by the police and suggested that Ingram had committed the false abuse events. Ingram readily confessed and, after praying on what he "remembered" and discussing the events with the minister, produced an elaborate written description of the false events. Following the interrogation, he continued to insist that the false events had really occurred. Although Ingram had no psychiatric history before his arrest, he was diagnosed by one psychologist involved in the case as suffering from MPD.

The Ingram case illustrates the importance of contextual factors in the construction and legitimation of satanic ritual abuse "memories." Eventually, both of Ingram's daughters, one of his sons, and his wife came to "remember" that they had been ritually abused by members of a satanic cult, and Ingram himself came to "remember" that he and several of his friends had perpetrated such abuse. The "memories" generated by Ingram's daughters influenced the shape of Ingram's own memories, and these, following Ingram's interactions with the police, minister, and psychologist, took on a satanic cast. When the satanic elements of Ingram's developing "memories" were made known to his daughters, they soon incorporated satanic elements into their own "memories." The similarities in the satanic fantasies of these different individuals served as evidence to all concerned that these fantasies were the memories of actual occurrences. Once this hypothesis was accepted, the many discrepancies among the varied accounts, and the changing nature and implausibilities in these accounts, tended to be ignored or explained away. Satanic abuse went from being the private fantasy of a man struggling to "make sense" out of accusations leveled at him by his daughters to a frightening shared reality for a substantial segment of those who lived in and around Olympia, Washington.

Disseminating the Satanic Abuse Mythology

Although the idea of a multigenerational satanic cult that ritually abuses children and brainwashes them into developing MPD has been rightfully challenged, the possibility of such abuse is nevertheless believed by many professionals. Professional conferences and workshops constitute the major vehicles for transmitting to the therapeutic community information about satanic ritual abuse and its ostensible connection to MPD (Mulhern, 1991b, 1992; J. Victor, 1993). Since 1984, the International Society for the Study of Dissociation has sponsored annual conferences. Some of the presenters at these conferences are internationally known psychiatric authorities on MPD and other dissociative disorders. Thus, the acceptance by some of these authorities (e.g., Braun & Sachs, 1988) of the reality of satanic child abuse has served to legitimate belief in such abuse and in the secret cult supposedly responsible for the abuse. Participating at these conferences are not only researchers and therapists who come to hear the latest ideas on the causes and treatment of MPD but also patients who participate in support groups, exchange ideas, and attend workshops and lectures. Satanism has become an increasingly prominent theme at each successive conference. In 1985, it was discussed informally by many participants, and in the following year papers describing satanic abuse, recovered abuse memories, and cult brainwashing and mind control procedures were a part of the scientific program. A survey of the conference participants in this year indicated that 25% of patients in treatment were recovering satanic abuse "memories." All of the conference presentations uncritically accepted both the veridicality of patients' satanic abuse memories and the existence of the large-scale cult that was purportedly responsible for the reported abuse (Mulhern, 1991b).

Most of the papers presented at these conferences are never published, and when distributed to attenders they are often marked "not for distribution or reproduction" (J. Victor, 1993). Thus, ideas about ritual abuse and its purported connection with MPD are disseminated by mental health experts to people already primed to believe these ideas. At the same time, by limiting the distribution of such conference papers, critical evaluation of these ideas by other professionals is minimized.

The legitimation by well-known psychiatric authorities of childhood satanic abuse as a cause of MPD has spawned a large number of small conferences and workshops on these topics. These workshops are held throughout North America (and more recently in parts of Europe as well) for the purpose of educating therapists and child protection workers on the dangers of satanism and its connection to MPD. The workshops are typically run by mental health professionals and cult "experts" and include films and lectures and sometimes first-hand presentations by MPD patients and other ritual-abuse "survivors." The presentations are characteristically uncritical. The existence of an international satanic cult conspiracy and the causal role of childhood satanic abuse in MPD are presented as fact. The importance of believing in the literal truth of survivor stories is repeatedly emphasized, and a parallel is frequently drawn between the disbelief that initially surrounded reports of child sexual abuse in the 1970s and the skepticism concerning recovered memories of satanic ritual abuse (Mulhern, 1992; J. Victor, 1993).

Purportedly, voicing disbelief at such workshops is looked on with evident disfavor by the workshop leaders, and various procedures may be used to limit the expression of such disbelief. For instance, at one workshop attended by J. Victor (1993), questions to speakers had to be posed in writing, and the speakers chose which questions they would answer and which they would ignore. In addition, critical questions raised in a small discussion group were sometimes met with obvious hostility by the discussion leader, who purportedly summoned the Bible as evidence for the existence of satanism and implied that to disbelieve survivor stories was to dismiss all that was good and holy.

The social norms that govern small-scale, face-to-face interactions often discourage confrontation and challenges to the veracity of the claims made by speakers or other participants. Because confrontations are often embarrassing and anxiety provoking for all concerned, people frequently fail to voice doubts or challenges in public contexts (Goffman, 1959). On the other hand, people who agree with a speaker often have no compunctions about publicly voicing agreement or about elaborating on and confirming what the speaker said with an example or two of their own. In short, norms that function to facilitate sociability in face-to-face interaction tend to discourage open disagreement and thereby generate in participants the impression of uniformity of belief. Because the only voices typically heard are those confirming the speakers and the accounts given by "survivors," the impression conveyed is that "everyone believes it, so it must be true."

The potency of conferences and workshops in influencing the practices of participants was recently demonstrated by a satanism panic initiated by child protection workers in Britain. Initially, several such workers with fundamentalist Christian backgrounds became concerned about ritual abuse after reading material from the United States on the subject. Several then went to the United States for "training" in the recognition of ritual abuse. After returning to Britain, they organized a conference on the subject and invited a number of American experts to speak. Soon afterwards, a number of the social workers who had attended the conference "discovered" that several children in a town near Manchester, England, had been abused in satanic rituals. Before the panic ended, 17 children were forcibly removed from their homes, made wards of the court, and allowed no visits from their parents. After interrogation, a number of the children told lurid stories of satanic rituals and abuse, including tales of babies being cooked in microwave ovens. Eventually, several investigative journalists began to lay bare the sequence of events that led to questions about alleged charges of abuse. A judicial inquiry that followed found no evidence of ritual abuse, and the fantastic claims made by the children (such as the cooking of babies in microwaves) were purportedly traced back to stories propagated by the American "experts" (J. Victor, 1993).

The effects of training seminars dealing with ritual abuse and MPD were also investigated by Bucky and Dallenberg (1992). These investigators found that therapists who had attended such training workshops were significantly more likely to see patients who reported ritual abuse memories than were therapists who had not attended such workshops. For instance, among therapists who held MA or PhD degrees, only 1% to 2% of the nonattenders had seen four or more ritual abuse patients, whereas 12% to 15% of the attenders had seen four or more such patients. Bucky and Dallenberg also assessed the frequency with which therapists had seen patients who displayed symptoms that are purportedly indicative of ritual abuse (e.g., preoccupation with cleanliness, fear of certain colors, premonitions of death). Correlations were then run separately for attenders and nonattenders between number of patients who exhibited the ritual abuse "syndrome" and the number who actually reported memories of having been ritually abused. The resultant correlation was significantly higher among therapists who had attended workshops ($r = .60$), than among nonattenders ($r = .32$). As pointed out by Bucky and Dallenberg, these correlational findings raise the possibility that workshop attendance influenced the likelihood with which therapists tied together a set of symptoms with "memories" of ritual abuse.

Taken together, the available data indicate quite clearly that recovered "memories" of ritual abuse are not memories at all; they are patient-generated fantasies. The generation of these fantasies is purportedly encouraged by therapists who then legitimate the fantasies as "real memories." These fantasies are consistent with the satanic cult mythology propagated by some evangelical and fundamentalist Christian sects, and when interpreted as the recovered memories of "survivors," they are used by some believers to support this mythology. However, belief in the existence of an international conspiracy of satanists that tortures children into developing hidden alter personalities is not restricted to fundamentalist sects. On the contrary, this idea has now been legitimated by prominent mental health professionals, and one offshoot of this professional legitimation has been the sprouting of conferences and workshops that serve to uncritically disseminate these ideas as established fact. As a consequence of such professional legitimation and resultant dissemination, there has been a growth in the number of therapists who use procedures aimed at recovering memories of satanic ritual abuse. In turn, these procedures are often effective in leading MPD and other patients to recover horrific "memories" of satanic ritual abuse that never occurred. These recovered "memories" then function as proofs to both therapists and the patients of the secret satanic organization that implemented the tortures that were so painfully remembered.

MPD theorists typically contend that alter personalities result from specific childhood traumas. During treatment, therapists "contact" and communicate with each alter to discover the particular trauma that caused the alter to split off in childhood from the remainder of the personality (e.g., Bliss, 1986). All of this theorizing is, of course, premised on the assumption that the memories reported by the alters are, in fact, accurate descriptions of actual childhood traumas. However, "memories" of childhood satanic ritual abuse do not appear to be memories of actual childhood traumas. The traumatic events "remembered" may never have happened. Consequently, the alters that purportedly formed at the time of these alleged traumas must, in fact, have other origins. As indicated in the last chapter, patients' alter personalities, like their satanic abuse memories, are most likely social constructions that, by and large, reflect the therapeutic procedures to which they have been exposed.

SUMMARY

The high rates of child abuse reported by MPD patients do not constitute good evidence that such abuse causes multiplicity. A number of different noncausal factors probably contribute to the high rates of child abuse reported by these patients (e.g., high base rates for abuse in chronic psychiatric populations, the use of abuse histories as a criterion for conducting MPD-eliciting hypnotic interviews, treatment-induced confabulation). No doubt many people who become MPD patients suffered some form of abuse during childhood. In fact, the high base rate in our culture for child abuse, broadly defined, ensures such a finding. Nevertheless, most people who suffer even severe child abuse do not exhibit MPD, and many people who have not been abused can easily and quickly be induced to display multiplicity (e.g., college students given past-life regression suggestions, mentally healthy spirit mediums). Taken together, these findings argue against a causal relationship between child abuse and later displays of multiplicity.

The role of psychotherapy and other social factors in creating a connection between MPD and confabulated memories of abuse is most clearly seen in the co-occurrence of MPD and recovered memories of satanic ritual abuse. These "memories" are, in all likelihood, therapy-induced fantasies; the events to which they refer never actually happened. The development in patients of alters who "hold" such "memories" involves a constructive process in which patients shape their experiences (including their "memories") to correspond with understandings and expectations derived largely from their therapists, but also from popular biographies, movies, television shows, and other cultural sources. In addition, the frequent recovery of satanic ritual abuse "memories" by MPD patients points to the importance of broad sociopolitical influences in the generation and maintenance of MPD enactments.

21

MULTIPLE PERSONALITY DISORDER, RECOVERED MEMORIES, AND SOCIOPOLITICAL CONSIDERATIONS

MPD AND THE MEDICALIZATION OF PROBLEMS IN LIVING

As indicated earlier, since the mid-1970s their has been an astronomical increase in the frequency of MPD diagnoses. In part, the huge growth in the use of this diagnosis reflects the widespread and expanding tendency in North American society to medicalize social problems and problems in living (Conrad, 1992; Zola, 1983). Medicalizing odd, deviant, or distressing behavior involves reconceptualizing the problem behavior as symptomatic of some medical (usually psychiatric) disorder. For example, behaviors such as heavy drinking (Schneider, 1978), excessive gambling (Rosencrance, 1985), and unusual eating habits (Brumberg, 1988; Ritenbaugh, 1982), which were previously explained in terms of sinfulness or other moral failings, are now commonly described as "addictions" that require psychological treatment.

The medicalization of problems implies that the causes of the problems are internal to the individual. The events that produce physical diseases like cancer and pneumonia occur inside the body. By metaphorical extension, the hypothetical events to which "mental diseases" are attributed occur inside the mind (e.g., repressed memories). Consequently, when problems like illegal drug use, nonnormative sexual behavior (e.g., transvestism), disruptive classroom behavior, and chronic criminal behavior

287

(e.g., psychopathy) are medicalized, the causes for these "disorders" are conceptualized as being internal to the individual (e.g., addictive personality, antisocial personality, attention deficit disorder). Relatedly, treatment for these "disorders" is usually conceptualized in terms of changing the "patient's" psychological functioning, and as requiring professional experts who specialize in providing psychological treatments (Conrad, 1992).

Growth in the medicalization of social and psychological problems requires increases in the number of mental health professionals to treat the new categories of "mentally disordered" individuals. Relatedly, increases in the number of mental health professionals create economic pressures to define more and more people as mentally disordered and requiring treatment. After all, without patients who are willing to pay (either directly or through third parties like insurance companies), mental health professionals cannot survive.

Since the early 1960s, there has been a huge increase in the United States in the number of psychiatrists, psychologists, and social workers. For example, between 1959 and 1989, membership in the American Psychiatric Association grew by a factor of 3.4, and during the same period, membership in the American Psychological Association grew by an astounding factor of 16. Since 1959, the number of clinical psychologists in the United States has doubled every 10 years (Dawes, 1994). This huge growth in the mental health professions has been paralleled by an increase in the number and types of problems that have been brought under the umbrella of mental disorder. Much criminal behavior is now defined in terms of mental illness, and mental health professionals have become a fixture in our legal system (Szasz, 1970, 1987). Heavy drinking, the use of illicit drugs, smoking, and even sex with numerous partners are increasingly defined as "addictions" that require psychological intervention. Troublemaking in school is often defined as hyperactivity or "attention deficit disorder," and self-starvation and purging out of fear of deviating from a cultural ideal of thinness have become "anorexia" and "bulimia" (purportedly often caused by early abuse). In fact, unhappiness, lack of personal fulfillment, relationship difficulties, and personal dissatisfactions of all stripes are, with increasing frequency, defined as psychological problems requiring the intervention of a mental health professional (Conrad, 1992; Dawes, 1994).

In an interesting paper, Blatner (1987) described the role of economic pressures in leading psychiatrists to admit increasing numbers of patients to psychiatric hospitals. According to Blatner, government-sponsored regulatory programs, which limited the number of hospital units that could be built on the basis of need, were allowed to lapse during the Reagan administration. This lapse led to competition within the health care industry and to the construction of new psychiatric and other hospital units. The proliferation of new psychiatric hospital units, in turn, "generates a significant pressure for admitting patients and keeping them in the hospital, a pressure which distorts our criteria for the indications for such costly treatments" (Blatner, 1987, p. 39).

Patients cannot be admitted to a hospital without being diagnosed, and, as Blatner (1987) suggested, the diagnoses utilized for this purpose are influenced by current psychiatric fashions. For instance, Blatner pointed out that the diagnosis of "borderline personality disorder" often functions as a justification for inpatient treatment, despite a lack of consensus concerning the causes and treatment of the "disorder" and despite the unreliability with which the diagnosis is made. The current popularity of dissociative disorders clinics suggests that the ubiquitous amalgam of odd behaviors subsumed under this category also functions to justify inpatient hospitalization and treatment. MPD is, of course, considered a dissociative disorder par excellence. As indicated earlier, MPD and borderline patients frequently exhibit similar behavioral styles, and MPD patients, like borderlines, are frequently defined as requiring inpatient hospitalization.

In short, mental health professionals have a vested interest in expanding the domain of behavior subsumed under the rubric of mental disorder. Consequently, problems in living and in relating that in previous eras were defined in moral, political, or religious terms are increasingly defined in psychiatric terms and dealt with by mental health experts (Dawes, 1994; Szasz, 1987). The explosion in psychiatric patients created by these practices requires further increases in the number of mental health professionals. These increases create economic pressures to expand still further the domain of mental health professionals, and so on.

The explanations for problems in living that are proffered by mental health professionals change to keep pace with changes in dominant cultural values and concerns. For example, in keeping with our current cultural emphasis on child abuse, problems of depression, somatic concerns, and personal dissatisfaction are frequently defined today as "symptoms" of early childhood sexual abuse (Blume, 1990; Fredrickson, 1992). A century or so ago, many physicians defined these same problems as caused by childhood masturbation and recommended a variety of harsh measures (e.g., clitoridectomy, tying the hands of children at bedtime) to prevent such "self-abuse" (Comfort, 1967; Hare, 1962).

Mental health professionals not only redefine existing problem behaviors as mental disorders and devise culturally consistent explanations for those "disorders" but sometimes also play an instrumental role in generating the behaviors that they then label as symptomatic of mental illness. As indicated in chapter 16, for example, the socially marginal and unhappy women who were institutionalized at the Salpetrière under the authority of Charcot learned through coaching, modeling, and selective reinforcement to display the intricate patterns of behavior that came to be designated as "grand hysteria." Relatedly, with the guidance of their therapists, some modern patients learn to develop fantasies of alien abduction, past lives, and satanic ritual abuse that are then legitimated by their therapists as memories. Others, as we have seen, learn to enact displays of MPD and to define themselves as possessing multiple selves.

The medicalization of problems in living, the consequent growth in the number of mental health professionals, and the growing public acceptance of the idea that a very wide range of social and interpersonal difficulties are "really" symptoms of psychological disorder are background factors that have allowed the MPD movement to expand. However, these factors alone do not explain why the MPD diagnosis (as opposed to other psychiatric diagnoses) has shown such a dramatic increase in popularity. Perhaps the most important determinant of this rise in popularity is the connection that has been developed between MPD and child sexual abuse.

SOCIOPOLITICAL IMPLICATIONS OF THE MPD–CHILD ABUSE CONNECTION

The regular co-occurrence of sexual abuse memories and MPD appears to have resulted from the confluence of several sociohistorical trends. The first aspect of this confluence involved a reawakening of interest in MPD during a period of intense societal interest in, and fascination with, the topic of child abuse. During the 1960s, a great deal of attention became focused on the physical abuse of children by their parents or guardians and led to the identification of the "battered-child syndrome" (J. Best, 1990, 1991). In the 1970s, largely as a function of the feminist movement, public attention also focused on sexual aggression against women and on the complicity of existing social institutions in fostering or at least tolerating such aggression (e.g., Brownmiller, 1975). The awakening of societal concern about the issues of childhood physical abuse and sexual violence toward women came together to produce a growing concern about the sexual abuse of children and, more specifically, a concern with the prevalence and consequences of such abuse.

It was in the context of these societal concerns that Sybil (Schreiber, 1973) became a best-selling psychiatric biography in the early 1970s. In the previous decade, the publication of The Three Faces of Eve (Thigpen & Cleckley, 1957) had aroused public interest and curiosity in the idea of MPD. However, sustained popular and professional interest in this topic occurred only with Sybil, who, unlike Eve, was reported as having suffered horrendous physical and sexual abuse during childhood. Thus, the idea of a causal relationship between MPD and early sexual abuse may have gained much of its credence because of the intense societal interest in the topic of child abuse that coincided with the publication of Sybil.

As indicated earlier, at least some of Sybil's memories of early abuse were quite clearly confabulations. These may have reflected the interests of her therapist, the societal emphasis on child sexual abuse common at that time, or both. Even if some of Sybil's abuse memories were accurate, the etiological significance assigned to them by her therapist was more a reflection of a zeitgeist in which such ideas appeared intuitively reasonable than of any empirical demonstration of a relationship between early abuse and Sybil's symptoms. Whatever the reason for the connection between Sybil's abuse memories and her MPD symptomatology, it was this combination that caught the attention of the public and made Sybil perhaps the best-known patient in the history of psychiatry. The result, of course, was a proliferation of MPD case histories in which child sexual abuse was assigned etiological significance (North et al., 1993). By 1980, child sexual abuse had gone from being considered one of the possible causes of MPD to the paramount and basic cause (Mulhern, 1991b). In turn, once this connection became established, public fascination with the topic of child sexual abuse and its consequences created a sustained interest in MPD and an increase in the use of the "diagnostic procedures" that generate displays of this phenomenon.

MPD "survivors" purportedly suffered abuse that was especially horrendous, and their shifts from one alter personality to another constitute particularly dramatic symptomatology. Therefore, within the abuse survivor movement that became increasingly prominent as the 1980s progressed, these patients became highly visible as prototypical helpless victims of male sexual aggression. For example, well-known feminist author Gloria Steinem (1992) endorsed the view that MPD is almost always caused by severe childhood sexual abuse that may be dissociated from conscious memory. In addition to these considerations, the notion that MPD stems from child abuse also fit comfortably with the long-held common assumption in psychiatric circles that adult problems stem from early childhood problems and with the reawakening in the 1970s of traumagenic theories for the etiology of psychiatric problems.

Also important both in strengthening the connection between abuse and MPD and in fostering the proliferation of MPD cases was the sociopolitical resurgence of the religious right in the 1980s. Some members of the religious right use the rhetoric of satanism to demonize social trends and values that threaten their underlying conservative ideology. The conservative ideology of the religious right focuses on the preservation of "family-oriented" middle-class values. Within this ideological system, the protection of women and children becomes a socially acceptable code term for the propagation of institutional arrangements that reinforce a traditional, male-dominated nuclear family structure. Institutions or activities that appear to threaten the values that underlie such a structure are thereby demonized (Richardson, Best, & Bromley, 1991). Thus, many of the political and social goals adopted by the feminist movement—the right to abortion, pay equity, encouragement of women to become economically self-sufficient, and so forth—were described by some leaders of the religious right as satanically inspired. The propagation of false rumors concerning satanic abuse of children in day-care centers is another example of such demonization. These rumors reinforce the guilt and anxiety working mothers often feel for not staying at home to be "real mothers." Such rumors also personify parents' fears that they have abandoned their children and through their own selfishness and neglect have put them in mortal danger (Nathan, 1991).

The resurgence of evangelical Christianity in the 1980s was infused into the MPD–child abuse movement in the form of ritual abuse "memories" recovered by adult survivors. The abuse "memories" obtained from adult "survivors" complemented and reinforced the similar stories elicited through leading interrogations from children caught in day-care ritual abuse panics. The central themes in the "memories" of the adult survivors appear to mirror some of the major concerns of the conservative political agenda cloaked in satanic imagery. These themes include concerns about the consequences of premarital and extramarital sex (e.g., illegitimate forced pregnancies at the hands of cultists) and a "pro-life" stance that includes concern about abortions and child protection issues (e.g., forced abortions, and the sacrifice and abuse of fetuses and young children by cultists). The stories, told by both the child day-care survivors and adult ritual abuse survivors, contained the same message: We are all endangered by a powerful but secret cult that threatens our very way of life. Women and children are in particular danger. If allowed outside the protected bosom of the God-loving, male-dominated nuclear family, they are in danger of mutilation, torture, and ritual death, and if they survive, they will suffer from MPD, severe depression, or other mental disorders.

Prominent psychiatric investigators in the MPD field legitimated the ritual abuse fantasies of patients as "real memories," and such legitimation led necessarily to the simultaneous legitimation of the idea of a secret satanic cult responsible for perpetuating the abuse. Legitimation of these ideas by psychiatric authorities spawned workshops and conferences for their dissemination to therapists throughout North America. The result was the creation and multiplication of MPD patients who "remember" the satanic ritual abuse that gave rise to their "splitting" into alter personalities.

The legitimation of satanic ritual abuse memories by psychiatric professionals may have occurred for several reasons. In some respects, the emergence of ritual abuse "memories" by newly discovered alters placed investigators who supported the MPD diagnosis in a position similar to that of the judges during the Salem witchcraft panic. Having legitimated what they considered to be the initial "reasonable" accusations of the possessed women and children, the judges could not refuse to legitimate the more questionable later accusations without discrediting their own earlier judgements. Relatedly, MPD proponents who legitimate the enactment of alters who "hold" memories of "conventional" child sexual abuse may have difficulty refusing to legitimate the outlandish memory reports of alters who describe satanic ritual abuse. After all, if satanic ritual abuse memories are not to be believed, then the ontological status of the alters that "hold" those memories is also called into question. By extension, the entire edifice of hidden alters purportedly created in childhood to "hold" intolerable memories is threatened with collapse.

Medical mythologies sometimes serve political functions by supporting the dominant ideology of those who hold social power. During the 19th century, for example, medical texts frequently described women as suffering from an inherent neurological weakness that was exacerbated by such practices as attaining a higher education or aspiring to any roles other than subservient wife and devoted mother. Obviously, these medical ideas served to support and legitimize patriarchal institutional arrangements that kept women economically and psychologically dependent on men (Smith-Rosenberg, 1985). Before the 19th century, these arrangements had been legitimated as God-given by religious mythologies. In the more secular 19th century, religious legitimation was at least partially replaced with scientific legitimation, and these institutional arrangements were thereby grounded as "natural" in the pseudobiology of the day.

The modern notion of abuse-created MPD may also function to support patriarchal institutional arrangements. By and large, MPD is a "disorder" of women. Supposedly, through some combination of inherited psychological predisposition (i.e., a tendency toward dissociation) and early wounding (satanic or other child abuse), these unhappy women are unable to "integrate" and function as full members of society. Looked at from a social–psychological rather than a medical perspective, this "disorder" can be conceptualized as a pattern of self-construal and interpersonal responding used by some chronically unhappy, troubled, women to express dissatisfactions, "make sense" of their troubled lives, and attain some succor by adopting a variant of the sick role. From this perspective, the political implications of the MPD diagnosis and its connection with satanic and other forms of child abuse can more readily be seen. By treating MPD as a disease caused by early abuse, the problems faced by women given this diagnosis and the strategies they have learned to use in dealing with these problems are explained in terms of internal psychological processes. As a result, these problems are isolated from broader social issues. These problems are not conceptualized as related to the economic and social inequities faced by women. No emphasis is placed on socialization practices that encourage women to adopt the language of sickness to express dissatisfactions, obliquely extract revenge (e.g., by becoming an economic or emotional burden), and seek solace or that encourage women to behave subserviently toward men and to limit their educational and professional attainments in favor of adopting traditional female roles. Relatedly, no emphasis is placed on the impediments institutionalized in our culture that make it difficult for women to achieve economic and psychological self-sufficiency (e.g., unequal pay, lack of adequate day care, job discrimination, sexual harassment at work, inadequate child support for divorced mothers). Within this medical framework the sociopolitical arrangements that maintain inequities between the sexes are not seen as relevant to the patterns of distress exhibited by these women. Instead, their current problems are conceptualized in terms of hypothetical causes that not only can be explored without questioning the sociopolitical status quo, but that, in fact, deflect attention away from any understanding in terms of sociopolitical factors (Culhane, 1993; Tavris, 1993). For example, to the extent that unhappy women attempt to understand their distress by devoting cognitive and emotional resources to uncovering alters who hold "memories" of early satanic cult abuse, they are unlikely to connect their problems to such structural considerations as lack of educational or employment opportunities, or socialization processes at home and in school.

In short, medical explanations of MPD that focus on early abuse may serve a political function similar to spirit possession explanations of peripheral possession in traditional cultures. By attributing the complaints and expressions of dissatisfaction proffered by unhappy and socially marginal women to indwelling spirits, an avenue is developed through which these women can attain some relief and succor and express anger and dissatisfaction with their personal plight. By the same token, however, the spirit-possession explanation that these women conspire to legitimate through their possession enactments serves to deflect attention away from the structural elements within their societies that maintain them and other women in positions of powerlessness and social marginality (I. M. Lewis, 1987). MPD enactments, and the explanations of those enactments in terms of early trauma, may constitute a secularized version of the possession hypothesis, which serves a similar social function: allowing expressions of dissatisfaction and the attainment of succor within a framework that prevents recognition of institutionalized social arrangements that are important to the creation of the initial dissatisfactions.

ALLEGATIONS OF FALSE MEMORIES AND THE BACKLASH AGAINST WOMEN

As pointed out by Faludi (1991), in the past 150 years there have been several periods during which women developed an identity of themselves as members of an oppressed group and engaged in political efforts that resulted in significant advancements toward social, political, and economic equality. In each case, these periods of political gain for women were accompanied and followed by a backlash from segments of the society that held a vested interest in maintaining women in subordinate positions. For example, the political gains of the 1970s that resulted largely from the activities of the feminist movement were followed in the 1980s by media depictions of professional, economically self-sufficient women as unhappy, as dealing poorly with the stresses of work, and as longing for a more traditional role as wife and mother.

Much media attention was also paid to scientific studies of questionable methodology that purported to show that women who were not married in their twenties would be very unlikely to find a husband when they became older (i.e., supporting the notion that women should not put off marriage to further their careers), that fertility in women fell off drastically when they reached their thirties (i.e., supporting the idea that women should have children while relatively young, even if this meant sacrificing or delaying a promising career), and so on (Faludi, 1991). Relatedly, a number of surveys (reviewed by Faludi, 1991) also revealed that many men were uncomfortable with the implications of economic equality between the sexes because these implications conflicted with their implicit conceptions of masculinity (e.g., "real" men do not do housework, do make important family decisions, do provide for the economic support of their families). Consequently, such men are often responsive to depictions that portray the ideal woman as a physically attractive but submissive creature who helps out economically when necessary but who really yearns to do the bidding of her husband and to provide emotional support for her family.

Recently, a number of investigators (Herman, 1991; Kristiansen, 1994) have suggested that publicity surrounding the notion that some women in therapy develop false memories of childhood sexual abuse constitutes another example of the backlash against women. According to this notion, powerful people with a vested interest in supporting the patriarchal status quo are threatened by the efforts of feminists to publicly proclaim that the sexual abuse of children is relatively common. Consequently, these individuals attempt to discredit such claims by describing them as exaggerated and as resulting from the unreliable reports of unstable and suggestible women who are led into developing false memories by their stupid, unscrupulous, or politically overcommitted therapists. According to proponents of the backlash hypothesis, parents who join the FMS Foundation after being accused of childhood sexual abuse by their grown children are prime examples of those who deny the reality of abuse and who blame the victims of abuse rather than accepting responsibility for the abuse that they perpetrated (Kristiansen, 1994).

The idea that claims about false memories of sexual abuse are likely to be used in support of a backlash against women undoubtedly contains much truth. Those with a vested interest in maintaining the subordination of women will undoubtedly use the phenomenon of false memories to paint a picture of women as mentally unstable and suffering from a childlike oversuggestibility. Moreover, the enthusiasm with which some aspects of the mainstream media have propagated the notion of false memories may, at least in part, reflect the relatively conservative ideologies of those who operate the corporate structures of these media organizations. These are, after all, the same media organizations that emphasize the importance of "family values" and that depict professional women as overstressed and unhappy.

Despite all of this, however, the notion that allegations of false memories can be explained solely in terms of a political backlash against women involves serious oversimplification of a complex social situation. To begin with, the backlash hypothesis assumes that allegations of false memories of childhood abuse are always or almost always untrue. As we have seen in various chapters, however, confusion between memories and fantasies commonly results when people are exposed to the kinds of situational contingencies that are used routinely in incest-resolution therapy. Moreover, there is no serious doubt that memory reports of abuse that arise for the first time in therapy are sometimes confabulated (e.g., reports of rape by space aliens, past-life abuse, and satanic ritual abuse) or that such reports are obtained regularly by therapists who search for such "memories." These considerations, along with others reviewed in earlier chapters, indicate that accused parents may frequently be correct when they allege that the "memories" of their accusing children are therapy-induced confabulations. To the extent that this is true, the establishment of support groups of accused parents that lobby to win political and media support can be better explained as reactions to the injustice experienced by these parents than as attempts to perpetuate patriarchy.

The establishment of groups such as the FMS Foundation in response to widespread accusations of abuse is similar to the response engendered by witchcraft panics in the 16th and 17th centuries. As described in chapters 13 and 14, witchcraft accusations were almost never true (occasionally, the people who were accused did, in fact, practice black magic and define themselves as witches). These accusations were, however, sometimes made on the basis of personal, economic, or political rivalries between accusers and the accused. In cases of large-scale accusations like the one that occurred at Salem, the panics were usually brought to an end when accusations spiraled up the social scale and involved the families of people who wielded social power. These prominant individuals used their political influence to organize countermovements that led eventually to the delegitimization of the accusations (Midelfort, 1972). At Salem, for example, prominant people became increasingly concerned about the spread of accusations and eventually helped to convince the Govenour General of the Coloney to disband the trial court (Spanos, 1983b).

Accusations of abuse based on "memories" that first arose during psychotherapy are usually made by relatively well-to-do women against their middle-class parents. These parents are often relatively well educated, sometimes politically sophisticated, and strongly committed to the belief that the accusations made against them are untrue. Therefore, it is hardly surprising that, with growth in their number, they have managed to organize into effective lobbying groups that have been successful at recruiting the legitimating support of respected academic experts and at swaying public opinion through the judicious use of media opportunities.

The backlash hypothesis is based on the assumption that the growth of the abuse survivor movement, with its emphasis on the purportedly widespread occurrence and catastrophic effects of childhood sexual abuse, benefits the political and social interests of women and effectively challenges the patriarchal status quo. Given the acceptance of these assumptions, it is natural to view allegations of false memories as necessarily detrimental to the political interests of women and as supportive of a conservative and partriarchial political ideology. As indicated earlier in this chapter, however, support for the notion that childhood sexual abuse is widespread and virulent can be used to support various social and political agendas. Strong advocacy of these ideas is voiced not only by certain aspects of the feminist movement, but also by some sections of the religious right with its support for false reports of satanic ritual abuse made both by adult survivors and by children trapped in day-care sexual abuse panics. In the case of the religious right, perpetuation of the idea that child sexual abuse is prevalent is used to support rather than challenge a conservative and antifeminist political agenda.

Relatedly, the propositions that one third to one half of women have experienced severe sexual abuse during childhood, that such abuse invariably produces serious psychological symptoms, and that half of these abused women suffer psychological sequelae without even being aware that they were abused could be said to undermine a view of women as mature and responsible adults who are as capable as men of economic self-sufficiency, professional attainment, and political acumen. On the contrary, the picture painted by these statistics serves to justify rather than challenge the political and economic inequality of women. After all, from this perspective, the problems of women stem not from economic and politically based discrimination that, with organized effort, can be changed. Instead, these problems are attributed to the "fact" that an astounding one third to one half of the female population has been psychologically and emotionally crippled by childhood events that cannot be altered.

It is difficult to see how the acceptance of such views is likely to alter the status quo or facilitate the economic and political emancipation of women. On the contrary, the group that most obviously and directly benefits from the perpetuation of such views is not women, but the professional therapists of both sexes who treat abuse "survivors" and thereby have a strong vested interest in maintaining a large client base (Culhane, 1993).

There is no evidence to suggest that women are more prone to the development of false memories than men. On the contrary, in experimental settings men appear to report false memories as frequently as women (Spanos, Burgess, Samuel, et al., 1994). Relatedly, men as well as women are led to develop false memories in police interrogation situations and in therapies aimed at uncovering memories of alien abduction. Most probably, then, allegations of false memories of childhood sexual abuse are more frequently leveled against women than men simply because women are much more likely than men to participate in incest-resolution therapies that contain the contextual elements that facilitate the occurrence of false memories of this type.

SUMMARY

The above considerations suggest that criticism of an abuse survivor movement that encourages women to view their abuse (either real or imagined) as the primary defining event of their lives, and the fundamental cause of their personal and interpersonal distress, need not be considered detrimental to the interests of women. On the contrary, such criticism, which includes recognition of false memories as a consequence of certain therapeutic practices, may be important in redirecting attention to the very real structural inequalities in our social system that hamper the political and economic advancement of women (Tavris, 1993).

V

CONCLUSION

22

FINAL THOUGHTS

Multiple identity enactments occur in most human societies. Nevertheless, the frequency of these enactments, their behavioral components, the conditions under which they occur, and the characteristics of those who display them differ dramatically among cultures and sometimes within cultures as well. When examined across cultures and historical eras, the rule-governed nature of multiple identity enactments and their embeddedness within a legitimating social matrix become clear.

Each culture develops its own indigenous theory of multiple-identity enactments. These local theories reflect local social structures and institutions, and they translate into culturally specific expectations that guide both the performance of multiple identity enactments and the reactions of audiences to these enactments. Thus, the theory that the Holy Ghost speaks through people, and in so doing endorses them spiritually, provides a local explanation for glossolalia and helps to establish motivations and expectations for its perpetuation. Relatedly, Catholic and Protestant theories of demonic possession served as explanations for deviant behavior and created the institutional contexts (e.g., exorcism procedures) that shaped demonic enactments in terms of the different requirements and expectations generated by each theory and its supporting social institutions. By definition, however, local theories of multiplicity are designed to explain only local displays of multiplicity, and their deficiencies as general theories of multiplicity enactments become obvious when these enactments are compared across historical and cultural contexts.

The disease theory of MPD is a local theory of multiple identity. Because the proponents of this theory are invariably mental health professionals, the displays of multiplicity that they observe are almost always limited to those distressed and unhappy people who go to them for help. This limitation profoundly influences the manner in which these investigators conceptualize multiplicity. The disease theory of MPD is based on the idea that unhappiness and/or behavioral deviance in adulthood stems from particular traumatic events occurring in childhood. The particular childhood traumas focused on by modern MPD proponents are physical abuse and especially sexual abuse. Because of its emphasis on childhood antecedents and on the notion that "symptoms" reflect unconscious defenses, this approach tends to greatly deemphasize the social and strategic nature of multiple identity enactments and the roles played by the institutionalized contexts that encourage, shape, and legitimate these enactments. In particular, this emphasis deflects attention away from the role the clinicians themselves play in cueing and legitimating manifestations of multiplicity. It also deflects attention from the marked charges in symptomatology that have occurred in MPD over the years, changes that clearly illustrate the role of social factors in shaping MPD displays. Since the 19th century, for example, the number of personalities per patient has jumped from 2 or 3 to frequently over 20, and sometimes into the hundreds. Many early cases were marked by displays of catalepsy, transitional periods of sleep, and often convulsions, which are uncommon today. The alter personalities of early patients were human. Recently, however, scholarly articles have been devoted to animal alters (e.g., Hendrickson, McCarty, & Goodwin, 1990) or reincarnated past lives (Krippner, 1986). Reports of child abuse have gone from occasional accompaniments of early cases to the ritual satanic abuse of today.

Changes of this kind are difficult to deal with from a disease perspective that explains identity enactments as "symptoms" caused by past traumas rather than as expectancy-guided, goal-directed displays that change as a function of new information concerning role demands. As indicated earlier, role changes of this kind are commonly seen in historical and cross-cultural displays of possession. Songhay mediums, for example, changed the characteristics of their possession displays in response to changes among the ruling elites (Stoller, 1989), and the characteristics of demonic possession changed to meet the different requirements of particular religious communities (Spanos, 1983a; D. P. Walker, 1981). Relatedly, the recent association of MPD with reports of ritual satanic abuse are much more likely to reflect therapy-induced confabulations generated by the infusion of fundamentalist Christian ideology into the MPD movement than the existence of a massive 50-year-old secret conspiracy that has murdered thousands of people without leaving a trace of evidence.

Like other local theories, the disease theory of multiplicity is unable to provide a general account of this phenomenon that takes into consideration its cross-cultural and trans-historical manifestations. I suggest that it is time to abandon the local theory of MPD and to view the phenomenon of multiplicity from a sociocognitive and historical perspective.

REFERENCES

Abhold, J. J. (1993). *The distortion of a distant and traumatic memory: Implications for eyewitness testimony and psychotherapy.* Unpublished doctoral dissertaion, University of Arkansas, Fayetteville.

Abse, D. W. (1987). *Hysteria and related mental disorders: An approach to psychological medicine* (2nd ed.). Wright, England: Bristol.

Ackerman, S. E., & Lee, R. L. M. (1981). Communication and cognitive pluralism in a spirit possession event in Malaysia. *American Ethnologist, 8,* 789–799.

Adamski, G. (1955). *Inside the space ships.* New York: Abelard-Schuman.

Adityhanjee, R., & Khandelwal, S. (1989). Current status of multiple personality disorder in India. *American Journal of Psychiatry, 146,* 1607–1610.

Agle, D. P., Ratnoff, O. D., & Wasman, M. (1967). Studies in autoerythrocyte sensitization: The induction of purpuric lesions by hypnotic suggestion. *Psychosomatic Medicine, 29,* 491–503.

Agle, D. P., Ratnoff, O. D., & Wasman, M. (1969). Conversion reactions in autoerythrocyte sensitization. *Archives of General Psychiatry, 20,* 438–477.

Aldridge-Morris, R. (1989). *Multiple personality: An exercise in deception.* Hillsdale, NJ: Erlbaum.

Alexander, P., & Lupfer, S. (1987). Family characteristics and long term consequences associated with sexual abuse. *Archives of Sexual Behavior, 16,* 235–245.

Allison, R. B. (1981). Multiple personality and criminal behavior. *American Journal of Forensic Psychiatry, 2,* 32–38.

Allison, R. B., & Schwarz, T. (1980). *Minds in many pieces.* New York: Rawson Wade.

Allison, R. M. (1991). Travel log: In search of multiples in Moscow. *American Journal of Forensic Psychiatry, 12*, 51–56.

Altrocchi, J. (1992). "We don't have that problem here": MPD in New Zealand. *Dissociation, 5*, 109–110.

American Psychiatric Associaion. (1994). *Diagnostic and statistical manual of mental disorders* (4th ed.). Washington, DC: Author.

Anderson, N. T. (1990). *The bondage breaker*. Eugene, OR: Harvest House.

Anderson, R. C., & Pichert, J. W. (1978). Recall of previously unrecallable information following a shift in perspective. *Journal of Verbal Learning and Verbal Behavior, 17*, 1–12.

Antens, E., Frischholz, E. J., Braun, B. G., et al. (1991, November). *The simulation of dissociative disorders on the Dissociative Experiences Scale*. Paper presented at the 8th annual meeting of the International Society for the Study of Multiple Personality Disorder and Dissociation, Chicago.

Anthony, D., & Robbins, T. (1992). Law, social science and the "brainwashing" exception to the first amendment. *Behavioral Sciences and the Law, 10*, 5–29.

Argyle, M. (1958). *Religious behavior*. London: Routledge & Kegan Paul.

Armstrong, J. G., & Loewenstein, R. J. (1990). Characteristics of patients with multiple personality and dissociative disorders on testing. *Journal of Nervous and Mental Disease, 178*, 448–454.

Asch, S. E. (1952). *Social psychology*. Englewood Cliffs, NJ: Prentice-Hall.

Asch, S. E. (1956). Studies of independence and conformity: I. A minority of one against a unanimous majority. *Psychological Monographs, 70*,(9, Whole No. 416).

Aubin, N. (1716). *Cruels effets del la vengeance du Cardinal de Richelieu ou histoire des diables de Loudun*. Amsterdam: Etienne Roger.

Bahnson, C. B., & Smith, K. (1975). Autonomic changes in a multiple personality patient. *Psychosomatic Medicine, 37*, 85–86.

Baker, A. W., & Duncan, S. P. (1985). Child sexual abuse: A study of prevalence in Great Britain. *Child Abuse and Neglect, 9*, 457–467.

Baker, R. A. (1992). *Hidden memories*. Buffalo, NY: Prometheus.

Barber, T. X. (1961). Experimental evidence for a theory of hypnotic behavior: II. Experimental controls in hypnotic age regression. *International Journal of Clinical and Experimental Hypnosis, 9*, 181–193.

Barber, T. X. (1965). Measuring "hypnotic-like" suggestibility with and without "hypnotic induction" psychometric properties, norms, and variables influencing response to the Barber Suggestibility Scale (BSS). *Psychological Reports, 16*, 809–844.

Barber, T. X. (1969). *Hypnosis: A scientific approach*. New York: Van Nostrand Reinhold.

Barber, T. X. (1979). Suggested "hypnotic" behavior: The trance paradigm versus an alternative paradigm. In E. Fromm & R. E. Shor (Eds.), *Hypnosis: Developments in research and new perspectives* (pp. 217–271). Chicago: Aldine.

Barber, T. X., & Calverley, D. S. (1964a). An experimental study of "hypnotic" (auditory and visual) hallucinations. *Journal of Abnormal and Social Psychology, 63*, 13–20.

Barber, T. X., & Calverley, D. S. (1964b). Experimental studies in "hypnotic" behavior: Suggested deafness evaluated by delayed auditory feedback. *British Journal of Psychology, 55*, 439–446.

Barber, T. X., & Calverley, D. S. (1966). Toward a theory of "hypnotic" behavior: Experimental analysis of suggested amnesia. *Journal of Abnormal Psychology, 71*, 95–107.

Barber, T. X., & Deeley, D. C. (1961). Experimental evidence for a theory of hypnotic behaviour: I. "Hypnotic" colour-blindness without "hypnosis". *International Journal of Clinical and Experimental Hypnosis, 9*, 79–86.

Barber, T. X., & Hahn, K. W., Jr. (1962). Physiological and subjective responses to pain producing stimulation under hypnotically suggested and waking-imagined "analgesia." *Journal of Abnormal and Social Psychology, 65*, 41–48.

Barber, T. X., & Ham, M. W. (1974). *Hypnotic phenomena.* Morristown, NJ: General Learning Press.

Barber, T. X., Spanos, N. P., & Chaves, J. F. (1974). *Hypnosis, imagination and human potentialities.* New York: Pergamon Press.

Barnier, A. J., & McConkey, K. M. (1992). Reports of real and false memories: The relevance of hypnosis, hypnotizability and context of memory test. *Journal of Abnormal Psychology, 101*, 521–527.

Baroja, J. (1964). *The world of witches* (O. N. V. Glendinning, Trans.). Chicago: University of Chicago Press.

Barthel, J. (1976). *A death in Canaan.* New York: Thomas Congdon Books.

Bartlett, F. C. (1932). *Remembering: A study in experimental social psychology.* Cambridge, England: Cambridge University Press.

Baskin, W. (1974). The devils of Loudon. In E. Nauman (Ed.), *Exorcism through the ages* (pp. 15–20). Secaucus, NJ: Citadel Press.

Bass, E., & Davis, L. (1988). *The courage to heal: A guide for women survivors of child sexual abuse.* New York: Harper & Row.

Becker, E. (1962). Toward a comprehensive theory of depression: A cross disiplinary appraisal of objects, games and meaning. *Journal of Nervous and Mental Diseases, 135*, 26–33.

Beer, L. (1988). The coming of the saucers. In J. Spencer & H. Evans (Eds.), *Phenomenon: Forty years of flying saucers* (pp. 19–25). New York: Avon.

Beitchman, J. H., Zucker, K. J., Hood, J. E., DaCosta, G. A., & Akman, D. (1991). A review of short term effects of child sexual abuse. *Child Abuse and Neglect, 15*, 537–556.

Beitchman, J. H., Zucker, K. J., Hood, J. E., DaCosta, G. A., Akman, D., & Cassavia, E. (1992). A review of long-term effects of child sexual abuse. *Child Abuse and Neglect, 16*, 101–118.

Bell, R. M. (1985). *Holy anorexia.* Chicago: University of Chicago Press.

Belli, R. F. (1989). Influences of misleading postevent information: Misinformation interference and acceptance. *Journal of Experimental Psychology: General, 118,* 72–85.

Bem, D. J. (1967). Self-perception: An alternative interpretation of cognitive dissonance phenomena. *Psychological Review, 74,* 183–200.

Bem, D. J., & McConnell, H. K. (1970). Testing the self-perception explanation of dissonance phenomena: On the salience of premanipulation attitudes. *Journal of Personality and Social Psychology, 14,* 23–31.

Bergasse, N. (1970). Idees générales sur le système du monde et l'accord des lois physiques et morales dans la nature [General ideas about the system of the world and the agreement of physical and moral laws in nature]. In R. Darnton (Ed.), *Mesmerism* (pp. 183–185). New York: Schocken Books. (Original work published 1785)

Bergin, A. E. (1971). The evaluation of therapeutic outcomes. In A. E. Bergin & S. L. Garfield (Eds.), *Handbook of psychotherapy and behavior change* (pp. 217–270). New York: Wiley.

Bernheim, H. (1900). *Suggestive theraputics.* New York: Putnam. (Original published 1886)

Bernstein, E. M., & Putnam, F. W. (1986). Development, reliability, and validity of a dissociation scale. *Journal of Nervous and Mental Disease, 174,* 727–735.

Bernstein, M. (1956). *The search for Bridey Murphy.* Garden City, NY: Doubleday.

Bertrand, L. D. (1989). The assessment and modification of hypnotic susceptibility. In N. P. Spanos & J. F. Chaves (Eds.), *Hypnosis: The cognitive-behavioral perspective* (pp. 18–31). Buffalo, NY: Prometheus.

Bertrand, L. D., & Spanos, N. P. (1985). The organization of recall during hypnotic suggestions for complete and selective amnesia. *Imagination, Cognition and Personality, 4,* 249–261.

Best, H. L., & Michaels, R. M. (1954). Living out "future" experiences under hypnosis. *Science, 120,* 1077.

Best, J. (1990). *Threatened children: Rhetoric and concern about child-victims.* Chicago: University of Chicago Press.

Best, J. (1991). Endangered children in antisatanist rhetoric. In. J. T. Richardson, J. Best, & D. G. Bromley (Eds.), *The satanism scare* (pp. 95–106). New York: Aldine.

Biderman, A. D. (1960). Social psychological needs and "involuntary" behavior as illustrated by compliance in interrogation. *Sociometry, 23,* 120–147.

Binet, A., & Fere, C. (1888). *Animal magnetism.* New York: Appleton.

Biscop, P. (1981). *By spirit possessed.* Unpublished master's thesis, Simon Fraser University, Burnaby, British Columbia, Canada.

Biscop, P. (1985). *There is no death: Belief and the social construction of reality in a Canadian spiritualist church.* Unpublished doctoral thesis, Simon Fraser University, Burnaby, British Columbia, Canada.

Black, S., & Wigan, E. R. (1961). An investigation of selective deafness produced by direct suggestions under hypnosis. *British Medical Journal, 2*, 736–741.

Blamary, M. (1979). *Psychoanalyzing psychoanalysis*. Baltimore: The John Hopkins University Press.

Blatner, A. (1987, November). Psychiatry's time bomb. *The Psychiatric Times, 8*, 39–41.

Bliss, E. L. (1980). Multiple personalities: a report of 14 cases with implications for schizophrenia and hysteria. *Archives of General Psychiatry, 37*, 1388–1397.

Bliss, E. L. (1984a). A symptom profile of patients with multiple personalities, including MMPI results. *Journal of Nervous and Mental Disease, 172*, 197–202.

Bliss, E. L. (1984b). Hysteria and hypnosis. *Journal of Nervous and Mental Disease, 172*, 203–206.

Bliss, E. L. (1986). *Multiple personality, allied disorders, and hypnosis*. New York: Oxford University Press.

Bliss, E. L., & Jeppsen, E. A. (1985). Prevalence of multiple personality among inpatients and outpatients. *American Journal of Psychiatry, 142*, 250–251.

Bliss, E. L., & Larson (1985). E. M. Sexual criminality and hypnotizability. *Journal of Nervous and Mental Diseases, 173*, 522–526.

Bliss, E. L., Larson, E. M., & Nakashima, S. R. (1983). Auditory hallucinations and schizophrenia. *Journal of Nervous and Mental Disease, 171*, 30–33.

Bloecher, T., Clamar, A., & Hopkins, B. (1985). *Summary report on the psychological testing of nine individuals reporting UFO abduction experiences*. Mt. Ranier, MD: Fund for UFO Research.

Blum, G. S. (1975). A case of hypnotically induced tubular vision. *International Journal of Clinical and Experimental Hypnosis, 23*, 111–119.

Blume, E. S. (1990) *Secret survivors: Uncovering incest and its after effects in women*. New York: Ballantine.

Boddy, J. (1988). Spirits and selves in northern Sudan: The cultural therapeutics of possession and trance. *American Ethnologist, 15*, 4–27.

Bonanno, G. A. (1990). Remembering and psychotherapy. *Psychotherapy, 27*, 175–186.

Bonke, B., Schmitz, P. I. M., Verhage, F., & Zwaveling, A. (1986). Clinical study of so-called unconscious perception during general anaesthesia. *British Journal of Anaesthesia, 58*, 957–964.

Boor, M. (1982). The multiple personality epidemic: Additional cases and inferences regarding diagnosis, etiology, dynamics and treatment. *Journal of Nervous and Mental Disease, 170*, 302–304.

Bothwell, R. K., Deffenbacher, K. A., & Brigham, J. C. (1987). Correlation of eyewitness accuracy and confidence: Optimality hypothesis revisited. *Journal of Applied Psychology, 72*, 691–695.

Bottoms, B. L., Shaver, P. R., & Goodman, G. S. (1991). *Profile of ritual and religion related abuse allegations reported to clinical psychologists in the United States*. Paper presented at the 99th annual convention of the American Psychological Association, San Francisco.

Bourguignon, E. (1976). *Possession*. San Francisco: Chandler & Sharp.

Bower, G. (1981). Mood and memory. *American Psychologist, 36*, 129–148.

Bowers, K. S. (1976). *Hypnosis for the seriously curious*. Monterey, CA: Brooks/ Cole.

Bowman, E. S. (1990). Adolescent multiple personality disorder in the nineteenth and early twentieth centuries. *Dissociation, 3*, 179–187.

Boyd, A. (1991). *Blasphemous rumors*. London: HarperCollins.

Boyer, P., & Nissenbaum, S. (1974). *Salem possessed: The social origins of witchcraft*. Cambridge, MA: Harvard University Press.

Brady, J. P., & Lind, D. L. (1961). Experimental analysis of hysterical blindness. *Archives of General Psychiatry, 4*, 331–339.

Brady, M. (1992). *Beyond survival*. New York: HarperCollins.

Braid, J. (1960). *Braid on hypnotism*. New York: Julian. (Originally published as *Neurypnology*, 1843)

Braid, J. (1970). The physiology of fascination and the critics criticized. In M. M. Tinterow (Ed.), *Foundations of hypnosis*. Springfield, IL: C. C. Thomas. (Original work published 1855)

Brandon, R. (1984). *The spiritualists*. Buffalo, NY: Prometheus.

Brandsma, J. M., & Ludwig, A. M. (1974). A case of multiple personality: Diagnosis and treatment. *International Journal of Clinical and Experimental Hypnosis, 22*, 216–233.

Braun, B. G. (1983). Neurophysiologic changes in multiple personality due to integration: A preliminary report. *American Journal of Clinical Hypnosis, 26*, 84–92.

Braun, B. G. (1990). Multiple personality disorder: An overview. *American Journal of Occupational Therapy, 44*, 971–976.

Braun, B. G., & Sachs, R. G. (1988). *Recognition of possible cult involvement in MPD patients*. Fifth International Conference on Multiple Personality/ Dissocitaion States (Tape # 436-88-IVD). Alexandria, VA: Audio Transcripts, Ltd.

Brende, J. O. (1984). The psychophysiologic manifestations of dissociation. *Psychiatric Clinics of North America, 7*, 41–50.

Breuer, J., & Freud, S. (1964). *Studies on hysteria*. (A. A. Brill, Trans.). Boston: Beacon Press. (Original work published 1895)

Brewster, W. F., & Treyens, J. C. (1981). Role of schemata in memory for places. *Cognitive Psychology, 13*, 207–230.

Briere, J., & Conte, J. (1989, August). *Amnesia for abuse in adults molested as children*. Paper presented at the annual convention of the American Psychological Association, New Orleans, LA.

Briere, J., & Conte, J. (1993). Self-reported amnesia for abuse in adults molested as children. *Journal of Traumatic Stress, 6,* 21–31.

Briere, J., & Elliot, D. M. (1993). Sexual abuse, family environment, and psychological symptoms: On the validity of statistical control. *Journal of Consulting and Clinical Psychology, 61,* 284–288.

Briere, J., & Zaidi, L. Y. (1989). Sexual abuse histories and sequelae in female psychiatric emergency room patients. *American Journal of Psychiatry, 146,* 1602–1607.

Brom, D., Kleber, R. J., & Defares, P. B. (1989). Brief psychotherapy for posttraumatic stress disorders. *Journal of Consulting and Clinical Psychology, 57,* 607–612.

Bromley, D. G. (1991). Satanism: The new cult scare. In J. T. Richardson, J. Best, & D. G. Bromley (Eds.), *The satanism scare* (pp. 49–72). New York: Aldine.

Bromley, D. G., & Shupe, A. D. (1981). *Strange gods.* Boston: Beacon Press.

Brooks, C. M., Perry, N. W., Starr, S. D., & Teply, L. L. (1994). Child abuse and neglect reporting laws: Understanding interests, understanding policy. *Behavioral Science and the Law, 12,* 49–64.

Brown, P. (1994). Toward a psychobiological study of dissociation. In S. J. Lynn & J. Rhue (Eds.), *Dissociation: Clinical, theoretical and research perspectives.* New York: Guilford.

Brown, R. (1986). *Social psychology* (2nd ed.). New York: Free Press.

Browning, D., & Boatman, B. (1977). Incest: Children at risk. *American Journal of Psychiatry, 134,* 69–72.

Brownmiller, S. (1975). *Against our will: Men, women, and rape.* New York: Simon & Schuster.

Brumberg, J. J. (1988). *Fasting girls: The emergence of anorexia nervosa as a modern disease.* Cambridge, MA: Harvard University Press.

Bucky, S. F., & Dallenberg, C. (1992). The relationship between training of mental health professionals and the reporting of ritual abuse and multiple personality disorder symptomatology. *Journal of Psychology and Theology, 20,* 233–238.

Bullard, T. E. (1991). Folkloric dimensions of the UFO phenomenon. *Journal of UFO Studies, 3,* 1–58.

Bulkley, J., & Horwitz, M. J. (1994). Adults sexually abused as children: Legal actions and issues. *Behavioral Sciences and the Law, 12,* 65–88.

Burgess, C. A., Spanos, N. P., Ritt, J., Hordy, T., & Brooks, S. (1993). *Compliant responding among high hypnotizables: An experimental demonstration.* Unpublished manuscript, Carleton University, Ottawa, Ontario, Canada.

Cacioppo, J. T., Claiborn, C. D., Petty, R. E., & Heesacker, M. (1991). General framework for the study of attitude change in psychgotherapy. In C. R. Snyder & D. R. Forsyth (Eds.), *Handbook of social and clinical psychology* (pp. 523–539). New York: Pergamon Press.

Calif, R. (1914). More wonders form the invisible world. In G. L. Burr (Ed.), *Narratives of the witchcraft cases, 1648–1706*. New York: Scribner's. (Original work published 1700)

Campbell, T. W. (1992). Theraputic relationships and iatrogenic outcomes: The blame and change maneuver in psychotherapy. *Psychotherapy, 29*, 474–480.

Cardeña, E., & Spiegel, D. (1993). Dissociative reactions to the San Francisco Bay Area earthquake of 1989. *American Journal of Psychiatry, 150*, 474–478.

Carlson, E. T. (1981) *Benjamin Rush's lectures on the mind*. Philadelphia: American Philosophical Society.

Carlson, E. B., Putnam, F. W., Ross, C. A., Anderson, G., Clark, P., Torem, M., Coons, P., Bowman, E., Chu, J. A., Dill, D., Loewenstein, R. J., & Braun, B. G. (1991). Factor analysis of the Dissociative Experiences Scale: A multicenter study. In B. G. Braun & E. B. Carlson (Eds.), *Proceedings of the Eighth International Conference on Multiple Personality and Dissociative States*. Chicago: Rush-Presbyterian.

Carstairs, G. M., & Kapur, R. L. (1976). *The great universe of Kota*. London: Hogarth Press.

Casey, G. A. (1966). *Hypnotic time distortion and learning*. Unpublished doctoral dissertation, Michigan State University, East Lansing.

Catherinet, F. M. (1972). Demoniacs in the Gospel. In F. J. Sheed (Ed.), *Soundings in satanism* (pp. 121–137). New York: Sheed & Ward.

Charcot, J. M. (1889). *Clinical lectures on the diseases of the nervous system* (Vol. 3). London: New Sydenham Society.

Cheyne, G. (1742). *The natural method of curing the disease of the body and the disorders of the mind, depending on the body*. London: Strahan & Leake.

Chordoff, P. (1987). More on multiple personality disorder [letter to the editor]. *American Journal of Psychiatry, 144*, 124.

Chu, J. A., & Dill, D. L. (1990). Dissociative symptoms in relation to childhood physical and sexual abuse. *American Journal of Psychiatry, 147*, 887–892.

Cialdini, R. B. (1984). *Influence: The new psychology of modern persuasion*. New York: Quill.

Cioffi, F. (1974). Was Freud a liar? *The Listener, 91*, 172–174.

Coe, W. C. (1964). Further norms of the Harvard Group Scale of Hypnotic Susceptibility, Form A. *International Journal of Clinical and Experimental Hypnosis, 12*, 184–190.

Coe, W. C. (1989). Posthypnotic amnesia: Theory and research. In N. P. Spanos & J. F. Chaves (Eds.), *Hypnosis: The cognitive-behavioral perspective* (pp. 418–436). Buffalo, NY: Prometheus.

Coe, W. C., Buckner, L. G., Howard, M. L., & Kobayashi, K. (1972). Hypnosis as role enactment: Focus on a role specific skill. *American Journal of Clinical Hypnosis, 15*, 41–45.

Coe, W. C., Kobayashi, K., & Howard, M. L. (1973). Experimental and ethical problems of evaluating the influence of hypnosis in antisocial conduct. *Journal of Abnormal Psychology, 82,* 476–482.

Coe, W. C., Peterson, P., & Gwynn, M. (1993). *Expectations and sequelae to hypnosis.* Unpublished manuscript, California State University at Fresno.

Coe, W. C., & Sarbin, T. R. (1977). Hypnosis from the standpoint of a contextualist. *Annals of the New York Academy of Sciences, 295,* 2–13.

Coe, W. C., & Sluis, A. S. E. (1989). Increasing contextual pressures to breach post-hypnotic amnesia. *Journal of Personality and Social Psychology, 57,* 885–894.

Cohn, N. (1975). *Europe's inner demons.* New York: Basic Books.

Cole, P. M., & Putnam, F. W. (1992). Effects of incest on self and social functioning: A developmental and psychopathological perspective. *Journal of Consulting and Clinical Psychology, 60,* 174–184.

Coleman, L. (1992). Creating "memories" of sexual abuse. *Issues in Child Abuse Accusations, 4,* 169–176.

Collins, L. N., Graham, J. W., Hansen, W. B., & Johnson, C. A. (1985). Agreement between retrospective accounts of substance use and earlier reported substance use. *Applied Psychological Measurement, 9,* 301–309.

Comfort, A. (1967). *The anxiety makers: Some curious preoccupations of the medical profession.* London: Nelson.

Condon, R. (1991). *The Manchurian candidate.* New York: Armchair Detective Library. (Original work published 1959)

Connery, D. S. (1977). *Guilty until proven innocent.* New York: Putnam.

Conrad, P. (1992). Medicalization and social control. *Annual Review of Sociology, 18,* 209–232.

Constantinides, P. (1977). Ill at ease and sick at heart: Symbolic behavior in a Sudanese healing cult. In I. Wilson (Ed.), *Symbols and sentiments* (pp. 61–84). New York: Academic Press.

Conway, M., & Ross, M. (1984). Getting what you want by revising what you had. *Journal of Personality and Social Psychology, 47,* 738–748.

Coons, P. M. (1980). Multiple personality: Diagnostic considerations. *Journal of Clinical Psychiatry, 41,* 330–336.

Coons, P. M. (1984). The differential diagnosis of multiple personality disorder. A comprehensive review. *Psychiatric Clinics of North America, 7,* 51–67.

Coons, P. M. (1993). *Confirmation of childhood abuse and adolescent cases of multiple personality and dissociative disorder NOS.* Unpublished manuscript, Laure D. Carter Memorial Hospital, Indianapolis, IN.

Coons, P. M., Bowman, E. S., & Milstein, V. (1988). Multiple personality disorder: A clinical investigation of 50 cases. *Journal of Nervous and Mental Disease, 176,* 519–527.

Coons, P. M., & Milstein, V. (1986). Psychosexual disturbances in multiple personality: Characteristics, etiology, and treatment. *Journal of Clinical Psychiatry*, *47*, 106–110.

Coons, P. M., Milstein, V., & Marley, C. (1982). EEG studies of two multiple personalities and a control. *Archives of General Psychiatry, 39*, 823–825.

Council, J. R. (1993a). Context effects in personality research. *Current Directions in Psychological Science, 2*, 31–34.

Council, J. R. (1993b). *The annoying itch of context effects*. Paper presented at the Nags Head Conference on Personality and Social Behavior, Highland Beach, FL.

Council, J. R., & Huff, K. D. (1990). Hypnosis, fantasy activity and reports of paranormal experiences in high, medium and low fantasizers. *British Journal of Experimental and Clinical Hypnosis, 7*, 9–16.

Courtois, C. A. (1988). *Healing the incest wound: Adult survivors in therapy*. New York: Norton.

Courtois, C. A. (1991, Fall). Theory, sequencing, and strategy in treating adult survivors. *New Directions for Mental Health Services, 51*, 47–60.

Cozolino, L. J. (1989). The ritual abuse of children: Implications for clinical practice and research. *The Journal of Sex Research, 26*, 131–138.

Crabtree, A. (1992). Dissociation and memory: A two-hundred year perspective. *Dissociation, 5*, 150–154.

Crawford, H. J., MacDonald, H., & Hilgard, E. R. (1979). Hypnotic deafness: A psychophysical study of response to tone intensity as modified by hypnosis. *American Journal of Psychology, 92*, 193–214.

Culhane, C. D. (1993, November). *Critical frameworks from contemporary anthropology and the case of adult survivors of sexual abuse*. Paper presented at the Clark Conference on Memories of Trauma, Worcester, MA.

Darnton, R. (1970). *Mesmerism*. New York: Schocken Press.

Davis, A. D. M., & Wagstaff. G. F. (1991). The use of creative imagery in the behavioral treatment of an elderly woman diagnosed as an hysterical ataxic. *Contemporary Hypnosis, 8*, 147–152.

Dawes, R. M. (1994). *House of cards: Psychology and psychotherapy built on myth*. New York: Free Press.

Deaux, K. (1993). Reconstructing social identity. *Personality and Social Psychology Bulletin, 19*, 4–12.

Decker, H. S. (1986). The lure of nonmaterialism in materialist Europe: Investigations of dissociative phenomena 1880–1915. In J. M. Quen (Ed.), *Split minds/split brains: Historical and current perspectives* (pp. 31–61). New York: New York University Press.

de Groh, M. (1989). Correlates of hypnotic susceptibility. In N. P. Spanos & J. F. Chaves (Eds.), *Hypnosis: The cognitive-behavioral perspective*. Buffalo, NY: Prometheus.

de Groot, H. P., & Gwynn, M. I. (1989). Trance logic, duality and hidden observer responding. In N. P Spanos & J. F. Chaves (Eds.), *Hypnosis: The cognitive-behavioral perspective* (pp. 187–205). Buffalo, NY: Prometheus.

Deleuze, J. P. F. (1879). *Animal magnetism* (T. Harshon, Trans.). New York: Wells. (Original work published 1825)

Dell, P. F., & Eisenhower, J. W. (1990). Adolescent multiple personality disorder: A preliminary study of eleven cases. *Journal of the American Academy of Child and Adolescent Psychiatry, 29,* 359–366.

Demos, J. P. (1982). *Entertaining Satan: Witchcraft and the culture of early New England.* New York: Oxford University Press.

Devereux, D. P. (1992). *Earth memory: Sacred sites—doorways into earth's mysteries.* St. Paul, MN: Llewellyn Publications.

Devereux, D. P., & McCartney, P. (1982). *Earth lights: Towards an explanation of the UFO enigma.* Wellingborough, Northamptonshire, England: Turnstone Press.

Devine, D. A., & Bornstein, P. H. (1980). Covert modeling—hypnosis in the treatment of obesity. *Psychotherapy: Theory, research, and practice, 17,* 272–267.

de Wohl, L. (1947). *The living wood.* London: Gollancz.

Deyoub, P. L., & Wilkie, R. (1980). Suggestion with and without hypnotic induction in a weight reduction program. *International Journal of Clinical and Experimental Hypnosis, 27,* 333–340.

Diamond, B. (1980). Inherent problems in the use of pretrial hypnosis on a prospective witness. *California Law Review, 68,* 313–349.

Diamond, M. J. (1974). Modification of hypnotizability: A review. *Psychological Bulletin, 81,* 180–198.

Dickes, R. A. (1974). Brief therapy for conversion reactions: An in-hospital technique. *American Journal of Psychiatry, 131,* 584–586.

Diethelm, O. (1970). The medical teaching of demonology in the seventeenth and eighteenth centuries. *Journal of the History of the Behavioral Sciences, 7,* 3–15.

Dillon, R. F., & Spanos, N. P. (1983). Proactive interference and the functional ablation hypothesis: More disconfirmatory data. *International Journal of Clinical and Experimental Hypnosis, 31,* 47–56.

Dingwall, E. J. (1968). *Abnormal hypnotic phenomena: A survey of nineteenth century cases* (Vols. 1–4). New York: Barnes & Noble.

DiTomasso, M. J., & Routh, D. K. (1993). Recall of abuse in childhood and three measures of dissociation. *Child Abuse and Neglect, 17,* 477–485.

Docter, R. F. (1988). *Trasvestites and transexuals: Toward a theory of cross-gender behavior.* New York: Plenum Press.

Drinka, G. F. (1984). *The birth of neurosis: Myth, malady and the Victorians.* New York: Simon & Schuster.

Dubreuil, D. L., Spanos, N. P., & Bertrand, L. D. (1983). Does hypnotic amnesia dissipate with time? *Imagination, Cognition and Personality, 2*, 103–113.

Du Maurier, G. (1992). *Trilby*. London: J. M. Dent. (Original work published 1895)

Durant, W., & Durant, A. (1961). *The story of civilization: Part IV. The age of reason begins*. New York: Simon & Schuster.

Early, L. F., & Lifschutz, J. E. (1974). A case of stigmata. *Archives of General Psychiatry, 30*, 197–200.

Edelson, J., & Fitzpatrick, J. L. (1989). A comparison of cognitive-behavioral and hypnotic treatments of chronic pain. *Journal of Consulting and Clinical Psychology, 45*, 316–323.

Edmonston, W. E., Jr. (1967). Hypnotic time distortion: A note. *American Journal of Clinical Hypnosis, 10*, 79–80.

Edmonston, W. E., Jr. (1981). *Hypnosis and relaxation: Modern verification of an old equation*. New York: Wiley.

Edmonston, W. E., Jr. (1991). Anesis. In S. J. Lynn & J. W. Rhue (Eds.), *Theories of hypnosis: Current models and perspectives* (pp. 197–240). New York: Guilford.

Edmonston, W. E., Jr., & Erbeck, J. R. (1967). Hypnotic time distortion: A note. *American Journal of Clinical Hypnosis, 10*, 79–80.

Ellenberger, H. F. (1970). *The discovery of the unconscious: The history and evolution of dynamic psychiatry*. New York: Basic Books.

Elliott, D. M., & Briere, J. (1992). Sexual abuse trauma among professional women: Validating the Trauma Symptom Checklist-40 (TSC-40). *Child Abuse and Neglect, 16*, 391–398.

Emslie, G. J., & Rosenfeld, A. (1983). Incest reported by children and adolescents hospitalized for severe psychiatric problems. *American Journal of Psychiatry, 140*, 708–711.

Epstein, S. (1973). The self concept revisited: Or a theory of a theory. *American Psychologist, 28*, 404–416.

Erickson, M. H. (1938a). A study of clinical and experimental findings on hypnotic deafness: I. Clinical experimentation and findings. *Journal of General Psychology, 19*, 127–150.

Erickson, M. H. (1938b) A study of clinical and experimental findings on hypnotic deafness: II. Experimental findings with a conditioned response technique. *Journal of General Psychology, 19*, 151–167.

Erickson, M. H., & Erickson, E. M. (1941). Concerning the nature and character of post-hypnotic behavior. *Journal of General Psychology, 24*, 95–133.

Esquirol, J. E. I. (1963). Mental maladies. In A. Esterson (Ed.), *Seductive mirage: An exploration of the work of Sigmund Freud*. Chicago: Open Court. (Original work published 1838)

Esterson, A. (1993). *Seductive mirage: An exploration of the work of Sigmund Freud*. Chicago: Open Court.

Evans, F. J., Reich, L. H., & Orne, M. T. (1972). Optokinetic nystagmus, eye movements, and hypnotically induced hallucinations. *Journal of Nervous and Mental Disease, 152*, 419–431.

Evans, H. (1988). The case for scepticism. In J. Spencer & H. Evans (Eds), *Phenomenon: Forty years of flying saucers* (pp. 373–386). New York: Avon.

Evans, M. B., & Paul, G. L. (1970). Effects of hypnotically suggested analgesia on physiological and subjective response to cold stress. *Journal of Consulting amd Clinical Psychology, 35*, 362–371.

Fahy, T. A. (1988). The diagnosis of multiple personality disorder: A critical review. *British Journal of Psychiatry, 153*, 597–606.

Fahy, T. A., Abas, M., & Brown, J. C. (1989). Multiple personality: A symptom of psychiatric disorder. *British Journal of Psychiatry, 154*, 99–101.

Faludi, S. (1991). *Backlash: The undeclared war against American women*. New York: Doubleday.

Farber, I. E., Harlow, H. F., & West, L. J. (1957). Brainwashing, conditioning and the DDD (Debility, Dependency and Dread) syndrome. *Sociometry, 29*, 271–285.

Feinstein, A. (1989). Posttraumatic stress disorder: A descriptive study supporting *DSM-III-R* criteria. *American Journal of Psychiatry, 146*, 665–666.

Fellows, B. (1986). The concept of trance. In P. L. N. Naish (Ed.), *What is hypnosis?* (pp. 37–58). Philadephia: Open University Press.

Femina, D. D., Yeager, C. A., & Lewis, D. O. (1990). Child abuse: Adolescent records vs. adult recall. *Child Abuse and Neglect, 14*, 227–231.

Fink, D. (1991). The comorbidity of multiple personality disorder and *DSM-III-R* Axis II disorders. *Psychiatric Clinics of North America, 14*, 547–566.

Finkelhor, D. (1979). *Sexually victimized children*. New York: Free Press.

Finkelhor, D. (1987). The sexual abuse of children: Current research reviewed. *Psychiatric Annals, 17*, 233–241.

Finkelhor, D., Hotaling, G., Lewis, I. A., & Smith, C. (1990). Sexual abuse in the national survey of adult men and women: Prevalence, characteristics and risk factors. *Child Abuse and Neglect, 14*, 19–28.

Fiore, E. (1989). *Encounters: A psychologist reveals case studies of abductions by extraterrestrials*. New York: Doubleday.

Firth, R. (1967). Ritual and drama in Malay spirit mediumship. *Comparative Studies in Society and History, 9*, 190–207.

Fisher, S. (1954). The role of expectancy in the performance of posthypnotic behavior. *Journal of Abnormal and Social Psychology, 49*, 503–507.

Fisher, S. (1962). Problems of interpretation and controls in hypnotic research. In G. H. Estabrooks (Ed.), *Hypnosis: Current problems* (pp. 109–126). New York: Harper & Row.

Flournoy, T. (1900). *From India to the planet Mars*. New York: Harpers.

Frank, J. D. (1973). *Persuasion and healing*. New York: Schoken.

Fraser, G. A. (1990). Satanic ritual abuse: A cause of multiple personality disorder [Special issue: In the shadow of Satan: The ritual abuse of children]. *Journal of Child and Youth Care*, 55–66.

Fredrickson, R. (1992). *Repressed memories*. New York: Fireside/Parkside.

Freud, S. (1896a). The aetiology of hysteria. In J. Strachey (Ed.), *The standard edition of the complete works of Sigmund Freud* (pp. 191–221). London: Hogarth Press.

Freud, S. (1896b). Further remarks on the neuropsychoses of defence. I. The "specific" aetiology of hysteria. In J. Strachey (Ed.), *The standard edition of the complete works of Sigmund Freud*. London: Hogarth Press.

Freud, S. (1898). Sexuality in the aetiology of the neuroses. In J. Strachey (Ed.), *The standard edition of the complete works of Sigmund Freud* (pp. 263–285). London: Hogarth Press.

Freud, S. (1905). Three essays on the theory of sexuality. In J. Strachey (Ed.), *The standard edition of the complete works of Sigmund Freud* (pp. 130–243). London: Hogarth Press.

Freud, S. (1933). New introductory lectures on psycho-analysis. In J. Strachey (Ed.), *The standard edition of the complete works of Sigmund Freud* (pp. 5–185). London: Hogarth Press.

Friesen, J. G. (1991). *Uncovering the mystery of MPD*. San Bernadino, CA: Here's Life.

Friesen, J. G. (1992). Ego-dystonic or ego-alien: Alternate personality or evil spirit. *Journal of Psychology and Theology, 20*, 197–200.

Frischholz, E. J., Braun B. G., Sachs, R. G., Schwartz, D. R., Lewis, J., Shaeffer, D., Westergaard, C., & Pasquotto, J. (1992). Construct validity of the Dissociative Experiences Scale (DES): I. The relationship between the DES and other self-report measures of dissociation. *Dissociation, 4*, 185–188.

Fromm, E. (1992). An ego-psychological theory of hypnosis. In E. Fromm & M. R. Nash (Eds.), *Contemporary hypnosis research*. New York: Guilford.

Fuller, J. G. (1996). *The interrupted journey*. New York: Dell.

Gach, J. (1980). Culture and complex: On the early history of psychoanalysis in America. In E. R. Wallace IV & L. C. Pressley (Eds.), *Essays in the history of psychiatry* (pp. 135–160). Columbia, SC: Wm. S. Hall Psychiatric Institute.

Galanter, M. (1990). Cults and zealous self-help movements: A psychiatric perspective. *American Journal of Psychiatry, 147*, 543–551.

Ganaway, G. K. (1989). Historical versus narrative truth: Clarifying the role of exogenous trauma in the etiology of MPD and its variants. *Dissociation, 2*, 205–220.

Ganaway, G. K. (1992). Some additional questions: A response to Shaffer & Cozolino, to Gould & Cozolino, and to Friesen. *Journal of Psychology and Theology, 20*, 201–205.

Ganaway, G. K. (1995). Hypnosis, childhood trauma, and dissociative identity disorder: Toward an integrative theory. *International Journal of Clinical and Experimental Hypnosis, 43*, 127–144.

Gardner, F. H., & Diamond, L. K. (1955). Autoerythrocyte sensitization: A form of purpura producing painful bruising following autosensitization to red blood cells in certain women. *Blood: The Journal of Hematology, 10,* 675–690.

Gardner, M. (1957). *Fads and fallacies in the name of science.* New York: Dover.

Garrett, C. (1975). *Respectable folly: Millinerianism and the French Revolution and England.* Baltimore: The John Hopkins University Press.

Garrison, V. (1977). Doctor, espiritista or psychiatrist? Health seeking behavior in a Puerto Rican neighborhood in New York City. *Medical Anthropology, 1,* 65–180.

Gauld, A. (1992). *A history of hypnotism.* Cambridge, England: Cambridge University Press.

Gavigan, M. (1992). False memories of child sexual abuse: A personal account. *Issues in Child Abuse Accusations, 4,* 246–247.

Gay, P. (1988). *Freud: A life for our time.* New York: Norton.

Glanville, J. (1689). *Saducimus triumphatus.* London: J. Collins & Lownds.

Goffman, E. (1959). *The presentation of self in everyday life.* New York: Doubleday.

Goldblatt, M., & Munitz, H. (1976). Behavioral treatment of hysterical leg paralysis. *Behavior Therapy and Experimental Psychiatry, 7,* 259–263.

Goldstein, E. (1992). *Confabulations.* Boca Raton, FL: SIRS Books.

Goldstein, E., & Farmer, K. (1993). *True stories of false memories.* Boca Raton, FL: SIRS Books.

Goodman, F. D. (1972). *Speaking in tongues: A cross-cultural study of glossolalia.* Chicago: University of Chicago Press.

Gorassini, D. R., Sowerby, D., Creighton, A., & Fry, G. (1991). Hypnotic suggestibility enhancement through brief cognitive skill training. *Journal of Personality and Social Psychology, 61,* 289–297.

Gott, P. S., Everett, C. H., & Whipple, K. (1984). Voluntary control of two lateralized conscious states: Validation by electrical and behavioral studies. *Neurophysiologia, 22,* 65–72.

Gould, C., & Cozolino, L. (1992). Ritual abuse, multiplicity and mind control. *Journal of Psychology and Theology, 20,* 194–196.

Graham, K. R. (1970). Optokinetic nystagmus as a criterion of visual imagery. *Journal of Nervous and Mental disorders, 151,* 411–414.

Graham, K. R., Wright, G. W., Toman, W. J., & Mark, C. R. (1975). Relaxation and hypnosis in the treatment of insomnia. *American Journal of Clinical Hypnosis, 18,* 39–42.

Greden, J. F., Genero, N., Price, L., Feinberg, M., & Levine, S. (1986). Facial electromyography in depression. *Archives of General Psychiatry, 43,* 269–274.

Greenleaf, E. (1969). Developmental state regression through hypnosis. *Dissertation Abstracts, 29,* 4365–4366.

Grescoe, P. (1980, October 27). Things that go bump in Victoria. *Maclean's* (Canada), 30–31.

Grimes, S. J. (1845). *Etherology: Or the philosophy of mesmerism and phrenology*. New York: Saxton & Miles.

Grosskurth, P. (1991). *The secret ring: Freud's inner circle and the politics of psychoanalysis*. Reading, MA: Addison-Wesley.

Gruenwald, D. (1971). Hypnotic techniques without hypnosis in the treatment of a dual personality. *Journal of Nervous and Mental Diseases, 153,* 41–46.

Guazzo, F. M. (1970). *Compendium maleficarum*. New York: Barnes & Noble. (Original work published 1608)

Gudjonsson, G. (1992). *The psychology of interrogations, confessions and testimony*. New York: Wiley.

Guillain, G. (1959). *J. M. Charcot 1825–1893: His life—his work*. (P. Bailey, Ed. and Trans.). New York: Hoeber.

Guze, S. B. (1970). The role of follow-up studies: Their contribution to diagnostic classification as applied to hysteria. *Seminars in Psychiatry, 2,* 392–402.

Guze, S. B. (1975). The validity and significance of the clinical diagnosis of hysteria (Briquet's syndrome). *American Journal of Psychiatry, 132,* 138–141.

Gwynn, M. I., Spanos, N. P., Gabora, N. J., & Jarrett, L. E. (1988). Long term and short term follow-up on the Harvard Group Scale of Hypnotic Susceptibility: Form A. *British Journal of Experimental and Clinical Hypnosis, 5,* 117–124.

Gwynn, M. I., & Spanos, N. P., Nancoo, S., & Chow, L. (1993). *Interrogative suggestibility and persuasability: Are they related?* Unpublished manuscript, Carleton University, Ottawa, Ontario, Canada.

Haaken, J. (1993, November). *The recovered memory debate as psychodrama: A psychoanalytic feminist perspective*. Paper presented at the Clark conference on Memories for Trauma, Worcester, MA.

Haaken, J., & Schlaps, A. (1991). Incest resolution therapy and the objectification of sexual abuse. *Psychotherapy, 28,* 39–47.

Hacking, I. (1986). The invention of split personalities. In A. Donagan, A. N. Perovich, Jr., & M. V. Wedin (Eds.), *Human nature and natural knowledge* (pp. 63–85). New York: D. Reidel.

Hacking, I. (1991). Double consciousness in Britain 1815–1875. *Dissociation, 4,* 134–146.

Hacking, I. (1992). Multiple personality and its hosts. *History of the Human Sciences, 5,* 3–31.

Hale, N. G., Jr. (1975). Introduction. In N. G. Hale, Jr. (Ed.), *Morton Prince: Psychotherapy and multiple personality* (pp. 1–18). Cambridge, MA: Harvard University Press.

Hall, G. S. (1918). A medium in the bud. *American Journal of Psychology, 29,* 144–158.

Hall, T. H. (1984). *The medium and the scientist*. Buffalo, NY: Prometheus.

Halleck, S. L. (1990). Dissociative phenomena and the question of responsibility. *International Journal of Clinical and Experimental Hypnosis, 38,* 298–314.

Ham, M. W., & Spanos, N. P. (1974). Suggested auditory and visual hallucinations in task motivated and hypnotic subjects. *American Journal of Clinical Hypnosis, 17,* 94–101.

Hammen, C., Marks, T., deMayo, R., & Mayol, A. (1985). Self-schemas and risk for depression: A prospective study. *Journal of Personality and Social Psychology, 49,* 1147–1159.

Hare, E. H. (1962). Masturbatory insanity: The history of an idea. *Journal of Mental Science, 108,* 1–25.

Harper, E. B. (1963). Spirit possession and social structure. In B. Ratman (Ed.), *Anthropology on the march.* Madras, India: Book Centre.

Harris, M. (1986). Are "past life" regressions evidence of reincarnation? *Free Inquiry, 6,* 18–23.

Harsch, N., & Neisser, U. (1989, November). *Substantial and irreversible errors in flashbulb memories of the Challanger explosion.* Poster presented at the Psychonomic Society annual meeting, Atlanta, GA.

Harsnett, S. (1599). *Discovery of the fraudulent practices of John Darrel.* London: John Wolfe.

Harsnett, S. (1603). *A declaration of egregious popish impostures.* London: I. Roberts.

Hart, B. (1910). The conception of the subconscious. *Journal of Abnormal Psychology, 4,* 351–371.

Hart, B. (1926). The conception of dissociation. *British Journal of Medical Psychology, 6,* 241–263.

Hart, E. (1898). *Hypnotism, mesmerism, and the new witchcraft.* New York: Appleton & Co.

Harter, S., Alexander, P., & Neimeyer, R. A. (1988). Long term effects of incestuous child abuse in college women: Social adjustment, social cognition, and family characteristics. *Journal of Consulting and Clinical Psychology, 56,* 5–8.

Hartshorn, T. C. (1879). In J. P. F. Deleuze (Ed.), *Animal magnetism.* New York: Wells.

Harwood, A. (1977). *Rx: Spiritist as needed: A study of Puerto Rican community mental health resourse.* New York: Wiley.

Hawksworth, H., & Schwarz, T. (1977). *The five of me.* Chicago: Henry Regnery.

Hecker, J. F. C. (1970). *The dancing mania of the Middle Ages.* New York: Franklin. (Original work published 1837)

Heimer, M. (1971). *The cannibal.* New York: Windsor.

Hendrickson K. M., McCarty, T., & Goodwin, J. M. (1990). Animal alters: Case reports. *Dissociation, 4,* 218–221.

Herman, J. L. (1992). *Trauma and recovery.* New York: Basic Books.

Herman, J. (1993). Recognition and treatment of incestuous families. *International Journal of Family Therapy, 5*(2), 81–91.

Herman, J. L., & Schatzow, E. (1987). Recovery and verification of memories of childhood sexual trauma. *Psychoanalytic Psychology, 4,* 1–14.

Hicks, R. D. (1991). *In pursuit of Satan*. Buffalo, NY: Prometheus.

Hilgard, E. R. (1963). Ability to resist suggestions within the hypnotic state: Responsiveness to conflicting communications. *Psychological Reports, 12*, 3–13.

Hilgard, E. R. (1965). *Hypnotic susceptibility*. New York: Harcourt, Brace & World.

Hilgard, E. R. (1977a). *Divided consciousness*. New York: Wiley.

Hilgard, E. R. (1977b). The problem of divided consciousness: A neodissociation interpretation. *Annals of the New York Academy of Sciences, 296*, 48–59.

Hilgard, E. R. (1979). Divided consciousness in hypnosis: The implications of the hidden observer. In E. Fromm & R. E. Shor (Eds.), *Hypnosis: Developments in research and new perspectives* (pp. 45–79). Chicago: Aldine.

Hilgard, E. R. (1986). *Divided consciousness: Multiple controls in human thought and action*. New York: Wiley.

Hilgard, E. R. (1991). A neodissociation interpretation of hypnosis. In S. J. Lynn & J. Rhue (Eds.), *Theories of hypnosis: Current models and perspectives* (pp. 83–104). New York: Guilford Press.

Hilgard, E. R., Hilgard, J. R., MacDonald, H., Morgan, A. H., & Johnson, L. S. (1978). Covert pain in hypnotic analgesia: Its reality as tested by the real-simulator design. *Journal of Abnormal Psychology, 87*, 655–663.

Hilgard, J. R. (1970). *Personality and hypnosis: A study of imaginative involvement*. Chicago: University of Chicago Press.

Hillman, R. G. (1981). The psychology of being held hostage. *American Journal of Psychiatry, 138*, 1193–1197.

Hine, V. H. (1969). Pentecostal glossolalia: Toward a functional reinterpretation. *Journal for the Scientific Study of Religion, 8*, 212–226.

Hine, V. H. (1970). Bridge burners: Commitment and participation in a religious movement. *Sociological Analysis, 31*, 61–66.

Hirt, E. R. (1990). Do I see only what I expect? Evidence for an expectancy guided retrieval model. *Journal of Personality and Social Psychology, 58*, 937–951.

Hoelscher, T. L., & Lichstein, K. L. (1984). Objective versus subjective assessment of relaxation compliance among anxious individuals. *Behavior Research and Therapy, 22*, 187–193.

Hoelscher, T. L., Rosenthal, T. L., & Lichstein, K. L. (1986). Home relaxation practice in hypertension treatment: Objective assessment and compliance induction. *Journal of Consulting and Clinical Psychology, 54*, 217–221.

Hole, C. (1947). *Witchcraft in England*. New York: Scribner's.

Holmes, D. A. (1974). Investigations of repression. Differential recall of material experimentally or naturally associated with ego threat. *Psychological Bulletin, 81*, 632–653.

Holmes, D. A. (1990). The evidence for repression: An examination of sixty years of research. In J. Singer (Ed.), *Repression and dissociation: Implications for personality theory, psychopathology and health* (pp. 85–102). Chicago: University of Chicago Press.

Hopkins, B. (1981). *Missing time*. New York: Putnam.

Hopkins, B. (1987). *Intruders: The incredible visitations at Copley Woods*. New York: Random House.

Horevitz, R. P., & Braun, B. G. (1984). Are multiple personalities borderlines? An analysis of 33 cases. *Psychiatric Clinics of North America, 7*, 69–87.

Horowitz, M. J. (1970). *Image formation and cognition*. New York: Appleton-Century-Crofts.

Hovland, C. I., Janis, I. L., & Kelley, H. H. (1953). *Communication and persuasion: Psychological studies of opinion change*. New Haven, CT: Yale University Press.

Howe, M. L., & Courage, M. L. (1993). On resolving the enigma of infantile amnesia. *Psychological Bulletin, 113*, 305–326.

Hudson, J., & Nelson, K. (1986). Repeated encounters of a similar kind: Effects of familiarity on children's autobiographical memory. *Cognitive Development, 1*, 253–271.

Hufford, D. (1982). *The terror that comes in the night*. Philadelphia: University of Pennsylvania Press.

Huizinga, J. (1954). *The waning of the middle ages*. New York: Anchor.

Hull, C. L. (1933). *Hypnosis and suggestibility: An experimental approach*. New York: Appleton-Century-Crofts.

Hunter, E. (1951). *Brainwashing in Red China*. New York: Vanguard.

Hunter, E. (1960). *Brainwashing: From Pavlov to powers*. New York: The Bookmaster.

Hutchinson, F. (1720). *A historical essay concerning witchcraft*. London: R. Knaplock.

Huxley, A. (1952). *The devils of Loudon*. New York: Harper & Row.

Hyland, M. E. (1990). The mood-peak flow relationship in adult asthmatics: A pilot study of individual differences and direction of causality. *British Journal of Medical Psychology, 63*, 399–384.

Hyman, G. J., Stanley, R. O., Burrows, G. D., & Horne, D. J. (1986). Treatment effectiveness of hypnosis and behavior therapy in smoking cessation: A methodological refinement. *Addictive Behavior, 11*, 335–365.

Hynes, S. (1968). *The Edwardian turn of mind*. Princeton, NJ: Princeton University Press.

Hyslop, J. H. (1917). The Doris case of multiple personality. *Proceedings of the American Society for Psychical Research, 11*, 5–866.

Hyslop, J. H. (1918). *Life after death: Problems of the future life and its nature*. New York: Dutton.

Iverson, J. (1977). *More lives than one?* London: Pan Books.

Jacobs, D. M. (1992). *Secret life: Firsthand accounts of UFO abductions*. New York: Simon & Schuster.

Jacobs, D. M., & Hopkins, B. (1992). *Suggested techniques for hypnosis and therapy of abductees*. Unpublished manuscript, Temple University, Philadelphia.

James, W. (1890). *The principles of psychology* (Vols. 1-2). New York: Holt.

James, W. (1909). *Essays in psychical research*. Cambridge, MA: Harvard University Press.

Janet, P. (1886). Les actes inconscients et le dedoublements de la personnalité pendant le somnambulisme provoquée [Unconscious acts and the splitting of personality during induced somnambulism]. *Revue Philosophique, 22,* 576–592.

Janet, P. (1889). *L'automatisme psychologique*. Paris: Centre National de la Recherche Scientifique.

Janet, P. (1907). *The major symptoms of hysteria: Fifteen lectures given in the medical school of Harvard University*. New York: Macmillan.

Janet, P. (1920). *Major symptoms of hysteria*. New York: Macmillan.

Janet, P. (1925). *Psychological healing* (Vols. 1-2). New York: Macmillan.

Jenkins, P., & Maier-Katkin, D. (1991). Occult survivors: The making of a myth. In J. T. Richardson, J. Best, & D. G. Bromley (Eds.), *The satanism scare* (pp. 127–144). New York: Aldine de Gruyter.

Jilek, W. G. (1989). Theraputic use of altered states of consciousness in contemporary North American Indian dance ceremonials. In C. A. Ward (Ed.), *Altered states of consciousness and mental health: A cross cultural perspective* (pp. 167–185). Newbury Park, CA: Sage.

Johnson, R. F. Q. (1989). Hypnosis, suggestion and dermatological changes: A consideration of the production and diminution of dermatological entities. In N. P. Spanos & J. F. Chaves (Eds.), *Hypnosis: The cognitive–behavioral perspective* (pp. 297–312). Buffalo, NY: Prometheus.

Johnson, R. F. Q., & Barber, T. X. (1976). Hypnotic suggestions for blister formation: Subjective and physiological effects. *American Journal of Clinical Hypnosis, 18,* 172–181.

Jones, B., & Spanos, N. P. (1982). Suggestions for altered auditory sensitivity, the negative subject effect and hypnotic susceptibility. *Journal of Personality and Social Psychology, 43,* 637–647.

Jones, W. J., & Flynn, D. M. (1989). Methodological and theoretical considerations in the study of "hypnotic" effects in perception. In N. P. Spanos & J. F. Chaves (Eds.), *Hypnosis: The cognitive–behavioral perspective* (pp. 149–174). Buffalo, NY: Prometheus

Kagan, D., & Summers, I. (1983). *Mute evidence*. New York: Bantam.

Kampman, R. (1976). Hypnotically induced multiple personality: An experimental study. *International Journal of Clinical and Experimental Hypnosis, 24,* 215–227.

Kampman, R., & Hirvenoja, R. (1978). Dynamic relation of the secondary personality induced by hypnosis to the present personality. In F. H. Frankel & H. S. Zamansky (Eds.), *Hypnosis at its bicentennial* (pp. 183–188). New York: Plenum Press.

Kardec, A. (1886). *The spirits' book*. Boston: Colby & Rich.

Kass, D. J., Silvers, F. M., & Abroms, G. M. (1972). Behavioral groups treatment of hysteria. *Archives of General Psychiatry, 26,* 42–50.

Kelly, H. A. (1974). *The devil demonology and witchcraft*. New York: Doubleday.

Kendall-Tackett, K. A., Williams, L. M., & Finkelhor, D. (1993). Impact of sexual abuse on children: A review and synthesis of recent empirical findings. *Psychological Bulletin, 113*, 164–180.

Kenny, M. G. (1981). Multiple personality and spirit possession. *Psychiatry, 44*, 337–357.

Kenny, M. G. (1986). *The passion of Ansel Bourne: Multiple personality and American culture*. Washington, DC: Smithsonian Institution Press.

Kern, T. (1994). Satanic ritual abuse: How real? *Issues in Child Abuse Accusations, 6*, 32–38.

Kerner, J. (1834). *Geschichten Besessener neurer Zeit* [Histories of possessed persons in recent times]. Karlsruhe, Germany: G. Braun.

Kerr, H. (1972). *Mediums, spirit rappers, and roaring radicals: Spiritualism in American literature, 1850–1900*. Urbana: University of Illinois Press.

Keyes, D. (1981). *The minds of Billy Milligan*. New York: Bantam.

Keyhoe, D. E. (1950). *The flying saucers are real*. New York: Fawcett.

King, B. T., & Janis, I. L. (1956). Comparison of the effectiveness of improvised versus non-improvised role-playing in producing opinion change. *Human Relations, 9*, 177–186.

Kirsch, I. (1992). The state of the altered state debate. *Contemporary Hypnosis, 9*, 1–6.

Kirsch, I., & Council, J. R. (1989). Response expectancy as a determinant of hypnotic behavior. In N. P. Spanos & J. F. Chaves (Eds.), *Hypnosis: The cognitive–behavioral perspective* (pp. 360–379). Buffalo, NY: Prometheus.

Kirshner, L. A. (1973). Dissociative reactions: An historical review and clinical study. *Acta Psychiatrica Scandanavia, 49*, 698–711.

Klass, P. J. (1974). *UFO's explained*. New York: Random House.

Klass, P. J. (1989). *UFO abductions: A dangerous game*. Buffalo, NY: Prometheus.

Kleeman, S. T. (1967). Psychiatric contributions in the treatment of asthma. *Annals of Allergy, 25*, 611–619.

Kline, M. V. (1951). Hypnosis and age progression: A case report. *Journal of Genetic Psychology, 78*, 195–206.

Kline, M. V., Guze, H., & Haggerty, A. D. (1954). An experimental study of the nature of hypnotic deafness: Effects of delayed speech feed-back. *Journal of Clinical and Experimental Hypnosis, 2*, 145–156.

Kluft, R. P. (1982). Varieties of hypnotic interventions in the treatment of multiple personality. *American Journal of Clinical Hypnosis, 24*, 230–240.

Kluft, R. P. (1984). Treatment of multiple personality disorder: A study of 33 cases. *Psychiatric Clinics of North America, 7*, 9–29.

Kluft, R. P. (1985a). Making the diagnosis of multiple personality disorder (MPD). *Directions in Psychiatry, 5*, 1–12.

Kluft, R. P. (1985b). The natural history of multiple personality disorder. In R. P. Kluft (Ed.), *Childhood antecedents of multiple personality* (pp. 197–238). Washington, DC: American Psychiatric Press.

Kluft, R. P. (1989). Iatrogenic creation of new alter personalities. *Dissociation, 2,* 83–91.

Kluft, R. P. (1992). Discussion: A specialist's perspective in multiple personality disorder. *Psychoanalytic Inquiry, 12,* 139–171.

Knox, R. A. (1950). *Enthusiasm.* New York: Oxford University Press.

Knox, V. J., Crutchfield, L., & Hilgard, E. R. (1975). The nature of task interference in hypnotic dissociation: An investigation of hypnotic behavior. *International Journal of Clinical and Experimental Hypnosis, 23,* 305–323.

Kohlenberg, R. J. (1973). Behavioristic approach to multiple personality: A case study. *Behavior Therapy, 4,* 137–140.

Korotkin, I., Pleshkova, T. V., & Suslova, M. M. (1969). Changes in auditory thresholds as a result of hypnotic suggestion. *Soviet Neurology and Psychiatry, 1,* 33–40.

Koss-Chioino, J. (1992). *Women as healers, women as patients.* Boulder, CO: Westview Press.

Kramer, E., & Tucker, G. R. (1967). Hypnotically suggested deafness and delayed auditory feedback. *International Journal of Clinical and Experimental Hypnosis, 15,* 37–43.

Krippner, S. (1986). Cross-cultural approaches to multiple personality disorder: Theraputic practices in Brazilian spiritism. *The Humanistic Psychologist, 14,* 177–193.

Krippner, S. (1989). A call to heal: Entry patterns in Brazilian mediumship. In C. W. Ward (Ed.), *Altered states of consciousness and mental health: Theoretical and methodological issues* (pp. 186–206). Newbury Park, CA: Sage.

Kristiansen, C. (1994). Bearing witness to the patriarchal revictimization of survivors. *SWAP Newsletter, 20,* 7–16.

Kutchinsky, B. (1992). The sexual abuse panic. *Nordisk Sexoligi, 10,* 30–42.

La Fontaine, J. (1990). *Child sexual abuse.* Cambridge, MA: Polity Press.

Laibow, R. E. (1990). *Experienced anomalous trauma: New directions.* Paper presented at the Mutual UFO Network Symposium.

Lambek, M. (1980). Spirits and spouses: Possession as a system of communication among the Malagasy speakers of Mayotte. *American Ethnologist, 7,* 318–331.

Lambek, M. (1988). Spirit possession/spirit succession: Aspects of social continuity among Malagasy speakers in Mayotte. *American Ethnologist, 15,* 710–731.

Lambek, M. (1989). From disease to discourse: Remarks on the conceptualization of trance and spirit possession. In C. A. Ward (Ed.), *Altered states of consciousness and mental health: Theoretical and methodological issues* (pp. 36–62). Newbury Park, CA: Sage.

Lang, P. J. (1969). The mechanisms of desensitization and the laboratory study of human fear. In C. M. Franks (Ed.), *Behavior therapy: Appraisal and status* (pp. 160–191). New York: McGraw-Hill.

Lanning, K. V. (1989). Satanic, occult and ritualistic crime: A law enforcement perspective. *Police Chief, 56*, 62–85.

Lanning, K. V. (1992). A law-enforcement perspective on allegations of ritual abuse. In D. K. Sakheim & S. E. Devine (Eds.), *Out of darkness: Exploring satanism and ritual abuse* (pp. 109–146). New York: Lexington.

Larmore, K., Ludwig, A. M., & Cain, R. L. (1977). Multiple personality: An objective case study. *British Journal of Psychiatry, 131*, 35–40.

Larner, C. (1981). *Enemies of God: The witch-hunt in Scotland.* Baltimore: The John Hopkins University Press.

Lasch, C. (1985). *The minimal self.* New York: Norton.

Laurence, J.-R., & Perry, C. P. (1988). *Hypnosis, will and memory.* New York: Guilford.

Law, T. G. (1894). Devil-hunting in Elizabethan England. *Nineteenth Century, 35*, 397–411.

Lawson, A. H. (1984). Perinatal imagery in UFO abduction reports. *The Journal of Psychohistory, 12*, 211–239.

Leacock, S., & Leacock, R. (1972). *Spirits of the deep: A study of an Afro-Brazilian cult.* New York: Doubleday Natural History Press.

Lee, R. L. M. (1989). Self-presentation in Malaysian spirit seances: A dramaturgical perspective on altered states of consciousness in healing ceremonies. In C. W. Ward (Ed.), *Altered states of consciousness and mental health: Theoretical and methodological perspectives* (pp. 251–266). Newbury Park, CA: Sage.

Leibowitz, H. W., Lundy, R. M., & Guez, J. R. (1980). The effect of testing distance on suggestion-induced visual field narrowing. *International Journal of Clinical and Experimental Hypnosis, 28*, 409–420.

Leonard, J. R. (1963). *An investigation of hypnotic age-regression.* Unpublished doctoral dissertation, University of Kentucky, Lexington.

Leventhal, H. (1976). *In the shadow of the enlightenment: Occultism and renaissance science in 18th century America.* New York: New York University Press.

Levitt, E. E., Aronoff, G., Morgan, C. D., Overley, T. M., & Parrish, M. J. (1975). Testing the coercive power of hypnosis: Committing objectionable acts. *International Journal of Clinical and Experimental Hypnosis, 23*, 59–67.

Levy, L. H. (1967). Awareness learning and the benificient subject as expert witness. *Journal of Personality and Social Psychology, 6*, 365–370.

Lewinsohn, P. M., & Rosenbaum, M. (1987). Recall of parental behavior by acute depressives, remitted depressives, and nondepressives. *Journal of Personality and Social Psychology, 52*, 611–619.

Lewis, I. M. (1987). *Ecstatic religion.* New York: Routledge.

Lewis, T. (1927). *The blood vessels of the human skin and their response*. London: Shaw.

Lifton, R. (1961). *Chinese thought reform and the psychology of totalism*. New York: Norton.

Lindsay, D. S. (1990). Misleading suggestions can impair eyewitnesses' ability to remember event details. *Journal of Experimental Psychology: Learning, Memory and Cognition, 16*, 1077–1083.

Lindsay, D. S., & Read, J. D. (1994). Psychotherapy and memories of childhood sexual abuse. *Applied Cognitive Psychology, 8*, 281–338.

Linton, M. (1982). Transformations of memory in everyday life. In U. Neisser (Ed.), *Memory observed* (pp. 77–91). San Francisco: Freeman.

Littig, L. W. (1994). Space alien hype, "science" and the end of the millennium. *Cosmos, 4*, 29–33.

Loftus, E. R. (1979). *Eyewitness testimony*. Cambridge, MA: Harvard University Press.

Loftus, E. R. (1993a). Desperately seeking memories of the first few years of childhood: The reality of early memories. *Journal of Experimental Psychology: General, 122*, 274–277.

Loftus, E. R. (1993b). The reality of repressed memories. *American Psychologist, 48*, 518–537.

Loftus, E. F., & Coan, J. (in press). The construction of childhood memories. In D. Peters (Ed.), *The child witness in context: Cognitive, social and legal perspectives*. New York: Kluwer.

Loftus, E. F., & Loftus, G. R. (1980). On the permanence of stored information in the human brain. *American Psychologist, 35*, 409–420.

Loftus, E. F., Polonsky. S., & Fullilove, M. T. (1994). Memories of childhood sexual abuse: Remembering and repressing. *Psychology of Women Quarterly, 18*, 67–84.

London, P. (1961). Subject characteristics in hypnosis research: Part I. A survey of experience, interest, and opinion. *International Journal of Clinical and Experimental Hypnosis, 9*, 151–161.

Lucas, W. B. (1987). Spontanious remissions. *The Journal of Regression Therapy, 2*, 109–114.

Ludwig, A. M., Brandsma, J., Wilbur, C., Bendfeldt, F., & Jameson, D. M. (1972). The objective study of multiple personality: Or, are four heads better than one? *Archives of General Psychiatry, 25*, 298–310.

Lukianowicz, N. (1972). Incest. *British Journal of Psychiatry, 120*, 301–313.

Lund, D., & Wilson, T. (1977). Brainwashing as a defense to criminal liability. *Criminal Law Bulletin, 13*, 341–382.

Lynn, S. J., & Nash, M. R. (1994). Truth in memory: Ramifications for psychotherapy and hypnotherapy. *American Journal of Clinical Hypnosis, 36*, 194–208.

Lynn, S. J., Nash, M. R., Rhue, J. W., Frauman, D. C., & Sweeney, C. A. (1984). Nonvolition, expectancies and hypnotic rapport. *Journal of Abnormal Psychology, 93*, 295–303.

Lynn, S. J., & Rhue, J. W. (1991). An integrative model of hypnosis. In S. J. Lynn & J. W. Rhue (Eds.), *Theories of hypnosis: Current models, and perspectives* (pp. 397–438). New York: Guilford.

Lynn, S. J., Rhue, J. W., & Green, J. P. (1988). Multiple personality and fantasy proneness: Is there an association or dissociation? *British Journal of Experimental and Clinical Hypnosis, 5*, 138–142.

Lynn, S. J., Rhue, J. W., & Weekes, J. R. (1989). Hypnosis and experienced nonvolition: A social-cognitive integrative model. In N. P. Spanos & J. F. Chaves (Eds.), *Hypnosis: The cognitive-behavioral perspective* (pp. 78–109). Buffalo, NY: Prometheus.

Lyons, A. (1988). *Satan wants you: The cult of devil worship in America*. New York: The Mysterious Press.

MacCracken, P. J., Gogel, W. C., & Blum, G. S. (1980). Effects of posthypnotic suggestion of perceived egocentric distance. *Perception, 9*, 561–568.

Mack, J. (1994). *Abduction: Human encounters with aliens*. New York: Scribner's.

Macmillan, M. (1991). *Freud evaluated: The completed arc*. New York: Elsevier.

Malony, H. N., & Lovekin, A. A. (1985). *Glossolalia: Behavioral science perspectives on speaking in tongues*. New York: Oxford University Press.

Maltz, W. (1990, December). Adult survivors of incest: How to help them overcome the trauma. *Medical Aspects of Human Sexuality*, 42–47.

Mancuso, J. C., & Sarbin, T. R. (1983). The self narrative in the enactment of roles. In T. R. Sarbin & K. E. Schiebe (Eds.), *Studies in social identity* (pp. 233–253). New York: Praeger.

Mandler, J. M. (1984). *Stories, scripts, and scenes: Aspects of schema theory*. Hillsdale, NJ: Erlbaum.

Mandrou, R. (1968). *Magistrats et sorciers en France au XVII siècle: Une analyse de psychologie historique* [Magistrates and sorcerers in 17th-century France: A historical psychological analysis]. Paris: Plon.

Marcus, G. B. (1986). Stability and change in political attitudes: Observe, recall and "explain." *Political Behavior, 8*, 21–44.

Marks, J. (1979). *The search for the "Manchurian candidate": The CIA and mind control*. New York: Dell.

Marx, O. M. (1970). Morton Prince and the dissociation of a personality. *Journal of the History of the Behavioral Sciences, 6*, 120–130.

Masson, J. M. (1984). *The assault on truth: Freud's suppression of the seduction theory*. New York: Farrar, Straus & Giroux.

Masson, J. M. (1985). *The complete letters of Sigmund Freud to Wilhelm Fliess 1887–1904*. Cambridge, MA: Harvard University Press.

Mather, C. (1914). A brand pluck't out of the burning. In G. L. Burr (Ed.), *Narratives of the witchcraft cases, 1648–1706*. New York: Scribner's. (Original work published 1693)

Mayer, R. S. (1991). *Satan's children*. New York: Avon.

McCasland, S. V. (1951). *By the finger of God*. New York: Macmillan.

McConkey, K. M. (1986). Opinions about hypnosis and self-hypnosis before and after hypnosis testing. *International Journal of Clinical and Experimental Hypnosis, 34*, 311–319.

McConkey, K. M. (1992). The effects of hypnotic procedures on remembering: The experimental findings and their implications for forensic hypnosis. In E. Fromm & M. R. Nash (Eds.), *Contemporary hypnosis research* (pp. 405–426). New York: Guilford.

McConkey, K. M., Labelle, L., Bibb, B. C., & Bryant, R. A. (1990). Hypnosis and suggested pseudomemory: The relevance of test context. *Australian Journal of Psychology, 42*, 197–206.

McCurdy, H. A. (1941). A note on the dissociation of a personality. *Character and Personality, 10*, 33–41.

McDougall, W. (1907). The case of Sally Beauchamp. *Proceedings of the English Society for Psychical Research, 19*, 410–431.

McDougall, W. (1920). Presidential address. *Proceedings of the English Society for Psychical Research, 31*, 105–123.

McFarlane, A. C. (1988). The phenomenology of posttraumatic stress disorders following a natural disaster. *Journal of Nervous and Mental Disease, 176*, 22–29.

Merskey, H. (1992). The manufacture of personalities: The production of multiple personality disorder. *British Journal of Psychiatry, 160*, 327–340.

Merskey, H., & Buhrich, N. A. (1975). Hysteria and organic brain disease. *British Journal of Medical Psychology, 48*, 359–366.

Mesel, E., & Ledford, F. F., Jr. (1959). The electroencephalogram during hypnotic age regression (to infancy) in epileptic patients. *Archives of Neurology, 1*, 516–521.

Mesmer, F. A. (1948). *Dissertation on the discovery of animal magnetism* (V. R. Myers, Trans.). London: Macdonald. (Original work published 1779)

Michaelis, S. (1613). *The admirable history of the possession and conversion of a penitent woman*. London: William Aspley.

Midelfort, H. C. E. (1972). *Witch hunting in Southwestern Germany 1562–1684*. Stanford, CA: Stanford University Press.

Milgram, S. (1974). *Obedience to authority: an experimental view*. New York: Harper & Row.

Miller, A. G. (1986). *The obedience experiments*. New York: Praeger.

Miller, R. J., Hennessy, R. T., & Leibowitz, H. W. (1973). The effects of hypnotic ablation of the background on the magnitude of the Ponzo perspective illusion. *International Journal of Clinical and Experimental Hypnosis, 21*, 180–191.

Miller, R. J., & Leibowitz, H. W. (1976). A signal detection analysis of hypnotically induced narrowing of the visual field. *Journal of Abnormal Psychology, 85,* 446–454.

Miller, S. D. (1989). Optical differences in cases of multiple personality disorder. *Journal of Nervous and Mental Disease, 177,* 480–486.

Miller, S. D., Blackburn, T., Scholes, G., White, G., & Mamalis, N. (1991). Optical differences in cases of multiple personality disorder: A second look. *Journal of Nervous and Mental Disease, 179,* 132–135.

Miller, S. D., & Triggiano, P. J. (1992). The psychophysiological investigation of multiple personality disorder: Review and update. *American Journal of Clinical Hypnosis, 35,* 47–61.

Modestin, J. (1992). Multiple personality disorder in Switzerland. *American Journal of Psychiatry, 149,* 88–92.

Moore, M. S. (1984). *Law and psychiatry: Rethinking the relationship.* Cambridge, England: Cambridge University Press.

Moore, R. L. (1977). *In search of white crows.* New York: Oxford University Press.

Morgan, A. H., Johnson, D. L., & Hilgard, E. R. (1974). The stability of hypnotic susceptibility: A longitudinal study. *International Journal of Clinical and Experimental Hypnosis, 22,* 249–257.

Morris, D. (1992). *The masks of Lucifer.* London: B. T. Batsford.

Morton, A. (1977). Dawit: Competition and integration in an Ethiopian Wuqabi cult group. In V. Crapanzano & V. Garrison (Eds.), *Case studies in spirit possession* (pp. 193–234). New York: Wiley.

Moss, P., & Keeton, J. (1979). *Encounters with the past: How man can experience and relive history.* London: Sidgwick & Jackson.

The most strange and admirable discovery of the witches of Warboys. (1972). In B. Rosen (Ed.), *Witchcraft* (pp. 239–297). New York: Taplinger. (Original work published 1593)

Mulhern, S. (1991a). Letter to the editor. *Child Abuse and Neglect, 15,* 609–611.

Mulhern, S. (1991b) Satanism and psychotherapy: A rumor in search of an inquisition. In J. T. Richardson, J. Best, & D. G. Bromley (Eds.), *The satanism scare* (pp.145–172). New York: Aldine.

Mulhern, S. (1992). Ritual abuse: Defining a syndrome versus defending a belief. *Journal of Psychology and Theology, 20,* 230–232.

Mulhern, S. (1994). *Le trouble de la personnalité multiple à la recherche du trauma perdu* [The trouble of multiple personality in the research of lost trauma]. In M. Gabel, S. Lebovici, & P. Mazet (Eds.), *Inceste.* Paris: Presses Universitaires de France.

Mulhern, S. (1995). Les aléas de la thérapie des réminiscences: Le trouble de la personalité. In Gabel, M., Lebovic, S., & Mazet, P. (Eds.), *Le traumatisme de l'inceste.* Paris: Presses Universitaires de France.

Mulholland, T., & Peper, E. (1971). Occipital alpha and accommodative vergence, pursuit tracking, and fast eye movements. *Psychophysiology, 8,* 556–575.

Munthe, A. (1929). *The story of San Michele*. London: John Murray.

Murphy, G. E. (1982). The clinical management of hysteria. *Journal of the American Medical Association, 247*, 2559–2564.

Murray, H. A. (1956). *Journal of Abnormal and Social Psychology, 52*, 291–295.

Myers, F. W. H. (1975). *Human personality and its survival of bodily death* (Vols. 1–2). New York: Longmans. (Original work published 1903)

Myers, S. A., & Austrin, H. R. (1985). Distal eidetic technology: Further characteristics of the fantasy-prone personality. *Journal of Mental Imagery, 9*, 57–66.

Nadon, R., Hoyt, I. P., Register, P. A., & Kihlstrom, J. F. (1991). Absorption and hypnotizability: Context effects re-examined. *Journal of Personality and Social Psychology, 60*, 144–153.

Nash, C. L., & West, C. D. (1985). Victimization of young girls. In D. West (Ed.), *Sexual victimization*. Hampshire, England: Gower.

Nash, M. R. (1987). What, if anything, is regressed about hypnotic age regression? A review of the empirical literature. *Psychological Bulletin, 102*, 42–52.

Nash, M. R., Hulsey, T. L., Sexton, M. C., Harralson, T. L., & Lambert, W. (1993a). Long-term sequelae of childhood sexual abuse: Perceived family environment, psychopathology, and dissociation. *Journal of Consulting and Clinical Psychology, 61*, 276–283.

Nash, M. R., Hulsey, T. L., Sexton, M. C., Harralson, T. L., & Lambert, W. (1993b). Reply to comment by Briere and Elliot. *Journal of Consulting and Clinical Psychology, 61*, 289–290.

Nash, M. R., & Lynn, S. J. (1986). Child abuse and hypnotic ability. *Imagination, Cognition and Personality, 5*, 211–218.

Nash, M. R., Lynn, S. J., & Givens, D. L. (1984). Adult hypnotic susceptibility, childhood punishment, and child abuse: A brief communication. *International Journal of Clinical and Experimental Hypnosis, 32*, 6–11.

Nathan, D. (1991). Satanism and child molestation: Constructing the ritual abuse scare. In J. Richardson, J. Best, & D. G. Bromley (Eds.), *The satanism scare* (pp. 75–94). New York: Aldine de Gruyter.

Neanon, G. M., & Hair, J. (1990). Imaginative involvement, neuroticism and charasmatic behavior. *British Journal of Experimental and Clinical Hypnosis, 7*, 190–192.

Neisser, U. (1967). *Cognitive psychology*. New York: Appleton-Century-Crofts.

Neisser, U. (1976). *Cognition and reality*. San Franscisco: Freeman.

Neisser, U., & Harsch, N. (1992). Phantom flashbulbs: False recollections of hearing the news about challenger. In E. Winograd & U. Neisser (Eds.), *Affect and accuracy in recall: Studies of "flashbulb" memories* (pp. 9–31). New York: Cambridge University Press.

Nelson, K. (1993). The psychological and social origins of autobiographical memory. *Psychological Science, 4*, 7–14.

Nelson, P. L. (1989). Personality factors in the frequency of reported spontaneous preternatural experiences. *Journal of Transpersonal Psychology, 21,* 193–209.

Newman, J. B. (1847). *Fascination.* New York: Fowler.

Nickell, J. (1993). *Looking for a miracle.* Buffalo, NY: Prometheus.

Nissen, M. J., Ross, J. L., Willingham, D. B., Mackenzie, T. B., & Shacter, D. L. (1988). Memory and awareness in a patient with multiple personality disorder. *Brain and Cognition, 8,* 117–134.

Nolan, R., Spanos, N. P., Hayward, A., & Scott, H. (1994). *Hypnotic and nonhypnotic imagery based strategies in the treatment of tension and mixed tension/migrane headache.* Unpublished manuscript, Carleton University, Ottawa, Ontario, Canada.

Norris, D. L. (1973). Barber's task-motivational theory and posthypnotic amnesia. *American Journal of Clinical Hypnosis, 15,* 181–186.

North, C. S., Ryall, J. M., Ricci, D. A., & Wetzel, R. D. (1993). *Multiple personalities and multiple disorders: Psychiatric classification and media influence.* New York: Oxford University Press.

Norton, G. R., Ross, C. A., & Novotny, M. E. (1990). Factors that predict scores on the Dissociative Experiences Scale. *Journal of Clinical Psychology, 46,* 273-277.

Notestein, W. (1911). *A history of witchcraft in England.* New York: Crowell.

O'Brien, D. (1985). *Two of a kind: The hillside stranglers.* New York: American Library.

Obstoj, I., & Sheehan, P. W. (1977). Aptitude for trance, task generalizability, and incongruity response in hypnosis. *Journal of Abnormal Psychology, 86,* 543–552.

O'Connell, D. N., Shor, R. E., & Orne, M. T. (1970). Hypnotic age regression: An empirical and methodological analysis. *Journal of Abnormal Psychology, 76*(3, Pt. 2).

Oesterreich T. K. (1966). *Possession: Demoniacal and other.* Secaucus, NJ: Citadel Press.

O'Faolain, J., & Martines, L. (Eds.). (1973). *Not in God's image.* New York: Harper & Row.

Ofshe, R. J. (1992a). Coercive persuasion and attitude change. In E. F. Borgatta & M. L. Borgatta (Eds.), *Encyclopedia of sociology* (Vol. 1, pp. 212–224). New York: Macmillan.

Ofshe, R. J. (1992b). Inadvertent hypnosis during interrogation: False confession due to dissociative state; mis-identified multiple personality and the satanic cult hypothesis. *International Journal of Clinical and Experimental Hypnosis, 40,* 125–156.

Olio, K. A. (1989). Memory retrieval in the treatment of adult survivors of sexual abuse. *Transactional Analysis Journal, 19,* 93–100.

Olio, K. A. (1994). Truth in memory. *American Psychologist, 49,* 442–443.

Ong, A. (1988). The production of possession: Spirits and the multinational corporation in Malaysia. *American Ethnologist, 15,* 28–42.

Orne, M. T. (1959). The nature of hypnosis: Artifact and essence. *Journal of Abnormal and Social Psychology, 58,* 277–299.

Orne, M. T. (1979a). On the simulating subject as a quasi-control group in hypnosis research: What, why and how. In E. Fromm & R. E. Shor (Eds.), *Hypnosis: Developments in research and new perspectives* (pp. 519–566). New York: Aldine.

Orne, M. T. (1979b). The use and misuse of hypnosis in court. *International Journal of Clinical and Experimental Hypnosis, 27,* 311–341.

Orne, M. T., & Evans, F. J. (1965). Social control in the psychological experiment: Antisocial behavior and hypnosis. *Journal of Personality and Social Psychology, 1,* 189–200.

Orne, M. T., Sheehan, P. W., & Evans, F. J. (1968). Occurrence of posthypnotic behavior outside the experimental setting. *Journal of Personality and Social Psychology, 9,* 189–196.

Owen, A. R. G. (1971). *Hysteria, hypnosis and healing: The work of J. M. Charcot.* London: Dobson.

Parfitt, D. N., & Gall C. M. C. (1944). Psychogenic amnesia: The refusal to remember. *Journal of Mental Science, 90,* 511–531.

Parrinder, E. G. (1963). *Witchcraft: European and African.* London: Farber.

Passantino, G., Passantino, B., & Trott, J. (1990). Satan's sideshow. *Cornerstone, 18,* 23–28.

Pattie, F. A. (1935). A report of attempts to produce uniocular blindness by hypnotic suggestion. *British Journal of Medical Psychology, 15,* 230–241.

Pattie, F. A. (1950). The genuineness of unilateral deafness produced by hypnosis. *American Journal of Psychology, 63,* 84–86.

Pattie, F. A. (1956). Methods of induction, susceptibility of subjects, and criteria of hypnosis. In R. M. Dorcus (Ed.), *Hypnosis and its therapeutic applications* (pp. 2/1–2/24). New York: McGraw-Hill.

Penfield, W., & Perot, P. (1963). The brain's record of auditory and visual experience: A final summary and discussion. *Brain, 86,* 595–696.

Penfield, W., & Roberts, L. (1959). *Speech and brain mechanisms.* Princeton, NJ: Princeton University Press.

Pennebaker, J. W. (1980). Self-perception of emotion and internal sensation. In D. M. Wegner & R. R. Vallacher (Eds.), *The self in social psychology* (pp. 80–101). New York: Oxford University Press.

Perlini, A. H., & Spanos, N. P. (1991). EEG alpha methodologies and hypnotizability: A critical review. *Psychophysiology, 28,* 511–530.

Perlini, A. H., Spanos, N. P., & Jones, B. (in press). Hypnotic negative hallucinations: A review of subjective, behavioral, and physiological methods. In R. G. Kunzendorf, N. P. Spanos, & B. Wallace (Eds.), *Hypnosis and imagination.* Amityville, NY: Baywood.

Perly, M. J., & Guze, S. B. (1962). Hysteria: The stability and usefulness of clinical criteria: A quantitative study based on a follow-up period of six to eight years in 39 patients. *New England Journal of Medicine, 266*, 421–426.

Perry, C. W. (1977). Is hypnotizability modifiable? *International Journal of Clinical and Experimental Hypnosis, 25*, 125–146.

Perry, N. E. (1992). *Therapists' experiences of the effects of working with dissociative patients*. Paper presented at the Ninth International Conference on Multiple Personality/Dissociation, Arlington, VA.

Persinger, M. A. (1980). Earthquake activity and antecedent UFO report numbers. *Perceptual and Motor Skills, 50*(3), 791–797.

Persinger, M. A. (1981). Geophysical variables and behaviour: III. Prediction of UFO reports by geomagnetic and seismic activity. *Perceptual and Motor Skills, 53*(1), 115–122.

Persinger, M. A. (1983). Geophysical variables and behaviour: IX. Expected clinical consequences of close proximity to UFO-related luminosities. *Perceptual and Motor Skills, 56*(1), 259–265.

Peters, L. G. (1981). A experiential study of Nepalese shamanism. *Journal of Transpersonal Psychology, 39*, 1–26.

Peters, S. D., Wyatt, G. E., & Finkelhor, D. (1986). Prevalence. In D. Finkelhor, S. Araji, L. Baron, A. Browne, S. D. Peters, & G. E. Wyatt (Eds.), *A sourcebook on child sexual abuse* (pp. 15–59). Beverly Hills, CA: Sage.

Peterson, E., Gooch, N. L., & Freeman, L. (1987). *Nightmare: Uncovering the strange 56 personalities of Nancy Lynn Gooch*. New York: Richarson & Steirman.

Phoon, W. H. (1982). Outbreaks of mass hysteria at workplaces in Singapore: Some patterns and modes of presentation. In M. J. Colligan, J. W. Pennebaker, & L. R. Murphy (Eds.), *Mass psychogenic illness: A social psychological analysis* (pp. 21–52). Hillsdale, NJ: Erlbaum.

Piccione, C., Hilgard, E. R., & Zimbardo, P. G. (1989). On the degree of stability of measured hypnotizability over a 25 year period. *Journal of Personality and Social Psychology, 56*, 289–295.

Pickett, R. (1952). *Mental affliction and church law*. Ottawa, Canada: University of Ottawa Press.

Pillemar, D. B., & White, S. H. (1989). Childhood events recalled by children and adults. In H. W. Reese (Ed.), *Advances in child development and behavior* (Vol. 21, pp. 297–340). San Diego, CA: Academic Press.

Pitblado, C., & Cohen, J. (1984). State-related changes in amplitude, latency, and cerebral asymmetry of average evoked potentials in a case of multiple personality. *International Journal of Clinical Neuropsychology, 6*, 69.

Plotkin, W. B. (1979). The alpha experience revisited: Biofeedback in the transformation of psychological state. *Psychological Bulletin, 86*, 1132–1148.

Podmore, F. (1902). *Modern spiritualism: A history and criticism*. London: Methuen.

Podmore, F. (1909). *Mesmerism and Christian Science: A short history of mental healing*. London: Methuen.

Poole, D. A., & Lindsay, D. S. (1993). *Psychotherapists' opinions, practices, and experiences with recovery of memories of incestuous abuse: A national survey of U.S. Ph.D. psychotherapists.* Paper presented at the annual meeting of the Midwestern Psychological Association, Chicago.

Pope, H. G., & Hudson, J. I. (1992). Is childhood sexual abuse a risk factor for bulimia nervosa? *American Journal of Psychiatry, 149,* 455–463.

Powell, R. C. (1980). James Hervey Hyslop (1854–1920) and the American Institute for Scientific Research, 1904–1934: An attempt toward the coordinated study of psychopathology and psychical phenomena. In E. R. Wallace IV & L. C. Pressley (Eds.), *Essays in the history of psychiatry* (pp. 161–171). Columbia, SC: W. S. Hall Psychiatric Institute.

Prince, M. (1908). The unconscious. *Journal of Abnormal Psychology, 3,* 261–297, 335–353, 391–426.

Prince, M. (1920). *The dissociation of a personality* (2nd ed.). London: Longmans Green. (Original work published in 1905)

Prince, W. F. (1915). The Doris case of multiple personality. *Proceedings of the American Society for Psychical Research, Part 1, 9,* 1–700.

Prince, W. F. (1916). The Doris case of quintuple personality. *Journal of Abnormal Psychology, 11,* 73–122.

Putnam, F. W. (1982, May). *Evoked potentials in multiple personality disorder.* Paper presented at the 135th annual meeting of the American Psychiatric Association, Toronto, Canada.

Putnam, F. W. (1984). The psychophysiologic investigation of multiple personality disorder. *Psychiatric Clinics of North America, 7,* 31–39.

Putnam, F. W. (1989). *Diagnosis and treatment of multiple personality disorder.* London: Guilford Press.

Putnam, F. W. (1993). Dissociative phenomena. In D. Spiegel (Ed.), *Dissociative disorders* (pp. 1–16). Lutherville, MD: Sidran.

Putnam, F. W., Guroff, J. J., Silberman, E. K., Barban, L., & Post, R. M. (1986). The clinical phenomenology of multiple personality disorder: Review of 100 recent cases. *Journal of Clinical Psychiatry, 47,* 285–293.

Putnam, F. W., Zahn, T. P., & Post, R. M. (1990). Differential autonomic nervous system activity in multiple personality disorder. *Psychiatric Research, 31,* 251–260.

Puysegur, A. M. J., de Chastenet, Marquis de. (1820). *Memoire pour servir a l'histoire et a l'establissement du magnetisme animal* (3rd ed.). Paris: J. G. Dentu. (Original work published 1784)

Rabinowitz, F. E. (1989). Creating the multiple personality: An experimental demonstration for an undergraduate abnormal psychology class. *Teaching of psychology, 16,* 69–71.

Rabkin, R. (1964). Conversion hysteria as social maladaptation. *Psychiatry, 27,* 349–363.

Rabkin, S. W., Boyko, E., Shane, F., & Kaufert, J. (1984). A randomized trial comparing smoking cessation programs utilizing behavior modification, health education or hypnosis. *Addictive Behaviors, 9,* 157–173.

Radtke, H. L., & Spanos, N. P. (1981). Was I hypnotized? A social psychological analysis of hypnotic depth reports. *Psychiatry, 44,* 359–367.

Ratnoff, O. D. (1969). Stigmata: Where mind and body meet. *Medical Times, 97,* 150–163.

Raulin, J. (1758). *Traité des affections vaporeuses du sexe avec l'exposition de leurs symptômes, de leurs différentes causes et la méthode de les guérir* [Treatise on the vaporous sex ailments, with an exposition of their symptoms, their different causes, and the way to cure them]. Paris: J. T. Herissant.

Ready, W. B. (1956). Bridey Murphy: An Irishman's view. *Fantasy & Science Fiction, 11,* 81–88.

Reiff, R., & Scheerer, M. (1959). *Memory and hypnotic age regression.* New York: International University Press.

Reiser, M. (1974). Hypnosis as an aid in a homicide investigation. *American Journal of Clinical Hypnosis, 17,* 84–87.

Reiser, M. (1980). *Handbook of investigative hypnosis.* Los Angeles: LEHI.

Richards, D. G. (1991). A study of the correlations between subjective psychic experiences and dissociative experiences. *Dissociation Progress in the Dissociative Disorders, 4*(2), 83–91.

Richardson, J. T. (1973). Psychological interpretations of glossolalia: A reexamination of research. *Journal for the Scientific Study of Religion, 12,* 199–207.

Richardson, J. T., Best, J., & Bromley, D. (1991). Satanism as a social problem. In, J. T. Richarson, J. Best, & D. Bromley (Eds.), *The satanism scare* (pp. 3–20). New York: Aldine de Gruyter.

Rickett, A. (1957). *Prisoners of liberation.* New York: Cameron Associates.

Ring, K., & Rosing, C. J. (1990). The omega project: A psychological survey of persons reporting abductions and other UFO encounters. *Journal of UFO Studies, 2,* 59–98.

Ritenbaugh, C. (1982). Obesity as a culture-bound syndrome. *Culture, Medicine and Psychiatry, 6,* 347–361.

Rivera, K. C. (1991). Multiple personality disorder and social systems: 185 cases. *Dissociation, 4,* 79–82.

Robbins, R. H. (1959). *The encyclopedia of witchcraft and demonology.* New York: Crown.

Rogers, M. L., & Brodie, L. (1993, April). *Front line providers in investigation of child abuse: Personal background, experience, knowledge base and attitudes of social workers regarding child sexual abuse survivors and recovered memories.* Paper presented at a conference on Memory and Reality: Emerging Crisis, Valley Forge, PA.

The Roman Ritual of Exorcism (1976). In M. Malachi (Ed. and Trans.), *Hostage to the devil*. New York: Reader's Digest Press. (Original work published 1614)

Rosenbaum, M. (1980). The role of the term schizophrenia in the decline of the diagnosis of multiple personality. *Archives of General Psychiatry, 37,* 1383–1385.

Rosencrance, J. (1985). Compulsive gambling and the medicalization of deviance. *Social Problems, 3,* 275–285.

Ross, C. A. (1984). Diagnosis of multiple personality during hypnosis: A case report. *International Journal of Clinical and Experimental Hypnosis, 32,* 222–235.

Ross, C. A. (1989). *Multiple personality disorder: Diagnosis, clinical features and treatment*. New York: Wiley.

Ross, C. A. (1991). Epidemiology of multiple personality disorder and dissociation. *Psychiatric Clinics of North America, 14,* 503–517.

Ross, C. A., Anderson, G., Fleisher, W. P., & Norton, G. R. (1991). The frequency of multiple personality disorder among psychiatric inpatients. *American Journal of Psychiatry, 148,* 1717–1720.

Ross, C. A., Anderson, G., Heber, S., & Norton, G. R. (1990) Dissociation and abuse among multiple personality patients, prostitutes, and exotic dancers. *Hospital and Community Psychiatry, 41,* 328–330.

Ross, C. A., Heber, S., Anderson G., Norton, G. R., Anderson, B. A., del Campo, M., & Pillay, N. (1989). Differentiating multiple personality disorder and complex partial seizures. *General Hospital Psychiatry, 11,* 54–58.

Ross, C. A., Heber, S., Norton, G. R., & Anderson, G. (1989a). Differences between multiple personality disorder and other diagnostic groups on structured interview. *Journal of Nervous and Mental Disease, 177,* 487–491.

Ross, C. A., Heber, S., Norton, G. R., & Anderson, G. (1989b). Somatic symptoms in multiple personality disorder. *Psychosomatics, 30,* 154–160.

Ross, C. A., Joshi, S., & Currie, R. (1990). Dissociative experiences in the general population. *American Journal of Psychiatry, 147,* 1547–1552.

Ross, C. A., Miller, S. D., Bjornson, L., Reagor, P., & Fraser, G. A. (1991). Abuse histories in 102 cases of multiple personality disorder. *Canadian Journal of Psychiatry, 36,* 97–101.

Ross, C. A., Norton, G. R., & Fraser, G. A. (1989). Evidence against the iatrogenisis of multiple personality disorder. *Dissociation, 2,* 61–65.

Ross, C. A., Norton, R., & Wozney, K. (1989). Multiple personality disorder: An analysis of 236 cases. *Canadian Journal of Psychiatry, 34,* 414–418.

Ross, M. W. (1980). Retrospective distortion in homosexual research. *Archives of Sexual Behavior, 9,* 523–531.

Roth, M. S. (1989). Remembering forgetting: Maladies de la memoire in ninteenth century France. *Representations, 26,* 49–68.

Rubenstein, R., & Newman, R. (1954). The living out of "future" experiences under hypnosis. *Science, 119,* 472–473.

Russell, D. (1988). The incidence and prevalence of interfamilial and extrafamilial sexual abuse of female children. In L. E. A. Walker (Ed.), *Handbook of sexual abuse of children: Assessment and treatment issues* (pp. 19–36). New York: Springer.

Russell, J. B. (1980). *A history of witchcraft.* London: Thames & Hudson.

Rutkowski, K. W. (1988). The terrestrial hypothesis: Geophysical alternatives. In J. Spencer & H. Evans (Eds.), *Phenomenon: Forty years of flying saucers* (pp. 301–307). New York: Avon.

Saltman, V., & Solomon, R. S. (1982). Incest and multiple personality. *Psychological Reports, 50,* 1127–1141.

Salzberg, H. C., & DePiano, F. A. (1980). Hypnotizability and task-motivating instructions: A further look at how they affect performance. *International Journal of Clinical and Experimental Hypnosis, 28,* 261–271.

Samarin, W. J. (1972). *Tongues of men and angels: The religious language of pentecostalism.* New York: Macmillan.

Sanders, B., McRoberts, G., & Tollefson, C. (1989). Childhood stress and dissociation in a college population. *Dissociation, 2,* 17–23.

Sansonnet-Hayden, H., Haley, G., Marriage, K., & Fine, S. (1987). Sexual abuse and psychopathology in hospitalized adolescents. *Journal of the American Academy of Child and Adolescent Psychiatry, 26,* 753–757.

Sarbin, T. R. (1950). Contributions to role-taking theory: I. Hypnotic behavior. *Psychological Review, 57,* 255–270.

Sarbin, T. R. (1962). Attempts to understand hypnotic phenomena. In L. Postman (Ed.), *Psychology in the making* (pp. 745–785). New York: Knopf.

Sarbin, T. R., & Coe, W. C. (1972). *Hypnosis: A social-psychological analysis of influence communication.* New York: Holt, Reinhart & Winston.

Sarbin, T. R., & Lim, D. T. (1963). Some evidence in support of the role taking hypothesis in hypnosis. *International Journal of Clinical and Experimental Hypnosis, 11,* 98–103.

Sarbin, T. R., & Slage, R. W. (1972). Hypnosis and psychophysiological outcomes. In E. Fromm & R. E. Shor (Eds.), *Hypnosis: Research developments and perspectives* (pp. 185–216). Chicago: Aldine-Atherton.

Sargent, W. (1957). *Battle for the mind.* New York: Doubleday.

Saunders, L. W. (1977). Variants in ZAR experience in an Egyptian village. In V. Crapanzano & V. Garrison (Eds.), *Case studies in spirit possession* (pp. 177–191). New York: Wiley.

Schachter, S., & Singer, J. E. (1962). Cognitive, social, and physiological determinants of emotional state. *Psychological Review, 69,* 379–399.

Schatzman, M. (1992, March). Freud: Who seduced whom? *New Scientist, 21,* 34–37.

Scheflin, A., & Opton, E. (1978). *The mind manipulators.* New York: Paddington Press.

Scheibe, K. E., Gray, A. L., & Keim, C. S. (1968). Hypnotically induced deafness and delayed auditory feedback: A comparison of real and simulating subjects. *International Journal of Clinical and Experimental Hypnosis, 16,* 158–164.

Schein, E. (1961). *Coercive persuasion.* New York: Norton.

Schieffelin, E. L. (1985). Performance and the cultural construction of reality. *American Ethnologist, 12,* 707–724.

Schimek, J. G. (1987). Fact and fantasy in the seduction theory: A historical review. *Journal of the American Psychoanalytic Association, 35,* 937–965.

Schneider, J. W. (1978). Deviant drinking as a disease: Deviant drinking as a social accomplishment. *Social Problems, 25,* 261–372.

Schreiber, F. R. (1973). *Sybil.* New York: Warner.

Schwaber, E. (1983). Psychoanalytic listening and psychic reality. *International Review of Psycho-Analysis, 10,* 379–392.

Schwarz, T. (1981). *The hillside strangler: A murderer's mind.* New York: New American Library.

Scobie, A. (1965). *Murder for magic: Witchcraft in Africa.* London: Cassell.

Segal, D., & Lynn, S. J. (1993). Predicting dissociative experiences: Imagination, hypnotizability, psychopathology, and alcohol use. *Imagination, Cognition and Personality, 12,* 287–300.

Segouin, A. (1853). *Les mystères de la magie, ou les secrets du magnetisme devoilés* [The mysteries of magic, or the secrets of magnetism revealed] (2nd. ed.). Paris: Author.

Shaffer, R. E., & Cozolino, L. (1992). Adults who report childhood ritual abuse. *Journal of Psychology and Theology, 20,* 188–193.

Sharp, L. A. (1990). Possessed and dispossessed youth: Spirit possession of school children in northwest Madagascar. *Culture, Medicine and Psychiatry, 14,* 339–364.

Sheaffer, R. (1986). *The UFO verdict: Examining the evidence.* Buffalo, NY: Prometheus.

Sheehan, P. W. (1971). A methodological analysis of the simulating technique. *International Journal of Clinical and Experimental Hypnosis, 19,* 83–99.

Sheehan, P. W. (1977). Incongruity in trance behavior: A defining property of hypnosis? *Annals of the New York Academy of Sciences, 296,* 194–207.

Sheehan, P. W., Garnett, M., & Robertson, R. (1993). The effects of cue level, hypnotizability and state induction on response to leading questions. *International Journal of Clinical and Experimental Hypnosis, 41,* 287–304.

Sheehan, P. W., & McConkey, K. M. (1982). *Hypnosis and experience.* Hillsdale, NJ: Erlbaum.

Sheikh, A. A., & Kunzendorf, R. G. (1984). Imagery, physiology and psychosomatic illness. In A. A. Sheikh (Ed.), *International review of mental imagery* (Vol. 1, pp. 95–138). New York: Human Sciences Press.

Sherif, M. (1936). *The psychology of social norms.* New York: Harper & Row.

Shor, R. E. (1959). Hypnosis and the concept of the generalized reality-orientation. *American Journal of Psychotherapy, 13*, 582–602.

Shor, R. E. (1970). The three-factor theory of hypnosis as applied to the book-reading fantasy and the concept of suggestion. *International Journal of Clinical and Experimental Hypnosis, 18*, 89–98.

Shorter, E. (1992). *From paralysis to fatigue: A history of psychosomatic medicine in the modern era.* New York: Free Press.

Shortt, S. E. D. (1984). Physicians and psychics: The Anglo-American medical response to spiritualism, 1870–1890. *The Journal of the History of Medicine and Allied Science, 39*, 339–355.

Silberman, E. K., Putnam, F. W., Weingartner, H., Braun, B. G., & Post, R. M. (1985). Dissociative states in multiple personality disorder: A quantitiative study. *Psychiatry Research, 15*, 253–260.

Silva, C. E., & Kirsch, I. (1987). Breaching hypnotic amnesia by manipulating expectancy. *Journal of Abnormal Psychology, 96*, 325–329.

Simpson, M. A. (1989) Correspondence "Multiple personality disorder." *British Journal of Psychiatry, 155*, 565.

Singer, J. L. (1966). *Daydreaming: An introduction to the experimental study of inner experience.* New York: Random House.

Slater, E., & Glithero, E. (1965). A followup of patients diagnosed as suffering from hysteria. *Journal of Psychosomatic Research, 9*, 9–13.

Smith, M., & Pazder, L. (1980). *Michelle remembers.* New York: Pocket Books.

Smith, M. C. (1983). Hypnotic memory enhancement of witnesses: Does it work? *Psychological Bulletin, 94*, 387–407.

Smith, S. E. (1993, April). *Body memories: and other pseudo-scientific notions of "survivor psychology."* Paper presented at the False Memory Foundation Conference, Valley Forge, PA.

Smith, V. L., & Ellsworth, P. C. (1987). The social psychology of eyewitness accuracy: Misleading questions and communicator expertise. *Journal of Applied Psychology, 72*, 294–300.

Smith-Rosenberg, C. (1972). The hysterical woman: Some reflections on sex roles and role conflict in 19th century America. *Social Research, 39*, 652–678.

Smith-Rosenberg, C. (1985). *Disorderly conduct: Visions of gender in Victorian America.* New York: Oxford University Press.

Snow, C. B. (1989). *Mass dreams of the future.* New York: McGraw-Hill.

Snow, L. (1979). The relationship between "rapid induction" and placebo analgesia, hypnotic susceptibility and chronic pain intensity. *Dissertation Abstracts International, 40*, 937.

Snyder, M., & Uranowitz, S. W. (1978). Reconstructing the past: Some cognitive consequences of person perception. *Journal of Personality and Social Psychology, 36*, 941–950.

Spanos, N. P. (1971). Goal-directed fantasy and the performance of hypnotic test suggestions. *Psychiatry, 34*, 86–96.

Spanos, N. P. (1978). Witchcraft in histories of psychiatry: A critical analysis and an alternative conceptualization. *Psychological Bulletin, 85,* 417–439.

Spanos, N. P. (1982). A social psychological approach to hypnotic behavior. In G. Weary & H. L. Mirels (Eds.), *Integrations of clinical and social psychology* (pp. 231–271). New York: Oxford University Press.

Spanos, N. P. (1983a). Demonic possession: A social psychological analysis. In M. Rosenbaum (Ed.), *Compliance behavior* (pp. 148–198). New York: Free Press.

Spanos, N. P. (1983b). Ergotism and the Salem witch panic: A critical analysis and an alternative conceptualization. *Journal of the History of the Behavioral Sciences, 19,* 358–368.

Spanos, N. P. (1985). Witchcraft and social history: An essay review. *Journal of the History of the Behavioral Sciences, 21,* 60–67.

Spanos, N. P. (1986a). Hypnosis and the modification of hypnotic susceptibility: A social psychological perspective. In P. L. N. Naish (Ed.), *What is hypnosis?* (pp. 85–120). Philadelphia: Open University Press.

Spanos, N. P. (1986b). Hypnotic behavior: A social-psychological interpretation of amnesia, analgesia and "trance logic." *Behavioral and Brain Sciences, 9,* 449–502.

Spanos, N. P. (1989). Hypnosis, demonic possession and multiple personality: Strategic enactments and disavowals of responsibility for actions. In C. A. Ward (Ed.), *Altered states of consciousness and mental health: Theoretical and methodological issues* (pp. 96–124). Newbury Park, CA: Sage.

Spanos, N. P. (1991). A sociocognitive approach to hypnosis. In S. J. Lynn & J. W. Rhue (Eds.), *Theories of hypnosis: Current models and perspectives* (pp. 324–361). New York: Guilford.

Spanos, N. P. (1994). Multiple identity enactments and multiple personality disorder: A sociocognitive perspective. *Psychological Bulletin, 116,* 143–165.

Spanos, N. P., Arango, M., & de Groot, H. P. (1993). Context as a moderator in relationships between attribute variables and hypnotizability. *Personality and Social Psychology Bulletin, 19,* 71–77.

Spanos, N. P., & Barber, T. X. (1968). "Hypnotic" experiences as inferred from subjective reports: Auditory and visual hallucinations. *Journal of Experimental Research in Personality, 3,* 136–150.

Spanos, N. P., & Barber, T. X. (1974). Toward a convergence in hypnosis research. *American Psychologist, 29,* 500–511.

Spanos, N. P., Barber, T. X., & Lang, G. (1974). Cognition and self-control: Cognitive control of painful sensory input. In H. London & R. E. Nisbit (Eds.) *Thought and feeling: Cognitive alteration of feeling states* (pp. 144–158). Chicago: Aldine.

Spanos, N. P., & Bodorik, H. L. (1977). Suggested amnesia and disorganized recall in hypnotic and task-motivated subjects. *Journal of Abnormal Psychology, 86,* 295–305.

Spanos, N. P., Brice, P., & Gabora, N. J. (1992). Suggested imagery and salivation in hypnotic and non-hypnotic subjects. *Contemporary Hypnosis, 9*(2), 105–111.

Spanos, N. P., & Bures, E. (1994). Pseudomemory responding in hypnotic, task-motivated subjects: Memory distortion or reporting bias? *Imagination, Cognition and Personality, 13,* 303–310.

Spanos, N. P., Burgess, C. A., & Burgess, M. F. (1994). Past-life identities, UFO abductions, and satanic ritual abuse: The social construction of memories. *International Journal of Clinical and Experimental Hypnosis, 42,* 433–446.

Spanos, N. P., Burgess, C. A., Cocco, L., & Pinch, N. (1993). Reporting bias and response to difficult suggestions in highly hypnotizable hypnotic subjects. *Journal of Research in Personality, 27,* 270–284.

Spanos, N. P., Burgess, C. A., & Perlini, A. H. (1991). Compliance and suggested deafness in hypnotic and nonhypnotic subjects. *Imagination, Cognition and Personality, 11,* 211–223.

Spanos, N. P., Burgess, M. F., Samuel, C., Blois, W. O., & Burgess, C. A. (1994). *False memory reports in hypnotic and nonhypnotic subjects.* Unpublished manuscript, Carleton University, Ottawa, Ontario, Canada.

Spanos, N. P., Burnley, M. C. E., Burgess, M. F., & Lacene, K. (1994). *The effects of hypnotic and nonhypnotic treatments on public speaking anxiety.* Unpublished manuscript, Carleton University, Ottawa, Ontario, Canada.

Spanos, N. P., Burnley, M. C. E., & Cross, P. A. (1993). Response expectancies and interpretations as determinants of hypnotic responding. *Journal of Personality and Social Psychology, 65,* 1237–1242.

Spanos, N. P., & Chaves, J. F. (1989). *Hypnosis: The cognitive-behavioral perspective.* Buffalo, NY: Prometheus.

Spanos, N. P., & Chaves, J. F. (1991). History and historiography of hypnosis. In S. J. Lynn & J. W. Rhue (Eds.), *Theories of hypnosis: Current models and perspectives* (pp. 43–78). New York: Guilford Press.

Spanos, N. P., Cobb, P. C., & Gorassini, D. (1985). Failing to resist hypnotic suggestions: A strategy for self-presenting as deeply hypnotized. *Psychiatry, 48,* 282–293.

Spanos, N. P., & Coe, W. C. (1992). A social psychological approach to hypnosis. In E. Fromm & M. R. Nash (Eds.), *Contemporary hypnosis research* (pp. 102–130). New York: Guilford.

Spanos, N. P., Cross, P. A., Dickson, K., & DuBreuil, S. C. (1993). Close encounters: An examination of UFO experiences. *Journal of Abnormal Psychology, 102,* 624-632.

Spanos, N. P., Cross, W. P., Lepage, M., & Coristine, M. (1986). Glossolalia as learned behavior: An experimental demonstration. *Journal of Abnormal Psychology, 95,* 21–23.

Spanos, N. P., de Groot, H. P., & Gwynn, M. I. (1987). Trance logic as incomplete responding. *Journal of Personality and Social Psychology, 53,* 911–921.

Spanos, N. P., de Groot, H. P., Tiller, D. K., Weekes, J. R., & Bertrand, L. D. (1985). "Trance logic" duality and hidden observer responding in hypnotic, imagination control and simulating subjects. *Journal of Abnormal Psychology, 94,* 611–623.

Spanos, N. P., & Flynn, D. M. (1989). Simulation, compliance and skill training in the enhancement of hypnotizability. *British Journal of Experimental and Clinical Hypnosis, 6,* 1–8.

Spanos, N. P., Flynn, D. M., & Gabora, N. J. (1989). Suggested negative visual hallucinations in hypnotic subjects: When no means yes. *British Journal of Experimental and Clinical Hypnosis, 6,* 63–67.

Spanos, N. P., Flynn, D. M., & Gwynn, M. I. (1988). Contextual demands, negative hallucinations and hidden observer responding: Three hidden observers observed. *British Journal of Experimental and Clinical Hypnosis, 5,* 5–10.

Spanos, N. P., Gabora, N. J., Jarrett, L. E., & Gwynn, M. I. (1989). Contextual determinants of hypnotizability and of the relationship between hypnotizability scales. *Journal of Personality and Social Psychology, 57,* 271–278.

Spanos, N. P., & Gorassini, D. (1984). Structure of hypnotic test suggestions and attributions of involuntary responding. *Journal of Personality and Social Psychology, 46,* 688–696.

Spanos, N. P., & Gottlieb, J. (1976). Ergotism and the Salem village witch trials. *Science, 194,* 1390–1394.

Spanos, N. P., & Gottlieb, J. (1979). Demonic possession, mesmerism and hysteria: A social psychological perspective on their historical interrelations. *Journal of Abnormal Psychology, 88,* 527–546.

Spanos, N. P., Gwynn, M. I., Comer, S. L., Baltruweit, W. J., & deGroh, M. (1989). Are hypnotically induced pseudomemories resistant to cross-examination? *Law and Human Behavior, 13,* 271–289.

Spanos, N. P., Gwynn, M. I., Della Malva, C. L., & Bertrand, L. D. (1988). Social psychological factors in the genesis of posthypnotic source amnesia. *Journal of Abnormal Psychology, 97,* 322–329.

Spanos, N. P., Gwynn, M. I., & Stam, H. J. (1983). Instructional demands and ratings of overt and hidden pain during hypnotic analgesia. *Journal of Abnormal Psychology, 92,* 479–488.

Spanos, N. P., & Ham, M. L. (1973). Cognitive activity in response to hypnotic suggestions: Goal-directed fantasy and selective amnesia. *American Journal of Clinical Hypnosis, 15,* 191–198.

Spanos, N. P., Ham, M. W., & Barber, T. X. (1973). Suggested ("hypnotic") hallucinations: Experimental and phenomenological data. *Journal of Abnormal Psychology, 81,* 96–106.

Spanos, N. P., & Hewitt, E. C. (1979). Glossolalia: A test of the "trance" and psychopathology hypotheses. *Journal of Abnormal Psychology, 88,* 427–434.

Spanos, N. P., & Hewitt, E. C. (1980). The hidden observer in hypnotic analgesia: Discovery or experimental creation? *Journal of Personality and Social Psychology, 39,* 1201–1214.

Spanos, N. P., Jones, B., & Malfara, A. (1982). Hypnotic deafness: Now you hear it—Now you still hear it. *Journal of Abnormal Psychology, 91,* 75–77.

Spanos, N. P., & Katsanis, J. (1989). Effects of instructional set on attributions of nonvolition during hypnotic and nonhypnotic analgesia. *Journal of Personality and Social Psychology, 56,* 182–188.

Spanos, N. P., Kennedy, S. K., & Gwynn, M. I. (1984). The moderating effect of contextual variables on the relationship between hypnotic susceptibility and suggested analgesia. *Journal of Abnormal Psychology, 93,* 285–294.

Spanos, N. P., Liddy, S. J., Baxter, C. E., & Burgess, C. A. (1994). Long-term and short-term stability of behavioral and subjective indexes of hypnotizability. *Journal of Research in Personality, 28,* 301–313.

Spanos, N. P., Liddy, S. J., Scott, H., Garrard, C., Sine, J., Tirabasso, A., & Hayward, A. (1993). Hypnotic suggestion and placebo for the treatment of chronic headache in a university volunteer sample. *Cognitive Therapy and Research, 17,* 191–205.

Spanos, N. P., Lush, N. I., & Gwynn, M. I. (1989). Cognitive skill training enhancement of hypnotizability: Generalization effects and trance logic responding. *Journal of Personality and Social Psychology, 56,* 795–804.

Spanos, N. P., Menary, E., Brett, P. J., Cross, W., & Ahmed, Q. (1987). Failure of posthypnotic responding to occur outside the experimental setting. *Journal of Abnormal Psychology, 96,* 52–57.

Spanos, N. P., Menary, E., Gabora, N. J., DuBreuil, S. C., & Dewhirst, B. (1991). Secondary identity enactments during hypnotic past-life regression: A sociocognitive perspective. *Journal of Personality and Social Psychology, 61,* 308–320.

Spanos, N. P., & McLean, J. M. (1986). Hypnotically created pseudomemories: Memory distortions or reporting biases? *British Journal of Experimental and Clinical Hypnosis, 3,* 155–159.

Spanos, N. P., McNeil, C., Gwynn, M. I., & Stam H. J. (1984). The effects of suggestions and distraction on reported pain in subjects high and low on hypnotic susceptibility. *Journal of Abnormal Psychology, 93,* 277–284.

Spanos, N. P., McNulty, S. A., DuBreuil, S. C., Pires, M., & Burgess, M. F. (1994). *The frequency and correlates of sleep paralysis in a university sample.* Unpublished manuscript, Carleton University, Ottawa, Ontario, Canada.

Spanos, N. P., Mondoux, T. J., & Burgess, C. A. (1995). Comparison of multicomponent hypnotic and nonhypnotic treatments for smoking. *Contemporary Hypnosis, 12,* 12–19.

Spanos, N. P., Mullens, D., & Rivers, S. M. (1979). The effects of suggestion structure and hypnotic vs. task-motivation instructions on response to hallucination suggestions. *Journal of Research in Personality, 13,* 59–70.

Spanos, N. P., Perlini, A. H., Patrick, L., Bell, S., & Gwynn, M. I. (1990). The role of compliance in hypnotic and nonhypnotic analgesia. *Journal of Research in Personality, 24,* 433–453.

Spanos, N. P., Perlini, A. H., & Robertson, L. A. (1989). Hypnosis, suggestion and placebo in the reduction of pain. *Journal of Abnormal Psychology, 98,* 285–293.

Spanos, N. P., Quigley, C. A., Gwynn, M. I., Glatt, R. L., & Perlini, A. H. (1991). Hypnotic interrogation, pretrial preparation, and witness testimony during direct and cross-examination. *Law and Human Behavior, 15,* 639–653.

Spanos, N. P., Radtke, H. L., & Bertrand, L. D. (1984). Hypnotic amnesia as a strategic enactment: Breaching amnesia in highly hypnotizable subjects. *Journal of Personality and Social Psychology, 47,* 1155–1169.

Spanos, N. P., Radtke, H. L., & Dubreuil, D. L. (1982). Episodic and semantic memory in posthypnotic amnesia: A reevaluation. *Journal of Personality and Social Psychology, 43,* 565–573.

Spanos, N. P., Radtke-Bodorik, H. L., Ferguson, J., & Jones, B. (1979). The effects of hypnotic susceptibility, suggestions for analgesia, and the utilization of cognitive strategies on the reduction of pain. *Journal of Abnormal Psychology, 88,* 282–292.

Spanos, N. P., Radtke, H. L., Hodgins, D. C., Bertrand, L. D., Stam, H. J., & Dubreuil, D. L. (1983). The Carleton University Responsiveness to Suggestion Scale: Stability, reliability, and relationships with expectancy and "hypnotic experiences." *Psychological Reports, 53,* 555–563.

Spanos, N. P., Radtke, H. L., Hodgins, D. C., Stam, H. J., & Bertrand, L. D. (1983). The Carleton University Responsiveness to Suggestion Scale: Normative data and psychometric properties. *Psychological Reports, 53,* 523–535.

Spanos, N. P., Rivers, S. M., & Ross. S. (1977). Experienced involuntariness and response to hypnotic suggestions. *New York Academy of Sciences, 296,* 208–221.

Spanos, N. P., Salas, J., Bertrand, L. D., & Johnston, J. (1989). Occurrence schemas, context ambiguity and hypnotic responding. *Imagination, Cognition and Personality, 8,* 235–247.

Spanos, N. P., Sims, A., de Faye, B., Mondoux, T. J., & Gabora, N. J. (1992). Comparison of hypnotic and nonhypnotic treatments for smoking. *Imagination, Cognition and Personality, 12,* 23–45.

Spanos, N. P., Stenstrom, R. J., & Johnston, J. C. (1988). Hypnosis, placebo and suggestion in the treatment of warts. *Psychosomatic Medicine, 50,* 245–260.

Spanos, N. P., Weekes, J. R., & Bertrand, L. D. (1985). Multiple personality: A social psychological perspective. *Journal of Abnormal Psychology, 94,* 362–376.

Spanos, N. P., Weekes, J. R., Menary, E., & Bertrand, L. D. (1986). Hypnotic interview and age regression procedures in the elicitation of multiple personality symptoms: A simulation study. *Psychiatry, 49,* 298–311.

Spanos, N. P., Williams, V., & Gwynn, M. I. (1990). Effects of hypnotic, placebo and salicylic acid treatments on wart regression. *Psychosomatic Medicine, 52,* 109–114.

Spear, N. E. (1979). Experimental analysis of infantile amnesia. In. J. F. Kihlstrom & F. J. Evans (Eds.), *Functional disorders of memory* (pp. 75–102). Hillsdale, NJ: Erlbaum.

Spence, D. P. (1982). *Narrative truth and historical truth*. New York: Norton.

Spence, D. P. (1993, August). *Narrative truth and putative child abuse*. Paper presented at the annual convention of the American Psychological Association, Toronto, Canada.

Spencer, J. (1989). *Suffer the child*. New York: Pocket Books.

Spinhoven, P., Linssen, A. C. G., Van Dyck, R., & Zitman, F. G. (1988, August). *Locus of control, cognitive strategies and hypnotizability in pain management: A preliminary report*. Paper presented at the 11th International Congress of Hypnosis and Psychosomatic Medicine, The Hague, The Netherlands.

St. Jean, R. (1978). Posthypnotic behavior as a function of experimental surveillance. *American Journal of Clinical Hypnosis, 20*, 250–255.

Stam, H. J. (1989). From symptom relief to cure: Hypnotic interventions in cancer. In N. P. Spanos & J. F. Chaves (Eds.), *Hypnosis: The cognitive-behavioral perspective* (pp. 313–339). Buffalo, NY: Prometheus.

Stam, H. J., McGrath, P. A., & Brooke, R. I. (1984). The effects of a cognitive-behavioral treatment program on temporo-mandibular pain and dysfunction syndrome. *Psychosomatic Medicine, 46*, 534–545.

Stava, L. J., & Jaffa, M. (1988). Some operationalizations of the neodissociation concept and their relationship to hypnotic susceptibility. *Journal of Personality and Social Psychology, 54*, 989–996.

Steinem, G. (1992). *Revolution from within: A book of self-esteem*. Boston: Little, Brown.

Stern, C. R. (1984). The etiology of multiple personalities. *Psychiatric Clinics of North America, 7*(1), 149–159.

Stevenson, I. (1994). A case of the psychotherapists falacy: Hypnotic regression to "previous lives." *American Journal of Clinical Hypnosis, 36*, 188–193.

Stevenson, J. H. (1976). Effect of posthypnotic dissociation on the performance of interfering tasks. *Journal of Abnormal Psychology, 85*, 398–407.

Stinson, M. H., & Hendrick, S. S. (1992). Reported childhood sexual abuse in university counseling center clients. *Journal of Counseling Psychology, 39*, 370–374.

Stoller, P. (1989). Stressing social change in Songhay possession. In C. A. Ward (Ed.), *Altered states of consciousness and mental health: A cross cultural perspective* (pp. 267–284). Newbury Park, CA.: Sage.

Story, R. D. (1980). Arnold sighting. In R. D. Story (Ed.), *The encyclopedia of UFOs* (p. 25). Garden City, NY: Dolphin Books.

Stratford, L. (1988). *Satan's underground*. Eugene, OR: Harvest House.

Streiber, W. (1987). *Communion: A true story*. New York: Avon.

Suengas, A. G., & Johnson, M. K. (1988). Qualitative effects of rehearsal on memories for perceived and imagined events. *Journal of Experimental Psychology: General, 117,* 377–389.

Sulloway, F. J. (1979). *Freud: Biologist of the mind.* New York: Basic Books.

Sutcliffe, J. P. (1960). "Credulous" and "skeptical" views of hypnotic phenomena: A review of certain evidence and methodology. *International Journal of Clinical and Experimental Hypnosis, 8,* 73–101.

Sutcliffe, J. P. (1961). "Credulous" and "skeptical" views of hypnotic phenomena: Experiments on esthesia, hallucination and delusion. *Journal of Abnormal and Social Psychology, 62,* 189–200.

Sutcliffe, J. P., & Jones, J. (1962). Personal identity, multiple personality and hypnosis. *International Journal of Clinical and Experimental Hypnosis, 10,* 231–269.

Szasz, T. S. (1961). *The myth of mental illness.* New York: Hoeber.

Szasz, T. S. (1970). *The manufacture of madness.* New York: Harper & Row.

Szasz, T. S. (1987). *Insanity: The idea and its consequences.* New York: Wiley.

Takahashi, Y. (1990). Is multiple personality disorder really rare in Japan? *Dissociation, 3,* 57–59.

Talamini, J. T. (1982). *Boys will be girls: The hidden world of the heterosexual male transvestite.* Washington, DC: University Press of America.

Tavris, C. (1993, January). Beware the incest-survivor machine. *New York Times Review of Books, 1,* 16–17.

Taylor, B. (1992, May 19). Therapist turned patient's world upside down. *Toronto Star,* p. C1.

Taylor, D. C. (1986). Hysteria, play-acting and courage. *British Journal of Psychiatry, 149,* 37–41.

Taylor, W. S., & Martin, M. F. (1944). Multiple personality. *Journal of Abnormal Psychology, 39,* 281–300.

Teasdale, J. D., Taylor R., & Fogarty, S. J. (1980). Effects of induced elation-depression on the accessibility of memories of happy and unhappy experiences. *Behavior Research and Therapy, 18,* 339–346.

Teoh, J., Soewondo, S., & Sidharta, M. (1975). Epidemic hysteria in Malaysian schools: An illustrative example. *Psychiatry, 38,* 258–268.

Terr, L. (1988). What happens to early memories of trauma? A study of twenty children under age five at the time of documented traumatic events. *Journal of the American Academy of Child and Adolescent Psychiatry, 27,* 96–104.

Terr, L. (1990). *Too scared to cry.* New York: Harper & Row.

Terr, L. C. (1991). Childhood traumas: An outline and overview. *American Journal of Psychiatry, 148,* 10–20.

Thigpen, C. H., & Cleckley, H. M. (1957). *The three faces of Eve.* New York: Fawcett.

Thigpen, C. H., & Cleckley, H. M. (1984). On the incidence of multiple personality disorder. *International Journal of Clinical and Experimental Hypnosis, 32,* 63–66.

Thomas, G. (1989). *Journey into madness*. New York: Bantam.

Thomas, K. (1971). *Religion and the decline of magic*. New York: Scribner's.

Thouret, M. A. (1784). *Recherches et doutes sur le magnetisme animal* [Research and doubts about animal magnetism]. Paris: Prault.

Tillman, J. G., Nash, M. R., & Lerner, P. M. (1994) Does trauma cause dissociative pathology? In S. J. Lynn & J. W. Rhue (Eds.), *Dissociation: Clinical and theoretical perspectives* (pp. 395–414). New York: Guilford Press.

Toews, J. (1991). Historicizing psychoanalysis: Freud in his time and for our time. *Journal of Modern History, 63*, 504–545.

Torrey, E. F. (1986). *Witchdoctors and psychiatrists: The common roots of psychotherapy and its future*. New York: Harper & Row.

Torrey, E. F. (1992). *Freudian Fraud: The malignant effect of Freud's theory on American thought and culture*. New York: HarperCollins.

Tourney, G. (1972). The physician and witchcraft in restoration England. *Medical History, 16*, 143–155.

Tozman, S., & Pabis, R. (1989). MPD: Further skepticism (without hostility we think) [Letter to the editor]. *Journal of Nervous and Mental Disease, 177*, 708–709.

Troffer, S. A. (1966). Hypnotic age regression and cognitive functioning. *Dissertation Abstracts, 26*, 7442–7443.

True, R. M. (1949). Experimental control in hypnotic age regression states. *Science, 110*, 583–584.

Ullman, L. P., & Krasner, L. (1969). *A psychological approach to abnormal behavior*. Englewood Heights, NJ: Prentice-Hall.

Ullman, M. (1947). Herpes simplex and second degree burn induced under hypnosis. *American Journal of Psychiatry, 103*, 828–830.

Usher, J. A., & Neisser, U. (1993). Childhood amnesia and the beginnings of memory for four early life events. *Journal of Experimental Psychology: General, 122*, 155–165.

Vallee, J. (1969). *Passport to Magonia: From folklore to flying saucers*. Chicago: Regnery.

Vallee, J. (1988). *Dimensions: A casebook of alien contact*. New York: Ballantine.

van Husen, J. E. (1988). The development of fears, phobias, and restrictive patterns of adaptation following attempted abortions. *Pre- and Peri-natal Psychology, 2*, 179–185.

Veith, I. (1965). *Hysteria*. Chicago: University of Chicago Press.

Velikovsky, I. (1950). *Worlds in collision*. New York: Doubleday.

Venkataramaiah, V., Mallikarjunaiah, M., Chandra shekar, C. R., Rao, C. K., & Reddy, G. N. (1981). Possession syndrome: An epidemiological study in West Karnataka. *Indian Journal of Psychiatry, 23*, 213–218.

Venn, J. (1986). Hypnosis and the reincarnation hypothesis: A critical review and intensive case study. *The Journal of the American Society for Psychical Research, 80*, 409–425.

Victor, G. (1975). Grande hysterie or folie deux [Letter to the editor]. *American Journal of Psychiatry, 132*, 202.

Victor, J. (1993). *Satanic panic: The creation of a contemporary legend*. Peru, IL: Open Court.

Wadden, T., & Flaxman, J. (1981). Hypnosis and weight loss: A preliminary study. *International Journal of Clinical and Experimental Hypnosis, 29*, 162–173.

Wagstaff, G. F. (1981). *Hypnosis, compliance and belief*. New York: St. Martin's Press.

Wagstaff, G. F. (1983). A comment on McConkey's "Challenging hypnotic effects: The impact of conflicting influences on response to hypnotic suggestion." *British Journal of Experimental and Clinical Hypnosis, 1*, 11–15.

Wagstaff, G. F. (1985). "The use of hypnosis by the police in the investigation of crime: Is guided imagery a safe substitute?": Comment. *British Journal of Experimental and Clinical Hypnosis, 3*, 39–42.

Wagstaff, G. F. (1986). Hypnosis as compliance and belief: A sociocognitive view. In P. L. N. Naish (Ed.), *What is hypnosis?* (pp. 59–84). Philadelphia: Open University Press.

Wagstaff, G. F. (1989). Forensic aspects of hypnosis. In N. P. Spanos & J. F. Chaves (Eds.), *Hypnosis: The cognitive-behavioral perspective* (pp. 340–357). Buffalo, NY: Prometheus.

Wagstaff, G. (1995). A tribute to Nick Spanos [Special issue]. *Contemporary Hypnosis, 12*, 39–41.

Wakefield, H., & Underwager, R. (1991). Female child sexual abusers: A critical review of the literature. *American Journal of Forensic Psychology, 9*, 43–69.

Wakefield, H., & Underwager, R. (1992). Recovered memories of alleged sexual abuse: Lawsuits against parents. *Behavioral Sciences and the Law, 10*, 483–507.

Walker, D. P. (1981). *Unclean spirits*. Philadelphia: University of Pennsylvania Press.

Wall, V. J., & Womack, W. (1989). Hypnotic versus active cognitive strategies for alleviation of procedural distress in pediatric oncology patients. *American Journal of Clinical Hypnosis, 31*, 181–189.

Wambaugh, H. (1979). *Life before life*. New York: Bantam.

Ward, C. A. (1982). A transcultural perspective on women and madness: The case of mystical affliction. *Women's Studies International Forum, 5*, 411–418.

Ward, C. A. (1989). Possession and exorcism: Psychopathology and psychotherapy in a magico-religious context. In C. A. Ward (Ed.), *Altered states of consciousness and mental health: Theoretical and methodological issues* (pp. 125–144). Newbury Park, CA: Sage.

Watkins, J. G. (1984). The Bianchi (L.A. Hillside Strangler) case: Sociopath or multiple personality. *International Journal of Clinical and Experimental Hypnosis, 32*, 67–101.

Watkins, J. G., & Watkins, H. (1980). Ego states and hidden observers. *Journal of Altered States of Consciousness, 5*, 318.

Watson, G. C., & Buranen, C. (1979). The frequency and identification of false positive conversion reactions. *Journal of Nervous and Mental Disease, 167,* 243–247.

Watson, J. B. (1913). Psychology as a behaviorist views it. *Psychological Review, 20,* 158–177.

Webb, J. (1974). *The occult underground.* La Salle, IL: Open Court.

Weekes, J. R., Lynn, S. J., Green J. P., & Brentar, J. T. (1992). Pseudomemory in hypnotized and task-motivated subjects. *Journal of Abnormal Psychology, 101,* 356–360.

Weinberg, S. K. (1955). *Incest behavior.* New York: Citadel.

Weisman, R. (1984). *Witchcraft, magic and religion in seventeenth-century Massachusetts.* Amherst: University of Massachusetts Press.

Weitzenhoffer, A. M. (1974). When is an "instruction" an "instruction"? *International Journal of Clinical and Experimental Hypnosis, 22,* 258–269.

Wells, G. L. (1993). What do we know about eye witness identification? *American Psychologist, 48,* 553–571.

Wells, G. L., & Murray, D. M. (1984). Eyewitness confidence. In G. L. Wells & E. F. Loftus (Eds.), *Eyewitness testimony: Psychological perspectives* (pp. 155–170). New York: Cambridge University Press.

Wells, W. R. (1940). Ability to resist artificially induced dissociation. *Journal of Abnormal and Social Psychology, 35,* 261–272.

White, R. W. (1941). A preface toward a theory of hypnotism. *Journal of Abnormal Psychology, 36,* 477–505.

White, T. B. (1990). *The believer's guide to spiritual warfare.* Ann Arbor, MI: Vine Books.

Whitley, G. (1992, January). Abuse of trust. *D. Magazine,* 36–39.

Whitlock, F. A. (1967). The aetiology of hysteria. *Acta Psychiatrica Scandinavia, 43,* 144–162.

Whorwell, P. J., Prior, A., & Faragher, E. B. (1984). Controlled trial of hypnotherapy in the treatment of severe refractory irritable bowel syndrome. *Lancet, 2,* 1232–1234.

Whytt, R. (1767). *Observations on the nature, causes, and cure of those disorders which have commonly been called nervous, hypocondriac, or hysteric.* Edinburgh, Scotland: J. Balfour.

Wijesinghe, C. P., Dissanayake, S. A. W., & Mendis, N. (1976). Possession trance in a semi-urban community in Sri Lanka. *Australian & New Zealand Journal of Psychiatry, 11,* 93–100.

Wilbur, C. B. (1984). Treatment of multiple personality. *Psychiatric Annals, 14,* 27–31.

Wilkins, K. (1972). The treatment of the supernatural in the Encyclopedie. *Miracles, Convulsions, and Ecclesiastical Politics in Early 18th Century Paris, 90,* 1757–1771.

Wilkins, K. (1974). Attitudes toward witchcraft and demoniacal possession in France during the 18th century. *Journal of European Studies, 3,* 349–362.

Willard, S. (1683). *The high esteem which God hath of the death of his saints: As it was delivered in a sermon preached October 7, 1683, occasioned by the death of the worshipful John Hull, Esq.: who deceased October 1, 1683.* Boston: Samuel Green.

Williams, L. M. (1993, October). *Recall of childhood trauma: A prospective study of women's memories of child sexual abuse.* Paper presented at the annual meeting of the American Society of Criminology, Phoenix, AZ.

Wilson, I. (1987). *The after death experience.* New York: William Morrow.

Wilson, S. C., & Barber, T. X. (1981). Vivid fantasy and hallucinatory abilities in the life histories of excellent hypnotic subjects (somnambules): Preliminary report with female subjects. In E. Klinger (Ed.), *Imagery: Concepts, results and applications* (pp. 133–149). New York: Plenum Press.

Wong, B., & McKeen, J. (1990). In the shadow of Satan: The ritual abuse of children. [Special issue]. *Journal of Child and Youth Care,* 1-26.

Woods, W. (1974). *A history of the devil.* New York: Berkley.

Woodward, W. E. (1969). (Ed.). *Records of Salem witchcraft copied from the original documents* (Vols. 1–2). New York: DaCapo Press.

Woolger, R. J. (1987). Aspects of past-life bodywork: Understanding subtle energy fields. Part II: Practical aspects. *The Journal of Regression Therapy, 2,* 85–92.

Wright, L. (1994). *Remembering satan.* New York: Knopf.

Wyatt, G. E. (1985). The sexual abuse of Afro-American and white American women in childhood. *Child Abuse and Neglect, 9,* 507–519.

Yant, M. (1992). *Presumed guilty: When innocent people are wrongly convicted.* Buffalo, NY: Prometheus.

Yapko, M. D. (1994a). Suggestibility and repressed memories of abuse: A survey of psychotherapists' beliefs. *American Journal of Clinical Hypnosis, 36,* 163–171.

Yapko, M. D. (1994b). *Suggestions of abuse: True and false memories of childhood sexual abuse.* New York: Simon & Schuster.

Yarmey, A. D. (1990). *Understanding police and police work.* New York: New York University Press.

Young, P. C. (1927). Is rapport an essential characteristic of hypnosis? *Journal of Abnormal and Social Psychology, 22,* 130–139.

Young, W. C. (1988). Observations on fantasy in the formation of multiple personality. *Dissociation, 1,* 13–20.

Young, W. C., Sachs, R. G., Braun, B. G., & Watkins, R. T. (1991). Patients reporting ritual abuse in childhood: A clinical syndrome. Report of 37 cases. *Child Abuse and Neglect, 15,* 181–189.

Zahn, T. P. (1986). Psychophysiological approaches to psychopathology. In M. G. H. Coles, E. Donchin, & S. W. Porges (Eds.), *Psychophysiology: Systems, processes and applications* (pp. 508–610). New York: Guilford.

Zamansky, H. S., & Bartis, S. P. (1985). The dissociation of an experience: The hidden observer observed. *Journal of Abnormal Psychology, 94,* 243–248.

Zimdars-Swartz, S. L. (1991). *Encountering Mary.* New York: Avon.

Zola, I. K. (1983). *Socio-medical inquiries.* Philadelphia: Temple University Press.

AUTHOR INDEX

355

McConkey, K. M., 34, 37, 92, 93, 94, 98
McConnell, H. K., 64, 65
McCurdy, H. A., 244
McDougall, W., 208
McFarlane, A. C., 219
McGrath, P. A., 24
McKeen, J., 45
McLean, J. M., 98
McNeil, C., 111
McNulty, S. A., 121
McRoberts, G., 253
Menary, E., 48, 135, 137, 139, 140, 141,
    239, 240, 278
Mendis, N., 145
Merskey, H., 233, 236
Mesel, E., 97
Mesmer, F. A., 184
Michaelis, S., 162, 174
Michaels, R. M., 97
Midelfort, H. C. E., 296
Milgram, S., 31, 52
Miller, A. G., 52
Miller, R. J., 31
Miller, S. D., 1, 248, 249, 250, 265, 268
Milstein, V., 1, 83, 84, 232, 235, 265
Modestin, J., 234, 253
Moore, M. S., 4, 204
Moore, R. L., 202, 203, 207
Morgan, A. H., 21, 26
Morgan, C. D., 26
Morris, D., 118
Morton, A., 149, 152, 154
Moss, P., 136
"Most strange and admirable discovery of
    the witches of Warboys, The,"
    165
Mulhern, S., 9, 58, 75, 106, 111, 245,
    256, 267, 270, 274, 281, 282,
    291
Mulholland, T., 248
Mullens, D., 24
Munitz, H., 220
Munthe, A., 195, 196
Murphy, G. E., 261
Murray,, D. M., 62
Myers, F. W. H., 206
Myers, S. A., 258

Nadon, R., 252, 259
Nakashima, S. R., 233, 251
Nancoo, S., 94, 257
Nash, C. L., 253

Nash, M. R., 58, 89, 95, 96, 253, 255
Nathan, D., 292
Neanon, G. M., 147
Neimeyer, R. A., 89
Neisser, U., 5, 60, 63, 80
Nelson, K., 80, 84
Nelson, P. L., 258
Newman, J. B., 186
Newman, R., 96
Nickell, J., 109
Nissen, M. J., 216, 217, 218
Nissenbaum, S., 178, 179, 180
Nolan, R., 24
Norris, D. L., 24
North, C. S., 110, 232, 241, 250, 259,
    261, 262, 266, 291
Norton, G. R., 1, 43, 232, 233, 235, 254,
    259, 261, 265, 267, 271
Notestein, W., 164, 165, 173
Novotny, M. E., 259

O'Brien, D., 242
Obstoj, L., 27
O'Connell, D. N., 26, 95, 96, 97
Oesterreich, T. K., 157, 158, 161, 162,
    163, 164, 165, 172
O'Faolain, J., 163
Ofshe, R. J., 51, 52, 58, 278, 280
Olio, K. A., 75, 129
Ong, A., 155
Opton, E., 51
Orne, M. T., 25, 26, 27, 47, 48, 52, 58,
    91, 92, 95, 96, 97
Overley, T. M., 26
Owen, A. R. G., 193, 194, 201

Pabis, R., 233
Parfit, D. N., 43, 44
Parrinder, E. G., 269
Parrish, M. J., 26
Pasquotto, J., 255, 259
Passantino, B., 270
Passantino, G., 270
Patrick, L., 24
Pattie, F. A., 30, 31
Paul, G. L., 24
Pazder, L., 269
Penfield, W., 58
Pennebaker, J. W., 109
Peper, E., 248
Perlini, A. H., 23, 24, 62, 94, 248, 250,
    257

SUBJECT INDEX